Praise for *Global Capitalism in Crisis:*
Profit System (2010)

"[Murray Smith] provides a rigorous accounting of Marx's argument that capitalism is always going to be governed by the economic law of the rate of profit to fall. This is not some philosophical abstraction. Rather it goes to the heart of why socialists believe that capitalism must be struggled against."

—Bryan Palmer, Professor, Canadian Studies, Trent
University, and Editor of *Labour-Le Travail*

"A timely scholarly achievement that establishes a *de facto* measure of the plethora of assessments on the global economic crisis.... Smith has outlined an account of the crisis that is theoretically coherent, self-conscious and unambiguous."

—Thom Workman, Professor, Political Science,
University of New Brunswick

"Smith provides a timely and important analysis of the global capitalist crisis from the Marxist perspective. In this reviewer's opinion, the book's basic argument—that capitalism is now in a historical-structural crisis, and has exhausted its potential to promote further human progress—correctly characterizes our current world-historical conjuncture. The book contributes to the preparation of the crucial subjective factor which, according to Smith, is urgently needed to match the objective historical conditions."

—Minqi Li, Associate Professor, Economics Department,
University of Utah

"Smith makes a significant contribution to [the labour theory of value] and our understanding of capitalist crisis."

—Graeme Reniers, PhD Candidate, Political Science, York University

"Smith poses a number of critical questions that provide a precise guidance to answer 'what is to be done' today, which I strongly encourage readers to engage with.... [H]is book deserves careful reading, which I also wish will be widespread."
—Esteban Castro, Professor, School of Geography, Politics, and Sociology, Newcastle University

"If the origins of the global economic crisis are indeed to be found in the 'decay of the profit system', as Smith persuasively argues, then this book cannot be dismissed or ignored by serious people."
—Josh Dumont, PhD in Political Science, York University

Praise for *Invisible Leviathan: The Marxist Critique of Market Despotism beyond Postmodernism* (1994)
"This is a formidable achievement, and Smith is to be congratulated for the rigor with which he has tried to demonstrate the probity and distinctiveness of Marx's original position."
—Noel Castree, Professor, School of Environment, Education, and Development, University of Manchester

"Murray E. G. Smith's book is an example of the excellent research being produced by a new generation of writers.... The author writes well, and his analysis is always penetrating, interesting and provocative."
—Alfredo Saad Filho, Professor, Department of Development Studies, SOAS University of London

Marxist Phoenix

Marxist Phoenix
Studies in Historical Materialism and Marxist Socialism

MURRAY E. G. SMITH

WITH CONTRIBUTIONS BY
JONAH BUTOVSKY AND JOSHUA D. DUMONT

Canadian Scholars' Press Inc.
Toronto

Marxist Phoenix: Studies in Historical Materialism and Marxist Socialism
by Murray E. G. Smith

First published in 2014 by
Canadian Scholars' Press Inc.
425 Adelaide Street West, Suite 200
Toronto, Ontario
M5V 3C1
www.cspi.org

Canadian Scholars' Press Inc. gratefully acknowledges financial support for our publishing activities from the Government of Canada through the Canada Book Fund (CBF).

Library and Archives Canada Cataloguing in Publication

Smith, Murray E. G. (Murray Edward George), author
Marxist phoenix : studies in historical materialism and Marxist socialism / Murray E.G. Smith; with contributions by Jonah Butovsky and Joshua D. Dumont.

Includes bibliographical references and index. Issued in print and electronic formats. ISBN 978-1-55130-625-4 (pbk.).--ISBN 978-1-55130-627-8 (pdf).--ISBN 978-1-55130-626-1 (epub)

1. Socialism--Textbooks. 2. Historical materialism-- Textbooks. I. Butovsky, Jonah, 1970-, author II. Dumont, Joshua D., author III. Title.

HX40.S55 2014   335.43   C2014-900092-8   C2014-900093-6

Cover design by Em Dash
Text design by Integra

Printed and bound in Canada by Webcom.

MIX
Paper from
responsible sources
FSC® C004071

DEDICATION

To Howard and Jack, whose struggles for a socialist perspective and a class-struggle program within the International Longshore and Warehouse Union have helped prepare the ground for the resurrection of the Marxist Phoenix; and to Elizabeth and Evan, whose generation will learn from their example.

TABLE OF CONTENTS

PREFACE AND ACKNOWLEDGEMENTS

This volume is a collection of new and previously published essays written between 1991 and 2013. Although unified by a common (Marxist) theoretical orientation, most were originally written as stand-alone pieces for a variety of scholarly journals, and, consequently, some degree of repetition in the questions discussed and the arguments advanced will be apparent. My hope is that this will not detract from the reader's experience, but rather serve to clarify and highlight the leading themes of a collection that covers a diverse array of topics in political economy, philosophy, social theory, and politics.

In preparing *Marxist Phoenix*, I was cognizant of its close relationship to my last book, *Global Capitalism in Crisis: Karl Marx and the Decay of the Profit System*, published in 2010. While *Marxist Phoenix* is decidedly more wide-ranging in its subject matter than *Global Capitalism in Crisis*, concentrating less on the political economy of the financial crisis and Great Recession of 2007–2009 and much more on the philosophy, history, and politics of Marxist socialism, I nevertheless regard the two books as companion volumes and as joint sequels to my (now out-of-print) 1994 work, *Invisible Leviathan: The Marxist Critique of Market Despotism beyond Postmodernism*.

Thanks are owed to a great many people who have influenced my thinking and given me various forms of assistance and encouragement with regard to the contents of the present volume. A non-exclusive list must include Jonah Butovsky (my co-author for Chapters 2 and 13), Ken Campbell, Noel Castree, Bob Chernomas, June Corman, Mohammed Dore, Josh Dumont (my co-author for Chapter 10), Adam Hanieh, Karen Hofman, Esther Kelly, Howard Keylor, David Laibman, John McAmmond, Bryan Palmer, Bob Ratner, Tom Reid, David Schweitzer, Errol Sharpe, Wayne Taylor, Henry Veltmeyer, and Thom Workman. Many thanks as well to my editors at Canadian Scholars' Press, Daniella Balabuk and James MacNevin, and to Emma Johnson and the CSPI production team.

Permissions to republish previously published pieces as chapters of this book are gratefully acknowledged. I should note that I have taken the liberty of minimally editing, updating, abridging, and/or supplementing most of these pieces with a view to producing a better integrated and, I hope, more readable book.

Murray E. G. Smith

December 2013

Whither the Marxist Phoenix?

The phoenix hope, can wing her way through the desert skies, and still defying fortune's spite; revive from ashes and rise.

—Miguel de Cervantes

Between 1989 and 1991, the leaders, ideologues, and publicists of world capitalism ecstatically proclaimed the collapse of Soviet-bloc communism as the final death knell of Marxist socialism. Twenty-five years on, the triumphalist euphoria and pro-capitalist optimism this evoked has all but dissipated.

By almost any measure, the record of world capitalism in the post-Soviet era has been an abysmal one. It is a record of burgeoning economic inequality and social malaise, an alarming resurgence of neo-colonialist adventurism and militarism, the productive torpor and escalating hubris of the sole remaining "superpower," and the steady erosion of average living standards and democratic rights in many of the richest capitalist countries. All this, and much more, has fostered a mounting interest in systemic alternatives to capitalism, as well as in strategies for its abolition, among a younger generation facing what many recognize to be a bleak and perilous future.

Although a majority of progressive-minded young activists remain attached, however tenuously, to various forms of left liberalism, radical populism, or anarchism, a growing number are discovering the indispens-able contribution that authentic Marxism can make to understanding the multiple crises and depredations of today's world, and to theoretically and programmatically guiding the social forces capable of fundamentally changing it. In the process, most are also rejecting the profoundly false identification of Marxism (the theory and practice of working-class self-emancipation) with Stalinism (the social phenomenon of bureaucratic, oligarchic rule on the basis of collectivized property forms), an identifica-tion that was long and assiduously promoted by pro-capitalist and Stalinist ideologues alike, and one that is directly targeted in the pages that follow.

The essays collected here address a broad range of issues in Marxist the-ory and socialist politics. Their unifying thesis can be stated synoptically as follows. After a brief efflorescence during and just following Russia's socialist revolution of 1917, authentic Marxism—a theoretical and prac-tical project that is at once scientific, revolutionary, internationalist, and emancipatory in its commitments—was marginalized and very nearly extinguished by the ascendancy of Stalinist policies and ideology in the international labour movement, a process that began in the mid-1920s with the bureaucratic degeneration of the Soviet workers' state under the tyrannical regime of Joseph Stalin. The protracted crisis of Stalinism in the post–World War II period, along with a rising tide of "anti-imperialist revolution" in Asia, Africa, and Latin America, created conditions that seemed favourable to a revival of revolutionary Marxism. But the continu-ing dominance of Stalinist, social-democratic, and liberal-nationalist ideas and practices within labour, anti-colonial, and other social movements, together with the persistent disorientation and weakness of the so-called Far Left (notably the ostensibly Trotskyist groups), precluded the emer-gence of a serious Marxist-socialist current to lead the fight against world capitalism as the latter entered into severe systemic crisis in the late 1960s and 1970s. The subsequent defeat of the working class and the putatively socialist left by the bourgeoisie's neoliberal offensive was followed up, and in a certain sense consolidated, by the collapse of Stalinism in the Soviet bloc and the pro-capitalist ideological triumphalism that accompanied it. As a result, working-class consciousness on a global scale suffered a profound regression—a problem that has persisted into the twenty-first century with ominous consequences for world politics.

Owing to the hugely disappointing and often disastrous results of capitalist restoration in the erstwhile "communist" countries, the troubling performance of Western capitalism in the post–Cold War era, the manifest inability of neoliberalism to address the severe ecological crisis confronting humankind, and, above all, the deep systemic crisis of the global capitalist economy that has become increasingly apparent since 2007–2008, the "End of History" announced by Francis Fukuyama in 1992 has acquired a meaning far removed from the one originally intended. Far from looking to a luminous future in which any serious challenge to liberal-democratic, free-market capitalism is unimaginable, sober-minded observers of the contemporary scene are now obliged to consider a terrifying alternative prospect: *Will the victory of world capitalism over what passed for communism in the Soviet bloc end up being a prelude to the wholesale destruction of human civilization?*

The very fact that such a question can be seriously posed today invites another that is far more hopeful in spirit: *Will the intensifying contradictions and multiple crises of the new world order fashioned by capitalism in the post-Soviet era incite the emergence of an insurgent socialist workers' movement committed not merely to the "reform" of capitalism but to its successful overthrow?* For profoundly moral as well as scientific reasons, this latter question, in my view, can only be answered in the affirmative. To be sure, such a "Marxist Phoenix"—a mass workers' movement, constituted from the ashes of its past and infused with the theory and program of Marxism— has been seen only fleetingly since the 1920s. And yet the current, perilous condition of humanity urgently *demands* its re-emergence. Indeed, its eventual triumph may well represent the last, best hope for the future of our species.

Taken together, the studies included in this volume marshal the principal arguments in support of the preceding interpretation of twentieth-century history and a Marxist-socialist vision of human progress for the twenty-first century. Nevertheless, it must be acknowledged that they fall short of demonstrating that a Marxist Phoenix will in fact take flight and ultimately

3

prevail over that intensifying menace to humanity and nature alike: the capitalist law of value, which I described some 20 years ago as an "Invisible Leviathan" (Smith 1994a). Certainly, as these lines are being written (in the summer of 2013), real doubts regarding the capacity and willingness of the international working class to embrace Marxism's emancipatory rationalism, scientific humanism, and commitment to revolutionary practice may seem all too warranted. Even so, in light of the objectively dire consequences of ongoing acceptance of the continuance of capitalism, a complacent "historical pessimism"—however realistic it may seem—is clearly an outlook that cannot be allowed to reign. Against such pessimism, a popular slogan of France's legendary worker-student uprising of May 1968 seems more apposite than ever: *Be realistic, demand the impossible! All power to the imagination!*

However "dead" the Marxist Phoenix may now appear to be, the overarching message of this book is that we must still do everything in our power to resurrect it and reconstitute it as the singular, indispensable force that can rescue human civilization from an increasingly zombie-like Capitalist Nemesis whose very lifeblood is, and always must be, the "surplus value" created through the ruthless exploitation of human labour and whose decaying flesh is nothing other than the desiccated ruins of the natural world.

The will to contribute to such a resurrection requires a specific kind of faith—not the fideistic faith of religion, which always involves a wilful suspension of reason and critical thought and a voluntary submission to forces beyond human control—but a faith, grounded in historical experience, inspired by the highest moral ambitions, and informed by scientific reason, in the ability of human beings to comprehend and then act to remedy our most pressing collective problems. In this sense, the purpose of this book is fully in accord with Antonio Gramsci's maxim that our remedial activity must be guided by "pessimism of the intelligence, optimism of the will"—a theme the celebrated Italian Marxist elaborated upon in his *Prison Notebooks*:

> It is certain that prediction only means seeing the present and the past clearly as movement. Seeing them clearly: in other words,

accurately identifying the fundamental and permanent elements of the process. But it is absurd to think of a purely "objective" prediction. Anybody who makes a prediction has in fact a "programme" for whose victory he is working, and his prediction is precisely an element contributing to that victory. (1971: 170–71)

And further:

The decisive element in every situation is the permanently organized and long-prepared force which can be put into the field when it is judged that a situation is favourable (and it can be favourable only in so far as such a force exists, and is full of fighting spirit). Therefore, the essential task is that of systematically and patiently ensuring that this force is formed, developed, and rendered ever more homogeneous, compact, and self-aware. (185)

The emphasis that Gramsci assigns to "the subjective factor"—to will, fighting spirit, and a revolutionary workers' party striving for the victory of its socialist program—is a defining characteristic of any properly dialectical conception of Marxism as the "unity of theory and practice." Moreover, it stands in irreconcilable opposition to that fatalism and objectivism that have so often been invoked by opportunist "radical leftists" to justify their compromises, their inept and short-sighted adaptations to the existing consciousness of the struggling masses, and their rejection or outright betrayal of the class-struggle principles of Marxist socialism. Little wonder, then, that Gramsci's famous concepts of "hegemony" and "war of position" are so often distorted and used to license a political practice that discounts the determined fight for a revolutionary Marxist program, and that emphasizes instead the need for incremental reforms and marginal alterations in the relationship of forces as necessary preconditions and preparations for the more advanced struggles that (might) lie ahead. Theories that provide a warrant to such a left-reformist orientation are theories that perennially insist upon *postponing* the struggle for a socialist program—that posit a more humane, more democratic capitalism as a necessary "stage" that must be secured before a socialist transformation can be undertaken, and/or that suggest that the "objective dynamic" of struggle against the oppressions and iniquities of capitalism absolves Marxists of the responsibility to fight for goals that go well beyond those immediate demands for social justice that are seen as winnable within its framework. Authentic Marxist theory provides no such warrant—and it never has.

This book is a work of social and political theory—and, for better or worse, it bears many of the traits and preoccupations of academic scholarship. Yet it is also infused with a fervent commitment to the idea of the dialectical unity of theory and practice. The Marxist unity of (historical-materialist) theory and (revolutionary-socialist) practice necessarily involves a conception of their *mutual* interaction and determination. In contrast to the false objectivity of purportedly value-free academic social science and the one-dimensional determinism of some (regrettably influential) versions of Marxism, Marx's own scientific socialism recognizes, as Gramsci's formulations suggest, that revolutionary practice—the fight for a program of social transformation—must have a decisive determining effect on the production of socialist theory, that is to say, on how we *understand* the world. To put the matter succinctly, *program generates theory*, at least as much as theory generates program—and usually more so.

But this last statement is true not only of Marxism, for every theory is ultimately a product of human activities that are directed toward affecting the world in definite ways, whether by preserving, reforming, or revolutionizing its existing conditions. Therefore, a key element in the struggle for the Marxist-socialist program must involve engaging with and defeating those competing theories and programs that are consciously opposed to the re-emergence of the Marxist Phoenix and thus to resolving what the great Marxist revolutionary Leon Trotsky called "the crisis of leadership" of the working class. Such opposition assumes many forms, only some of which are overtly hostile to the socialist idea. All the same, what unites all such perspectives is the false notion that the fight for a revolutionary socialist program—and the construction of a party determined to win over the most advanced layers of the working class—is a sectarian and ultimately futile enterprise, whether or not it is also considered, in some sense, well intentioned.

The essays collected here engage with and critique a good number of such perspectives, some of them avowedly anti-Marxist, some postmodernist, and some ostensibly Marxist or "neo-Marxist." In many cases, I have sought to tease out the political-programmatic impulses or appetites informing them in addition to providing serious critical assessments of their substantive arguments. But it is important to appreciate that my critiques are by no means simply exercises in intellectual one-upmanship. Rather they are offered in defense of a series of propositions that are fundamental to my own understanding of authentic Marxism as a unity of theory and practice. These core propositions can be enumerated as follows:

1. The capitalist system is based upon institutions and social relations that serve the interests not of humanity as a whole but of a small social class—the bourgeoisie or capitalist class—that is determined to maintain its dominance at all costs. This class monopolizes the ownership of the major means of production, distribution, and exchange and is therefore in a position to subordinate economic activity, and most other aspects of social life, to the reproduction of its dominant, privileged position and the material inequalities that are its foundation. In other words, social and economic life under capitalism is organized in such a way as to perpetuate the wealth and power of a tiny class of profit-seekers. Consequently, social need is systematically sacrificed to private profit.

2. This situation is not simply morally objectionable. The institutional arrangements and social relations of production intrinsic to capitalism give effect to objective economic laws that point to the increasing irrationality of capitalism as a mode of production. The most striking expression of this irrationality is the way in which capitalism simultaneously promotes improvements in the productivity of labour, through labour-saving and labour-displacing technological innovation, while continuously measuring material wealth (the "use-values" created by living labour) in accordance with a class-antagonistic "law

of value"—that is to say, in terms of quantities of money representing "abstract social labour." Technology-based improvements in labour
productivity at the micro level undercut the creation of new value at
the macro level. The result is a *tendency for the average rate of profit to
fall*—a tendency that sets the stage for severe systemic crises and that
calls forth a variety of class-based responses.

3. As a consequence of the growing contradiction between the social
   relations of production constitutive of capitalism and the ever-more
   powerful forces of production it brings into being, the capitalist system is prone to severe instabilities and economic crises, the magnitude of which tend to increase over time. The capitalist class and its
   more affluent underlings try to resolve these problems while defending
   their privileges and preserving the fundamental features of the system.
   They do so primarily by shifting the costs of repairing the system onto
   the working class—through wage and benefit cuts, austerity, and pit-
   ting their own workers against those of other countries in wars. The
   working class, or proletariat, strives to resist such "solutions," but it can
   be truly effective in doing so only when it understands that it has an
   objective interest, one consciously grasped unevenly and discontinu-
   ously by working people, in replacing the capitalist system with a more
   rational, egalitarian, and truly democratic social order: socialism (and
   eventually, at a higher stage, advanced communism).

4. Only a class-conscious movement of the proletariat has the potential
   social power and historical interest to overthrow the bourgeoisie and
   inaugurate a new, more progressive stage in the social evolution of
   humanity. Such a movement can only emerge and fulfill its historic
   task to the extent that socialists are able to win a decisive segment of
   the working-class population to a revolutionary socialist party that
   promotes the idea that working people must organize themselves *independently* of the capitalist class—in opposition to the latter's values,
   priorities, and fundamental interests, and in the struggle for an egalitarian-socialist future.

5. The emancipation of humanity from material insecurity and debilitating toil, as well as from age-old prejudices, oppressions, and iniquities,

depends upon the ascendancy of these Marxist-socialist ideas among the international masses of working people—and so too does the very survival of the human species. The existing capitalist world-system is shot through with bitter antagonisms that will inevitably engender worsening economic and ecological conditions as well as catastrophic wars if it is not abolished and replaced with socialism in a timely fashion. The difficulties and risks involved in such a revolutionary transformation are certainly great. The dangers flowing from our failure to carry it through are incomparably greater.

Only through the widespread promulgation of these fundamental propositions, and the arguments supporting them, can there be any hope that the Marxist Phoenix will eventually take flight. This book is, above all, a contribution to that project. And yet it must be said that it falls short of addressing *all* of the outstanding controversies surrounding Marxist theory and politics in recent years. Its particular concerns and emphases reflect my own understanding of what is of greatest importance to the revival of Marxism as a unified theoretical-political project. Once again, *program generates theory.* Accordingly, the theoretical interests and preoccupations displayed here are *not* dominated by questions pertaining to how the capitalist state might be incrementally "democratized," or how the capitalist economy might be made more "stable" and its distribution of income more "just," or how the phenomena of racial and gender oppression within particular wealthy nations might be mitigated while leaving intact the structures of capitalism, imperialism, and oppression on a world scale. Rather they are shaped by my intention to make the case that a mass socialist workers' movement must be built—and built soon!—to rescue humanity, once and for all, from the perils and increasingly onerous burdens of a rapidly decaying capitalist order.

PART I
Capitalism, Value, and Crisis

CHAPTER 1

The Unbearable Burdens of Capitalism: A Marxist Perspective

In the opening decades of the twenty-first century, a disturbing paradox has become apparent in the way that a great many seemingly intelligent people, including those living in relatively comfortable circumstances in the so-called developed world, are thinking about the current state of humanity. On the one hand, there is a strong and quite realistic sense that we are sliding into a global era of ever-worsening social, economic, and environmental conditions—an era that could end with the extinction of our species either through high-tech wars or an accumulation of ecological catastrophes. On the other hand, there remains a persistent and remarkably pervasive unwillingness to assign the blame for this perilous situation to the operations of capitalism, the globally dominant socioeconomic system, and a still greater unwillingness to seek a solution to it through fundamental systemic change.

The explanation for this paradox—and for the crisis in human problem-solving it reflects—can be traced to *the power of ideology*, that is to say, to the ability of powerful forces within contemporary society to obscure social reality and deflect attention from the demonstrable connections that

exist between the capitalist profit system and the multiple crises of the contemporary world. One can only expect that once an understanding of the
unbearable burdens that capitalism is now inflicting on humanity becomes
more widespread, the emergence of a mass movement toward socialism
will become altogether irrepressible.

This book is a contribution to reloading the most powerful *scientific*
weapon ever fashioned against capitalism and the ideologies supporting
it: the body of theory and program known as Marxism. In this regard, the
present chapter serves a limited, twofold purpose: first, to review the fundamentals of Marxist theory, and second, to outline its unique ability to
account for the outstanding problems and unbearable burdens that threaten
the future of humanity. This purpose is primarily a critical one, but it is not
simply critical. For Marxism is not merely a scientific critique of ideologies
that seek to depict capitalism more favourably than it deserves; it is also a
program—a practical project—for achieving a qualitatively superior form
of human society, the *classless society* known as socialism or communism.
Indeed, by negating in thought the conditions of human exploitation and
oppression and the social practices that breed deprivation, war, and the
ruination of the natural world, Marxism also posits the prerequisites for
their universal transcendence and for securing the conditions of genuine
human progress into the future. This "negation of the negation"—to use a
Hegelian expression favoured by Karl Marx and Frederick Engels—is powerfully evoked by Marx in a famous passage toward the end of the first
volume of *Capital*:

> [The expropriation of the capitalist] is accomplished through the
> action of the immanent laws of capitalist production itself, through
> the centralization of capitals. One capitalist always strikes down
> many others. Hand in hand with this centralization, or this expro-
> priation of many capitalists by a few, other developments take place
> on an ever-increasing scale, such as the growth of the co-operative
> form of the labour process, the conscious technical application of
> science, the planned exploitation of the soil, the transformation
> of the means of labour into forms in which they can only be used

in common, the economizing of all means of production by their use as the means of production of combined, socialized labour, the entanglement of all peoples in the net of the world market, and, with this, the growth of the international character of the capitalist regime. Along with the constant decrease in the number of capitalist magnates, who usurp and monopolize all the advantages of this process of transformation, the mass of misery, oppression, slavery, degradation and exploitation grows; but with this there also grows the revolt of the working class, a class constantly increasing in numbers, and trained, united and organized by the very mechanism of the capitalist process of production. The monopoly of capital becomes a fetter upon the mode of production which has flourished alongside and under it. The centralization of the means of production and the socialization of labour reach a point at which they become incompatible with their capitalist integument. This integument is burst asunder. The knell of capitalist private property sounds. The expropriators are expropriated.

The capitalist mode of appropriation, which springs from the capitalist mode of production, produces capitalist private property. This is the first negation of individual private property, as founded on the labour of its proprietor. But capitalist production begets, with the inexorability of a natural process, its own negation. This is the negation of the negation. It does not re-establish private property, but it does indeed establish individual property on the basis of the achievements of the capitalist era: *namely* cooperation and the possession in common of the land and the means of production produced by labour itself.

The transformation of scattered private property resting on the personal labour of the individuals themselves into capitalist private property is naturally an incomparably more protracted, violent and difficult process than the transformation of capitalist private property, which in fact already rests on the carrying on of production by society, into social property. In the former case, it was a matter of the expropriation of the mass of the people by a few usurpers; but in this case, we have the expropriation of a few usurpers by the mass of the people. (1977: 929–30)

From our present historical standpoint, Marx's stirring, almost lyrical, summation of the processes whereby the capitalist mode of production prepares its own burial strikes one as both extraordinarily prophetic and oddly insensible to the enormous obstacles to a successful revolt of the working class and therefore to the universal dissolution of capitalist private property and the reclamation of the social wealth created by socialized labour and hitherto claimed by the capitalist expropriators. This dissonance reflects something rather significant about Marx's theoretical contribution: its juxtaposition of a masterful comprehension of the objective dynamics and fundamental "laws of motion" of the capitalist mode of production with a strikingly incomplete understanding of *how* a "trained, united, and organized" working class could eventually expropriate the capitalist class as a whole and inaugurate a new society.

Precisely because the latter question was addressed far more adequately by many of his successors than by Marx himself, it must be acknowledged that the call for a "return to Marx" raised by many Marxist academics in recent years is profoundly misleading to the extent that it involves a rejection of the later contributions of such pre-eminent revolutionary Marxists as Vladimir Lenin, Rosa Luxemburg, and Leon Trotsky. Basing themselves on a much broader and richer set of historical experiences than those available to Marx and Engels, these figures made crucially important extensions to "authentic Marxism" in the twentieth century—above all, through their elaboration of the key programmatic, strategic, organizational, and tactical considerations confronting a serious socialist workers' movement. Against the hasty dismissals they are so often accorded by those who reject "vanguardism" in favour of a romanticized "original Marxism," whose historically determined *vagueness* concerning the conditions for a proletarian victory over capitalism is too often seen as a virtue rather than as a weakness that had to be overcome through the hard-won lessons of class struggle and the creative development of revolutionary Marxist theory and strategy, these contributions should be regarded as entirely *indispensable* to a serious twenty-first-century socialist praxis.

That said, none of these contributions, several of which are considered in the chapters that follow, would have been possible without the theoretical inspiration and guidance provided by Marx and Engels' scientific socialism. And so it is with the key elements of this original legacy, as well as its burning practical relevance to the *objective* problems of the twenty-first century, that we need to begin.

Scientific Socialism and the Materialist Conception of History

For Marx and Engels, in contrast to their socialist predecessors as well as many of today's putative "radical leftists," the question—capitalism or socialism?—was not primarily an ethical one, and still less was it a question of axiological preferences (for example, the "values" of possessive individualism versus those of egalitarian collectivism). Instead, it was a question of which social system can better sustain the human species in the future and promote human flourishing—goals to which only the most misanthropic among us could possibly be hostile. But for this question to be resolved clearly in favour of socialism, it was necessary for the founders of Marxist socialism to develop an objective, scientific understanding of the specific "laws of motion" of capitalism: the laws governing its emergence, its structural dynamics, and the ways in which it prepares the ground for socialism as it enters into historical decline. On the basis of such an understanding, socialism could then be viewed not simply as a moral or humanitarian protest against the iniquities of capitalism, but as the only fully *rational* response to the intensifying contradictions and maladies of the capitalist social order and the exhaustion of its historically progressive mission.

By raising the productivity of labour to historically unprecedented levels, unleashing an ongoing scientific and technological revolution, creating a worldwide division of labour, and sponsoring a process of "objective socialization of production" alongside the capitalist appropriation of the social surplus product, capitalism distinguishes itself as the most progressive of all hitherto existing "class-antagonistic" modes of production. Marx paid this tribute to capitalism without hesitation, even though he was fully aware that capital (understood as an intrinsically *exploitative* social relation) came into the world "dripping from head to toe, from every pore, with blood and dirt" (1977: 926) and, further, that this "anarchic" and crisis-prone system can only inflict great harm on the mass of humanity so long as it continues to exist.

In light of this seemingly contradictory assessment of capitalism, how then are we to understand the Marxist conception of human progress?

For Marx, human history has a pattern and a meaning, to the extent that the rational attempt to raise the productivity of labour, and human creative capacities in general, holds sway. The human propensity toward labour-saving, technical-scientific forms of rationality is the key to social progress and foundational to Marx's philosophical anthropology. This propensity promises, in his view, to permit the eventual emergence of a mode of human existence in which all individuals will be able to develop their many-sided talents and capabilities unconstrained by either material hardship or social antagonism.

Since the breakup of "primitive communism" (the classless "mode of life" that prevailed for tens of thousands of years before the advent of private property) and the emergence of class-divided societies, the rational impulse to reduce the burden of human toil through labour-saving innovation has been both frustrated and perversely served by socially antagonistic forms of rationality that promote inequality and relations of domination/subordination. Indeed, human beings have been driven to seek material security in the face of both adverse natural conditions (the conditions of scarcity of particular geophysical environments) and antagonistic social forms—above all, the *class divisions and relations* that confer special privileges and powers upon a dominant class that appropriates the social surplus product created by the "direct" producers.

Modes of production are geographically and historically variable. However, they always involve the interpenetration and interplay of forces of production (defined broadly to include individual labour-powers, tools, machines, skills, technologies, etc.) and relations of production and reproduction (class relations, property forms, methods of resource allocation, family forms, etc.). Marx judged the capitalist mode of production to be the most progressive of the class-antagonistic modes of production for one reason above all others: its ability to create the "material premises" for a technologically advanced society of material abundance in which antagonistic class divisions disappear and "the free development of each is the condition for the free development of all" (Marx & Engels 1998: 41). In this sense, capitalism begets its socialist negation. The productive forces that the capitalist mode of production brings into being become increasingly incompatible with the social forms that define it and that distinguish it in fundamental ways from both precapitalist modes—such as medieval feudalism and the ancient mode based on chattel slavery—and the future communist mode.

The Capitalist Mode of Production

Capitalism is the only class-antagonistic mode of production possessing a set of social relations that systematically promotes the development of labour productivity and the extension of human capacities through the progress of science and technology. Societies in which it dominates economic life are characterized by three dynamically interrelated relations of production: an exploitative relation existing between the capitalist owners of the means of production/circulation and the class of wage-labourers who must sell their labour-power in order to live; a competitive relation between individual capitalist firms in "the market" (the sphere of commodity exchange); and a formally equalitarian relation between economic actors as determined by the normative imperative to respect the principle of the "exchange of equivalents" within so-called free markets. These relations act and interact in ways that unleash technical forms of rationality and encourage labour-saving and labour-displacing innovation within production. And yet, in so doing, they also drive the capitalist system to evolve in ways that undercut its ability to create sufficient quantities of "surplus value"—the "social substance" that is the very lifeblood of the system.

Like all other class-antagonistic modes of production, capitalism involves the extraction of surplus labour from the direct producers and the appropriation of the resulting surplus product by a dominant class of property owners. It is characterized, in other words, by the systematic exploitation of one class by another. But there are also essential differences that distinguish capitalism from other modes of production in this regard. In the first and third volumes of *Capital*, Marx writes:

> What distinguishes the various economic formations of society—the distinction between for example a society based on slave-labour and a society based on wage-labour—is the form in which this surplus-labour is in each case extorted from the immediate producer, the worker. (Marx 1977: 325)

> The specific economic form in which unpaid surplus labour is pumped out of the direct producers determines the relationship of domination and servitude, as it grows directly out of production itself and reacts back on it in turn as a determinant. On this is based the entire configuration of the economic community arising from the actual relations of production, and hence also its specific political form. It is in each case the direct relationship of the owners of the conditions of production to the immediate producers—a relationship whose particular form naturally corresponds always to a certain level of development of the type and manner of labour, and hence its social productive power—in which we find the innermost secret, the hidden basis of the entire social edifice, and hence also the political form of the relationship of sovereignty and dependence, in short, the specific form of state in each case. (Marx 1981: 927)

According to Marx, the "direct relationship of the owners of the conditions of production to the immediate producers" as found under capitalism is one defined by the generalization of commodity production—the transformation of the major means of production into capitalist property seeking to enlarge itself through the profitable sale of commodities, as well as the transformation of labour-power into a unique commodity that is sold to capitalists on an ever-widening scale. The "commodity form" assumed by more and more of the products of labour is indeed the "innermost secret" of the capitalist social structure and "the hidden basis" of such phenomena as wage-labour, capitalist competition, the "exchange of equivalents in the marketplace," the formal equality of citizens before the law, and all the most essential features and functions of the capitalist state. To be sure, Marx acknowledged that this "economic basis" can display "endless variations and gradations in its appearance" due to "innumerable different empirical circumstances, natural conditions, racial relations, historical influences acting from the outside, etc. and these can only be understood by analyzing these empirically given conditions" (1981: 927–28). That said, the study of these variations should not obscure the fundamental processes at work in what is an increasingly globalized socio-economic system. The overarching programmatic goal of Marxist socialism—the proletariat's expropriation of the capitalist class politically and economically, and the construction, not simply in one country but on a world scale, of a democratically administered socialist economy—flows logically from those fundamental processes and their scientific comprehension rather than from detailed analyses of "empirically given" conditions in particular times and places.

The starting point of such a scientific understanding is precisely the individual commodity, what Marx refers to as the "elementary form" of the "wealth of societies in which the capitalist mode of production prevails" (Marx 1977: 125). To be a commodity, an external object or thing must be useful to a potential purchaser, and must therefore have a *use-value*. At the same time, it must have the power to command remuneration in a market, and therefore an *exchange-value*. Hence, a commodity has a dual character: a value in use and a value in exchange, something that had already been recognized by the classical political economists who preceded Marx. For Marx, however, a third and essential feature of each and every commodity needed to be recognized: *its ontological status as a product of human labour and a societal division of labour.*

The dual aspects of the individual commodity—its "natural" use-value aspect and its "social" exchange-value aspect—find their unity in its value, which refers to the quantitative and qualitative relationships of the individual commodity to all other commodities produced by the capitalist division of labour.[1] The value of a commodity (as distinct from its exchange-value or final market price) is therefore not determinable by analyzing it in isolation from all the other commodities that are being produced at any given time and to which it is necessarily compared in the sphere of exchange. On the contrary, the value of a commodity is determined by the amount of socially necessary labour time required for its production (or reproduction). To express this idea a little differently, a commodity's value is not determined by the actual concrete labour expended in its production, but by the amount of abstract labour time that is required to produce it "under the conditions of production normal for a given society and with the average degree of skill and intensity of labour prevalent in that society" (Marx 1977: 129).

A detailed discussion and defense of Marx's theory of labour-value will be found in Chapters 3 and 7 of this volume (see also Smith 1994a, 2010). For our present purposes, however, what needs to be stressed is that this theory—which is not only an account of how the products of labour acquire value, but also, crucially, an interrogation of the "value form" of human labour under conditions of generalized, capitalist commodity production—is fundamental to his analysis of the "economic law of motion" of capitalist society. It is the analytical tool with which Marx probes the anatomy of an economy increasingly dominated by a specifically capitalist law of value—a law that posits living labour as the sole source of new value and whose operations demand that wealth be measured in terms of "abstract labour" and its phenomenal form, money. While Marx was certainly interested in how a commodity's "individual value" is transformed into a definite market price (as a result of several processes that determine that its final exchange-value will rarely coincide exactly with its intrinsic value), his main aim was to disclose the crisis tendencies and historical limits of capitalism as a mode of production—in other words, the ways in which the forces of production and relations of production come into conflict with one another under capitalism, thereby announcing the need for a social revolution to inaugurate a non-antagonistic, communist mode of production.

The Irrationality of Capitalism: Marx's Theories of Surplus Value and Capitalist Crisis

One of the most obvious ways that the capitalist mode of production signals its historical distinctiveness and limits is through the form assumed by its economic crises. Precapitalist societies are prone to crises of underproduction: too little is produced to meet the needs of the community, usually due to natural inclemencies or disasters such as drought, flooding, or pestilence. In a capitalist economy, however, an apparently opposite problem arises as a regular feature of its recurrent "boom and bust" cycles: too many commodities are produced in relation to the demand that exists for them; that is to say, in relation to demand that is backed by money in the hands of a would-be purchaser. This form of capitalist economic crisis—namely *overproduction*—results from a lack of purchasing power to absorb the total material output of society. Commodities cannot be sold (or markets cleared) at prices that permit an adequate profit margin; and since profit drives capitalist investment, the economy slows and ultimately contracts, throwing large numbers out of work and rendering much productive capacity idle.

Marx wanted to show that the underlying cause of these crises of overproduction was not "underconsumption" or "disproportionalities" in the sphere of exchange resulting from a problematic distribution of income between capital and labour, but rather insufficient production of new value—above all surplus value. This problem of *valorization* is the ultimate source of the "realization" problems associated with cyclical overproduction phenomena (Smith 2010: 77–79). Moreover, inadequate valorization is also at the root of the evolving manifestations of the historical-structural crisis of capitalism: the pronounced tendency for the average rate of profit to fall in the long term; the growing concentration and centralization of capital; the absorption by "unproductive capital" and the capitalist state of ever-larger shares of social wealth; and the growing importance of fictitious capital in an increasingly debt-burdened global economy.

To develop his theory of capitalist crisis, Marx set himself the task of explaining how surplus value was generated under capitalism—the specific way in which surplus labour was pumped out of the direct producers in an economy based on the "free-market" principle of the exchange of equivalents—as well as the money form assumed by it. In the first volume of *Capital*, he demonstrates that, even if we accept the limiting assumption that commodities exchange according to their "values," the capitalist economy operates in such a way as to involve and compel the systematic exploitation of the wage-labourer class by the owners of capital. The specifically capitalist mechanism for the exploitation of labour does not involve unequal exchanges between capital and wage-labour in the sphere of circulation. Rather it involves the extraction of surplus (unpaid) labour from workers in the sphere of commodity production, under conditions where the capitalist owners are continuously compelled to reduce their labour costs in order to meet the challenges of inter-capitalist competition.

According to Marx, what the capitalist purchases from the wage worker is not the actual concrete labour she or he performs, but rather the worker's ability to work—the commodity labour-power. The value of this unique commodity, the price of which is the wage, is determined by what it costs the working-class household to produce it. Accordingly, following its purchase, the commodity labour-power is the one major input to capitalist production that is not itself a product of profit-seeking capitalist production.

The wage is determined *primarily* by what it costs to continually reproduce the ability to work—that is, by what is required for workers to survive, and to work, and to support a few dependents in historically and culturally determined circumstances—and *not* by the value actually created by labour on the job. In general, the labour performed within the capitalist workplace, carried out under the supervision and compulsion of the agents of capital, will produce a mass of commodities representing a magnitude of value that exceeds the total costs of their production. Thus, the difference between the total value of the output and the total value of the inputs to production—a difference referred to as "value added" by mainstream economists—resolves itself into the difference between the value of labour-power (wages) and the value newly created by living wage-labour. Labour-power is therefore the only input commodity that can create the new value that finds expression in the wages of productive workers as well as in the surplus value realized by capitalists as profit of enterprise, interest, and rent.

Having revealed the mechanism through which capital exploits wage-labour, Marx was unwilling to rest his case against capitalism on purely "moral" grounds. Exploitation is certainly a morally charged term, but exploitation, defined as the appropriation of someone else's labour or property in order to serve one's own interests (or, even more simply, as the act of taking advantage of others), is a phenomenon that can take many different forms in human societies and one that doesn't always produce such irrational results as a crisis of overproduction. Moreover, if all that Marx wanted to accomplish was to demonstrate that capitalists exploit workers, he could have done so without relying on a theory of labour-value (see Chapter 3).

This returns us to the question posed earlier: why did Marx consider his theory of value (and surplus value) to be so pivotal to his critical analysis of capitalism?

One of the central claims made by virtually all proponents of the capitalist system is that the private pursuit of individual profit has the unintended and unanticipated consequence of promoting the welfare of society as a whole—and that, consequently, no real contradiction exists between profitability and the growth of material productivity. Thus, according to Adam Smith, profit seeking in the context of expanding "free markets" necessarily leads to an improved division of labour and a continuous expansion of material wealth. This thesis finds concise expression in a famous passage from Smith's *The Wealth of Nations* (1776): "[Every individual] intends only his own security; and by directing that industry in such a manner as its produce may be of the greatest value, he intends only his own gain, and he is in this, as in many other cases, led by an invisible hand to promote an end which was no part of his intention" (1986: 265).

From the Marxian standpoint, however, Smith's defense of the profit system finds a more revealing—and deeply problematic—expression in his earlier work, *The Theory of Moral Sentiments* (1759): "[The rich] are led by an invisible hand to make nearly the same distribution of the necessities of life, which would have been made, had the earth been divided into equal portions among all its inhabitants, and thus without knowing it, without intending it, advance the interest of the society, and afford means to the multiplication of the species" (Smith 1976: 184–85). It was Marx's great achievement to show, on the basis of his value-theoretic analysis of capitalism, that Smith, along with all other celebrants of capitalist rationality, fails to recognize a significant unintended consequence of the individual pursuit of profit under capitalism: it promotes developments in the productivity of labour that are profoundly *inimical* to the profitability and stability of the system as a whole.

Economic growth in capitalist societies is fundamentally regulated by the average rate of profit (the rate of return on invested capital), and this is defined by the relationship of surplus value (s) to the capital advanced—that is, the value of what Marx calls the "constant capital" stock (c). Again, new value, encompassing both surplus value and the value represented in the wages of *productive* workers, can only be created by living labour.[2] And yet two of the fundamental features of capitalism—the competition between capitalist firms and the antagonism between capitalists and workers—encourage labour-displacing technological innovation within individual enterprises. The result is a rise in the "organic composition of capital"—the ratio of dead to living labour in the overall process of production and reproduction. Productivity-enhancing innovation leads to an economy-wide decline in investment in living labour-power (the variable capital, or v)—the sole input to capitalist production that creates new value. As the pool of currently produced surplus value shrinks relative to the total investment in the constant-capital stock, the average rate of profit (s/c) falls.

It should now be clear why Marx considered his theory of value as crucially important to his critical analysis of capitalism. For if surplus value, as the unique product of exploited human labour, is indeed the lifeblood of the capitalist system, and if the system operates in ways that reduce the magnitude of surplus value produced in relation to the overall capital investment, then it is apparent that capitalism moves in contradiction to its own most basic requirements. The micro-level activities of competing individual capitalist firms to limit their dependence on living labour generate the unintended consequence of a "crisis of valorization"—a macro-structural crisis in the production of surplus value on an economy-wide scale. The pool of social surplus value, which is divided up by a multitude of capitalist firms competing with one another in the market, fails to expand sufficiently to warrant the ever-growing investment in fixed constant-capital stocks (the capital tied up in increasingly sophisticated tools, machinery, equipment, etc.). Hence, the eminently rational efforts of individual capitalist firms to reduce their unit costs of production by means of labour-saving technological innovation—and to thereby increase the productivity of their workers and improve their competitive positions—has the unintended and seemingly perverse consequence of reducing the amount of new value being produced and depressing the average rate of profit for the social capital as a whole, setting the stage for capitalist economic crises and the class struggles these provoke (see Chapter 2).

This law of the tendency of the rate of profit to fall, which Marx considered "the most important law of political economy," directly confutes Adam Smith's notion that what is rational at the micro level for the individual capitalist firm must also produce rational macroeconomic results. More to the point, it demolishes the assumption that, in principle, the growth of productivity under capitalism must eventually work to the benefit of all members of society. Contrary to Smith, Marx recognized that the relationship between profitability, productivity, and economic crisis is not only complex and counterintuitive, but also substantively irrational within a mode of production founded upon class exploitation and ruthless competition:

The barriers to the capitalist mode of production show themselves as follows: 1) in the way that the development of *labour productivity* involves a law, in the form of the falling rate of profit, that at a certain point confronts this development itself in a most hostile way and has constantly to be overcome *by way of crises*; [and] 2) in the way that it is the appropriation of unpaid labour in general ... that determines the expansion of and contraction of production, instead of the proportion between production and social needs, the needs of socially developed human beings…. Production comes to a standstill not at the point where needs are satisfied, but rather where the production and realization of profit impose this. (1981: 367, emphasis added)

Global Capitalism in Crisis: The Relevance of Marx in a "Neoliberal" Era

What needs to be emphasized is that capital's governing logic is *not* the expansion of material productivity, and, still less, the satisfaction of human needs in general, but the maximization of wealth in the class-antagonistic form of surplus value (profit). And the latter can only be generated through the exploitation of wage-labour by capital—the appropriation of unpaid labour.[3] Faced with a falling average rate of profit (s/c), the capitalist class (or social capital) of every country must resort to methods of increasing the rate of surplus value (the ratio of surplus value to variable capital, s/v) that rely less on productivity-enhancing technical innovation or increases in the composition of capital ($c/s+v$) and more on intensifying the labour process, reducing the real wages and benefits of working people, manipulating financial markets, redirecting government revenues and assets from popular social programs to schemes that benefit the rich, and extending their efforts to capture a larger share of an increasingly internationalized pool of social surplus value through foreign trade and investment.

Over the past 30 to 40 years, these are precisely the methods that have been employed by capitalists and governments to overcome the severe profitability problems that began to afflict the advanced capitalist world in the 1970s. They are the methods of neoliberalism, globalization, financialization, accumulation by dispossession, military Keynesianism, and austerity—phenomena that are all associated with what Marx calls the "counteracting factors" to a falling rate of profit. As capital retreats, albeit hesitantly and unevenly, from raising labour productivity through technological innovation, it has resorted, ever more desperately, to tactics that exhaust the worker and undermine the security and quality of life of the great majority of the population. The result has been a pronounced decline in the dynamism of the worldwide capitalist economy, a decline reflected in the slowdown in global GDP growth over the past few decades, as indicated in Tables 1.1 and 1.2.

Table 1.1: Average Annual Growth Rates of Global GDP by Decade

1960s	1970s	1980s	1990s	2000–09
4.9%	3.93%	2.95%	2.70%	2.58%

Source: World Bank

Table 1.2: Average Annual Growth Rates of Global GDP Per Capita by Decade

1960s	1970s	1980s	1990s	2000–09
3.5%	2.4%	1.4%	1.1%	1.3%

Source: World Bank

It is well known that a crucial factor in preventing an even greater slowdown in the world economy than that revealed in these tables has been the contribution of China to global economic growth. Not only has this "deformed workers' state" become a significant new site of surplus value production (due to an enormous expansion of capitalist enterprise since the 1980s), but the hybrid or transitional nature of its economy, combining elements of capitalism with features of a planned "socialist" economy, has allowed it to grow in ways that have insulated it, at least partially, from the constraints of the law of value (Smith 2010).

While it is clearly impossible to remove the contradictory impact of China from our analysis entirely, it is nevertheless illuminating to consider the specific growth performance of the leading advanced capitalist economies over the past three decades. Table 1.3 reveals that this performance has been a strikingly non-dynamic one, with the average annual growth rates of the combined GDPs of the top 35 advanced capitalist economies slipping well below the average global rates since 1990.

Table 1.3: Average Annual Growth Rates of the Combined GDPs of the Top 35 "Advanced" Capitalist Economies by Decade

1980–89	1990–99	2000–09
3.09%	2.64%	1.75%

Source: International Monetary Fund, World Economic Outlook Database

The upshot should be clear to all who are willing to discard the distorting lens of pro-capitalist ideology and examine social reality in an objective and scientific spirit. The global capitalist economy (seen through its own optic for measuring wealth, the money value of Gross Domestic Product) has been experiencing a deep malaise since the 1970s. Moreover, the capitalist system under these conditions is revealing itself more and more to be decisively geared toward further enriching and perpetuating the capitalist class—the tiny fraction of the population that owns and controls the major means of production, distribution, and exchange. Far from being guided, as Adam Smith believed, by an invisible hand that makes "nearly the same distribution of the necessities of life, which would have been made, had the earth been divided into equal portions among all its inhabitants," the accumulation of capital, under the domination of the capitalist law of value, is producing an ever-greater concentration of wealth at one pole of an increasingly globalized class structure and a massive growth of misery at the other. This "general law of capitalist accumulation," as Marx calls it, is a wrenching, discontinuous, and crisis-ridden process, one that *must* awaken the "workers of the world" to the historic necessity of abolishing capitalism and constructing a new socialist society capable of placing the productive forces at the disposal of those who labour.

The Unbearable Burdens of Capitalism in Crisis

The idea that capitalism is an essentially rational system in which the interests of capital and labour can be reconciled has been refuted definitively by historical experience. Since its consolidation in North Western Europe over two centuries ago through brutal processes of "primitive accumulation" involving the separation of the direct producers from their means of production, the pillage and colonization of much of the non-European world, and the trade and exploitation of millions of chattel slaves abducted from Africa, capitalism has demonstrated conclusively that even its more "normal" or "mature" operations can purchase progress only at a very heavy price to the mass of humanity.

Over the past two centuries, capitalism has produced dozens of economic crises and upheavals that have inflicted untold hardships on billions of working people. Over the past century (since the advent of what Lenin called the "imperialist epoch"), the intensifying crisis tendencies of the capitalist mode of production and the growing contradiction between the international character of production and the antagonistic logic of the capitalist nation-state system have brought about three severe economic slumps (in the 1930s, the 1970–80s, and the opening decades of the twenty-first century); two devastating world wars that cost the lives of at least 70 million people; dozens of bloody regional conflicts that claimed tens of millions more; highly distorted patterns of development and chronic underdevelopment across much of Asia, Africa, the Caribbean, and Latin America resulting in an average *annual* death toll from starvation and easily preventable disease of around 40 million; serious and potentially catastrophic ecological disturbances, including climate change and the depletion of non-renewable natural resources; and the squandering of enormous amounts of social wealth on armaments, advertising, the maintenance, policing, and surveillance of the indigent, and a host of other wasteful activities. Furthermore, since the 1970s, the living standards of the bottom 80% to 90% of wage- and salary-earners in even the richest capitalist countries have declined appreciably, notwithstanding continuously rising levels of labour productivity. Over the same period, a rapidly expanding global "surplus population," now constituting about a third of the world's population, has been condemned to a remorseless cycle of dispossession, unemployment, underemployment, and starvation.

31

The price paid by humanity as a whole to maintain the capitalist ruling class has always been a steep one. But as the irrationality of the capitalist system has become more pronounced and as the disastrous long-term ecological effects of capital's need for continuous expanded reproduction have become increasingly manifest, that price has assumed truly monstrous proportions. Indeed, the multiple crises engendered by capitalism and the burgeoning costs to humanity of perpetuating an economy and social order based on class antagonism, capitalist exploitation, competition among nation-states, and reckless disregard for the biosphere are now altogether unbearable.

The acute crises confronting humankind now include:

- the deepening malaise of the global capitalist economy and the related employment crisis faced by the world's youth
- the yawning social chasm between the super-rich and the bottom 90% of the world's population
- the decline and hollowing out of capitalist democracy—which has never been much more than a façade for the dictatorship of the bourgeoisie—as the dogmas of neoliberalism and the authoritarian precepts of the "war on terror" have drastically narrowed the terms of "official" political discourse and eroded the hard-won rights and liberties that were the product of generations of struggle by ordinary working people
- the crisis in science and technology, as several hundred transnational corporate entities press ever more aggressively to subordinate research and innovation to the specific requirements of capital
- the crisis in culture, as the mass media of a morally bankrupt capitalist order attempt to hypnotize and "dumb down" the population with entertainment products promoting trivial, misanthropic, dystopian, militaristic, and even psychopathic messages
- the crisis in education, as school curricula increasingly discourage critical thought while celebrating and glamorizing "entrepreneurial" profiteering

- the crisis in the production, distribution, and quality of food, as malnourishment is increasingly associated not simply with starvation but with the proliferation of obesity and chronic illnesses, and as human consumption relies more and more on the most monstrous treatment of non-human animals and the production of genetically modified crops
- the growing crisis in international relations, as the time-honoured efforts of the imperialist capitalist nation-states to resolve their deepening economic problems at the expense of their main rivals as well as the so-called "developing world" prepare the ground for a new world war
- the global environmental crisis, a phenomenon that must be seen as the inevitable result of capitalism's need to promote constant economic growth as a condition of valorization, to recklessly exploit what Marx called "the natural conditions of production" without regard to any long-term consequences, and to measure wealth solely in ways that comport with the "law of value"—that is, in terms of abstract labour and its phenomenal expression as money.[4]

The first of these grave crises—the global economic malaise of the early twenty-first century—will be explored further in the remainder of this chapter. The ability of Marx's theory to illuminate it, which I consider fundamentally and inseparably linked to all of the other crises identified above, will be discussed in greater detail in Chapter 2.

The Global Economic Malaise

In my analysis of the global economic crisis of 2007–09 (Smith 2010), two observations made by US presidential candidate John McCain in September 2008, as stock markets were crashing in the wake of the bankruptcy of the Lehman Brothers investment bank, proved to be useful as a starting point. The first of these—that "the fundamentals of our economy are strong"—was so absurd that it had armed Barack Obama with a convenient means to dismiss his Republican rival as "out of touch" with economic realities. Replying to Obama, an indignant McCain then implied that the most fundamental indicator of an economy's health is its labour productivity. "Our workers," he observed, "are the most innovative, the hardest working, the best skilled, most productive, most competitive in the world."

McCain's second observation was more or less accurate, even if his implication that high and rising levels of labour productivity were enough to guarantee the strength and stability of a capitalist economy was utterly wrong. Nevertheless, the reasoning behind McCain's "bullish on America" stance was apparent. From his right-wing, pro–"free market" perspective, it was simply inconceivable that a truly *severe* economic crisis could afflict the world's dominant capitalist country given the historical context of strong productivity growth, declining real wages, and the recent "defeat" of Soviet "communism."

In spite of these facts, and in defiance of McCain's ideological convictions, the US economy was indeed slipping into just such a crisis. As I went on to comment:

> [W]orker productivity is at an all-time high and wages have lagged badly behind productivity growth for a whole generation. Data furnished by the US Bureau of Labor Statistics reveal that productivity and real hourly wages in the private, non-farm US economy grew in lock step between 1947 and the early 1970s, but diverged significantly [in favour of productivity] over the next thirty years. Referring to the growing income gap between wage earners and investors, US billionaire Warren Buffett remarked candidly in 2005: "It's class warfare, and my class is winning."
>
> Since the 1970s, labour has indeed lost considerable ground in what has been a decidedly one-sided class war. Capital has had its way, in the US and globally; and yet, despite that, capital has still found a way to shoot itself in the foot—and rather badly at that. With Soviet-style "communism" out of the way, with unions decimated and lacking in strategic vision, with the welfare state a receding memory,

with China partially reopened to capitalist exploitation, and with most of the world's masses seemingly resigned to the inevitability of free-market economics, the global capitalist order is nevertheless now mired in what is clearly the worst economic crisis since the 1930s. (Smith 2010: 3)

To anyone who has grasped the fundamentals of Marx's crisis theory, the source of McCain's error should be abundantly clear. The assumption that a high level of labour productivity in a capitalist economy means that its "fundamentals" are sound presupposes that capitalism is a rationally ordered economic system. However, as Marx explains, the exact opposite is the case: under capitalism, the most "progressive" methods of increasing labour productivity become increasingly incompatible with capital's need to exploit living labour in order to produce surplus value, and this incompatibility leads inexorably to a deepening systemic crisis.

Of course, it is quite possible to reject McCain's particular version of free-market economic orthodoxy without embracing Marx, and that is precisely what most liberal economists and "progressives" did as they rushed headlong to revive and popularize the theories of John Maynard Keynes and Hyman Minsky. Virtually all such commentators agreed that the cause of the "Great Recession" of 2007–09 was to be found in the excessive greed of corporate and financial elites. For a generation or more, they argued, capital had succeeded in claiming ever-larger shares of national income at the expense of labour. Concurrently, the deregulation of financial institutions and markets had freed up the big banks to engage in ever-riskier practices that had allowed the rate of profit in the financial sector to soar to unprecedented heights. In view of these undeniable trends, it was by no means obvious that Marx's "law of the tendency of the rate of profit to fall" had very much relevance. In contrast, Keynes, with his theory of "deficient aggregate demand," and Minsky, with his notions of financial fragility, surprise events, and debt deflation, seemed to have anticipated the principal contours of the first great recession of the twenty-first century. What's more, Keynes and Minsky had offered seemingly "practical" solutions to the crisis—a redistribution of national income in favour of labour, increased taxation on the rich, stimulation of aggregate demand through increased government spending, and more stringent regulation of banks and financial markets—solutions that were aimed at stabilizing and "saving the economy" (read, *the capitalist system itself*) from the avarice and irresponsibility of the rich. Even many ostensible Marxists joined the bandwagon, petitioning the US Congress to adopt a left-Keynesian economic policy and "re-regulate" the banks.

President Obama's administration and a supposedly dysfunctional Congress soon dashed the hopes of these reform-minded "progressives." The bailout of the big investment banks and the economic policies pursued in the aftermath of the financial crisis brought about a greater centralization of financial capital, a further widening of the income gap between the "top 1%" and the great majority of the population, a resurgence of stock market values predicated on successive rounds of "quantitative easing" (the US Federal Reserve's injection of massive liquidity into the banks at near 0% interest), depressed wages, eviscerated social services, and a ballooning national debt.

Despite all this, and to some extent because of it, the appeal of "reformist" prescriptions to address the crisis has persisted. Since the official end of the Great Recession in 2009, soaring stock markets, record corporate profits, and reports of massive tax evasion by the wealthy have given credence to the notion that the system is far from broken and that capitalists are continuing to find ways to claim an ever-larger share of the enormous wealth that remains in circulation. Not surprisingly, in light of all this, many conclude that a big improvement in the "economic fundamentals" is attainable within the capitalist framework through progressive reforms centred on a *redistribution* of wealth and income.

The problem with this perspective is that much of the new-found wealth and income in the US (as well as in Europe and Japan) has a decidedly fictitious character: it is money arising not from the production of new value (in Marx's sense) but from governmental efforts to print money and to make it cheaply available to "too-big-to-fail" banks. As national debt levels rise (providing politicians with convenient excuses for starving the public sector and cutting popular social welfare programs), the private banks are appropriating government-generated liquidity and then making loans at interest rates that guarantee windfall financial profits. The result of these policies and practices is quite clear: to shift ever-more wealth toward the corporate and financial elites through the deliberate impoverishment of the working population.

This massive redistribution of wealth in favour of the rich is occurring precisely because the agents of capital have determined that productive investment is no longer the surest route to profitability. The resurgence of booked profits since the Great Recession is based to a considerable extent on the increasing importance of "fictitious" profits—profits based not on a relation of production (that is, upon surplus value created by living labour) but on a "relation of debt/credit" (to borrow Carchedi's phrase, 2011a, 2011b). Moreover, this is hardly a recent phenomenon, as it represents the continuation of a financialization of the global economy that extends back to the 1980s. The effects of this process are strikingly illustrated in Figure 1.1.

Figure 1.1: "Real" GDP Wealth and Global Financial Assets—1980, 1990, and 2000–07

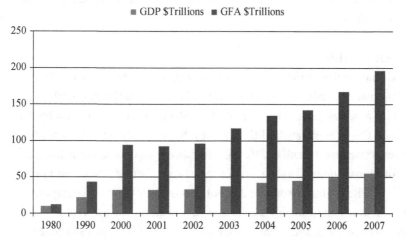

Source: McKinsey Global Institute

Given how entrenched the financialization phenomenon has become, it is far from clear that a major redistribution of income from capital to labour could have a beneficial effect on the "real" rate of profit—that is to say, the rate of profit excluding fictitious profits based on rising debt. Indeed, there is every reason to believe that it could lower the rate of profit and destabilize the financial system without doing much to stimulate productive investment.

A far more radical solution is clearly needed. If the underlying reason for the malaise of global capitalism is indeed a persistent crisis of valorization, then the only truly progressive way forward is to liberate economic life from the tyranny of the capitalist law of value. Daunting as the task may seem, this can only be accomplished in one way: through the expropriation of capital by the working class and the establishment of a democratically administered and rationally planned socialist economy geared toward the satisfaction of human needs.

The hypothesis of a crisis of valorization, underlying persistently low rates of return on productive capital, is analyzed in greater depth in Chapter 2. Before turning to that analysis, however, it will be useful to consider some other recent studies that provide some support to the hypothesis, beginning with several Marxist analyses that have focused on trends in the US rate of profit.[5]

ANWAR SHAIKH

Shaikh has analyzed the before-tax rate of profit in the US from 1947 to 2010. However, unlike many economists, he excludes the financial sector from his analysis, calculating a "rate of profit-of-enterprise" (the difference between the interest rate and the rate of return on active investment) that "drives active investment" (2010: 46). His rate of profit for US non-financial corporations is defined as the ratio of their profit "before interest and profit taxes" to "the beginning of year current cost of their plant and equipment" (48). On this basis, Shaikh discloses a falling trend for the rate of profit from 1947 to 1983 and a very modestly rising trend from 1983 to 2010, with a steep fall in 2006–09 followed by a jump in early 2010. He then points to two main factors responsible for the rise in the rate of profit after

1983: "an unparalleled slowdown in real wage growth" and "the extraordinary sustained fall in the interest rate which began at more or less the same time" (50). The first factor suggests a considerable increase in the rate of surplus value, as does his graph showing a continuously widening gap between hourly productivity gains and hourly real compensation after 1983 (49). However, Shaikh makes no attempt to assess the trend for the organic composition of capital, and consequently provides no clear explanation for the crisis of valorization that his analysis implicitly suggests.

ERGODAN BAKIR AND AL CAMPBELL

Bakir and Campbell report findings that are broadly similar to those of Shaikh. Their analysis focuses on "structural changes" in capitalism resulting in an after-tax rate of profit that has been "lower in the neoliberal period than in the previous period" (2010: 324). These changes are associated with an increased transfer of profits from the productive circuits of capital into financial circuits, with a simultaneous drop in the rate of capital accumulation—findings that refute "the neoliberal claim that increased finance has improved the conditions for accumulation" (325). Bakir and Campbell provide no explanation either for the "increased finance" of the neoliberal period or for the profitability crisis that preceded—and likely encouraged—the process of financialization. Even so, their analysis lends support to the idea that the robust performance of the "financial rate of profit" was purchased, to some extent, at the expense of productive capital, and that the crisis of valorization has only been exacerbated by the financialization process.

SIMON MOHUN

Mohun is concerned with trends in "aggregate capital productivity" in the US economy from 1964 to 2001, and their relationship to the rate of profit, the profit share of national income, and the rate of surplus value. His major focus is on "the ratio of labour productivity to capital intensity" (2009: 1025). He takes seriously Marx's vital distinction between productive and unproductive labour (see Chapter 2 of this volume), and his findings are clearly relevant to an evaluation of so-called "capital intensity," which is indirectly related to Marx's concept of the organic composition of capital.

Reporting a before-tax rate of profit that fell sharply between 1964 and 1982 and rose gradually from 1982 to 2001, Mohun argues that the 1964–82 period "has some elements of a classical period *à la Marx*," by which he means that "capital productivity fell steeply because a rising technical composition of capital [the ratio of dead to living labour in "material" terms] could only generate rising labour productivity at a lower rate (and the rate of surplus value was constant)" (1041). The rate of profit was driven down by both falling capital productivity and the rising wage-share of unproductive labour. These empirical findings are broadly consistent with Marx's theoretical expectations.

In addition, Mohun finds that in the second period (1982–2001) the technical composition of capital "was roughly constant, but labour productivity was rising so that real capital productivity rose sharply, driving up the rate of profit" (1041). This is in general accord with my argument that, in response to the crisis of profitability, the capitalist class and the state effectively mobilized many of the counteracting tendencies to the falling rate of profit, among them various methods for increasing "absolute surplus value" through the intensification and reorganization of the labour process (such as speed-up, "lean production" methods, etc.). What Mohun calls the "exceptionalism" of the later period—characterized by "sustained annual increases in labour productivity in the absence of capital deepening" (1041)—was precisely what was needed to arrest the decline in the rate of profit during that conjuncture. In the 1980s, the only viable alternative strategy from the perspective of capital would have been to allow a massive devaluation of capital assets, risking a descent of the US and global economies into a severe depression at a time when the capitalist West was still facing down its Soviet adversary.

ANDREW KLIMAN (VERSUS MICHEL HUSSON)

Kliman's analysis (2010a, 2010b) provides support to the claims that "the long-term build-up of debt that led to the current crisis is in turn the result of a longstanding profitability problem," and that "capital was not destroyed during the slumps of the 1970s and early 1980s to a degree sufficient to reverse the decline in the rate of profit" (2010b: 9). The first claim is certainly correct, but the second should be approached with considerable caution. While, for a variety of reasons (the Cold War, the strength of organized labour during the 1970s and 1980s, etc.), the strategists of the social capital sought to avoid a slaughtering of capital values on a scale adequate to quickly restore a dramatically higher rate of profit, the evidence is overwhelming that the rate of profit was stabilized in the 1980s and began a gradual rise thereafter. This was accomplished by extracting greater surplus labour from productive workers through methods that did not require large increases in the technical and organic compositions of capital, the result being a considerable rise in the rate of surplus value.

While he denies the reality of an increase in the rate of surplus value, Kliman is able to do so only by entirely ignoring the distinction between productive and unproductive labour, treating tax revenues as either surplus value or variable capital, and failing to disaggregate after-tax wages and salaries into their variable capital, surplus value, and constant-capital components.

To his credit, Kliman is critical of analysts like Dumenil and Levy (2004) who had insisted that "the structural crisis is over" and that poor accumulation rates could be blamed simply on neoliberal economic policies (a position that lends itself to reformist political prescriptions). But his refusal to recognize the "exceptionalism" of the post-1982 period cannot be justified with the implied claim that his analysis is uniquely resistant to the idea that the crisis is a "purely financial one." Analytically, a middle position between Dumenil and Levy on the one side and Kliman on the other is not only possible but scientifically indicated—and such a position is clearly occupied by proponents of a variety of political perspectives.

Kliman also makes much of his commitment to "historical-cost" measures of the capital stock and therefore of the rate of profit, as opposed to the "current-cost" measures that are more commonly used among Marxists. Arguably, it is useful to measure, analyze, and compare *both* historical-cost and current-cost rates of profit. At the same time, however, Husson is right to observe that choosing between them "does not have enormous empirical implications" (2010: 2).

Husson is also correct to observe that Kliman's claim that the wage-share of national income in the US has remained essentially constant is badly compromised by his failure to recognize that a sizable and rising share of "wages and salaries" in the national income accounts is actually a disguised form of profit (surplus value), namely, the salaries of corporate executives. As he correctly observes: "It is enough to exclude one per cent of the highest wages to find a fall in the share of wages as marked in the US as in Europe" (6).

Each of the above studies by Marxist economists lend strong support to the "crisis of valorization" hypothesis, even if they do so in ways that are incomplete or depart from the approach adopted in Chapter 2. What is perhaps more surprising is that a recent study by two mainstream economists provides some (indirect) support for it as well.

ERIK BRYNJOLFSSON AND ANDREW McAFEE

In 2011, Brynjolfsson and McAfee published a much-publicized and widely discussed book entitled *Race Against the Machine: How the Digital Revolution is Accelerating Innovation, Driving Productivity, and Irreversibly Transforming Employment and the Economy*. The book presents an array of statistics and evidence to support the argument that technological innovation has not slowed in recent years as some have argued, but is actually accelerating at a pace that is bound to create a long-term "jobs crisis" in the US and other advanced capitalist economies. This prediction is, of course, disastrous in its implications for a younger generation already hard hit by a global economic slump that has produced historically unprecedented youth unemployment rates around the world, including rates of over 60% in such "developed countries" as Greece and Spain.

The two economists provide numerous examples revealing how digital technology is leading to a rapid "deskilling" of the workforce. They acknowledge that this deskilling process has been a perennial feature of capitalist economic development—a principal means whereby firms reduce their labour costs in the long term to more effectively compete in the market. But the acceleration of the process they describe portends an ever-widening gap between the number of new jobs that will be created and the number of new entrants to the workforce. Unlike previous eras of robust labour-saving technological innovation, they argue, the period ahead will be marked by a "structural" jobs crisis and persistently high levels of unemployment and underemployment.

One might think that Brynjolfsson and McAfee's analysis would have led them to at least consider Marx's general law of capitalist accumulation and his related predictions concerning the growth of a surplus population. Instead, they present a strangely optimistic view according to which "digital innovation increases productivity, reduces prices (sometimes to zero), and grows the overall economic pie," while also proposing that "employment prospects are grim for many today ... because we humans and our organizations aren't keeping up" (Amazon, n.d.). The problem, from their point of view, is not with the capitalist system as such, but with the failure of individuals, private organizations, and governments to adapt to these exciting new technologies. Their attitude might well be summed up by paraphrasing a famous one-liner by US President John Kennedy: Ask not what the economy can do for you, ask what you can do for the economy!

Whither Twenty-First-Century Capitalism?

Like Adam Smith, John McCain, and all those who believe in the perennial "rationality" of capitalism, Brynjolfsson and McAfee fail to understand that, so long as the capitalist law of value holds sway, "the economic pie" must always be measured in terms of labour time (via its phenomenal money form) and not by abstract "material productivity." By this yardstick, the economic pie is *not* growing, even if the money supply currently is, albeit through extraordinarily "artificial" means. The illusion of growth is being sustained by a fantastic and ultimately unsustainable expansion of debt, the "value" of which will need to be seized from the working class through a variety of draconian measures if the capitalist system is to avoid a catastrophic depression.

The continuing technological revolution occurring within the global economy will certainly *not* lead to the sort of capitalist utopia that Brynjolfsson and McAfee, along with other bourgeois "futurists,"[6] would like us to envision. On the contrary, it can only exacerbate the crisis of valorization that has long signalled the historic bankruptcy of the capitalist mode of production. To develop a better understanding of that crisis, it is essential to explore the deepest roots of the first global slump of twenty-first-century capitalism, a task taken up in Chapter 2.

Notes

1. Marx recognizes that not everything sold in a market is a commodity. Land untouched by human hands, for example, can command a price, but has no "value" in Marx's sense. Similarly, an individual work of art created by a renowned master painter can command a price that has no clear connection to its cost of production reckoned in labour time. Strictly speaking, products of private labour that are individually unique and that are not strictly reproducible are not really commodities at all in Marx's sense, even though they may assume the commodity form.
2. In Marx's theory, not all wage-labourers are productive for capital. Only those directly involved in the production of goods and services in the commodity form create surplus value. Unproductive wage-labourers (in the sphere of circulation and in state and parastatal sectors) nevertheless play a necessary role in realizing the value of commodities in circulation and otherwise reproducing the conditions for capital accumulation (see Chapter 2 and Smith 2010).
3. Marx uses the terms "unpaid labour" and "surplus labour" interchangeably. "Paid labour" corresponds to the necessary labour required to create the value received by workers in their wages, while unpaid labour is the labour that is performed above and beyond the necessary labour and that allows for the creation (or transfer) of surplus value. See Chapter 10 of Marx (1977) on "The Working Day" for an elaboration of these distinctions.
4. Apart from the imperative of avoiding a global thermonuclear war, if we were to be permitted just one argument on behalf of socialism, it might well be this: only the triumph of global socialism has the potential to arrest and reverse the worsening environmental crisis by subordinating production to

the requirements of *sustainable human need* and by regulating the metabolic relation between human productivity and non-human nature through rational global planning, as informed by the fruits of scientific discovery. For some important discussions of this topic, see Minqi Li (2008, 2010).

5. The next few pages are taken from Smith and Butovsky (2012), the greater part of which is reproduced as Chapter 2 of this volume.

6. See, for example, Diamandis and Kotler (2012).

Profitability and the Roots of the Global Crisis: Marx's "Law of the Tendency of the Rate of Profit to Fall" and the US Economy, 1950–2007

Co-authored with Jonah Butovsky

Since the onset of the financial crisis of 2007–08 and the ensuing global economic slump, radical political economists have debated the role of profitability in what has been the most severe systemic crisis of world capitalism since the 1930s. While few, if any, have argued that the downturn that began in 2007 was triggered exclusively by a conjunctural fall in the average rate of profit (either globally or in the United States), most radical-left commentators have generally adopted one of two divergent positions:

1. The severe profitability crisis of the 1970s and early 1980s instigated changes in capitalist investment strategies, state regulatory practices, and patterns of capital accumulation that have not (or not yet) resolved the crisis entirely, but that did pave the way for a much-enlarged role for financial capital and therewith for the financial turbulence that crested in late 2008; or

2. The profitability crisis was substantially overcome by the late 1980s, and therefore the current crisis of world capitalism has much more to do with the contradictions of "financialization," conceived as a process

that has been integral to the neoliberal project and largely beneficial to profitability in a new era of finance-driven capitalism.[1]

Proponents of Marx's "law of the tendency of the rate of profit to fall" (LTRPF) tend to support the first position, while most of its critics on the radical left tend to support some variant of the second.[2] Complicating matters further, the proponents of each of these positions are divided over the causes of the 1970s profitability crisis, with some citing a wage-push/profit-squeeze and declining productivity, others overcapacity resulting from heightened inter-capitalist competition, and still others a rising organic composition of capital associated with a crisis of "valorization" (that is, a crisis of surplus-value production).

In this chapter, we defend a particular version of the first position—one that takes seriously Marx's LTRPF and regards it as central to a satisfactory account of the origins of the current crisis, but also recognizes that this "most important law of modern political economy" (Marx 1973: 748) has found evolving concrete expressions over the history of capitalism. Building on an earlier analysis (Smith 2010), the chapter reports our attempt to chart the fundamental Marxian ratios for the US economy between 1950 and 2007. In doing so, it serves to reinforce three central propositions of that analysis: (1) the current crisis has its deepest roots in *the persistent profitability problems of productive capital* on a world scale; (2) these problems are an expression of Marx's LTRPF in an era that has been marked both by a persistently high organic composition of capital (involving the displacement of living labour from production) and by the growing weight of unproductive capital and "socially necessary unproductive labour"; and (3) the profitability problems of productive capital, the hypertrophy of unproductive capital and the capitalist state, and the unprecedented growth of global debt over the past decade are interrelated expressions of an "historical-structural crisis" of the capitalist mode of production (CMP).

The Marxian theoretical presupposition of this argument is that economic value originates in social labour and must be conceptualized both in terms of the *class dynamics* of capitalism and *temporally*. For Marx, value is above all a *social relation*, the substance of which is abstract labour, the measure of which is socially necessary labour time, and the form of appearance of which is money. Marx's fundamental value categories of constant capital, variable capital, and surplus value are key to conceptualizing the specifically capitalist mode of class exploitation, the process of capital accumulation, and the distribution of value in national income and gross output. But the Marxian theory of capitalist crisis—and especially any Marxian theory of the historical-structural crisis of the CMP—must also distinguish between three *temporal modes* of value: previously existing value (PEV), new or currently produced value (NV), and anticipated future (not-yet-existing) value (AFV).

In Marx's theory, the concept of constant capital corresponds to PEV, while variable capital and surplus value are two forms of NV whose relative magnitudes are, within certain limits, determined by class struggle. The concept of AFV is not developed by Marx in any systematic way but is nevertheless implicit in his discussions of the credit system and "fictitious capital." Stocks, bonds and debt obligations, together with more recent innovations in fictitious capital such as credit default swaps, constitute claims on current and previously existing value (NV and PEV) but also wagers on AFV—value that has yet to be, and that may never be, produced.[3]

Fictitious capital has long played an important role in the operations of capitalist economies, and should not be regarded as purely parasitic or predatory. Fundamentally, however, it is money capital seeking to enlarge itself through speculative claims on future income, signifying an attempt on the part of a fraction of the social capital, centred in the financial sector but involving other sectors as well, to liberate itself from the problems of the "productive economy" and the constraints of the law of value. *Our claim is that the proliferation of forms of fictitious capital whose "temporal value composition" is weighted more and more toward AFV has emerged as a hallmark of the historical-structural crisis of capitalism in the neoliberal era.*[4]

As the flow of constant capital (PEV) grows relative to the flow of NV (due to the declining role of productive labour in the capitalist economy), there is a corresponding tendency for representations of AFV to acquire increased importance. This process is manifested in the proliferation of *increasingly fictitious* forms of financial capital and a malignant growth of unsustainable debt. The result is that the true extent of the valorization crisis of late capitalism—*the crisis in the production of surplus value*—is concealed by the false appearance of (some) AFV as part of the "profit" component of currently produced surplus value. Consequently, booked profits, as these appear in conventional national income accounts, reflect not only a determinate share of the new value produced by productive living labour, but also fictitious profits that have no substantial foundation in the value creation process.

To be sure, some profits that do not arise from the current exploitation of living labour represent *transfers* within the circuits of capitalist revenue (NV) or from certain streams of constant capital (for example, PEV flows originally earmarked for state expenditures). Such profits can be conceptualized as "profit upon alienation" or "profit through dispossession." But alongside such (non-NV) profits exists a growing mass of fictitious profits (above all in the financial sector) that constitute claims on AFV in the form of debt obligations—and therefore claims on income whose actualization depends upon the future performance of productive labour (or, failing that, upon the appropriation of previously existing values represented in workers' pensions and in "public assets"; that is, through various processes of "accumulation through dispossession").[5]

The mechanisms whereby booked profit is bolstered by transfers involving one or another form of AFV are myriad and cannot be examined in detail here. Nevertheless, theoretical acknowledgement of this reality is vitally important to registering the significance of the long-term divergence between the rate of profit on productive capital and the rate of profit on financial capital. The more robust performance of the latter compared to the former has been one of the most striking features of capitalism in the neoliberal era. At the same time, however, it can be seen as constituting a new and rather significant "adulteration" of Marx's LTRPF—one that further complicates the already daunting task of evaluating this law through empirical analysis.

Notwithstanding these difficulties, we are convinced that Marxist analysis of the historical dynamics of the capitalist world economy ought not to dispense with serious attempts to measure such fundamental Marxian (value-theoretic) ratios as the average rate of profit, the rate of surplus value, and the organic composition of capital. To be sure, such attempts can never offer much more than rough approximations. Even so, we think they are vitally important to charting and comprehending essential trends in the CMP—trends that can usefully inform, if only in a very general sense, the political-programmatic perspectives and educative tasks of Marxist socialists in relation to the broader working-class movement.

Our itinerary is as follows. In Section I, we discuss the main elements of Marx's LTRPF, the theoretical controversy surrounding it, and some of the major problems involved in empirically evaluating the actuality of the law. We then outline our own approach to theoretically specifying the value categories that comprise the Marxian ratios and discuss some of the controversial issues posed by this specification. In Section II, we consider these issues in greater depth and explore their implications for an analysis of the current crisis that traces the roots of the financial crisis of 2007–08 in the longer-term crisis of profitability of the advanced capitalist world. In Section III, we present the findings of our own "case study" of the US economy between 1950 and 2007, concluding in Section IV with a few observations concerning the political-programmatic implications of our findings.

I. The Rate of Profit and the Crisis of Global Capitalism

MARX'S LAW OF THE TENDENCY OF THE RATE OF PROFIT TO FALL

Capitalism is dominated by historically specific laws that are rooted in its fundamental social relations of production, relations that are at once class exploitative, competitive, and formally egalitarian. The capitalist law of value regulates socio-economic reproduction by allocating resources in accordance with the principle that only living, commodity-producing labour (that is to say, "productive labour") can create new value. This new value finds expression in the wages of *productive* wage-labourers (variable capital, or v) and in the surplus value (s) appropriated by the class of capitalist property owners. As the competitive dynamics of capitalist accumulation assert themselves, individual capitalist enterprises seek to improve their productivity and lower their costs of production/doing business by reducing their dependency on living wage-labour and relying on labour-saving technologies. The result is an increase in the technical composition

51

of capital (TCC)—the ratio of the means of production and circulation (the "constant capital stock" [c]) to living labour, as well as an increase in the rate of surplus value (s/v)—the rate of exploitation of productive labour. To the extent that the increase in the former ratio finds expression in value/money terms, the consequence will be increases in the "value composition of capital" (VCC, measured as c/v) and the "organic composition of capital" (OCC, measured as $c/s+v$).

An increase in c/v will only lead to a fall in the average rate of profit (measured as s/c) if it rises faster than the rate of surplus value (s/v). However, inasmuch as any change in $c/s+v$ already manifests changes in s/v, an increasing organic composition of capital (OCC) *must* be associated with a falling rate of profit.[6] This is the essence of Marx's LTRPF.

The capitalist law of value and the LTRPF are understood by Marx to involve and reflect a deepening structural contradiction between the development of the productive forces and the reproduction of capitalist social relations. Indeed, they inform and give expression to a growing incompatibility between the "technical-natural" and "social" dimensions of capitalism as an historical mode of production (Marx 1859; Smith 2010). Thus, while playing an important (though not always central) role in periodic crises of capitalist economies, the LTRPF also finds long-term "secular" expressions and can be viewed as integral to capitalism's historical-structural crisis.

Marx's LTRPF provides a simple and remarkably compelling foundation for the argument that capitalism's capacity to develop the productive forces and promote human progress is historically limited. But precisely because it stands opposed to any notion that capitalism can enjoy a progressive, "crisis-free" evolution, it has been the target of repeated criticism from both defenders of the capitalist order and reformist leftists who envision a gradual, incremental transition to socialism. Having noted this important dialectic of program and theory, we are nevertheless obliged to consider the scientific merit of the major theoretical objections to the LTRPF, since no empirical demonstration can establish its veracity so long as significant doubts about it remain at the theoretical level.

THE CONTROVERSY SURROUNDING THE LTRPF[7]

The most important objections to Marx's exposition of the LTRPF are to be found in four (somewhat overlapping) arguments: (1) the argument that the tendencies that Marx himself identifies as "counteracting" the fall in the rate of profit are sufficient to effectively negate the "law as such"; (2) the neutral technological progress argument, according to which technological innovation under capitalism can evince a "capital-saving" bias just as easily as a "labour-saving" one; (3) the "rising technical composition/stable organic composition" argument, according to which the displacement of living labour from production and any concomitant increase in the TCC need not result in a rising OCC; and (4) the "choice of technique" argument, according to which Marx's theory fails to establish why individual capitalist firms would adopt techniques of production that lower the average rate of profit. Let's consider each of these in turn.

(1) The Law and Its Counteracting Tendencies

In evaluating what Marx cites as counteracting tendencies to a falling rate of profit, we can begin by distinguishing those factors that contribute to an increase in the rate of surplus value from those that pertain directly to the OCC. The former includes (1) "increases in the intensity of exploitation," (2) "reduction of wages below their value," and (3) "relative overpopulation," while the latter involves (4) "the cheapening of the elements of constant capital" and (5) "foreign trade" (Marx 1981, Ch. 14).

"Increasing the intensity of exploitation" encompasses two distinguishable modes of increasing exploitation, only one of which can counter a fall in the average rate of profit. In this connection, Marx points to methods employed by capitalists to improve labour productivity that do *not* involve investments in labour-saving technology conducive to a rising OCC. Such methods are generally associated with the production of "absolute surplus value" and include speed-up and a prolongation of the working day—methods that run up against physiological limits, worker resistance, and pressures to increase wages. Marx also mentions productivity-enhancing technical innovations as these are applied by individual capitalists before they are universally applied and, presumably, before they have an impact on the economy-wide OCC.

As with the methods employed to increase the intensity of labour exploitation, "the reduction of wages below their value" is generally an *ephemeral* factor in countering the fall in the rate of profit—for any permanent reduction would amount to a lowering of the value of the commodity labour-power, thereby compromising workers' performance within the labour process and eventually inciting serious worker resistance. Thus, a long-term reduction of wages below their value can be envisioned only under conditions of severe anti-labour repression.

"Relative overpopulation" can also have a positive impact on the rate of exploitation by pushing down wages, but it encounters a significant barrier in the limited size of the working population. Only in situations where capital is in the process of uprooting non-capitalist modes of production and constantly replenishing a massive "reserve army" of the unemployed is it likely to have anything more than a short-term impact as a counteracting factor.

Conjuncturally, all three of the above factors can play a role in increasing the rate of surplus value without inducing a rise in the OCC. Even so, Marx's apparent expectation that the rate of surplus value will show a *secular* tendency to rise is inseparable from his view that it will rise mainly due to an increased TCC. And such an increase, Marx assumed, will find a value expression in a rising OCC. Only if a rising TCC occurs without a concomitant increase in the OCC can this lead to a situation of rising productivity and exploitation with no falling rate of profit.

It is in just this connection that "the cheapening of the elements of constant capital" assumes its exceptional significance as a counteracting factor. Marx writes:

> [The] same development that raises the mass of constant capital in comparison with variable reduces the value of its elements, as a result of a higher productivity of labour, and hence prevents the value of the constant capital, even though this grows steadily, from growing in the same degree as its material volume, i.e., the material volume of the means of production that are set in motion by the same amount of labour-power. (Marx 1981: 343)

Marx suggests here that the OCC will rise less impetuously than the TCC, but he does *not* assert that a rise in the OCC will be *prevented* by "a higher productivity of labour." For a rise in the OCC to be fully blocked, the elements of constant capital must "increase [in mass] while their total value remains the same or even falls" (1981: 343). While the limitations of "constant-capital-saving" as a factor inhibiting the fall in the profit rate are not clearly specified, it is reasonable to assume that Marx considered labour-saving innovation a *greater priority* for capitalists. After all, the drive by capitalist enterprises toward labour-saving innovation is deeply rooted in the *totality* of social production relations in which they are enmeshed—relations that impel them not only to cut costs per unit of output in order to meet the challenges of competition, but to do so in ways that simultaneously strengthen capital's hand in relation to labour.

Marx's fifth counteracting factor is "foreign trade and investment"—a factor that is clearly germane to the performance of *national* rates of profit, but much less so to an increasingly internationalized rate of profit. However, this factor can play a role in elevating the average rate of profit of particular national economies only to the extent that the terms of trade *continue* to improve and/or the rate of return on capital invested abroad *continues* to rise from the standpoint of a given "national" social capital. Accordingly, the results of foreign trade and investment need to be viewed as a two-edged sword, capable of depressing as well as raising national rates of profit.

This survey of the tendencies counteracting the TRPF suggests that "the law as such" and the counteracting tendencies to the law are not *co-equal* "tendential laws" (as suggested, for example, by Albo, Gindin, & Panitch 2010: 39). While the "countertendencies" are certainly key components of capitalist dynamics, all of the counteracting tendencies cited by Marx—with the possible exception of the cheapening of the elements of constant capital—have clearly defined *limits* as means to stemming a fall in the average rate of profit. On the other hand, the "law as such"—a rising OCC, accompanied by a falling rate of profit—finds its limit only in economic crises that bring about a devaluation of capital assets. In Marx's theory, it is *capitalist crisis* that creates the conditions for a recovery of the profit rate and resumed accumulation. Moreover, it is precisely the *recurrence* of capitalist crises that induces the capitalist class to deploy ever-changing "tactics" to increase the rate of profit, ensure the conditions of accumulation, and mitigate the destabilizing influences of severe economic dislocations on capitalist society's "class equilibrium."

(2) The Neutral Technological Progress Argument

Marx's LTRPF postulates that technological progress under capitalism has an inherently *labour-saving bias*. Against this, several of his critics argue that, *given a constant real wage,* there are no good reasons to believe that capitalists will economize more on labour than on constant capital. But it is precisely the real-world possibility of wage increases outstripping the growth of labour productivity that ensures that technological progress must exhibit a labour-saving bias.

What needs to be emphasized here is that the labour-saving bias of capitalist innovation has its most fundamental roots in the "real subsumption of labour by capital."[8] Labour-saving technical innovation—the utility and purpose of which is to increase "relative surplus value"—strengthens capital's position by rendering it as independent as possible of living labour in general and skilled labour in particular.

A second benefit of labour-saving innovation was alluded to earlier. Since the limited size of the working population is an obvious barrier to the accumulation process, capitalists must find ways to increase output in the face of labour shortages. Labour-saving technological innovation is by far the most effective solution to this problem. If technical change were to exhibit a neutral tendency or a constant capital-saving bias, capital's dependence on the available working population would become ever greater, depleting the reserve army of labour and forcing up wages.

If Marx's TCC refers to "what modern economists call 'capital intensity', the quantity of capital goods in real terms co-operating with each worker at some 'normal' level of full employment" (Mage 1963: 72), then the TCC can be defined as the ratio of means of production expressed in "constant dollars" to the number of production workers, or, better still, as the constant-dollar value of capital stock employed per hour worked. All theoretical speculation aside, empirical studies establish unmistakably that technological change does indeed exhibit a pronounced labour-saving bias in the long term and furthermore that this tendency entails a marked increase in the TCC.[9]

(3) The "Rising TCC—Stable OCC" Argument

The most frequently encountered theoretical objection to the LTRPF concerns Marx's expectation that a rise in the TCC (a ratio of "use-value" magnitudes) will be accompanied by a rise in the OCC (a ratio of "value" magnitudes). As noted previously, Marx acknowledges that the rise in the OCC will be less pronounced than the rise in the TCC owing to productivity increases associated with the latter. His critics go further, however, arguing that productivity increases in industries producing means of production have the effect of reducing the value of constant capital, in this way deflating the value of the capital stock, the numerator of the OCC.

However, productivity increases cannot *completely* negate the tendency of the OCC to rise along with the TCC. The rise in the TCC is attributable to a labour-saving bias in capitalist technical innovation—a notion rooted in Marx's explicit recognition of the capital-labour relation as *antagonistic*. Such a notion is absent from the neoclassical theory of technical progress, and for just this reason it is difficult to see from the latter perspective that the use-value of a "capital good" is a function not only of its "capacity-increasing effect" but of its "labour-saving effect" as well (Mage 1963: 159). Once this *dual* function of capitalist means of production is recognized, it becomes clear that the TCC is neither proportional to nor quantitatively co-extensive with labour productivity.

Labour productivity is the ratio of *the mass of use-values produced* (output or capacity) to the number of hours worked. The TCC, on the other hand, refers to the ratio of *the use-value of the means of production* in relation to the number of hours worked. Accordingly, the use-value of the numerator of the TCC (the capital stock) encompasses *both* output/capacity-expanding and labour-saving effects. If technical innovation displays a labour-saving bias, for all the reasons pointed to by Marx, then the numerator of the TCC should increase at a *faster* rate than the numerator of labour productivity—since all positive changes in the latter will be reflected in the former but not all positive changes in the former will find expression in the latter. Since the OCC is the value expression of the TCC, it follows that a rise in the OCC will be restrained by increased labour productivity *but not entirely blocked* (Smith 1984: 144–48).

(4) The Choice of Technique Argument

If a rising OCC is compatible with a stable or rising rate of profit *for particular capitals*,[10] the precise microeconomic criteria by which individual capitalist firms choose different techniques of production need to be established. The much-cited "Okishio theorem" attempts to show that the criteria actually employed by capitalists would rule out a fall in the *general* rate of profit (Okishio 1961).

Under competitive conditions, a capitalist enterprise will only adopt a specific technique of production if it lowers per-unit production costs or increases per-unit profits at prevailing prices. Such innovation enables the firm to achieve a "transitional" rate of profit higher than the prevailing "general" rate. The Okishio theorem assumes that "the new average rate will be higher than the old average, due solely to the introduction of a cheaper technique (real wages being given)" (Shaikh 1978: 242).

In his response to this "choice of technique" argument, Shaikh suggests that Okishio's theorem merely underscores Marx's own thesis that "the battle of competition is fought by the cheapening of commodities" and that "the cheapest method of production will win out in the wars among capitals" (Marx 1978: 245). But there is a crucial difference between the "cheapest method of production" *per unit of output* and the "cheapest method" from the standpoint of *capital invested*. In order to grasp this, the distinction between *flows* and *stocks* must be appreciated. The cheapening of commodities is predicated on the lowering of unit cost-price—that is, a reduction in the *flow* of capital used up in producing each unit of output. Marx's argument is precisely that this reduction is generally accomplished through increased investment in the fixed-capital *stock*. Elaborating on Marx's point, Shaikh argues:

> Once the difference between production costs and investment costs is grasped, it immediately follows that there in fact exist two different

measures of profitability; profits in relation to capital used up in production ... which I shall call profit-margin on costs, and profits in
relation to capital advanced, or the profit rate. The former is a ratio
of two flows, the latter a ratio of flow to stock. (1978: 242–43)

Since the Marxian rate of profit is a ratio of the surplus-value flow to
the constant-capital stock, the increased fixed capital needed to cheapen
commodities "will lower not only the maximum but also the actual rate of
profit—precisely because this cheapening 'necessitates a costly and expen-
sive apparatus' [Marx]" (1978: 244).[11]

THEORETICAL ISSUES IN EMPIRICAL MEASUREMENT

The above discussion establishes, we think, that the major theoretical
objections to the LTRPF are by no means conclusive and that substantial
grounds exist for affirming that this law has a real and significant impact on
the macroeconomic dynamics of capitalist economies and the actual history of capitalism. Nevertheless, significant problems still confront those
seeking to empirically test the major hypotheses suggested by the LTRPF.

The first problem concerns the value-theoretic rectitude of measuring
the value categories and the Marxian ratios in magnitudes of money. Some
readings of Marx posit a dualism of labour-values and money-prices that
enjoins the theorist either to reject in principle *any* empirical measurement
of "value" or to insist upon the measurement of value in units of labour.
In counterpoint to such readings, we affirm our general agreement with
Moseley that Marx's concepts of constant capital, variable capital, and surplus value "can be defined in terms of sums of money which function as
capital. In principle, these concepts correspond to entries in the income
statements and balance sheets of capitalist firms" (1991: 30).

A second problem has to do with the appropriate theoretical specification of the value categories of Marx's system and the empirical translation
of these categories using conventional data sets (as furnished by capitalist states)—data sets that tend to be recalcitrant to Marxist concepts and
especially to the critical distinction between productive and unproductive

labour. As this problem is central to our concerns in the rest of this chapter, we will not dwell on it at this point.

The third problem concerns the appropriate "unit of analysis" for establishing the real trends of the fundamental Marxian ratios. Can meaningful results be achieved by analyzing *national* capitalist economies, or must the analysis be conducted at the level of the world economy—a postulated "international rate of profit"?

Certainly, as the internationalization of capital proceeds, manifested through increased international capital mobility and more pronounced tendencies toward profit rate equalization across national lines, one must acknowledge that processes of international surplus-value redistribution and "unequal exchange" will play an increasingly important role in the realization of profits within individual capitalist nation-states. Such processes will necessarily obscure *the transnational origin* of *some* of the surplus value that appears as "domestic profit"—and, to a certain extent, "delink" the (increasingly "internationalized") category of surplus value from the "nationally measured" value categories of constant-capital stock and variable capital.[12]

However, the globalization of capitalist economy has not reached a point where one can speak of a "general" international rate of profit, and it is impossible, in any case, to measure an average rate of profit on an international scale. What's more, it can be assumed that, to the extent that processes involving transfers of surplus value through unequal exchange are operative on a world scale, these would tend to favour national capitalist economies exhibiting the highest rates of labour productivity and the highest organic compositions of capital. Therefore, if the LTRPF can be measured and recognized as operative in the most powerful and productive national economy, the United States, there can be little doubt that it is also operative on a world scale.[13]

Transfers of surplus value across national lines do not occur entirely or even mainly through processes of unequal exchange. They also occur through foreign direct investment and the "repatriation" of corporate profits earned abroad. Over the past twenty years, US corporate profits earned "in the rest of the world" have increased considerably as a percentage of total corporate profits. This too complicates any empirical test of Marx's LTRPF because the capital investments "standing behind" these profits are not easily measured. We note, however, that the greatest share of these foreign investments was made in high-wage countries exhibiting already high compositions of capital.[14]

The foregoing considerations suggest that empirical measurement of the Marxian ratios in any national framework, even the United States, must always be scrutinized carefully and with many caveats in mind. That said, we think the exercise is still well worth doing.

THE LTRPF AND THE HISTORICAL-STRUCTURAL CRISIS OF CAPITALISM

As previously indicated, the burden of the present study is to defend, on the basis of a value-theoretic analysis of the laws of motion of capital in the US economy, several arguments advanced by Smith in his 2010 book *Global Capitalism in Crisis*. Smith's overarching thesis was that "the current crisis should be viewed against the backdrop of a historical-structural crisis of capitalism—as an extreme conjunctural expression of the decay of the profit system" (2010: x).[15]

To support this thesis, Smith explores three issues pertaining to the "deepening structural contradiction between the development of the productive forces and the reproduction of capitalist social relations" (2010: 6). The first is the negative impact on profitability of a rising or persistently high organic composition of capital in the capitalist core—the issue highlighted by Marx in his LTRPF.

The second issue is the impact of the growing specific weight of unproductive capital and of "socially necessary unproductive labour" in the advanced capitalist economies—an issue that not only enormously complicates any empirical evaluation of the LTRPF, but also points to a certain corruption or *adulteration* of Marx's law and to the declining dynamism of the capitalist mode of production:

If capitalism's tendency to promote the "objective socialization" of labour and of production once reflected its historically progressive role in developing the forces of production, it now *also* reflects a hypertrophy of the capitalist state and the sphere of circulation—

a hypertrophy which impedes the advance of the productive forces by diverting enormous economic resources *away from* production. (2010: 90)

The third issue stressed by Smith is that the *growing systemic overhead costs* associated with the expansion of unproductive capital relative to productive capital should be regarded as elements of the *constant-capital flow*: "[If] the growth of constant capital in relation to newly created value once signified a growth in the productivity of labour, it now *also* signifies a relative diminution of *productive* labour in relation to socially necessary unproductive labour" (1994a: 181). As a manifestation of an historical-structural crisis of capitalism, this phenomenon reveals that a growing share of economic resources is being used to sustain and perpetuate the distinctive institutional and class-antagonistic structures of capitalism. It signifies, in other words, that the social relations of capitalist production and reproduction are standing more and more as an obstacle to the progressive development of productive *capacities.*

II. The Specification of Marx's Value Categories and the Origins of the Current Crisis

Originally proposed by Mage, the value-theoretical specification of the unproductive "overhead costs" of the capitalist system as elements of constant capital is controversial and stands opposed to an entrenched convention to treat such costs (that is, tax revenues and the wages of unproductive workers in general) either as non-profit elements of social surplus value or as part of variable capital (if the relevance of the unproductive-productive distinction is denied).[16] In a series of publications, Smith (1991, 1993, 1994a, 1999, and 2010) has documented the uncertain status of these costs in Marx's own writings and defended a constant-capital specification of socially necessary unproductive labour (SNUL) and tax revenues. Table 2.1 provides a schematic representation of how productive labour is defined in Marxist theory along with three alternative specifications of what we call SNUL.

Table 2.1: Productive Labour (PL), Socially Necessary Unproductive Labour (SNUL), and the Marxian Value Categories (Variable Capital, Surplus Capital, and Constant Capital)

PRODUCTIVE LABOUR (PL)						
PL & PL wage costs as value	Does PL produce surplus value?	Does PL produce new value?	Does PL preserve previously existing value?	Does PL function as variable capital?	Are PL wages a component of social-surplus value?	Are PL wages a component of constant-capital flow?
As variable capital	Yes	Yes	Yes	Yes	No	No
SOCIALLY NECESSARY UNPRODUCTIVE LABOUR (SNUL)						
SNUL & SNUL wage costs as value (alternative conceptions)	Does SNUL produce surplus value?	Does SNUL produce new value?	Does SNUL preserve previously existing value?	Does SNUL function as variable capital?	Are SNUL wages a component of social-surplus value?	Are SNUL wages a component of constant-capital flow?
As variable capital (denies u-p distinction)	Yes	Yes	Yes	Yes	No	No
As surplus value (upholds u-p distinction)	No	No	Unclear	No	Yes	No
As constant capital (upholds u-p distinction)	No	No	Yes	No	Yes	Yes

Without exploring the finer points of this debate, it is sufficient to note here that the Mage-Smith approach allows us to agree with the critics of the unproductive-productive (u-p) distinction that costs associated with government taxation and the employment of unproductive labour are indeed *systemically necessary* from the point of view of the social capital (and are therefore *not* elements of surplus value easily convertible to profits), while also agreeing with our fellow defenders of the distinction that it is incorrect to treat the wages of workers employed in supervisory activity, bookkeeping, finance, trade, and many service industries as part of variable capital—that is to say, as capital exchanged with *productive labour* (Moseley 1991; Shaikh & Tonak 1994; Shaikh 1999; Mohun 1996). Thus, the constant-capital specification of these systemic overhead costs allows us to recognize that state expenditures, unproductive capital, and SNUL are at once *necessary* to overall capitalist profitability and *hazardous* to it. But to theoretically sustain this specification we are obliged to conceptualize the category of constant capital as the value expression not only of physical means of production (its definition at the level of abstraction of the first volume of *Capital*) but also of *all* the expenses and investments implicated in the total process of capitalist production, circulation, and reproduction, *with the singular exception of living, productive labour*, which is the sole creator of the new value that enters into profit-of-enterprise, interest, and rent (the principal components of surplus value), as well as the productive-labour wage bill.

Such a conceptualization of constant capital has enormous implications for empirical Marxist analysis. For it suggests that the *flow* of constant capital represents a much larger share of the total value of gross output than is usually thought—and this is especially true for the most developed capitalist economies with expansive state, commercial, service, and financial sectors. Other things being equal, real growth in the SNUL wage-bill and in tax revenues must produce an increase in the "value composition of output"—$c^f/(c^f + v^f + s^f)$—that is, the ratio of the annual flow of constant capital to the total value of gross product—an increase "likely to be associated with a declining average rate of profit."[17]

These observations have found some indirect support in a number of studies that establish a strong statistical correlation between movements in the rate of profit and in the "output-capital ratio" (the ratio of GDP to the value of the total capital stock) (Brenner 1998; Dumenil & Levy 2004; Freeman 2009). Freeman, for example, has shown that the output-capital ratio accounts for "75.7 per cent of the variation [in the US profit rate] between 1929 and 1996" (2009: 8).

In light of the theoretical perspective defended here, the reason that the output-capital ratio accounts for so much of the variation in the rate of profit over time might well be that it captures the effects of movements in *both* the OCC (defined as $c^s/[s^f+v^f]$: the ratio of the *stock* of constant capital to the sum of the two flows of new value) and the value composition of output (which reflects changes in such "overhead costs" of systemic reproduction as state expenditures and SNUL wages). However, assuming that total output is equal to the sum of the *three flows* of value identified by Marx (constant capital, variable capital, and surplus value), analysis of movements in the output-capital ratio (in value-theoretical terms, $[c^f+v^f+s^f]/c^s$) cannot tell us whether Marx's theory of a rising OCC leading to a falling rate of profit is empirically verifiable, even though a falling output-capital ratio is entirely consistent with Marx's theory and may well reflect a rising OCC.[18]

How then does this analysis assist us in understanding the process of financialization and the proximate causes of the financial crisis of 2007–08? In brief, the profitability crisis of the 1970s, particularly as it afflicted productive capital in the core capitalist countries, was never fully resolved due to the determination of capital and capitalist states to (a) avoid the kind of deep global depression that would involve widespread bankruptcies and a significant devaluation of capital stocks, and (b) restore profitability through a *gradual* increase in the rate of exploitation, but in ways that would not provoke a major politico-ideological crisis for world capitalism in the era of the Cold War. Furthermore, to sustain effective demand and to mitigate crises of overproduction, the credit system was overhauled and extended in ways that allowed for the accumulation of dramatically larger volumes of debt across the world economy. Along with the globalization of capitalist production and the creation of significant new sites of surplus value production in Asia and Latin America, the expansion of the debt bubble helped restore profitability and conferred upon financial capital a much enhanced role in maintaining the conditions of capital accumulation and economic growth, even as the rate of new capital formation and the growth rate of global GDP slowed in the 1980s and the 1990s.[19] In these circumstances, fictitious capital and profits became much more significant phenomena within the global circuits of capital.

The proliferation of fictitious capital and the buildup of ever-greater debt between 2001 and 2007 stimulated an anomalously high rate of profit in the US and robust global economic growth. But the escalating financial panic of 2007–08 signalled a growing recognition that the rising value of an array of dubious financial assets (collateral debt obligations and other derivatives) was wildly out of line with the "economic fundamentals" (the precarious realities of the US sub-prime mortgage market, the profitability problems of productive capital, the stagnancy of real wage growth, etc.). In the end, the capitalist law of value asserted itself as a kind of gravitational force, pulling down the financial house of cards and precipitating the worst global recession since the 1930s.

This analysis suggests that the current slump is by no means a typical periodic crisis of capitalism, but rather an extreme manifestation of a longer-term crisis of capitalist profitability rooted in a persistently high organic composition of capital in the "advanced capitalist" core of the world economy. Short of a complete collapse of the latter into deep depression, the immediate prospect is for a major escalation of the offensive by capital against labour on a world scale in order to both boost surplus-value production and reduce systemic overhead costs, all with a view to restoring the conditions of profitability and arresting the burgeoning debt crisis.[20]

III: The Rate of Profit, the Rate of Surplus Value, and the OCC in the US Economy, 1950–2007

This case study represents the first attempt of which we are aware to "test" Marx's LTRPF for the US economy in a way consistent with a constant-capital specification of tax revenues and SNUL since Mage's pioneering study of 1963. The results, however, have a somewhat inconclusive character owing to numerous technical problems associated with the translation of official economic data into the Marxian value categories. This translation problem is especially evident in our calculations of surplus value (*after-tax* profits and elite salaries) and variable capital (after-tax wages of productive workers).

The National Income and Product Accounts (NIPA) tables published by the US Bureau of Economic Analysis (BEA) include no data for after-tax wages or for *the corporate-officer share* of "wage and salary accruals" (an income stream that properly belongs to surplus value), rendering the calculation of after-tax wages of productive workers (variable capital, or v) problematic. Nor do these data sets allow us to easily discriminate between productive and unproductive labour, either within economic sectors/ industries or between them.

In addressing these problems, we have been obliged to apply a crude "average tax rate on personal income" in order to derive our estimates of variable capital (v). In addition, we have derived a rough estimate of corporate-officer compensation by defining the top 1% of wage and salary earners as recipients of such compensation for every year from 1950 to 2007. This estimate, based on figures provided by Saez (2011), was subtracted from after-tax wage and salary incomes and added to after-tax corporate profits to obtain our measure of surplus value (s). Inasmuch as the proportion of total wage and salary accruals received by the top 1% increased considerably between the 1960s and the 2000s, the growth of this (revenue) component of surplus value contributed to the upturn in the rate of profit over the past 30 years while doing little to improve the rate of capital accumulation.

To distinguish between productive and unproductive labour, the classification system suggested by Shaikh and Tonak (1994) and Mohun (2005) has been employed. Defined as *entirely unproductive* are the following divisions represented in the BEA/NIPA tables: wholesale trade, retail trade, finance, insurance and real estate, business services, legal services, miscellaneous professional services, other services, private households, and general government. All other divisions, including construction, manufacturing, transportation, and several service industries, were defined as *entirely productive*.[21] This compromise procedure—that is to say, the treatment of *all* labour employed by productive capital as productive—may skew our results for the rate of surplus value and the composition of capital to the extent that the ratio of supervisory to non-supervisory labour and, more generally, the ratio of unproductive to productive labour in these productive divisions vary over time. Nevertheless, we think it is reasonable to assume that the basic long-term *trends* revealed for these ratios would not be affected substantially by more exact measurements that captured such changing ratios within the productive divisions.

Notwithstanding these difficulties and compromises, our estimates should be of considerable interest to those who recognize the importance of empirically operationalizing the productive-unproductive distinction in the analysis of the fundamental Marxian ratios, and particularly to those persuaded of the need for a constant-capital specification of taxes and SNUL wages—a specification that effectively *removes* these flows from the calculation of the rate of profit, the rate of surplus value, and the OCC.

A detailed account of our methods and sources for calculating the basic variables of this study is provided in the Appendix at the end of the chapter.

THE MAIN FINDINGS

The principal findings of our study can be summarized concisely and are presented in a series of figures below.

First, with respect to the rate of profit (ROP), the current-cost ROP and the historic-cost ROP both display a downward trend over the entire period from 1950 to 2007 (see Figure 2.1, which depicts the current-cost ROP). As expected, both ROPs fall rather dramatically between 1950 and the 1980s, but then begin to climb sharply from 1990 to 2007, the eve of the Great Recession.[22] Furthermore, a truly remarkable increase in both ROPs is observable following the recession of 2001. Indeed, each approaches a postwar peak (14.5% and 24%, respectively) in 2006.

Figure 2.1: The Rate of Profit, US, 1950–2007 (*s/c*)

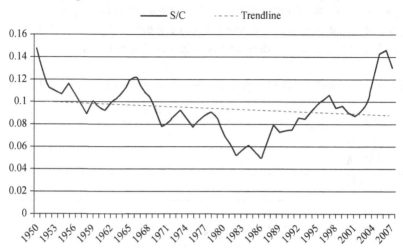

Source: See Appendix to this chapter.

That said, there are compelling grounds for regarding the strong per-formance of the ROP between 2002 and 2006 as *anomalous* and based to a considerable extent on "fictitious profits" booked in the finance, insur-ance, and real estate sectors, and perhaps also by many firms operating in the productive economy whose profits relied increasingly on the sale of "financial services." This suspicion is reinforced by the performance of Shaikh's (2010) before-tax "non-financial" ROP, which shows a steep rise between 2002 and 2006 but only to a peak of 12%, a level that remains about one-third below its postwar high in 1966.[23] Our own *after-tax* non-financial ROP (presented in Figure 2.2 below) reaches a peak during this period of just under 7% in 2006, fully *half* its postwar highs in 1950 and 1966. Moreover, the unprecedented growth in the mass of profits during this period was accompanied by rates of new capital formation that were unusually sluggish in the context of an allegedly booming economy (Bakir & Campbell 2010), as well as by a relatively low taxation rate on corpo-rate profits (McIntyre & Nguyen 2004). As investment in capital stocks stagnated, already-high levels of public and private debt soared under the combined impact of the costly Iraq War and the expanding housing bubble.

And so, of course, did profits. The conclusion is obvious: the anomalously high mass and rate of profit of the 2002–06 period was made possible only by the accumulation of an enormous volume of debt obligations—that is to say, of fictitious capital understood as claims on future income.

Figure 2.2: Non-Financial Corporate Rate of Profit (After-Tax), US, 1950–2008

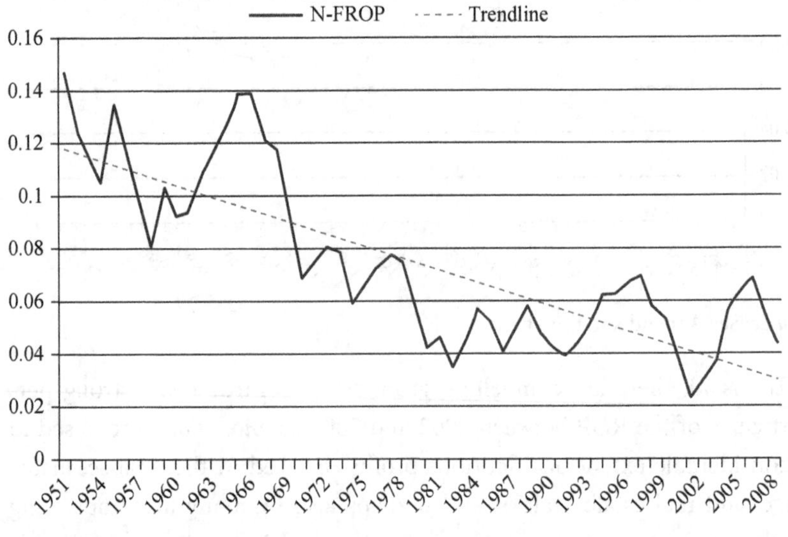

Source: See Appendix to this chapter.

The anomalous 2002–06 ROP was, then, both illusory and unsustainable. The ROP was bound to fall dramatically, and this was duly accomplished over 2007–09. With higher profits in 2009–10, the ROP returned to a level closer to its long-term trend line. Overall corporate revenues remained low, however, suggesting that enterprise cost-cutting (and some devaluation of capital stock) was responsible for the improved profit rate. The NIPA estimates for after-tax domestic corporate profits of $614 billion in 2008 and $710 billion in 2009 stood well below the record $1.09 trillion registered in 2006. A sharp spike to an estimated $1.04 trillion in 2010, however, suggested continuing volatility in the mass of profits, the ratio of financial to non-financial profits, and the average ROP.[24] Indeed, this spike was due in good part to the remarkable recovery of financial profits made possible by the government-funded bailout of the big banks as well as the massive infusion of liquidity into the banking system by the US Federal Reserve at 0% interest.

Second, with respect to the rate of surplus value (s/v), we find an overall increase in the trend line from 27% to 50% between 1950 and 2007 (see Figure 2.3). While s/v is essentially flat between 1950 and the 1970s, it falls after 1978, reaching its lowest point in 1986. It then embarks on a strongly upward trend between 1986 and 2007. These findings support the proposition that the decline in the ROP was arrested in good part due to a significant increase in the rate of exploitation of productive labour (s/v), with a long-term decline in corporate taxation playing a supplementary role. This increased exploitation, as we have seen, is reflected in the widening gap between the growth of labour productivity and the growth of hourly real wages, which itself must be explained in terms of changes in the labour process, on the one hand, and falling or stagnant real wages, on the other. Again, however, to the extent that it reflects a massive growth of fictitious financial profits, the sharp spike in s/v between 2002 and 2006 should be viewed as anomalous.[25]

Figure 2.3: The Rate of Surplus Value, US, 1950–2007 (s/v)

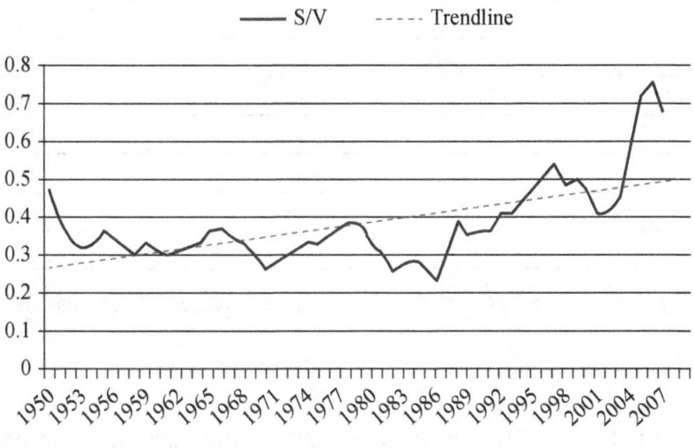

Source: See Appendix to this chapter.

Finally, with respect to the organic composition of capital (OCC), which is understood by Marx to be the value expression of the ratio of "dead to living labour in production,"[26] we find that the current-cost OCC displays a strong upward trend between 1950 and 2007, reaching a peak of 3.93 in 1982 compared to a postwar low point of 2.18 in 1950 (see Figure 2.4). The upward trend for the historical-cost OCC is even more pronounced, with the latter reaching a peak of 2.43 in 2000 compared to 1.16 in 1950. Much of this increase occurred after the onset of the profitability crisis of the 1970s. However, the OCC exhibits a very gradual, long-term declining trend between 1982 and 2007. The stabilization of the OCC during this period (in a range that is nevertheless well above that of 1950–75) suggests that one of the underlying causes of the profitability malaise of the past 30 to 40 years continues to assert itself. This conclusion is reinforced by the upward trends of both current-cost and historic-cost estimates of the value composition of capital (c/v), which effectively remove both actual and fictitious profits from the picture (see Figure 2.5 for the current-cost c/v).[27]

Figure 2.4: The Organic Composition of Capital, US, 1950–2007 ($c/s+v$)

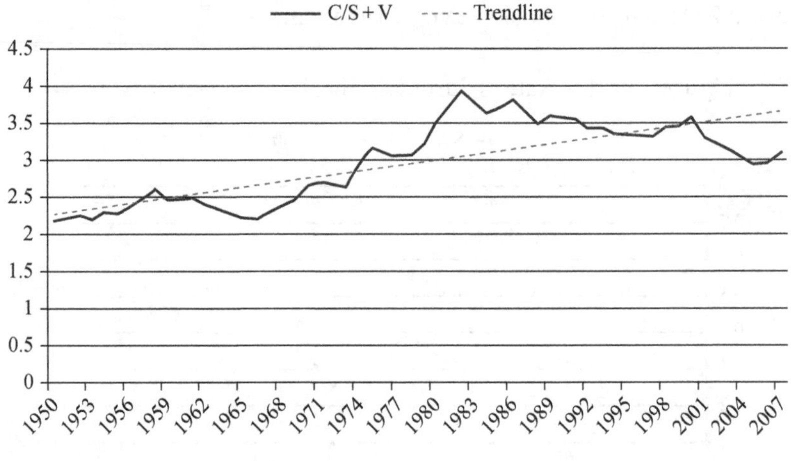

Source: See Appendix to this chapter.

The steep fall in the OCC in the early 2000s coincides with comparably steep rises in the ROP and s/v. We think that this fall is associated with the proliferation of fictitious capital and profit, the super-profits realised by US "defense" contractors following the invasions of Afghanistan and Iraq, and the anomalously slow pace of new capital formation during the Bush-era "boom." With the mass of profits and wages falling after 2007, the path of the OCC, like that of the ROP, seems to be returning to its historic trend line, at least in the short term.

Figure 2.5: The Value Composition of Capital, US, 1950–2007 (*c*/*v*)

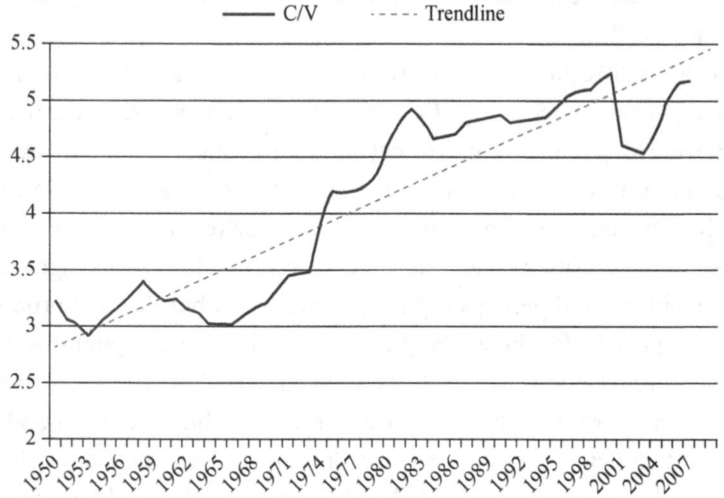

Source: See Appendix to this chapter.

IV: Concluding Remarks

The results of this case study of the US economy lend considerable support to the thesis that the crisis of global capitalism that erupted in 2007–08 is due to the persistent profitability problems of productive capital, and that these problems are at the root of the financialization phenomenon and debt crises that are now destabilizing the world system. Furthermore, our findings reinforce the argument that the global capitalist slump is unlikely to be overcome without much more savage attacks on labour by capital than those that characterized the pre-2008 neoliberal era, and without a quite significant devaluation of capital stocks involving widespread bankruptcies and persistently high levels of unemployment. In some significant measure, the super-profits reaped by Wall Street and European banks in the wake of the government bailouts of 2009 must also be seen as having been purchased through an increase in state debt obligations, a form of fictitious capital. To stem this rising tide of debt, draconian austerity measures and increased levels of exploitation are now being imposed on the international working class.[28]

Reports for 2010 and 2011 concerning profits, wages, and the value of the capital stock in the US suggest that the period we are now entering marks a critical turning point within (or beyond) the neoliberal era. Barring the eruption of serious working-class resistance and the emergence of a consciously anti-capitalist labour movement, a major restructuring of capital values and class relations seems imminent—one that is likely to augur well for profitability (and perhaps capital accumulation) but that will produce devastating results for the working class of the developed capitalist world. This new period—one that might be dubbed "neoliberalism with a vengeance"—is clearly fraught with great perils, including the likelihood of intensified rivalry among the major economic powers, the rise of right-wing populism, and an accelerated assault on the rights and living standards that working people took for granted in the liberal-democratic West for decades after World War II (and even well into the neoliberal era).

The conclusion is unavoidable. Now, more than ever, socialists must declare boldly and without equivocation that the time has arrived to replace a socio-economic order geared toward generating profits for the few with a socialist system of production to meet the needs of the many.

Notes

1. Albo, Gindin, and Panitch argue, *inter alia*, that the "onset of the crisis in 2007 was not rooted in any sharp profit decline or collapse of investment.... Rather it was rooted in the dynamics of finance" (2010: 42). Choonara (2009) provides a survey of other accounts of the crisis that share this general approach.

2. A third, intermediate position is occupied by McNally (2011), who embraces Marx's value-theoretic strategy and the LTRPF while agreeing with Albo, Gindin, and Panitch that the neoliberal era has been a "very dynamic period of capitalism" (2010: 33). McNally argues that "while neoliberal expansion (1982–2007) did not reach the heights of the Great Boom [of 1948–73], it compares most favorably with every other phase of capitalist history" (2011: 38). However, McNally's comparative historical analysis is based on figures for *world economic growth* for four discrete periods, and fails to discriminate between GDP growth in capitalist, precapitalist, semi-capitalist and post-capitalist regions of the world economy—regions whose specific weights and roles have varied enormously over the 130-year "capitalist history" that he surveys. For example, China's growth performance during its Maoist period is treated no less problematically as a component of *capitalist* "world economic growth" than its performance since 1979 (the post-Maoist period) or its performance between 1870–1949, when it was burdened by feudalism and imperialist subjugation. Through this legerdemain, McNally obscures the historical significance of the sluggish rate of global capitalist growth in the neoliberal era. For a quite different assessment, one linked to the proposition that capitalism entered into historical-structural crisis in the period leading up to World War I and that emphasizes the role of China's hybrid (semi-capitalist or post-capitalist) economy in helping to stabilize world capitalism during the neoliberal era, see Smith (2010). Many aspects of McNally's analysis are nevertheless complementary to our own and we note that his discussion of the neoliberal financialization process is particularly valuable in rounding out analyses of the current global slump that call attention to the LTRPF.

3. Marx writes: "With the development of interest-bearing capital and the credit system, all capital seems to be duplicated, and at some points triplicated, by the various ways in which the same capital, or even the same claim, appears in various hands in different guises. The greater part of this 'money capital' is purely fictitious" (1981: 601). A contemporary instance is the appearance of "money-capital" at first as a mortgage and subsequently as a mortgage-backed security. Further on, Marx observes that "commodity capital largely loses its capacity to represent *potential* money capital in time of crisis, and generally when business stagnates. The same is true of

fictitious capital, *interest-bearing paper,* in as much as this itself circulates as money capital on the stock exchange. As the interest rate rises, its price falls. It falls further, owing to the general lack of credit, which compels the owners of this paper to unload it onto the market on a massive scale in order to obtain money" (1981: 624–25, emphasis added). Carchedi observes: "Titles of credit/debt have no intrinsic value. However, they have a price. Take a bond. Its price is given by the capitalization of future earnings and thus depends on the rate of interest. Marx refers to this as the 'most fetish-like form' of capital because it seems that it is capital that creates surplus value, not labour.... If loan capital is fictitious, loan (financial) profits are fictitious too. They are fictitious not because they do not exist (as in some fraudulent accounting practices). They are the appropriation of a representation of value (money), and in this sense they are real. But they are fictitious because this appropriation is based upon a relation of debt/credit rather than of production. Financial capital sells valueless titles of debt for money (2011a: 5–6).

4. One of the consequences of the new investment strategy of the social capital in this era was "financialization—significantly increased investment in financial activity, the appearance of new financial instruments like derivatives and hedge funds, frenzied speculation surrounding a growing volume of fictitious capital, a massive overloading of the credit system and a generalized 'irrational exuberance'" (Smith 2010: 15).

5. The continual repackaging and reselling of derivatives in recent years undoubtedly generated financial profits (upon alienation) of an especially fictitious character. Lapavitsas and Levina (2010) suggest that "financial profit remains redistributed loanable capital, hence, a part of the existing flows of value." Thus, while it encompasses redistributed profit from production, "it retains elements of profit upon alienation or expropriation" as well. In official national income accounts, no effort is made to distinguish financial profits that originate in flows of value newly created in production from those that represent a mere paper claim on future income or from those that represent a transfer of previously existing values (for example, through the privatization of "public" assets as a means of servicing government debt to banks).

6. This conceptualization of the relationship between the fundamental Marxian ratios follows the approach suggested by Mage (1963) and differs from the influential treatment by Sweezy (1968). Smith summarizes as follows: "The rate of surplus-value is the ratio of two *flows* of living labour (L), which together constitute the 'net value' of the commodity product: surplus value and variable capital. Hence, $s' = s/v$. It follows from this that $s = L - v = L - (s/s') = L/(1+1/s') = L(s'/1+s')$. Now, if the OCC is Q and this equals $C/s+v$, then $Q = C/L$, and the capital stock C equals L x Q ($C = LQ$). If the rate of profit is the ratio of surplus value to the capital stock (s/C), then through substitution we arrive at $r = L(s'/1 = s')/LQ = s'/Q(1+s')$. In this formula, changes in the rate of surplus value will impact on both the rate of profit and the OCC, so that if the OCC increases, this must mean a fall in the rate of profit. An increase in the rate of surplus value contributes to maintaining or increasing the rate of profit only if it occurs without an increase in the OCC defined as $C/s+v$" (1994a: 149). Marx's original representation of the relationships between these ratios in *Capital* does not distinguish between stock and flow expressions of constant capital. Variable capital is treated by Marx as part of the "capital advanced," contrary to his observation that wages are paid out only after the value they represent is produced. On the latter point, see Mage (1963) and Reuten (2006).

7. The following discussion borrows heavily, though incompletely, from Smith (1994a: Ch. 7). The collections edited by Bellofiore (1998) and Campbell and Reuten (2002) also provide useful surveys of many of the controversial issues surrounding Marx's LTRPF.

8. See "The Results of the Immediate Process of Production," appendix to Marx (1977).

9. See Leontieff (1982), Shaikh and Tonak (1994), and Webber and Rigby (1996).

10. High OCC firms are able to achieve higher than average rates of profit due to their ability to capture surplus value produced by other firms. Capitalists tend to realize as profit a share of socially produced surplus value commensurate with their share of the total economy-wide capital investment. But individual capitals may realize above-average shares due to their

superior competitive performance in the market—and this may be due to a higher TCC.

11. For insightful critiques of the choice of technique argument that are complementary but not identical to Shaikh's, see Freeman (1998) and Reuten and Williams (1989).

12. For extended discussions of these issues, see Smith (1994a: Ch. 9) on "international and inter-regional value transfers" and Carchedi (1991: Ch. 7) on "production and distribution as worldwide processes."

13. In this regard, Moseley has argued that the "most likely source of bias resulting from [estimating the Marxian variables more narrowly in terms of the US economy] is that the composition of capital may have increased slower in the US than in the world capitalist economy" (1991: 182).

14. According to one analyst: "In the last half of the 1990s, US direct investment abroad experienced a dramatic shift from developing countries to the richest developed economies: the share of US direct investment going to developing countries fell from 37% in 1996 to 21% in 2000. [In 2009, d]eveloped countries received nearly 70% of the investment funds of US multinational firms, while developing countries received about 30%" (Jackson 2011: 4).

15. The discussion on the next few pages borrows from Smith (2011).

16. Mage argues that the costs associated with unproductive labour in the spheres of production, circulation, and the state should all be treated as part of constant capital, noting that the "difference between variable capital and constant capital is founded on their differing modes of transferring value to the commodity-product; and in the case of constant capital this characteristic mode is precisely '*the addition of previously existing value*'" (1963: 66).

17. Smith (2010: 89); see also Smith (1984). It should be noted that massive amounts of constant capital, understood as PEV, are also stored up in physical assets whose value is not represented in annually measured gross output.

18. In defending Marx's account of a rising OCC leading to a falling rate of profit, Smith (2010) refers to the results of his own empirical study of the Canadian economy from 1947 to 1991 (Smith & Taylor 1996). This study,

based on the specification of Marx's value categories outlined above, produced an almost "ultra-Marxist" set of conclusions regarding the long-term dynamics of capitalist development between 1947 and 1975: a falling rate of profit, a gradually increasing rate of surplus value, and an impetuously rising OCC. In the 1976–91 period of capitalist restructuring in response to the profitability crisis (a period marked by a determined mobilization of the "counteracting tendencies" to the LTRPF), the trend lines for the rate of profit and the OCC stabilize and the rate of surplus value rises sharply.

19. Between 1981 and 2008, credit market debt in the US increased from 164 percent to 370 percent of GDP (Smith 2010: 9).

20. "Confidence" must not only be restored in the ability of the system to generate adequate profits but also in its ability to "make good" on the anticipated future value (AFV) represented by a mountain of debt—estimated in 2011 at over $40 trillion for the OECD countries alone.

21. Integrating estimates of the ratio of productive to unproductive labour in different sectors and industries is a notoriously difficult and arduous task. Clearly, the financial, insurance, and real estate (FIRE) sector is reasonably regarded as unproductive in Marxist terms, as are retail and wholesale trade, whose workers are involved essentially in "changing titles of ownership" to commodities that have already been produced. But it is certainly true that many "personal service" firms produce "useful effects" that assume the commodity form and represent surplus value. Likewise, however, many workers employed by productive capital (from bookkeepers and marketing specialists to supervisory personnel) are clearly not involved directly in producing commodities or surplus value and should therefore be treated as SNUL. Among the NIPA divisions producing "service commodities" that we have defined as productive and as employing productive labour are hotels, personal services, auto repairs, motion pictures, amusement and recreational services, miscellaneous repair services, health services, educational services, and social services. This classification system represents an advance over the system used by Smith and Taylor (1996) and reported in Smith (1999, 2010), which involved the treatment of *all* Canadian service divisions as entirely unproductive.

22. The trend line for the current-cost rate of profit (s/C) between 1950 and 2007 falls slightly, while the historic-cost rate of profit (s/C2) registers a marginally steeper decline. If we distinguish between two phases of this 57-year period, we find that in the first, longer phase (1950–82) the un-standardized regression coefficient for s/C is 0.002, a statistically significant result. In the second, shorter phase (1983–2007), the coefficient is 0.003.

23. Figure 2.2 displays our modified version of Shaikh's (2010: 48) "Profit-of-Enterprise" ROP—the rate of profit for US non-financial corporations measured as the ratio of *after-tax* profits to the beginning-of-year current cost of their plant and equipment.

24. This estimate of after-tax domestic profits for 2010 was calculated from data provided in a Bureau of Economic Analysis News Release on corporate profits (to 3rd quarter of 2010) released on December 22, 2010.

25. The trend line for s/v is flat in the 1950–82 phase, but registers a strong, statistically significant rise in the 1983–2007 phase (its unstandardized regression coefficient in the latter phase is 0.016).

26. Marx writes: "I call the value composition of capital, in so far as it is determined by its technical composition and mirrors the changes in the latter, the *organic composition* of capital. Wherever I refer to the composition of capital, without further qualification, its organic composition is always understood" (1977: 762, emphasis added). For the OCC to mirror changes in the TCC in value terms, it needs to be conceived as the value ratio of "the mass of the means of production employed" to "the mass of labour necessary for their employment"—that is, as the value of the constant-capital stock in relation to the total new value (s+v) produced by living labour. Means of production include circulating constant capital (such as raw materials) as well as fixed capital—but it is the tendency for the value of the fixed constant capital to rise in relation to the living labour performed that is the cornerstone of the LTRPF. Smith (1984) found that a calculation of the capital stock that included circulating constant capital did not produce *trends* for the rate of profit or the OCC between 1947 and 1980 in Canada that were different from those which included only fixed capital. In the present study of the US economy, as in Smith and Taylor (1996), only a fixed-capital measure of the capital stock was employed.

27. For the first (1950–82) phase, the regression coefficients for the OCC and the VCC are 0.04 and 0.05 respectively, while for the second (1983–2007) phase it is 0.03 for the OCC. In the second phase, the VCC registers a flat trend.

28. After fluctuating between 69% and 76% between 1993 and 2005, the total financial liabilities of OECD governments as a percentage of the OECD's combined GDP rose rapidly between 2006 and 2011, from 74.5% to 102.4%. The total deficit for OECD countries saw a sixfold increase as a percentage of combined GDP between 2006 and 2010 (-1.3% to 7.7%) (OECD 2011).

Appendix

DATA SOURCES AND METHODS FOR FIGURES 2.1–2.5

Constant-capital stock (C): Value of the Net Stock of Private Assets measured according to current-cost (C) and historic-cost (C2) criteria. C = current-cost net stock of private fixed assets, year-end estimates (BEA Fixed Assets, Table 6.1, line 2). C2 = historic-cost net stock of private assets, year-end estimates (BEA Fixed Assets, Table 6.3, line 2). Figures in our spreadsheet for each year correspond to the historic-cost figure at the beginning of the year, i.e., the end of the prior year. For example, the 1980 figure in the BEA table is our spreadsheet figure for 1981. This is the procedure also followed by Kliman (2010b).

Surplus value (s): Corporate Profits after Tax, for Domestic Industries, taken from BEA NIPA Table 6.19 B, line 2, plus the after-tax earnings of the top 1% of the recipients of "wage and salary accruals" = s. The proportion of earnings represented by the top 1% of wage and salary earners was obtained from Saez (2011).

Variable capital (v): Total Wages and Salary Accruals (NIPA Table 6.3B, Line 1) *minus* line 50 (wholesale trade), line 51 (retail trade), line 52 (finance, insurance and real estate), line 63 (business services), line 69 (legal services), line 74 (miscellaneous professional services/other services), line 74 (private household services), and lines 72 and 83 (general government services, federal, state, and local) = before-tax wage-bill of productive labour. v = before-tax wage-bill of productive labour *minus* estimated tax deductions calculated by multiplying the "effective tax rate on income" by the productive-labour wage-bill. The effective tax rate was calculated as the ratio of personal current taxes (NIPA Table 3.1, line 3) to personal income (NIPA Table 2.1, line 1).

CHAPTER 3

Alienation, Exploitation, and Abstract Labour: A Humanist Defense of Marx's Theory of Value

The years leading up to the Soviet-bloc collapse of 1989–91 saw a notable effort to revive the notion of a fundamental opposition between a humanistic "young Marx" and the scientific "mature Marx" of *Capital*. Works by Kitching (1988) and Macy (1988), drawing upon "neo-Marxist" criticisms of Marx's theory of value and exploitation (Steedman 1977; Elster 1978; Cohen 1981; Roemer 1982, 1988), were representative of an outlook that reaffirmed the enduring importance of Marx's theory of alienation and his philosophy of praxis while rejecting his mature economics. This view was by no means new in its fundamentals.[1] What was new, however, was its specific form—one heavily influenced by neo-Ricardian and post-Sraffian critiques of the labour theory of value as well as the then-current academic vogue of Analytical Marxism.[2]

My purpose here is by no means to revisit the now-hoary question as to whether Marx's concept of alienation constituted a link of continuity between the young socialist humanist of 1844–47 and the older "scientific socialist" who, from the 1850s onward, analyzed the "economic law of motion" of capitalist society. To my mind at least, this question has long since been resolved in the affirmative by Marx's own testimony in the *Grundrisse* (his brilliant manuscripts of 1857–58 that remained largely unknown until the 1970s) as well as by the scholarship of an impressive roster of Marxist scholars (among them, Mészáros 1970; Mandel 1971a; Colletti 1972; Walton & Gamble 1972; Ollman 1976). My concern is rather with the claims of neo-Marxists like Kitching and Macy that Marx's mature economic theory is inconsistent with the humanist philosophy of praxis and critique of alienation articulated by the young Marx, that in any case it is logically flawed, and that it fails in its intended purpose to serve Marx's goal of human emancipation.

In rejecting these claims, I want to defend the proposition that Marx's "mature" theory of economic value is not only logically and scientifically sound, but also deeply informed by the methodological and ontological principles that guided Marx from 1844–45 onward. Following a summary of Kitching's and Macy's indictments of the Marx of *Capital*, the standard "neo-Marxist" critiques of Marx's theory of value and exploitation will be answered on the basis of a "fundamentalist" reading of that theory. This will be followed by discussions of the main concepts and principles that unite Marx's theory of value with his philosophy of praxis, and by way of conclusion, the politico-ideological context in which the relationship of the young to the mature Marx re-emerged as a contentious issue toward the end of the Soviet era.

Alienation and Exploitation: The Neo-Marxist Articulation

Kitching and Macy share the view that Marx's labour theory of value and his value-theoretic account of the exploitation of workers by capitalists are scientifically unsustainable. At the same time, both champion the youthful Marx of the mid-1840s as having enunciated that which is most important and enduringly relevant in Marx's thought. Their common claim is *not* that the Marx of *Capital* broke from his early concepts of alienation and praxis, as famously argued by Louis Althusser (1969). Rather it is that the humanist concerns of the young Marx were *adulterated* by his engagement with Ricardian political economy and his subsequent adoption of a labour theory of value. As Macy puts it, "Despite its grounding in Marx's general theory of alienation, Marxian value theory fundamentally diverts the critique from its earlier line of development, in a direction that is both logically flawed and normatively inappropriate from Marx's own perspective" (1988: 131).

For Macy, Marx's theory of alienation—that is, the theory of alienation elaborated before he embraced the "labour theory of value"—implies an account of labour exploitation as a necessary "distributional consequence of alienated labour" (1988: 151). In this view, workers suffer exploitation not because the labour they perform is the unique source of the surplus value appropriated by capitalists, but because their relationship to the means of production is that of an "object manipulated and consumed as a factor input" rather than that of a "purposive, reflexive subject" (147). Further, Marx's pre-value-theoretic account of alienation suggests that "to be exploited is to be used," whereas his later economic theory attempts, unsuccessfully, to show that "it is labour, not capital, that 'lays golden eggs'" (139). Macy views this difference as especially significant because the value-theoretic premise that "labour is uniquely productive" has "normative implications closer to the entrepreneurial work ethic than to socialist standards of distributive justice" (131). It is therefore something of a mystery that Marx should have adopted the labour theory of value as the basis for developing his critique of capitalism.

Kitching's purview is broader than Macy's, but there is a fundamental consonance of purpose. What needs to be salvaged from the wreckage of Marx's scientific project, according to Kitching, is the "philosophy of praxis" that runs through the entirety of Marx's work. However, Kitching also argues that, contrary to a view he (wrongly) imputes to Marx, "classical political economy was not the perfect completion of [Marx's] philosophy of praxis" and that "it narrowed that philosophy in a damaging way" (1988: 115). Once again, we are confronted with a rather odd paradox: why would Marx come to embrace a system of ideas so alien to his own most basic philosophical premises and so inappropriate to advancing his project of human emancipation? Kitching offers the following answer: "[Marx] thought that an economics which treated all commodities as embodiments of varied quantities of human labour was the perfect complement to a theory of history which treated both the world and thought as 'objectifications' of human activity or practice" (115). In this, however, he was quite simply mistaken. Accordingly, Marx's essentially humanist theory of history became entangled with a system of ideas that lacked both scientific credibility and humanist motivation.

Before proceeding, it will be useful to briefly review the principal elements of the philosophy of history and theory of alienation that Macy and Kitching (largely correctly) attribute to Marx. Marx's humanism is grounded on an insight enunciated in *The German Ideology*: "The premises from which we begin are ... the real individuals, their activity and the material conditions of their life, both those which they find already existing and those produced by their activity" (1989d: 22). In the course of "making their own history," human beings must, before all else, secure the material conditions of their existence. "The first historical act is thus the production of the means to satisfy these needs, the production of material life itself" (23). But this in turn leads to new needs, since the satisfaction of such elementary needs as food and clothing (the means of subsistence) requires the continuous production and development of means of production, forms of co-operation, and determinate, yet changeable, social relations of production and reproduction (including family forms).

By objectifying their labour, Marx asserts in his Paris manuscripts of 1844, human beings embark on a project of transforming nature through praxis (purposive, self-directing activity), thereby affirming their "species being." Accordingly, Marx rejects Hegel's idealist view that the material objectification of human capacities (labour) is the basis of human alienation. He proposes instead that such objectification entails the alienation of "the worker" (the direct producer) only under historically specific social conditions. Thus, the alienation of labour occurs where labour is "external" to the worker in the sense that it "belongs to another," is "coerced" or "forced" labour, and performed only as a means "to satisfy needs external to it" (1964: 111); where the worker experiences the product of labour as "an alien object exercising power over him and the objects of nature as an alien world inimically opposed to him" (111); where the worker experiences the labour process as an "activity which is turned against him, independent of him and not belonging to him" (111–12); and where human beings are generally estranged from their "species life" and from one another due to a compulsion to transform their capabilities into a means of "individual existence" (114). In short, for the young Marx, the alienation of labour is not an eternal anthropological condition, but is bound up with the presence of class-antagonistic social relations of production, in particular those associated with capitalism.

At the heart of the critiques advanced by Kitching and Macy is the view that the labour theory of value fails utterly to serve Marx's "real" objective. Macy defines that objective essentially as a protest against "the coercive character of 'voluntary exchange' between market actors with unequal discretion over the utilization of productive forces" (1988: 147). Not only does the asymmetric interdependence between capital and labour within the division of labour result in unequal market capacities and rewards; it creates a situation in which the subjectivity of living labour is negated, and a "loss of what Baudrillard refers to as the capacity to speak" (150). For Macy, the theoretical basis for this critique is much weaker in Marx's mature "economics" than in his youthful writings, and this is so because his attachment to the labour theory of value encourages the older Marx to reassert the centrality of labour to production rather than to depict the real process of its degradation, dehumanization, and exploitation. With some ingenuity, Macy argues in this regard that the concept of exploitation cannot be meaningfully applied to a value-theoretic conception of "alienated labour" (as abstract labour) if by exploitation we understand the capitalist appropriation of the subjective human capacities necessary for the production of use-values. In other words, labour that is already alienated—and therefore "stripped of all individual or human features that might distinguish it individually" (143)—cannot possibly be the "subjective factor" in "production." Yet, by treating alienated labour as the sole source of surplus value, while also positing human subjectivity as the basis of living labour's unique capacity to create exchange-value, Marx effectively identifies alienated labour as the subject of exploitation.

For Macy, this alleged contradiction in Marx's thinking can only be resolved by recognizing that, insofar as the worker's subjectivity survives in capitalist production (above all, under conditions of machinofacture and deskilling), it is oriented not toward creation but toward resistance.

Exploitation in such a context can only refer to capital's real subsumption of labour—its denial of a subjectively creative role to living labour in the immediate process of production:

> Contrary to Marx, labour's subjectivity in capitalist production is not its capacity to "realize what first is imagined" [Marx 1977: 283–284] but its capacity to *resist*. The more their labour power is separated from any traces of human subjectivity, the more reluctant are the sellers of labour power to part with what they have sold. Ironically, having asserted the dubious singularity of labour as the uniquely productive factor, value theory then misses what truly distinguishes labour from other factors—its capacity to resist its consumption by capital, necessitating the forcible extraction of work. The essential distinction between human and nonhuman factors of production is not that the former is uniquely creative; it is that machines and raw materials do not fight back.... The magic of extracting "surplus value" depends not on the subjectivity of human labour but on its negation. (Macy 1988: 143–44)

Here Macy's argument dovetails neatly with Kitching's insistence that the mature Marx recoils against the commodification of "human capabilities" while failing to see that the capabilities that are being alienated are often of the most mundane sort:

> Since for Marx the essence of human beings (their "species being") is their capacity for creative activity, then in selling this, in reducing this to a commodity, they quite literally "sell their soul." ... [On] the other hand, however, it does not seem to me that there is much human creativity involved in mining coal, or packing cakes into boxes, or assembling transistor radios from standard components. (Kitching 1988: 110, 119)

"Critical" social theory of this sort is hardly in need of Marx's value-theoretical account of exploitation. Indeed, Marx's theory of surplus value can only be an embarrassment for theorists who wish to identify the process of exploitation entirely with the *subjective* experience of alienation and ignore its "objective" dimensions (Schweitzer 1982). These latter dimensions, rooted in the operations of the law of value and other "structural" imperatives of capitalist production, can only serve to obscure what is most significant from this "humanist" (or, more precisely, *subjectivist*) perspective: the fashion in which the "purposive activity" of capitalists in exploiting (read, dominating) workers, and of workers in resisting this exploitation/domination, "make history" within capitalist society. In other words, if Marx's theory of value and surplus value can be dismissed as logically incoherent, the basis is conveniently removed for any consideration of those "objective aspects" of alienation that originate in specifically *social* relations. It is not surprising, therefore, that Macy and Kitching are not content to assert the incompatibility of Marx's ideas concerning alienation and praxis with his mature economics; they are also determined to demonstrate the "unscientific" character of the latter.

The Neo-Marxist Critique of Marx's Theory of Surplus Value

Kitching and Macy ground their critiques of Marx on the argument that his identification of value with "socially necessary abstract labour" is both arbitrary and demonstrably false insofar as it entails the proposition that living labour is the *sole* source of surplus value. Their arguments are remarkably similar and may be summarized as follows.

According to Marx, the "magic of accumulation"—the ability of capitalist production to generate a surplus, an increment beyond the value of the inputs to production—is due to the unique ability of a single commodity, the commodity labour-power, to produce more value than it represents. Against this, Kitching and Macy argue that Marx arrives at this conclusion through a sleight-of-hand, as an artifact of his value-based accounting system (Macy 1988: 140; Kitching 1988: 100–101). There is no reason, in principle, why *any* input commodity could not serve as a source of incremental value, with energy or machines being especially good candidates for this role. For Macy, "in a market economy with a net social product, whatever commodity is identified with value will thereby appear to be endowed with unique powers of crescive self-regeneration, replenishing itself faster than it depreciates" (1988: 141). The problem, quite simply, is that Marx "applies one accounting procedure to machines and another to living labour power" (Kitching 1988: 101) without providing any compelling justification for this inconsistency. Thus, while living labour-power may certainly contribute to the production of new value, there is no reason to deny the productive contributions of other factors of production as well. Indeed, in today's world, the contribution of fixed capital is, by any reasonable standard, far greater than that of living labour. None of this adds up to the conclusion that labour is not exploited; only that the phenomenon of the exploitation of labour by capital cannot be understood "scientifically" in the terms proposed by Marx.

In Defense of Marx's Theory of Value and Surplus Value

An appropriate place to begin the task of disentangling Kitching's and Macy's myriad confusions is with some simple points concerning the actual relationship of Marx's theory of value (and the *unified* scientific and humanist project which it reflects) to the "classical" labour theory of value. For, contrary to Kitching, Marx's engagement with classical political economy was, from the outset, highly critical and one deeply informed by a philosophical position that Kitching has only partially defined; and, contrary to Macy, Marx did not simply adopt David Ricardo's theory of labour value (after abandoning his earlier criticisms of it), but instead radically transformed it in ways that reflected his profound philosophical differences with the whole tradition of classical political economy.

After a century of intense discussion surrounding Marx's value theory, it is remarkable that these elementary points should find no place in the accounts of Macy and Kitching. Remarkable, but perhaps not surprising: for these are precisely the points that remain most incomprehensible to those committed to neoclassical or neo-Ricardian critiques of Marx.

Kitching's and Macy's commitments in this respect are clear and unequivocal. For all their avowed sympathy for Marx's politics, their philosophical
and methodological horizons are nevertheless close to what Marx called
"vulgar economy." Evidence of this is unmistakably given by their mutual
failure to consider Marx's analyses of the value-form and of commodity
fetishism, analyses that point to a concept of value that is very remote from
the one to which they are attached.

Whereas for Kitching and Macy "value" is a *quality* that inheres to commodities and a synonym for "exchange-value," for Marx value is fundamentally a *social relation* that finds material expression through the products of
labour. By conflating the Ricardian and Marxian theories of value, the two
authors not only ignore the fundamental discontinuity between them; they
also set up Marx's theory for a series of criticisms that are wholly inappropriate and misdirected. This is nowhere more obvious than in their insistence that Marx's identification of value with labour is "arbitrary" and that
therefore an inconsistency exists in his value-based "accounting procedure."

Let's begin with the charge of inconsistency. Kitching complains that
Marx asserts (without proving) that the means of production (machinery,
raw materials, fuel, etc.) can only contribute their own "previously existing"
value to the new commodity product, and can never create "new value."
The role of "adding new value" to the commodity product is reserved for
living labour in Marx's theory: "While the labourer preserves and transfers to the product the value of the means of production, he at the same
time, by the mere act of working, creates each instant an additional or new
value" (Marx 1965: 208, quoted in Kitching 1988: 99). Kitching insists that
it is no less reasonable to say that, by simply being in operation, a machine
can also create additional or new value. Marx's "reply" to such an argument, according to Kitching, would be that "living labour power, unlike
'dead labour', unlike machines, can work for a period of time in excess of
the [socially necessary abstract labour] time required for its production"
(1988: 100). But Kitching denies this difference, arguing that machines too
can remain in operation for a period of time "well exceeding the labour
time embodied in them" (101). It is here that Kitching joins a long tradition
of *capital-fetishistic* argumentation, one endorsed by the analytical Marxist

economist John Roemer: "Labour power as a commodity is not unique in its magical property of producing more value than it embodies.... Any commodity has this magical property" (1982: 273, quoted in Macy 1988: 141).

There are several problems with this argument, but the most fundamental is that it attributes to Marx a position he simply does not hold. Labour power, for Marx, is a *capacity*—an "ability to work"—that wage-workers sell to capitalists in the labour market. However, what confers new value on the commodity product is the labouring *activity* of these workers. Of course it is quite true that Marx holds that the value created by this activity will in general exceed the "socially necessary abstract labour" represented by the workers' wages (the price of the commodity labour-power), and that this makes labour-power "unique" in comparison with the "capacities" of other input commodities. But this uniqueness cannot be grasped simply in *material-technical* terms, as Kitching's post-Sraffian "physical-magnitudes" argument testifies. Nor can it be grasped by invoking the idea that the subjectivity of wage-labourers is the basis of production, as Macy shows. Rather it can only be grasped once value is understood as a *social relation*—a relation of *people to people,* not a (subjective) relation of people to things, or, still worse, a (technical) relation of things to things.

Marx's crucial distinction between "labour-power" and "labour performed" is precisely a distinction between a commodity input with a determinate "value" (cost of reproduction) and a human activity that forms part of the societal division of labour. Such a distinction is not applicable to other factors of production for two very good reasons. The first is that capitalists are generally in a position to exact prices for their commodities that approximate the value released and transferred by the consumption of their use-values in capitalist production. In other words, capitalists have a very hard time "exploiting" other capitalists by buying input commodities at prices that fail to reflect the *full* potential contribution of these commodities to the formation of the value of newly produced commodities. Moreover, the inter-capitalist relation is a relation established entirely within the sphere of exchange, whereas the capital-labour contract concerns activity within the sphere of production. Since the law of the conservation of value in exchange excludes the generation of surplus value at the aggregate level through "buying cheap and selling dear," the *social surplus value* that is appropriated by the social capital as a whole can only be the product of activity occurring within production (Marx 1977: 247–80).

The second consideration is still more fundamental. Machines and other non-labour inputs to production do not and cannot generate any "new value" because they form no part of the *social division of living labour*, to which value, conceived as a social relation, refers. This may seem enigmatic at first. But the fundamental idea suggested here is really at the heart of Marx's theory. Not only does it explain why Marx is not inconsistent when he treats labour-power differently from other commodity inputs in his so-called "accounting procedure"; it also explains why he is not at all arbitrary in insisting that human labour (conceived in a certain way) is both the sole measure and unique source of value.

Marx's "Abstract Labour" Theory of Value

Broadly speaking, there are today three main schools of Marxian value theory: an "orthodox" school that adheres to an essentially "Ricardian"-embodied labour theory of value (with some qualifications, it is this account of value theory that Kitching and Macy set up for criticism); a "neo-orthodox" (or "value-form") school that rejects the notion of "embodied labour" as the measure of a commodity's value and emphasizes Marx's thesis that "money as the measure of value is the *necessary* form of appearance of the measure of value which is immanent in commodities, namely labour-time" (Marx 1977: 188); and a "fundamentalist" school that criticizes the tendency of the neo-orthodox value theorists to *dissociate* Marx's "value-form" and "value-magnitude" analyses, insisting instead upon a conceptualization of "abstract labour" as the reflection in thought of the real social processes through which commodities are produced for the purpose of sale and the realization of profit.[3]

In my view, Marx's own value theory is closest to the fundamentalist account, the key postulates of which may be summarized as follows:

1. The value of a commodity, as distinct from its exchange-value, refers *quantitatively* to the amount of socially necessary labour time required for its production.
2. The necessary form of appearance of this measure of value is the money-price of commodities.
3. Money-price (the value form) is pre-eminently a microeconomic category referring to the exchange ratios of particular commodities.
4. Value refers *qualitatively* to the large-scale social processes and relations out of which the value-form emerges.
5. When Marx refers to "abstract labour" as the substance of value, he is referring to the structure of relations that links and mediates the "value-form" and "value-magnitude" expressions of labour-value.
6. This structure of relations (articulating the various and multitudinous fractions of commodity-producing labour into a complex social division of labour) finds expression both in the money-price of individual commodities *and* in the macroeconomic processes of capitalist economy.
7. Abstract labour, as a universal structure of relations standing behind the myriad exchange-values of individual commodities, is by no means "physically incorporated" into commodities within the labour process; rather commodities, as products of social labour, stand in a specific relation to "abstract socially necessary labour time"—as vendible items representing a more or less efficient allocation of the labour time of society.
8. Therefore, commodities do not *physically embody* either value or its abstract-labour substance, despite Marx's occasional use of this verb; instead, they represent a definite fraction of the "aggregate" value magnitude.
9. The value represented by a commodity is always measured in terms of the amount of socially necessary labour time required for its production *in the here and now* (Marx 1977: 528).
10. Marx's value-form analysis establishes that "the money-form is merely the reflection thrown upon a single commodity by the relations between all other commodities" (Marx 1977: 184).

11. Marx's value-magnitude analysis establishes that value exists as an "objective, quantitatively determined magnitude" (Hilferding 1975: 159) and that its sole source is *living labour.*

12. This latter postulate is fundamental to the capitalist law of value and the key to discovering not only the secret of accumulation under capitalism (capital's specific mode of extracting surplus labour) but the "laws of motion" of the capitalist mode of production as well.[4]

To be sure, some aspects of this interpretation of Marx's value theory are controversial. But the more important point is that such an account is not vulnerable to many of the *particular* criticisms that have been traditionally made of the "Ricardian-Marxist orthodoxy." To illustrate this, it is useful to consider the critique of Marx's value theory advanced by G. A. Cohen, a leading Analytical Marxist whose views on this matter are close to those of Kitching and Macy. The following passage constitutes the core of Cohen's critique:

[Marx's] theory entails that past labour is irrelevant to how much value a commodity now has. But past labour would not be irrelevant if it created the value of the commodity. It follows that *labour does not create value, if the labour theory of value is true.* (1981: 209–210)

Although Cohen distinguishes between a "popular" version of the labour theory of value, according to which value is embodied or congealed labour, and a "strict" version, according to which value is determined by socially necessary labour time, his argument is crucially predicated on a basic misunderstanding of the proposition that "labour creates value." We are alerted to this in the first instance by Cohen's discussion of "socially necessary labour time" in the absence of any mention of the concept of "abstract labour." This omission is of critical importance, because Marx's position is not that "labour creates value" in some direct and unmediated sense, but that abstract labour creates value, a statement that is closely related to but also distinguishable from the statement that living labour is the sole *source* of value.[5]

95

Cohen proposes that "past labour is irrelevant to how much value a commodity now has." By this he means that the amount of socially necessary labour time that was required for its production in the past cannot be relevant to determining its present value. But the misleading implication of this statement is that the socially necessary labour time "physically incorporated" into a commodity in the past *was* relevant to the amount of value it "had" *at that point* in the past.

That Cohen understands the value of a commodity to be determined by the socially necessary labour time physically incorporated into it (the value a commodity literally "has") is even clearer when he proceeds to state that "past labour would not be irrelevant if it created the value of the commodity." But this proposition only makes sense if we understand Cohen to mean that value is created at the same time and by the same labour as the "physical body" of the commodity. Cohen's Ricardian conception of *embodied* socially necessary labour is rendered still more explicit when he asserts that the proposition "labour and labour alone creates value" necessarily belongs to the popular version of the labour theory. Significantly, Cohen refers to this proposition as one that speaks of "value as embodied or congealed labour." *But this is only true if the labour referred to is concrete labour rather than abstract labour.*

Let's consider Cohen's argument as it would need to be amended to reflect Marx's actual position (that is, the position of what I have called *fundamentalist* value theory):

> The theory entails that past *abstract* labour is irrelevant to how much value a commodity now has. But past *abstract* labour would not be irrelevant if it created the value of the commodity. It follows that *abstract* labour does not create value, if the labour theory of value is true.

Cohen's legerdemain can now be more easily exposed. It is of course quite true that past abstract labour does not create the value that a commodity presently represents. But it does not follow from this that abstract labour does not create value, provided that abstract labour is understood to be a real structure of relations determining the value of that commodity on the basis of the social production norms *currently* required for its (re)production. Cohen's "logical argument" against Marx rests, then, upon fundamentally specious premises.

To be sure, Marx erects several terminological obstacles to a proper understanding of his theory of value. As previously noted, he himself sometimes uses the term "embodied labour" while nevertheless making it clear that what is relevant to a commodity's value is its current cost of reproduction reckoned in socially necessary labour time. Furthermore, when Marx speaks of a transfer of "previously existing value" from machinery or raw materials within production to the new commodity product, he would seem to be inviting the notion that the magnitude of this value is determined by the labour time that was socially necessary to the production of these inputs "in the past." Yet the value of a given stock of raw materials or machinery is just as subject as any other group of commodities to continuously occurring adjustments within the structure of abstract labour (that is, the changing standards of socially necessary labour time required for the production of its manifold elements). The expression "previously existing value " can only refer to the *current* value represented by commodities that were produced in the past; in this sense it is a mere shorthand expression for the *contribution* of the objectified elements of the process of production (the "constant capital") to the value formation of the new commodity product. The magnitude of this contribution, it bears repeating, is not at all determined by past events, but always by the current configuration of abstract labour. Accordingly, all of the value of the new commodity product is a reflection of the prevailing "social division of living labour"—the socially necessary labour time required to (re)produce its inputs as well as the socially necessary labour being performed by living labourers within its production process. Marx simply insists that a distinction must be made between those inputs whose contribution to the value process is essentially "constant" (and whose value is now subject, if anything, to a process of negative redefinition) and that productive input which is always "variable" in its contribution to the magnitude of value: *the living labour performed*, which, depending upon the concrete conditions of its performance, may contribute very little or a great deal to the production of new value. The value represented by the former (the constant-capital inputs) reflects the changing realities of the social division of living labour while the latter (the living labour performed) is *constitutive* of it.

There is nothing arbitrary in this so-called accounting procedure once the fundamental postulates of Marx's theory of value are understood. Arguably Marx may be faulted for having used shorthand expressions (embodied labour, previously existing value, etc.) borrowed from classical political economy that sometimes obscure his meaning. All the same, the content of these expressions should be clear to anyone who has studied the fundamentals of his value theory with some care. Indeed, in my opinion, there should be no problem with their continued use, precisely as shorthand, so long as their real theoretical content is properly grasped.

Philosophical Foundations of Marx's Theory of Value

The key to understanding Marx's value theory is to understand the way in which he apprehends social reality. This is an ontological question, but one that entails methodological issues as well, since every methodology expresses definite ontological commitments.

There is, perhaps, no better place to begin than with that seminal historical-materialist text upon which Kitching and Macy base so much of their humanist interpretations of Marx. In *The German Ideology*, Marx and Engels write: "The production of life, both of one's own in labour and of fresh life in procreation … appears as a twofold relation: on the one hand as a natural, on the other as a social relation—social in the sense that it denotes the co-operation of several individuals, no matter under what conditions, in what manner and to what end" (Marx 1989d: 23).

The "twofold relation" involved in the "production of life" (the "first premise" of human existence) is here defined as embracing both a natural aspect and a social aspect (involving different forms of human co-operation). With this statement Marx announces that the study of specific concrete forms of human existence (modes of life) must take as its starting point a focus on the internal dialectical relation between the Natural and the Social.

Such an approach fundamentally distinguishes Marx's analytical project from the great majority of social theories that begin with a focus on a presumed external opposition between "the material" and "the ideal" (or, similarly, "the objective" and "the subjective"). Marx's dialectical social ontology stands irreconcilably opposed to the ontological dualisms sponsored by this material-ideal opposition—dualisms that posit discrete "levels of reality" or even "different worlds" as they problematize the relationship between facts and values, subjects and objects, structure and agency, noumena and phenomena, what is and what ought to be, science and philosophy, and so on.

Of course, Marx does not deny that dualities are a persistent feature of human existence. But he nevertheless insists upon approaching these dualities with due regard to their singular (monistic) foundation: the "materialist connection of men with one another, which is determined by their needs and their mode of production, and which is as old as men themselves" (1989d: 24). This "materialist connection" holds pride of place in Marx's social ontology because it, and not "consciousness" or "ideas" springing from a realm considered "independent" of the material world, is the real basis upon which the nature-society relation is mediated: "This connection is ever taking on new forms, and thus presents a 'history' irrespective of the existence of any political or religious nonsense which would especially hold men together" (24).

This concept of an internal, dialectical relation between the Natural and the Social is the actual starting point of Marx's critique of political economy, a matter he makes abundantly clear in *Notes on Adolph Wagner*, written late in his career. Here Marx asserts that his analysis does not begin with "the concept of value" but with the "simplest social form in which the labour-product is presented in contemporary society ... the commodity," something that is revealed to have both a "natural form" (a use-value) and a "form of appearance" (an exchange-value) which is the "autonomous mode of appearance of the *value* contained in the commodity" (1989b: 41–42). Thus, 34 years after *The German Ideology*, Marx explicitly restates the methodological principle that consistently guided him in his critique of political economy: that the objectifications of human praxis simultaneously express a relation to nature (a natural form) and a relation to society (a social form). If the inner anatomy of capitalism is to be fathomed, then the elementary form in which human praxis (labour) is manifested in capitalist society, *the commodity,* must be seen for what it is: *a contradictory unity of natural and social aspects,* an expression of the concrete (mental and manual) labour that fashions its natural form and an individual manifestation of the larger social processes that define its value (its status in relation to all other products of labour) and its price (its power to command remuneration in exchange).

Marx's methodological concern with the analysis of "forms" in relation to different "contents" reflects the enduring influence of Hegelian dialectics on his thought. The Hegelian provenance of Marx's understanding of the "value form" is highlighted by Rubin (1973), who argues convincingly that Marx adhered to a conception (descending from Hegel and opposed to Kant's dualist approach) that regards form as "internally related" to content and as growing out of it (1973: 117). The upshot is that the value form (exchange-value, money-price) must be considered in its *internal* dialectical relationship to the content (or "substance") of value: "socially equalized labour," or, as this exists under capitalism, "abstract labour."

Rubin also highlights the importance of "commodity fetishism" to Marx's theory of value, emphasizing the fact that Marx is concerned with *distinguishing* the Social from the Natural—even as he recognizes their dialectical interpenetration. A *fetishistic* error, for Marx, is one that *confuses* the Natural and the Social—and this is precisely the sort of error that the classical political economists commit time and again.

By indulging precisely this error, Kitching and Macy evince an attachment to a social ontology diametrically at odds with that of Marx. Repeatedly, both fall victim to *conflating* the analytical categories that Marx sought to distinguish as "internally related" yet distinct aspects of his investigation: concrete labour and abstract labour, use-value production and value production, exchange-value and value, the labour process and the valorization process. Thus, when Macy attributes to Marx the premise that "labour is alone productive," he commits the cardinal fetishistic error of conflating the material/natural and the social dimensions of production while ignoring the fact that Marx asserts the centrality of "labour" only to *surplus-value production* and not to "material production" in general.

Marx's dialectical social ontology involves not only a focus on the natural-social relation internal to the "materialist connection" existing between human beings but also a philosophically *realist* position according to which real structures enjoying a holistic ontological status are understood to mediate the relationship between "natural laws" (such as the imperative of a distribution of social labour to different economic branches) and "concrete particulars" (such as the market prices of individual commodities or the performance of specific concrete labour tasks in production). Such a conception suggests a theoretical space for "abstract labour" understood not merely as "an undifferentiated raw material" (Macy 1988: 143) but as the sort of "non-particular entity" (Fischer 1982) that exists as a social-structural *universal* and whose expression is money.[6] Not only do Kitching and Macy fail to recognize this dimension of the mature Marx's social ontology, but they also tend to present his ideas as if they were formulated in a spirit of methodological individualism and nominalist empiricism—and then "expose" their incompatibility with same!

It is an old dilemma. How does one answer a critic who insists upon interpreting and judging a theory on the basis of a method and ontology that are fundamentally alien to it? The most reasonable way, it would seem, is by insisting that no "scientific method" or "social ontology" can be taken as "given" and none justified on the basis of *a priori* considerations. For Marx, *what finally distinguishes a truly scientific approach from a "metaphysical" one is the recognition that the criterion of "truth" is a practical one.* As he observes in his second thesis on Feuerbach: "Man must prove the truth, i.e., the reality and power, the this-worldliness of his thinking in practice" (Marx 1989a: 8). This eminently humanist observation fits well with a famous comment in defense of value theory: "Even if there were no chapter on 'value' in my book [*Capital*], the analysis of the real relations which I give would contain the proof and demonstration of the real value relations" (Marx 1989c: 53). In short, the "proof" of Marx's ontology, and *inter alia* of his theory of value, can only be determined by how well it enables us to understand the "real history" of the capitalist mode of production, and, on that basis, to formulate a workable program of social transformation and human emancipation.

Praxis, Alienation, and Value: Toward an Articulation

Kitching and Macy simultaneously indict the older Marx for a starry-eyed failure to see that capitalism extinguishes the creative flame of human praxis within production and for a sentimental attachment to the idea that the sale of labour-power represents a Faustian alienation of human creative abilities, even though it usually amounts to little more than a sale of the capacity to endure drudgery and toil. Yet, both of these (partially complementary, partially contradictory) criticisms appear strangely misdirected—for Marx was never under any illusion as to how capital concretely treats the "capacity to labour" embodied in living wage-workers. The Marx of *Capital* no less than the Marx of 1844 understood only too well the immanent tendency of capitalist production to subordinate the "subjective" aspects of the process to the "objective." But if there is a discernible shift in Marx's thinking it surely concerns the fact that the Marx of 1844 is far more concerned with the subjective experience of the individual worker than is the Marx of *Capital*. In *Capital*, the human subjectivity requisite to *use-value* production (the material labour process) is now assigned to the "collective worker" (that is, to a workforce increasingly characterized by segmentation and a divorce between mental and manual functions). At the same time, however, the "subjectivity" requisite to securing surplus-value production (the valorization process) is assigned to the managerial agents of capital—if only tenuously. "Tenuously" because these agents (from corporate directors to workplace supervisors) are unable to assert full "control" over the macroeconomic processes governing the magnitude and rate of surplus-value production and capital accumulation. Indeed, the mutual powerlessness of both labour and capital in the face of "free" and "unconscious" market forces is the necessary point of departure of any attempt to adequately articulate Marx's theories of alienation and value on the basis of his philosophy of praxis.

Marx's "decentring" of the human subject in *Capital* is in no sense a repudiation of his humanism or his concept of praxis—that is to say, the idea that human beings are purposive, reflexive agents with the capacity to consciously transform their circumstances. Rather it is a theoretical expression of the *result* of an "alienation" of human beings from a condition of mastery over the societal division of labour—of a fragmented and necessarily *partial* praxis. Indeed, the whole of *Capital* can be read as an extended analysis of a phenomenon of "objective alienation" that is much more profound and far more encompassing than the phenomena identified by Marx in 1844. The alienation of the producer from the (appropriated) product, from other human beings, from nature, and from "species life" (praxis) constitute the dimensions of an alienated condition *apprehended from the point of view of the producer as a "real living individual."* But in the *Grundrisse* and in *Capital*, Marx shows that these are simply aspects of a larger "alienation"—the alienation of human beings from a condition of mastery over their social and economic life process: what might be called the "collective alienation of the species."

Under the sway of the capitalist law of value and the laws of motion of capital, human praxis is necessarily *partial* and therefore *alienated*. The socio-economic mechanism operates outside the control of capitalist and worker alike, regulated not by conscious and purposive human agency but by objective forces. Marx's theory of value is nothing other than an attempt to explain the operations of these forces—these "objective laws"—with a view to exposing their socio-historical specificity (that is, their non-inevitability) and thereby enlarging the scope of a scientifically informed human praxis, which, under prevailing conditions, can only be a *revolutionary political practice*.

"Abstract labour"—the social substance of value—is precisely alienated labour, as Colletti (1972: 84) long ago pointed out; it is "labour separated or estranged with respect to man himself." But abstract labour is also a concept that bridges and mediates the subjective-particularistic and objective-holistic aspects of alienation. The young Marx's theory of alienation remained incomplete to the extent that it failed to identify the dialectical unity of these aspects, a task conforming to the methodological imperative to overcome any dualism of the general and the particular. The *implicit* theory of value of the Marx of 1844 was an obstacle to this, not because he rejected Ricardo's labour theory of value (for this theory too posits a dissociation of the particular and the general) but because any value theory other than that fashioned by Marx on the basis of his later *transformation* of Ricardo's theory must focus on the value of the individual commodity in abstraction from the "world of commodities." It must therefore tend toward a simple conflation of "price" and "value" rather than encourage an exploration of their complex, dialectical interrelationship. In coming to adopt the labour theory of value, then, Marx did not abandon his youthful standpoint; on the contrary, he radically transformed the content of the labour-value theory in light of the results of his critique and critical appropriation of Hegel's and Feuerbach's philosophies.

In *Capital*, the concept of abstract labour appears precisely as a "shorthand" expression for the unconscious and reified processes through which social labour is distributed in capitalist economies and through which the products of labour are quantitatively related. At the same time, however, it refers to the process of the reduction of concrete (that is, utility-shaping, more or less "creative") labour(s) to a common standard (the abstract aspect of the activity performed by the labourers). To quote Colletti, "individual labour powers are equalized [in the reality of the world of commodities] precisely because they are treated as abstract or separate from the real empirical individuals to whom they belong" (1972: 84). This process of real abstraction permits the articulation of privately undertaken concrete labour(s) into a social division of labour regulated by market exchange, while also decisively subordinating the labour process to the "value-expansion" process. In this way, the governing aim of production becomes the alienated and socially antagonistic one of continuously creating surplus value in magnitudes adequate to "justify" use-value production and the application of concrete labour. In other words, the labour process is subordinated to the valorization process and continuously transformed in line with its requirements.

In a society lacking conscious regulation of its economic life, the unconscious principle represented by "value" comes to dominate all human activity, continually shaping it in accordance with its imperatives. This consideration returns us to Marx's discussion of commodity fetishism—to the theoretical problems associated with a confusion of the Natural and the Social, but also to Marx's observation that under conditions of commodity production and exchange "private labours appear ... as material relations between persons and social relations between things" (1977: 166). This appearance is not illusory; indeed, private labours appear here "as what they are." The mediation between private labours and the aggregate labour of society is provided by the market exchange of privately produced commodities; consequently, as *producers,* persons relate to one another through the mediation afforded by "things."

Marx's analyses of the fetishism of commodities, the value-form and the alienated social power of money (the universal equivalent) are replete with observations strongly reminiscent of the alienation critique of 1844.[7] This suggests not only the obvious fact of "continuity"; it also establishes that *Capital* represents the *completed* version of this critique. The alienation of the producer is revealed to be a manifestation of the alienation of *all* human beings from social control over their own affairs, and this *collective alienation* results from economic laws rooted in principles of social organization that are by no means immutable. By exposing the historically-specific character of the pillars of human alienation, Marx points the way to an historical resolution of the problem of alienation and to a future in which the field of praxis will be generalized—for collective humanity and for the individual human being.

Conclusion

There are two very good reasons why the foregoing restatement of Marx's "mature" theory of alienation became less compelling in the politico-ideological climate associated with the collapse of Soviet bloc "socialism." The first is that its attention to the objective-universal dimension of alienation under capitalism appears to have a certain affinity with a "structuralist" and "deterministic" reading of Marx's theoretical project. By the 1990s, however, structuralism had suffered a major decline within Marxist discourse because its deterministic (and non-dialectical) view of the "march of history" had been belied by a series of events that established that the victory of socialism was by no means inevitable. Indeed, the vital element of *purposive human agency*, which looms so large in Marx's youthful writings, had strikingly demonstrated its capacity to deflect the objectivist juggernauts of a rigidly deterministic version of Marxism in a most unexpected way. In the 1980s, the "purposive agency" of viciously anti-labour and anti-communist governments (Reagan's and Thatcher's in particular) succeeded in redefining the relationship of class forces and in re-stabilizing the regime of capital in the process. On a world scale, this rightist offensive found expression in increased imperialist pressure on the Soviet bloc and China, and an indirect reflection in the emergence there of pro-Western political movements and pro-market economic policies. No less than the October Revolution of 1917, which a young, praxis-minded Antonio Gramsci wryly dubbed the "revolution against Marx's *Capital*," the pro-"free-market" tempests of the 1980s and early 1990s seemed, through sheer human cunning and determination, to have undone the basic scenario of Marxist objectivism: the inexorable progression of human history through determinate "stages" in accordance with unyielding "historical laws."

Just as Bolshevik "human agency" permitted a telescoping of bourgeois-democratic and proletarian-socialist tasks in 1917—an unexpected surge toward a "post-capitalist" society in backward Russia, the purposive agency of capitalist reaction found the resources to push certain well-established expressions (in reality, fundamental distortions) of the "socialist project" (social democracy, Eurocommunism, Stalinist "real socialism," etc.) severely off course as it threatened to capsize them completely. The association of Marx's economics with the fatalism and objectivism that characterized the *failed* projects of parliamentary socialism and Stalinism encouraged a reappraisal of the former that subverted an understanding of the *unified* theoretical and political project that was Marx's chief legacy.

Related to this is a second consideration. If, as argued earlier, Marx's own criterion for truth is a practical one, the collapse of "actually existing socialism" in the Soviet bloc could only have called into question the plausibility of Marx's theory of value, his critique of capitalism, and his emancipatory program. The crisis of Stalinist rule in the bureaucratized workers' states found partial but unmistakable expression as a crisis of "actually existing planned economy." The lesson drawn here—concerning the supposed indispensability of "free market mechanisms" to the optimization of economic efficiency—seemed to decisively vitiate Marx's programmatic goal: the realization of a society in which the relations of "people to people" are no longer dominated by "objective bonds" and in which "universally developed individuals, whose social relations, as their own communal relations, are ... subordinated to their own communal control" can fulfill the promise of a non-alienated "individuality" marked by "universality and the comprehensiveness of ... relations and capacities" (Marx 1973: 162). In short, if the Soviet experience of building socialism was any indication, Marx's project of "disalienation" appeared to be in serious trouble as a guide to changing the world—and with it the value theory upon which it was at least partially predicated.

This general line of thought, it should be stressed, assumed that the dominant forms of Marxist practice from the 1930s to the 1980s *were informed* by Marx's mature theory of value, if not by his youthful theory of alienation. But on this score there is ample room for doubt. Indeed, there is really no reason to believe that Marx would have endorsed the view that his theory of value enjoins the working class to conciliate the bourgeoisie with a program of reforms *within* the framework of capitalism, or the view that progress toward a rationally planned socialist economy can be made *without* the democratic involvement of the "associated producers" and *without* the benefit of an international socialist division of labour. Indeed, value theory points socialist practice precisely in the direction of a revolutionary confrontation with a capitalist order that relies on the operations of the law of value to divide, disorient, and blackmail the working class into playing by capital's "rules of the game." And just as decisively, Marx's value-theoretic critique of alienation suggests that the material and social bases for authentic socialism can only be laid through a commitment to internationalist (universalist) principles and an *extension* of individual human capacities—something which is impossible so long as post-capitalist society remains in the grip of a bureaucratic dictatorship.

Even so, Marx's programmatic vision can only seem utopian to those, like Macy and Kitching, who take their ground on the fetishistic concepts of neoclassical or neo-Ricardian economics. Here the alienation of the wage-labourer can be construed as the unique condition of a social agent unfavourably placed within the social division of labour; but there can be no meaningful discussion of the alienated character of capitalist production as a whole. Here the subjective consequences of working-class alienation can be diagnosed and partial remedies (such as Macy's "socialist distributive justice") proffered; but there can be no question of fundamentally altering the relations of the producers and all humanity to the socio-economic life process.

It is indeed ironic that those who reject the alleged "determinism" of Marx's theory of value in the name of praxis must end up as prisoners of a still-more remorseless determinism: the one that asserts that the basic economic laws of capitalism are timeless and ineradicable, and that Marx's goal of radical disalienation is therefore beyond humanity's reach. Such pessimism is in no sense an affirmation of Marx's philosophy of praxis; it is its negation. The point, however, is that this pessimism has its basis not in any alleged errors of Marx's economic theory, but in the inability of his critics to break definitively from a worldview that conceives of material wealth only in terms of monetary value and that, consequently, regards social progress as inseparably and eternally linked to capitalist accumulation.

Notes

1. See Mandel (1971a) and Schweitzer (1982) for comprehensive summaries of earlier rounds of debate on these issues.
2. Neo-Ricardianism refers to an approach (descending from the classical political economist David Ricardo) that regards capitalist profit as determined,

above all, by the direction of the real wage. Unlike Ricardo, however, the neo-Ricardians reject all versions of the labour theory of value, with many subscribing to the "physical magnitudes" approach of Piero Sraffa. In this view, wage growth that exceeds productivity increases must impact negatively on profitability. This was a common way of seeing the profitability crisis of the 1970s. However, the neo-Ricardian Marxists (including most "Sraffians") often viewed the "wage-push/profit squeeze" of that period as an expression of successful proletarian class struggle and even as a harbinger of socialist revolution.

3. For a detailed analysis of these schools of value theory, see Smith (1994a); summaries are available in Smith (1991, 2010) and in Chapter 7 of this volume. This particular classification is my own and is meant to encompass only the most prominent of the standpoints existing within Marxian value theory. The "orthodox" Ricardian-Marxist value theorists include Meek (1956), Sweezy (1968), and Dobb (1973). Among the "neo-orthodox" theorists are Elson (1979), Himmelweit and Mohun (1981), and Reuten and Williams (1989). The "fundamentalist" group includes Shaikh (1981), Foley (1986), Carchedi (1991, 2011b), and Smith (1994a, 2010). Due to its possible, though unintended, association with religious fideism, the term "fundamentalist" in the present context should be understood as referring simply to a commitment to clarifying and defending the importance of *all three of the fundamental elements of Marx's value theory*: the measure, the form, and the substance of labour-value.

4. For Marx, the most important of these "from the historical standpoint" is the law of the falling tendency of the rate of profit.

5. Strictly speaking, the dialectical conception of the relationship between abstract labour and value as an "internal relation" enjoins us from speaking of the "creation" of value by "abstract labour." I do so here only to facilitate clarity in my argument with Cohen.

6. Key to this interpretation of value theory is an extension of the ontological "reversals" discussed by Marx in his analysis of the value-form to include the relation between abstract labour as a real universal structure and commodities as sensuously concrete particulars.

7. For example, "[the commodity-form] reflects the social relation of the producers to the sum total of labour as a social relation between objects, a

relation which exists apart from and outside the producers" (Marx 1977: 165). The language of "alienation" is certainly more conspicuous in the *Grundrisse*. One passage among many reads: "as the [social character of production grows], so grows the power of *money*, i.e., the exchange relation establishes itself as a power external to and independent of the producers. What originally appeared as a means to promote production becomes a relation *alien* to the producers" (Marx 1973: 146, emphasis added).

PART II
Human Progress and the Materialist Dialectic

CHAPTER 4

Against Dualism: Marxism and the Necessity of Dialectical Monism

Introducing a special issue of *Science & Society* devoted to "Dialectics: The New Frontier," Bertell Ollman and Tony Smith wrote: "There are serious limits to how dialectical our thinking can become in capitalist society. With its frequent upheavals of all kinds, no society requires dialectics as much, but it is also true that with its reified social forms and constantly expanding consciousness industry, no society makes it so difficult for its inhabitants to think dialectically" (1998: 335). It is, of course, commonplace among Marxists to view dialectics as the indicated antidote to prevailing impressionistic, faith-based, and one-sidedly rationalistic or positivist methods of explanation and understanding. Among other things, to "think dialectically" means to break with the static and mechanical ways of seeing things that are so pervasive in capitalist society. What often receives insufficient attention, however, is the necessary connection that exists between epistemological commitments and ontological ones. For the methods and theoretical strategies that we use to understand the world are shaped in good part by our tacit assumptions concerning its underlying reality—its "ontological structure"; and these assumptions in turn are heavily influenced by the "social being" that Marx says "determines consciousness."

This chapter explores one aspect of the problem to which Ollman and Smith allude: the influence and persistence of *ontological dualism* within capitalist society, and the challenge that materialist dialectics, conceived as a monistic alternative at the level of social ontology, pose to the ideologically dominant—that is, dualistic—ways in which social reality and human problems are apprehended, framed, and analyzed. Ontological dualism is to be understood here as a metaphysical worldview that divides reality into two substantially opposed and "estranged" spheres: the natural and the supernatural; the physical and the spiritual; and the material and the ideal. Following a brief discussion of the controversy surrounding the place of dialectics in Marxism, the chapter surveys the sources of dualistic thinking and some of its expressions in modern social theory. This is followed by an examination of Marx's materialist conception of history and its basis in a monistic ontology that encompasses three dialectically interpenetrated aspects or fields: the Natural, the Social, and conscious Activity. The idea of an historical-materialist system of "dialectical triads" is then proposed, and the usefulness of this system is illustrated through a brief survey of competing concepts of economic value.

Marxism and the Controversy Surrounding Dialectics

Three broad positions are discernible among Marxists with regard to the place of dialectics in Marxist thought.[1] The first, traditional position is that dialectics is a set of methodological principles for grasping the interconnections of the various aspects and elements of reality, their mutual relations, and the contradictions within and among them that generate forces for change and development (Engels 1970b; Lefebvre 1968; cf. Ollman 2003). On this view, dialectic is the "logic of change," and its methods are useful precisely because they "map on" to the actual nature and movement of reality. Dialectic as method is deemed necessary because the reality that it helps to explain and to understand is itself dialectical in its ontological structure. Although controversial and susceptible to different readings, Engels' exposition of the "three laws of the dialectic" in *Dialectics of Nature* captures the traditional Marxist conception of the "internal" connection between dialectical reason and a dialectical reality. Descending from Hegel, the three laws are: "the unity of opposites" (every concrete totality comprises contradictory elements), "the transformation of quantity into quality" (changes in degree eventuate in changes in type), and "the negation of the negation" (the clash of contradictory elements produces changes that both preserve and radically transform them) (Engels 1954: 83). For Engels, as for most traditional defenders of "materialist dialectics," these three laws find application in the analysis of nature and society alike (Engels 1954, 1969; Novack 1978; see also Foster 2000: 226–36).

The second broad position on the status of dialectics in Marxist thought maintains that dialectic can refer only to the interplay of a subject and an object. Where human consciousness or subjectivity is absent, there can be relations of causality but no truly dialectical relations. On this view, dialectic is relevant to the methodology of the social sciences and to a variety of epistemological issues, but it is not an ontological category. In other words, dialectic is *only* a method (of a conscious subject), and ontological dialectics (whether in its idealist-Hegelian or its materialist-Engelsian guise) is a variety of "metaphysics" that Marxists ought to avoid. Thus, Engels' elaboration of a "dialectics of nature" is dismissed as spurious, while Marx's more modest focus on "human society" is applauded as the appropriate frame of reference for a dialectical theory (Lukács 1971; Schmidt 1971).

The third position is in line with the view of anti-Marxist thinkers like Popper (1974) that dialectic is an irredeemably muddled or idealist concept with no place in a theoretical system aspiring to scientific rigour. The key dialectical category of "contradiction" is rejected as logically untenable, whether applied to natural or social processes (Colletti 1973). This position has been associated with various structuralist, analytical, or positivist Marxists who argue for the incorporation into Marxism of "state-of-the-art" methods borrowed from structural anthropology, neoclassical economics, linguistic philosophy, or other disciplines. Such methods, it is argued, are more precise and less prone to metaphysical obfuscation or manipulation than the dialectical principles deployed by Hegel, Engels, or even Marx (Rosenthal 1999).

For his part, Marx insisted that a vast gulf separated the idealist dialect-ical method of Hegel from his own materialist dialectic.[2] Nevertheless, he asserted that it was possible and even necessary to discover the "rational kernel" within the "mystical shell" of the Hegelian system (1977: 103). But of what does that rational kernel consist? Among contemporary Marxists there is a notable lack of consensus, but it nevertheless appears that a list of its possible constituents would include Engels' "three laws," a philosophy of "internal relations" (Ollman 1976), a commitment to the systematic dia-lectical ordering of concepts (Murray 1988; T. Smith 1990; Arthur 1998), and a rejection of "metaphysical dualism" in favour of ontological monism (Caudwell 1971; Mészáros 1970, 2010).

What is all too frequently absent from the debates between (and within) the three "camps" identified above is the recognition that the question of "dialectic" cannot be separated from two critically important philosophical issues confronting a truly emancipatory social science: the defense of real-ism in epistemology (the theory of knowledge) and the defense of monism in ontology (the theory of being/what exists). Sean Sayers has addressed the first issue admirably in his 1985 book *Reality and Reason: Dialectic and the Theory of Knowledge* by showing how dualistic presuppositions subvert the realist proposition that an objective, material world exists independently of consciousness and is also knowable by consciousness. For Sayers, only a dialectical approach can break through the dualistic, anti-realist tendencies in the theory of knowledge and overcome their disorienting and paralyzing implications for human practice.

The argument I wish to make is in many respects parallel and comple-mentary to that of Sayers. If dialectic is essential to the defense of realism within epistemology (that is, to the *possibility* of the identity—or "iso-morphism"—of thought and reality), it is no less essential to the defense of monism within ontology. And the defense of monism is *imperative* for the very good reason that monism is the only effective "antidote" to the ontological dualism that pervades the culture of bourgeois society and obscures the roots of human misery in the prevailing social relations of production and reproduction. If "the critique of religion is the beginning of all criticism" as Marx famously argued, it is no less true that the critique of dualism is an urgent task of contemporary Marxist criticism. Thus, dialectical monism is a "necessity" just because the struggle against dualistic ways of understanding the world is essential to the emancipatory project of Marxist socialism.

Once dualism is consciously rejected and the necessity of dialectical monism is grasped, it becomes much easier to navigate the controversy surrounding dialectics in Marxist thought. The "anti-dialectic" position of analytical, structuralist, and positivist Marxists can be seen as an attempt to avoid, in "agnostic" fashion, the central ontological position defended by materialist dialectics: the *materially grounded* but also internally differentiated and contradictory nature of reality. At the same time, proponents of the "subject-object dialectic" who reject ontological dialectics (and, *mutatis mutandis*, "the dialectics of nature") can be seen as succumbing to a dualism of human and natural worlds. Against such dualism, defenders of the materialist dialectic must insist that, notwithstanding the important differences that exist between the human and natural realms, they are best viewed as a "unity of opposites" rather than as *absolutely* different and opposed. While the ontological "fields" of the human and natural realms are certainly different (with the former far more complex than the latter), dialectical principles are an indispensable aid to understanding both realms in anti-metaphysical (that is to say, non-dualistic) ways.

Dualistic Social Ontology versus Marxism

One of the most pervasive notions in non-Marxist social thought—and one that has long exerted a hegemonic, if generally unacknowledged, influence on the major intellectual and political debates of our time—is the dualistic notion that "the human condition" or "social being" is riven between and, in some sense, co-determined by two metaphysically different worlds, substances, or principles. This notion finds popular expression in myriad ways but perhaps most tellingly in the widespread concern that "moral progress" is lagging badly behind scientific and technological advancements, with potentially disastrous consequences for human society (such as nuclear war or ecological collapse). Just as the "dualistic social ontology" implied in this lament provides the implicit philosophical framework of nature-versus-nurture controversies that tacitly regard existing social relations and institutions as inevitable or insurmountable, so does it encourage reliance on scientific progress and technological innovation, on one side, and moral education (and perhaps some notion of distributive justice), on the other, as the *sole* available solutions to pressing human problems. Despite its basically conservative implications, however, the dualistic perspective has received surprisingly little explicit critical attention from Marxists.

Dualism, as ontology, finds its most secure and perennial expression in a worldview that insists that "the material" and "the spiritual" constitute entirely separate domains with an indeterminate relationship to one another. Despite its obvious connection to religion, however, such a fully developed dualistic conception is present only in comparatively recent religious doctrines. Animistic and naturalistic religions regard reality as a unity, with spiritual and natural entities coexisting in the *same* world, albeit at different "levels." The "disenchantment of the world"—the human mind's dualistic separation of the spiritual/eternal and the mundane/temporal into absolutely separate spheres—involved an uneven and historically protracted process that was decisively associated with the rise and "rationalization" of the monotheistic religions. But this separation was only completed under the impact of the modern scientific revolution, which entrenched the idea that natural events and processes are better comprehended in terms of predictable natural laws than as the whims of supernatural beings. To be sure, not all modern religions consistently endorse this separation, even when they allow for an independent role for science in human affairs. Idealism—the view that mind or spirit is the foundation of all that exists—remains the preferred ontology of those who affirm the active and ongoing intervention of a god or gods in the temporal world (true theism), while ontological dualism appeals most strongly to those who entertain the existence of a creator-god whose direct involvement with humanity is in doubt and who may have disengaged from the material universe after setting it in motion and decreeing the natural laws of its operation (deism).

Across a succession of class-divided societies, historically specific conditions of social being have provided continuous and systematic reinforcement to the dualist worldview.[3] These conditions include the division of intellectual and manual labour, which is emblematic of all "civilized" social formations, and which is initially associated with the emergence of state religions and priesthoods; the separation of exchange and use inherent in the process of commodity production and exchange, which has become a generalized phenomenon with the consolidation of capitalism as the globally dominant mode of production; and, most recently, the functional imperative of capitalist society to create a relatively free space for the progress of modern science (as the indispensable means of raising the productivity of labour and furthering the accumulation of capital), while also preserving a role for religion and superstition in pacifying the subaltern classes and countering the influence of emancipatory trends in the social sciences, above all Marxism. The critique of dualism is therefore not only a useful but a necessary starting point for revealing the historically limited (and increasingly perilous) character of these conditions of social being and for suggesting an alternative theoretical strategy—one informed by a dialectical-monistic social ontology—that complements a program and practice for their progressive dissolution.

Fundamental to a Marxist, historical-materialist critique of dualism is an insistence upon the role of the social relations of production (and reproduction) in *mediating* (dominating and regulating) the dynamic relationship between the material-natural (encompassing human "corporeal organisation," the forces of production, and the invariant laws of nature) and human conscious Activity (encompassing ideas and agency).[4] In this view, the social is not immediately reducible to either the material or the ideal (as in dualistic thought), but plays a relatively autonomous role within an ontological unity. Thus, Marxism rejects any supposition of principled indeterminacy in the relationship between the material-natural and human consciousness/activity, positing each as relatively distinct aspects or moments of a dialectical (monistic but also internally diverse and contradictory) unity in which the social plays a significant *determining* role.

Dualism in Modern Philosophy and Social Theory

Dualism, in both ontology and epistemology, has ancient roots, finding its best-known early expression in Plato's Allegory of the Cave. In the history of philosophy, down to the Enlightenment, only idealism has been more influential, owing to the overweening influence of religion in pre-modern cultures. Dualism emerged as the dominant perspective of early modern European intellectuals under the influence of Descartes' mind-body dualism and Locke's empiricist theory of knowledge (the latter involving a dualism of "ideas" and real objects). To be sure, some Enlightenment thinkers (Helvetius, D'Holbach, La Mettrie, and others) championed a vigorously materialist (and more or less explicitly atheist) position, while the rationalist philosopher Spinoza defended an elaborate pantheistic (and perhaps surreptitiously materialist) monism as against Descartes. But most Age of Reason and Enlightenment philosophers adopted a dualistic position—with some emphasizing material factors and others "the ideal." Propelled by the capitalist drive for scientific innovation and by the intellectual revolt against religious dogma, the modern era saw the gradual displacement of traditional, religiously grounded idealism by dualism, and the burgeoning influence of dualistic perspectives within the wider culture.

Immanuel Kant's philosophy represented the culmination of this trend in early modern philosophy and social theory. Kant defended the view that the human mind can know phenomena (sense experience as categorized and organized by the mind) but not things in themselves (the "noumena" existing independently of human thought), and that reality, from the standpoint of human consciousness, is riven between "what is" (*Müssen*) and "what ought to be" (*Sollen*). Despite Kant's avowed intent, the result of his epistemological assault on traditional ontology was a dualistic metaphysics: a speculative division of reality into material-natural and ideal-spiritual worlds, the former conceived as subject to deterministic physical laws and the latter to "free will." Science and religious faith were understood to be the legitimate concerns of two different types of human reason: science with "what is"—*a priori* knowledge and the empirically given as conceptualized by "pure reason," and religion with "what ought to be"—those transcendent spiritual goals and moral precepts that are divinely inscribed in the human mind (above all, the "categorical imperative") and that are the intuitive pre-occupations of "practical reason."

Kant's dualism met with considerable resistance from the idealist and materialist philosophers of the nineteenth century, but by century's end it had established a growing following among social theorists and phil-osophers alike, particularly in continental Europe. In Germany, a Kantian revival, led by Rickert and Windelband, eclipsed Hegel's absolute idealism and challenged the growing influence of a decidedly mechanistic under-standing of Marx's materialism in the era of the Second International. The neo-Kantians insisted upon a radical separation of facts and values in what they called the human or cultural sciences—an opinion that exerted a par-ticularly strong influence on Max Weber, whose methodological principles and dualistic social ontology were to leave a lasting imprint upon European and Anglo-American social theory (Weber 1949; Giddens 1971; Therborn 1980).

Weber's sociology may be seen as providing a dualistic template for an influential body of modern and postmodern social theory, includ-ing some neo-Marxist and post-Marxist variants broadly associated with what might be called the "power-conflict paradigm." In brief, his theoretical project offered an alternative to Marx's handling of the char-acteristic preoccupations of modern social theory (capitalism, social con-flict, inequality, rationality, community) by effacing the determinative role of historically specific social relations of production/reproduction and by reinstating a metaphysical indeterminacy as between the material/natural and the ideal/cultural.[5] This is perhaps best exemplified by his famous thesis concerning the "independent" contribution of Protestant theological and ethical ideas to the emergence of "rational asceticism"—the "spirit of capitalism"—and thus to the rise of the modern capitalist economic order; however, his dualistic perspective is no less evident in his theories of domination and the distribution of power within society (Weber 1958; 1978).

Within the rising academic discipline of sociology in twentieth-century Europe and America, Weber's thesis was widely hailed by non-Marxists as a devastating blow to Marx's purportedly "economic interpretation" of history. Yet, an alternative, historical-materialist account of the relationship between Protestantism and capitalism had already been suggested by Engels in an under-appreciated passage from his 1892 introduction to the English edition of *Socialism: Utopian and Scientific*. This passage points to the ability of historical materialism to not only affirm the "role of ideas in history" (the task Weber set for himself) but also their "material" provenance. At the same time, it serves to illustrate the very different social-ontological presuppositions underlying the Marxian and Weberian appreciations of an event of singular importance to the forging of the modern world.

Engels wrote: "Calvin's creed was one fit for the boldest of the bourgeoisie of his time. His predestination doctrine was the religious expression of the fact that in the commercial world of competition success or failure does not depend upon a man's activity or cleverness, but upon circumstances uncontrollable by him" (1970b: 104). From Engels' perspective, Calvinist and other Protestant ideas were hardly an "independent" force in stimulating the "spirit of capitalism." On the contrary, they were a product of, as well as reinforcement to, the process of transition to the modern, capitalist order—a transition that had begun with the *prior* emergence of a "commercial world of competition." The material and social conditions of this commercial world, Engels suggests, were to decisively *mediate* the relationship between the spread of Protestant ideas (such as "predestination" and "the work ethic") and the rise of what Weber called "modern capitalism."

As against this eminently dialectical approach, Weber conceived human social action, and the institutions to which it gives rise, as the product of two ontologically independent sets of factors: on the one side, natural laws and technical necessity (the concerns of formal rationality), and, on the other, the spiritual and ethical orientations of human individuals (the province of value rationality). On this view, value rationality is disconnected from the material facts of life associated with production and economics, flowing instead from a seemingly mystical connection between human subjectivity and an immaterial, spiritual domain. Accordingly, Weber's dualistic social theory allows a significant role for mysterious (spiritual or supernatural) factors in human affairs, even though it is not motivated by any explicit religious purpose.

Weber's dualism has been reproduced by many later thinkers associated with a variety of currents, including "left-critical" ones, within social theory. From the camp of Critical Theory, for example, Jürgen Habermas proposes a correction of Marx and a reconstruction of historical materialism that involves a dualistic separation of "production" and "communicative interaction" (Habermas 1971; cf. Sensat 1979). In elaborating his theory of structuration, Anthony Giddens (1981) develops a critique of historical materialism based on a dualism of "allocative resources" and "authoritative resources"—corresponding respectively to distinct material and social worlds. While "social power" is considered to be generated at the "intersection" of these two worlds, Giddens suggests that their relations are necessarily indeterminate—in contrast to the deterministic relations that Marx allegedly posits between the "forces" and "relations" of production.[6] From the camp of postmodernism, Jean Baudrillard (1975) establishes an ontological opposition between an ideal-social realm of symbolic exchange/"sacrificial economy" and a material realm of "political economy," conferring an ontological privilege to symbolic exchange over the production of commodity values, and positing an irreconcilable, transhistorical opposition of material wealth and symbolic wealth.

Michael Hardt and Antonio Negri's (2000, 2004) much-celebrated attempt to combine a post-Marxist understanding of "economic postmodernization" with Michel Foucault's concept of biopolitics provides yet another example of dualistic thinking in recent social theory, one relevant to the discussion of economic value later in this chapter. Hardt and Negri argue that two developments have combined to "explode" the "value form" that Marx analyzed in *Capital*, thereby negating the law of (labour) value as the pre-eminent regulatory principle of contemporary capitalism. On the one hand, "immaterial labour" (essentially, intellectual and service-producing labour) has prevailed over "material labour" (the "industrial labour" that produces "material goods") owing to the increasingly dominant role played by science and technology in the productive metabolism with nature. On the other hand, capital "subsumes" under its control not only labour and the productive process in general, but also the "biopolitics" of social reproduction (education, communication, sexuality, and so on). Marx's capitalist law of value—according to which new value is created solely by living labour and exists as a definite quantitative magnitude that sets limits on wages, prices, and profits (Smith 1994a)—is replaced by a vague notion of value as "determined by humanity's own continuous innovation and creation" (Hardt & Negri 2000: 356).

In making their argument, Hardt and Negri succumb to the *capital fetishism* that is engendered by what Marx (in the *Resultate*) called the "real subsumption of labour under capital" and by the ever-increasing role of science and technology (defined by Marx as "the general product of social development") in modern capitalism (Marx 1977, appendix). At bottom, capital fetishism (like commodity fetishism) involves the confusion and conflation of the Natural and the Social in the human mind, and the concomitant failure to recognize that the production of value and surplus value under capitalism remains decisively dependent upon the exploitation of wage-labour, however technologically sophisticated the productive metabolism with nature may become. Such fetishism obscures the fact that capitalism, as a mode of production, is geared fundamentally to the creation of surplus value, the accumulation of capital, and the (expanded) reproduction of the capital/wage-labour relation, and not to the creation of "wealth" as such or to the development of the "independent powers" of technology.

Ironically, Hardt and Negri's capital fetishism attests to the residual influence of a dualistic metaphysics in their thinking, despite their disavowal of "the great Western metaphysical tradition" (2000: 355)—for the inescapable result of their effective conflation of the material-natural and the social dimensions of capitalist production is the reinstatement of the material-ideal opposition that is the hallmark of dualistic thinking. By heralding the dominance of so-called "immaterial labour" over "material labour" in "postmodern capitalism," Hardt and Negri not only oppose, in dualistic fashion, types of labour with "intellectual" and "affective" functions to those more mundane types that create material goods; they also imply that capital has won its independence from the *living labour* that Marx identifies as the sole source of *new value*. Thus, Hardt and Negri transform value, conceived by Marx as both a social relation and a definite quantitative magnitude specific to capitalism, into a transhistorical and immeasurable "quality" and "product" of the human intellect. Yet, as David Camfield points out in a searching critique, their "argument depends on both a faulty premise and theoretical confusion about the relationship between concrete labour, abstract labour and value," and fails to "offer any compelling reason to question the belief that value continues to regulate the global economy" (2007: 47; see also Chapter 3 of this volume for a response to earlier "neo-Marxist" critiques of Marx's theory of value similar to those of Hardt and Negri).

This very limited survey reveals that, notwithstanding their diversity, dualist critics of Marxism are remarkably united in their insistence that Marxism "misses something" of great importance to human social life, whether defined as the "independent role of ideas" in history, the contribution of science and technology to creating "value," or a human propensity to symbolism, playfulness, deference, mysticism, or domination. Yet, this sort of indictment can be quite easily reversed. For what distinguishes Marxism from virtually all versions of dualistic social theory is not a constitutive blindness to culture, extra-class conflict, religious sentiment, language, racism, gender, sexuality, communication, or symbolic exchange, but rather an insistence upon approaching all such phenomena with due attention to the historically specific and alterable material and social conditions in which they are manifested. Marxists can legitimately insist that there is nothing in the theoretical constitution of historical materialism that prevents, or compromises, the analysis of any and all of the phenomena that preoccupy the various styles of dualistic theorizing, even though political priorities ("program") will inevitably influence the selection of those problems that attract greater attention and those less.

On the contrary, it is precisely dualistic social theory that necessarily "misses something" that is of utmost significance to the "human condition": namely, the social relations of production in the dialectical mediation of what dualism posits as the "material/natural" and "ideal/cultural" aspects of human existence.[7] Accordingly, the real issue is not whether the defining shibboleths of non-Marxist or post-Marxist social theory should be addressed, but whether they should be addressed in connection with an analysis of the social relations of production (and historically specific forms of human labour), or whether they should be invoked as a rationale for either ignoring the latter or treating them as mere "epiphenomena" of natural laws, an "independent" (perhaps "spiritually influenced") human consciousness, or both. To fully appreciate this difference, along with its ontological foundation, a number of key themes in Marx's critique of hitherto existing philosophy deserve review.

Marx's Dialectical-Monistic Ontology: Against the Metaphysics of Idealism and Dualism

Against all forms of idealism and dualism, Marx embraced a materialist-monist perspective, one distinguished by the idea that reality is unified and that its manifold elements are dialectically interrelated within a material world. When we speak of a Marxist dialectical ontology, therefore, we are speaking, minimally, of an ontology with materialist, monist, and therefore anti-dualistic commitments—an ontology, moreover, which regards all the elements of a dynamic and ever-changing reality as implicated in complex processes of *mediation* with one another.[8]

The foundation of this singular, unified reality is a material universe governed by natural laws. In this view, human life forms have emerged over the course of natural history that acquire consciousness and the capacity for agency, and that enter into definite social relationships with one another. Humans constitute society as a kind of "second nature"—an ontological condition that remains subject to eternal natural laws and constraints, but which is also shaped by historically and geographically specific social forms and laws. From the standpoint of Marx's social theory, then, the reality occupied by human beings—the "human condition" in the most general sense—is one that embraces three aspects: the Natural, the Social (people-to-people relations/interactions), and conscious Activity (the latter encompassing labour, "sensuous activity," creative practice, subjectivity, "self-consciousness," and "the ideal"). These three aspects are by no means independent of one another. Rather, they interpenetrate with and shade into each other in complex ways, even as they remain relatively distinct and distinguishable from one another. Nevertheless, their common ontological ground is precisely a unified, material reality.

In his "Theses on Feuerbach," Marx famously registers the superior historical contribution of idealist philosophy (compared to traditional materialism) in illuminating the human capacity for creative practice. However, according to Marx, the "active side" of human affairs has always been "set forth abstractly by idealism—which, of course, does not know real, sensuous activity as such."[9] The revolutionary new materialism that he advocates emphasizes "human activity itself as objective activity" while also affirming the relative autonomy of human consciousness from mechanically conceived natural processes. Already implicit in Marx's formulation of the problem, then, was the role of "the social" in mediating the relation between the "sensuous objects" and "distinct conceptual objects" of Feuerbach's philosophy (that is to say, between the material-natural and the "ideal" components of human consciousness). Marx writes: "Feuerbach, not satisfied with abstract thinking, wants [sensuous] contemplation; but he does not conceive sensuousness as practical, human-sensuous activity." Such practical, human activity is necessarily *social* in form. At the same time: "All social life is essentially practical. All mysteries which lead theory to mysticism find their rational solution in human practice and in the comprehension of this practice." For Feuerbach, "Essence ... can be regarded only as 'species,' as an inner, mute, general character which unites the many individuals in a natural way...." But for Marx, "the essence of man is no abstraction inherent in each single individual. In its reality it is the ensemble of the social relations."

Thus, as against any naturalistic conception of the human essence, Marx's new materialism takes "human society" or "social humanity"—"the ensemble of the social relations"—as its point of departure. Marx goes on to insist that "the standpoint of the old materialism is civil society; the standpoint of the new is human society, or social humanity." This latter standpoint affirms the crucial role of the social in mediating the relation between nature and conscious human activity—the better to not only interpret the world, but also to change it in definite ways. Accordingly, the "practical materialism" affirmed here by Marx is one which regards "the Social" as an irreducible dimension of the unified material reality of which humanity is a part.

Marx's theoretical strategy was motivated not by an arbitrary theoretical preference, but by the eminently practical consideration that the key to changing the world is to transform—that is to say, to revolutionize—the Social. In taking this position, he distanced himself not only from Feuerbach's more traditional materialism (that posited a complete separation of "sensuous objects" and "conceptual objects" and which was therefore still infected with dualistic and idealistic tendencies), but also from the idealism of the Left Hegelians, for whom a changed consciousness (understood narrowly as a definite set of ideals—a mere "ideality") was sufficient to revolutionize the world.

The special attention accorded to the Social within Marx's new materialism fundamentally distinguishes his approach from all dualistic philosophies and social theories that proceed from a presumed opposition between nature ("the material-natural") and the ideal (understood as the "spiritually rooted" contents of human consciousness). Indeed, it was precisely from the ontological standpoint of "social humanity" that Marx berated Proudhon for "a dualism between life and ideas, between soul and body, a dualism which recurs in many forms" (1989c: 12).

As we have seen, the "recurrence" of dualism is endemic to modern, non-Marxist social theory in general. Indeed, a formal, unmediated opposition of the material-natural and the ideal is foundational to a dualistic outlook that necessarily considers the relations between facts and values, objects and subjects, structure and agency, as eternally problematic, and that persistently treats the terms of these dualities as separated and externally related. While Marx's social theory certainly distinguishes the terms of such dualities, it nevertheless also insists upon approaching them with due attention to their common, monistic foundation: the "materialist connection of men with one another, which is determined by their needs and their mode of production, and which is as old as men themselves" (Marx & Engels 1968: 42). This "materialist connection" is central to Marx's social ontology because it, and not consciousness, spirit, or ideas springing from a putatively "non-material" realm, is the real basis of the "second nature" constituted as human society. "This connection is ever taking on new forms, and thus presents a 'history' irrespective of the existence of any political or religious nonsense which would especially hold men together" (42).

As against the hard metaphysical opposition of the material-natural and the ideal that is emblematic of modern dualistic (bourgeois) social theory and philosophy, Marx invites a focus on a dialectically conceived *distinction* between the Social and the Natural,[10] while defining ideas as "the independent expression in thought of the existing world" (102). In doing so, he elevates "the Social" to the status of a determining (as well as determined) moment or aspect of an ontological unity in which the Natural and conscious Activity form the other two moments. The Social emerges from the shadows of both the "material-natural" and "the ideal," taking its place as an irreducible element of what might be regarded as a distinctively historical-materialist "dialectical triad."

Historical Materialism and the Dialectical Triad

The essential feature of the syllogism is the unity of the extremes, the middle term which unites them, and the ground which supports them.
—Hegel, *Science of Logic*

I have been arguing that Marx's ontology is both dialectical and monistic in its underlying structure. To speak of dialectic is to posit the interrelations of two or more terms, while to speak of monism is to affirm a fundamental "oneness." Within the oneness that is material reality, Marxist ontology posits the dialectical interplay of three distinguishable and yet interpenetrated "ontological fields": the Natural, the Social, and conscious Activity. Accordingly, the dialectical-monist ontology of Marxism has a definite "triadic" structure, one which ought to be both explicitly theorized and consciously applied in Marxist-socialist theory, practice, and pedagogy.

The triadic conceptual structure of Marx's social theory should come as no surprise to those familiar with Marx's writings as well as the Marxist secondary literature. István Mészáros (1970) has observed that Marx's *Economic and Philosophic Manuscripts of 1844* describe the dialectical interrelations within a triad involving Industry, Man, and Nature. In Marx's 1859 Preface to *The Contribution to the Critique of Political Economy*, we encounter a triad involving (material-natural) forces of production, (social) relations of production, and a (political and ideological) superstructure.[11] Norman Fischer (1982) has argued that Marx's value theory in *Capital* is informed by a "three-tier ontology"—one involving a *natural* law (the human imperative to allocate labour in definite proportions to different socio-economic tasks), a holistic *social* structure (abstract labour, conceived as a macroeconomic regulator of commodity production and exchange), and the *activities* of conscious individuals. Perhaps most strikingly of all, Marx and Engels refer in *The German Ideology* to "three moments—the forces of production, the state of society, and consciousness" that "can and must come into contradiction with one another" (Marx & Engels 1968: 44). The immanent contradictions of these moments point immediately to the need to understand the ontological triad not as a *seamless* or *static* structure but as a *structure in process*—as one subject to both quantitative and qualitative change. Indeed, a truly dialectical conception of "social being" demands an appreciation of this ontological triad's own historical movement. Such an account is to be found in the *Grundrisse*—where Marx sketches a three-stage conception of human social development involving a progression from "community" (the most "natural" of human conditions) to "individuality and external sociality" (the stage most heavily laden with reified "social" forms) to "communal individuality" (the future communist society in which conscious Activity comes fully into its own) (Marx 1973; Gould 1978).

In an especially suggestive discussion, Tony Smith (1993a) has sought to establish the relevance of Hegel's theory of the syllogism and its triadic structure to Marxism (Hegel 1969, 1975). For Hegel, the totality that is modern society can be grasped in terms of the relations between universality ("objective spirit" as represented by the state), particularity (the socio-economic institutions of civil society), and individuality (the sovereign individual, as identified in Locke's political philosophy). Smith argues that this U-P-I syllogism is applicable to Marx's analysis of capitalism, with capital forming the moment of universality, the distinct structural tendencies of capital forming the moment of particularity, and the acts of individuals, as determined by these tendencies and mediated by the inner nature of capital, forming the moment of individuality (cf. Rosenthal 1999).

Smith's fertile argument reveals the formal relevance of Hegel's U-P-I syllogism to the interrogation of the capitalist mode of production and the inner logic of bourgeois society. Yet two reservations need to be registered concerning this Hegelian-Marxist argument. The first is that Hegel's theory of the syllogism belongs to a thoroughly idealist and teleological philosophical system that conceives of human history as unfolding in accordance with a certain logical (even "deductive") necessity. Marx's materialist conception of history, to the contrary, conceives "real, living individuals" (and not any transcendental *logos*) as the true subject of history, and accordingly considers "the development of social relations from one stage to the next [as] a contingent one" that "follows from human choices and actions" (Gould 1978: 21; Smith 1994b; see Chapter 6 of this volume). Owing to the triadic ontological structure of social reality, the real movement of human society may have parallels to the "spiral" movement of negation described in Hegel's philosophy of history and supported deductively by his idealist dialectic. For Marx, however, a materialist conception of history is incompatible with any such idealist teleology, and the dialectical interaction of the three fields of his ontology has no necessary, ineluctable outcome.[12]

This brings us to the second reservation. Marx's historical materialism is not concerned exclusively with the analysis of modern, capitalist society. Indeed, as we have seen, Marx defines the general standpoint of his "new materialism" as "human society" or "social humanity"—rejecting Feuerbach's naturalistic standpoint of "species essence" and the "old materialist" (political-economic) standpoint of "civil society," as well as Hegel's standpoint of the modern state (conceived as the highest expression of "objective spirit"). This implies two things: in the first place, the social relations, structures, and forms *specific to particular human societies* are the necessary starting point of historical-materialist inquiry; and secondly, the notion that either the state or civil society can be seen as representing the principle of universality must be rejected.

Within Marx's ontology *taken as a whole*, the concept of universality is most appropriately aligned with the Natural, the concept of particularity with the Social, and the concept of individuality with the conscious Activity of "real, living individuals." Although it is perhaps tempting to speak of a distinctive "historical-materialist dialectical syllogism" that can be derived from the "rational kernel" of Hegel's logical theory, it is more in keeping with Marx's materialist and anti-teleological commitments to speak instead of a "dialectical ontological triad"—or, better yet, a *system* of dialectical triads.[13]

This system of triads begins with S<–N->A, where N (the natural conditions and aspects of human existence) mediates S (the social relations of production/reproduction) and A (conscious Activity, encompassing ideas and agency). In the grand sweep of human history, S<–N->A highlights the role that natural circumstances and laws play in determining the range of specific features and forms available to conscious Activity and to concretely existing societies. But this triad cannot stand alone as an explanatory principle. It must be supplemented by two others: N<–S->A and N<–A->S. In disclosing the specific "logic" of a particular type of society (always the principal concern of historical-materialist inquiry), N<–S->A assumes pre-eminence: for here, the social relations of production/reproduction dominate and mediate all aspects of a historically specific totality. Furthermore, in revealing the effects of the deliberate and intentional activities of individual agents (as well as the collective projects/movements formed by them), S<–A->N takes its turn at centre stage: for here, conscious Activity mediates the relations and seeks to attenuate, overcome, or transcend the contradictions arising between the Social and the Natural.

From the standpoint of historical materialism, the consequence of considering only one of these triads in the analysis of a given social totality (and eliding the other two) is a necessarily *partial* view. Thus, S<–N->A, taken in isolation, lends itself to "vulgar" or "mechanical" versions of materialism, to one-sidedly "naturalistic" explanations of social phenomena of the type associated with sociobiology, evolutionary psychology, and memetics, or to a spurious universalism (such as technological determinism). A fixation on N<-A->S, on the other hand, tends to be associated with subjective idealism, relativism, and a voluntaristic social constructionism. Although central to and definitive of historical-materialist inquiry, the N<-S->A triad, when considered alone, is also inadequate to the extent that it understates the essential role of material-natural conditions in shaping the Social and the necessary role of conscious Activity in effecting social change. Thus, as Tony Smith has argued on behalf of Hegel's theory of the syllogism, the practical effect of considering the *system* of dialectical syllogisms, and allowing each term to take the position of the middle term, is the avoidance of vulgar reductionism in theory (T. Smith 1993a: 14).

The historical-materialist system of dialectical triads may be represented, somewhat schematically, as follows:

S<-N->A   [<-]   N<-S->A   [->]   S<-A->N

Within each triad, the middle term dominates the outlying terms and regulates their relations; and, within the system of triads, the middle triad dominates the outlying triads and regulates their relations.

In accordance with the method of materialist dialectics, each of the individual triads comprising the historical-materialist system of triads must be seen as open-ended in character—with each term (or ontological field) referring to a historically variable and site-specific content that is subject to concrete empirical investigation. This circumstance makes general definitions of these fields difficult to specify with precision, all the more so since each "shades into" the others in dialectical fashion. Nevertheless, some general definitions are mandatory to render the system of triads more transparent and operationally useful.

THE NATURAL

Earlier in this chapter, the Natural was described as "encompassing human corporeal organization, the forces of production, and the invariant laws of nature." The "invariant laws of nature" refer to the universal physical laws that humans seek to understand and bring under their control, but which they can neither repeal nor escape. Some examples are the laws of thermodynamics, evolution through natural selection, and the allocation of labour time within human communities. The "forces of production" refer to the capacities that humans have devised to subdue nature, manipulate its laws, and reduce the burden of toil and material insecurity that afflicts humankind. They mediate the relationship of social humanity to its natural environment and are central to the metabolic relation between conscious Activity and nature. The development of such capacities *follows* from what Marx and Engels called "the first fact" of the materialist conception of history: "human corporeal organization" (Marx & Engels 1968).

Joseph Fracchia has drawn attention to the undeserved neglect that has attended Marx and Engels' passing reference to this "first fact," as well as its potential to illuminate many issues in historical-materialist theory, including the satisfactory articulation of the Natural and the Social aspects of "human nature." He writes:

> The construction of the categorial framework for a historical-materialist taxonomy [as "a categorial replacement for 'human nature'"] begins with the generic category of *anlagen* denoting the general predispositions embedded in human corporeal organisation. It then moves to the two sub-categories that together establish the range of human corporeal predisposition: one delineating those aspects of human corporeal organisation that allow us to make our own history—the bodily instruments, capacities, and dexterities; and the other delineating those bodily attributes that prevent us from making our history as we please—bodily needs, (socio-culturally mediated) wants and desires, and bodily limits and constraints which themselves could be transformed into challenges that humans solve through the production of artifice. (Fracchia 2005: 53)[14]

Impetus to human creativity and to the diversity of socio-cultural forms is provided not only by our "bodily instruments, capacities, and dexterities" but also by our "bodily needs," which are, among other things, a "positive provocation to people inhabiting particular geographical sites to develop commensurately particular cultural forms" (59). On the basis of such a historical-materialist taxonomy of human capacities and needs, we can proceed more successfully "to study the modes of human being, of socio-cultural forms, in their infinite though not unlimited diversity" (59–60). From the standpoint of the dialectical triad S<–N–>A, such a taxonomy would form a key element defining the "material-natural" field of Marx's ontology.[15]

Drawing on Spinoza, Andrew Brown has developed an interesting critique of the principle of the "non-isomorphism" of thought and its object (as posited by Bhaskar's critical realism) that is strikingly relevant to the issues raised by Fracchia. He writes:

> The thinking body is an active material body, amongst other active material bodies, and so, through its spatial activity, the thinking body comes into direct contact with other objects. The faculty of self-awareness of spatial activity is the key that enables the thinking body to turn such direct contact into direct acquaintance with the object.... By acting spatially and transforming its schema of action when external objects intervene, it is possible for the thinking body to achieve and recognise an identity between its own spatial activity and that of external objects.... According to Spinoza, an adequate idea of an object is then nothing but the self-awareness of the spatial activity of the body identical in shape (isomorphic) to the object. (Brown 1999)[16]

The self-transformation of the thinking, material body through spatial action is a process rooted in human corporeal organization and in the faculty of self-awareness of spatial activity, which this organization makes possible. As such it points to a vital "materialist connection" between the Natural and the Social, on the one hand, and the Natural and "the ideal," on the other—connections, it bears emphasizing, that are always and necessarily mediated by conscious Activity.[17]

THE SOCIAL

In *The German Ideology*, Marx and Engels wrote: "the production of life, both of one's own in labour and of fresh life in procreation ... appears as a double relationship: on the one hand as a natural, on the other as a social relationship. By social we understand the cooperation of several individuals, no matter under what conditions, in what measure and to what end" (Marx & Engels 1968: 41).

For Marx, human co-operation can assume many forms: voluntary and coerced, egalitarian and class-antagonistic, solidaristic and exploitative; it can involve "bonds of personal dependency" as well as "objective bonds"— and, in the future, the universal communal bonds of an advanced communist society. Moreover, the goals of human co-operation can range from the production of the material necessities of life, to the creation of semiotic artifacts, to the reproduction of structures of inequality.

In historical materialism, "the Social" refers to the people-to-people relations and structures that confer particular forms upon the material-natural content of "social humanity." Social structures are nothing other than relatively enduring patterns of inter-human relations—relations through which human beings transform the natural world and themselves. Human labour and the process of objectification are central to these transformations. For this reason, the Social refers pre-eminently to modes of co-operation as constituted by definite relations of production and reproduction.

Closely connected to "cooperation" in Marx's thought is the concept of "division of labour." Marx writes:

> Within the division of labour, relationships are bound to acquire independent existence in relation to individuals. All relations can be expressed in language only in the form of concepts. That these general ideas and concepts are looked upon as mysterious forces is the necessary result of the fact that the real relations, of which they are the expressions, have acquired independent existence. (Marx & Engels 1968: 46)

In a similar vein, Marx insists that "society, irrespective of its form" is "the product of man's interaction upon man" (1989c: 29).

The social relations of production and reproduction are at the heart of the Social; they are both defined by and constitutive of such social forms as commodity exchange, wage-labour, capital, social class, gender, race, citizenship, and the family. At the most fundamental level, they define the mechanisms for articulating a division of labour, distributing the material wealth of society, and producing "fresh life in procreation" (economic, political, and family forms). At the same time, they produce and reproduce social forms that give concrete material definition to structures of exploitation and oppression (class, state, race, gender). Accordingly, a "production relation" can have legal, political, and familial aspects as well as more narrowly conceived "economic" ones. The category is inherently open-ended, requiring "in each separate instance," as Marx insists, "empirical observation [to] bring out ... the connection of the social and political structure with production" (Marx & Engels 1968: 36; Sayer 1987).

The social field of the S<–N–>A triad "grows out" of the natural field, as form to content. While the relationship is an internal one, social form is ultimately dependent upon natural content. Indeed, the natural content of "social humanity" or "human society" defines the limits and potentialities of its forms. But once the social field adopts the middle position within the triad (corresponding to a shift in the focus of analysis to a particular *type* of society), it is also true that S defines and sets limits on N. Indeed, within the N<–S–>A triad, the Natural is altered and "formed" in accordance with the logic and imperatives of the constitutive social relations. The domination of a particularly constituted social field within a given totality must persist until such time as structural contradictions arise between N and S (and are registered and addressed by A). Such structural contradictions will manifest themselves as serious threats to the integrity or further development of the natural field posed by the continuation of the prevailing social relations of production and reproduction.

(CONSCIOUS) ACTIVITY

Dualism in social theory involves a specific form of reductionism— the reduction of the social to one of two ontological spheres that are regarded as incommensurable and absolutely distinct from one another: the "material-natural" and "the ideal." That is to say, within dualistic social ontology, the social aspects of the human condition are understood to be either the immutable manifestations or epiphenomena of the natural laws of the material universe (encompassing non-human as well as human nature) or an objectification of those elements of human consciousness that are considered to have a transcendent and essentially non-material origin. Notwithstanding the tremendous diversity in the forms of dualistic thought (some instances of which may appear to give priority to material factors over ideal ones), all dualisms remain committed to the idealist proposition that mind, ideas, and spirit can and do exist apart from the domain of the "material-natural."

Marx's historical materialism categorically rejects this idealist proposition, insisting that "ideas" spring not from any "immaterial" realm but from the material-natural and social conditions of human existence; they are "the independent expression in thought of the existing world" in both its material-natural and social dimensions. What may give "ideas" the appearance of an independent ontological status is their ability to endure long after the conditions that gave rise to them have disappeared. Their origin in human engagement with concrete practical problems—pertaining either to people's relations to nature or to each other—can be "forgotten" and yet their hold on human thinking may still persist. For this reason, even the most implausible and practically suspect of ideas can nevertheless remain a real "material force."

In historical materialism, however, consciousness is not merely co-extensive with "ideas in people's heads" or with "the ideal" as this is understood in idealist or dualistic ontologies. Consciousness involves the *active relations* that humans establish toward nature and toward each other, as well as the capacities they develop through these relations. It is important to note that intellectual capacities, as grounded in "human corporeal organization" and as related to "self-awareness in spatial activity," include forms of thought that are engendered by determinate social relations. The categories of thought arise from social intercourse and are not simply hard-wired into the human brain. Marx's reproach of Proudhon's dualism, referred to earlier, was predicated on just this consideration:

138

[The] categories are no more eternal than the relations they express. They are historical and transitory products.... Because Mr. Proudhon posits on the one hand eternal ideas, the categories of pure reason, and, on the other, man and his practical life which, according to him, is the practical application of these categories, you will find in him from the very outset a dualism between life and ideas, between soul and body—a dualism which recurs in many forms. (1989c: 11-12)

The categories of human thought—whether political-economic, philo-sophical, or scientific in character—are "historical and transitory products" of human practical activity and, potentially at least, veritable "forces of pro-duction" in their own right. Just as social forms can become productive forces (Marx insists, for example, that a "mode of cooperation is itself a 'productive force'"), so too can cognitive forms sometimes assume such a role (Marx & Engels 1968: 41; Smith 1994a; see Chapter 5 of this volume).

Language, of course, is one of the most powerful and fundamental com-ponents of human conscious Activity, possessing both a natural basis and a practical function as a means of social co-operation.[18] Neither circum-stance precludes it from acquiring a relatively autonomous logic or from becoming a means to dissimulation and oppression rather than authentic communication (a central preoccupation of twentieth-century philosophy and social theory). But the question as to whether it develops as a creative or destructive capacity must turn in large part on whether it assists or impedes conscious Activity in resolving adequately the immanent struc-tural contradiction between N and S referred to above.

Ideas, cognitive categories, language, and moral values are the means through which conscious Activity fulfills its role as the middle term of the dialectical triad S<-A->N. In mediating the relationship between S and N, conscious Activity may obscure and seek to attenuate the contradictions arising between them; and indeed in "normal times" this will be a predomi-nant tendency. Yet Activity is always executed by individual social agents differentially located within class and other social structures. It is, of course, the optimistic expectation of the founders of historical materialism that, as growing numbers of conscious agents come to recognize the destructive consequences of these contradictions, human (class) consciousness and agency will seek to overcome them in the only progressive way open to them: through the revolutionary transformation of the Social.

Dualism versus Historical Materialism: The Case of "Economic Value"

The usefulness of the historical-materialist system of dialectical triads can now be illustrated by considering the problem of "value" as it is approached by economic theories informed by dualistic ontology, on the one hand, and by dialectical monism, on the other.

The concept of "economic value," conceived as the basis of the price mechanism within a market economy, has been a notoriously elusive and controversial one in the history of economic thought. Three basic approaches to the concept are distinguishable in this history: a first approach, associated with classical political economy and in particular with David Ricardo, that treats value as an objective relation of things to things; a second, associated with neo-classical marginal utility theory, that sees value as a subjective relation of people to things; and a third, distinctive to Marx and his followers, that regards value as a relation of people to people (Marx 1977; Rubin 1973; Engels 1941; Clarke 1982).

The first two approaches are united in conceiving economic value as rooted in a material world governed by unalterable natural laws. Value is therefore considered eternal—a category necessarily present in all conceivable human societies. In the classical theory, human labour itself is treated as a thing, a force of nature, that is related to other things within the economic life process in a purely objective way (that is, on the basis of a common measure for determining the costs of production). Value theory, from this perspective, is a way of determining natural prices on the supply side—that is, from the standpoint of costs incurred or resources expended in the material production process. To the extent that subjectivity or consciousness enters into this approach at all, it pertains mainly to the decisions made by capitalists or their managerial agents with respect to micro-level investments, choices of technique, and the management of labour processes.

In the marginalist theory of value, the problem of determining the "natural prices" of commodities is displaced and an attempt is made to specify the mechanisms of supply and demand that determine actual market prices. The emphasis, however, is characteristically on the "demand side." Since the level of demand is based on subjective perceptions of the uses to which commodities can be put, marginalists propose an essentially subjectivist theory of value. In this view, the production of a commodity may entail definite costs that have their basis in a material "object" world characterized by scarcity; but the actual price of a commodity cannot be predicted solely or even mainly by "supply side" considerations. Rather, given a determinate level of supply, actual prices are finally determined on the demand side, that is, by the psychological relation of prospective buyers to particular goods or services. From this standpoint, the value of a commodity is pre-eminently a function of its marginal utility (the intensity of consumer preference for it), and value is conceived to be an essentially subjective category, detached from any "material" or properly "social" determinations.

The subject-object dualism that is either latent or openly expressed in classical and marginalist theories of value follows ineluctably from a more fundamental ontological dualism that considers "the ideal" (ideas in people's heads, including their "preferences") and the material (the use-values produced and consumed by people) as *unmediated* by specifically social relations and forms. This leads to a common microeconomic focus on the formation of individual prices. In both of these bourgeois approaches to value, the constitution of individual prices is considered in isolation from the historically determinate forms and processes that imbricate commodity values and prices in a structure of specifically social relations. Value and price are treated essentially as either "material-natural" or "ideal" categories. Thus, from the standpoint of the historical-materialist system of dialectical triads, one might say that classical value theory is fixated on A<-N->S and marginal utility theory on N<-A->S, with both schools treating S as an afterthought, a mere derivative of N or A.

141

These two approaches to the question of economic value have long dominated bourgeois ("mainstream") economic thought. To be sure, some economists have sought to dispense with a theory of value entirely while continuing to account for the formation of prices in allegedly more "concrete" ways. But the predominant tendency within non-Marxist economic thought has been to embrace one or both of the approaches outlined above.

Now, by way of contrast, what does it mean to regard value, in the Marxist way, as a "social relation of people to people"?

In one of his last works, *Notes on Adolph Wagner*, Marx defines his own conceptual starting point in *Capital* as "the simplest social form in which the labour-product is presented in contemporary society ... the commodity." The commodity reveals both a "natural form" (a use-value) and a "form of appearance" (an exchange-value) that is the "autonomous mode of appearance of the value contained in the commodity" (1989b: 41–2). In adopting the commodity as his starting point, Marx was evidently guided by a fundamental principle of his social ontology and materialist conception of history: a focus on the internal dialectical relation of the Natural (material labour process and use-value production) and the Social (exchange process) to the scientific analysis of a concrete socio-economic formation and its laws of motion. Indeed, it would seem that Marx selected the real abstraction "commodity" as his starting point in *Capital* because the commodity constitutes the simplest expression of the dialectical unity and opposition of the categories "use-value" and "value," the first corresponding to the material-natural content (the "wealth") of human societies and the second corresponding to the social forms of capitalist production—the specific production relations of "people to people" under capitalism.

A full rehearsal of Marx's analysis of the "value-form" is hardly necessary to establish that specifically capitalist social relations of production are a presupposition of his analysis.[19] Before turning to the question of money (the fully developed form of value), Marx had already identified the "social substance" of value as abstract labour, and the measure of this value-creating substance as "socially necessary labour time." Moreover, in his discussion of the relative and equivalent forms as the two poles of the simple expression of value, Marx had already identified three peculiarities of the "value relation": the appearance of use-value as value; the appearance of concrete labour as abstract labour; and the appearance of social labour as private labour. The ontological inversions or reversals revealed by these peculiarities presuppose the presence of the social conditions and relations of a system of generalized commodity production and exchange, that is, the capitalist mode of production (Smith 1994a, 2010).

The upshot of Marx's theory of value are two postulates that are of central importance to his critical analysis of capitalism: (1) living labour is the sole source of all new value (including surplus value), and (2) value exists as a definite quantitative magnitude that establishes parametric limits on prices, profits, wages, and all other expressions of the "money-form" (Smith 1994a). The distinctive categories of bourgeois political economy (capital, wage-labour, surplus value) are *internally related* to "value" and can exist only where capitalist relations of production (the capital-labour relation, inter-capitalist competition, etc.) mediate the relationship between the satisfaction of human needs (as registered by consciousness) and the creation of use-values (the material-natural production process). Value (in its fully developed form) can have neither theoretical pertinence nor concrete existence outside of these relations.

From even this brief synopsis we can readily see that Marx's value theory is fully in accord with the historical-materialist focus on the triad N<-S->A, where S is the dominant, mediating term. For the purposes of historical-materialist inquiry this focus is the appropriate and necessary starting point, since the overriding purpose of Marx's theory of value (in contrast to the classical and marginalist theories) is to disclose the historical laws of motion of a determinate social totality, the capitalist mode of production, and not the mechanisms of individual price formation.

Even so, it would be a disservice to the historical-materialist theoretical agenda to stop there. For the historical-materialist system of triads also involves S<-A->N and S<-N->A, albeit in supporting roles. The first of these suggests, among other things, the need to recognize the role of conscious Activity in mediating the relationship between the material-natural "costs" of production and the imperatives of capital (valorization, accumulation, the exploitation of wage-labour, etc.). This places on the agenda the traditional marginalist preoccupation with the immediate subjective determinants of price formation (a subject taken up but not fully explored by Marx).

The second supporting triad focuses attention on the role of N in mediating between S and A; among other things, the "natural conditions of production" mediate the relationship between capitalist imperatives and human consciousness/activity. In doing so, it places on the research agenda a host of issues pertaining to the "hidden costs" of capitalist production, among them: damage to the biosphere, unsustainable consumption of natural resources, the injuries and deformities inflicted on wage-labourers by capitalist production, and the uncompensated domestic labour performed by women in the social reproduction of wage-labour and the "capacity to work" (the commodity labour-power).

Hence, a historical-materialist research agenda proceeding from the system of dialectical triads is, in principle, capable of addressing many of the central concerns and preoccupations of non-Marxists in relation to the problem of economic value. But because it also (and uniquely) addresses the dominant role of the capitalist relations of production in mediating the Natural and conscious Activity, and exposes the growing contradiction between the Social and the Natural under capitalism (above all, between the imperatives of valorization and productivity), it leads inexorably to the conclusion that "value" must be abolished as the central organizing principle of social life. It is precisely on this point that it parts company with all agendas that seek merely to reform or fine-tune the capitalist price mechanism, whether from a marginalist, an ecological, or a feminist perspective.

The foregoing discussion points to how the historical-materialist system of dialectical triads can illuminate ecological and feminist concerns while also highlighting the crucial role of specifically *capitalist* social forms in exacerbating environmental problems or in sustaining "family values" as the ideological bulwark of a structure of unpaid female domestic labour. In principle, the system can be extended and applied to a wide range of contentious issues in social theory, public policy, and socialist strategy, serving as a persistent reminder that the supersession of capitalist social relations constitutes a *necessary condition* of human progress.

Conclusion: The Pedagogy and Politics of Socialist Anti-Dualism

In setting forth the key elements of a dialectical-monistic social ontology and proposing the idea of a historical-materialist system of dialectical triads, the purpose of this essay has been to suggest a systematic strategy for combating the obfuscations of dualistic thinking and for sharpening the methods that Marxists can bring to the practical tasks of socialist education, political mobilization, and programmatic elaboration. Our task, at one level at least, must be to make materialist dialectical monism the "common sense" of the working-class movement and its allies.

The perennial oscillation of bourgeois thought between vulgar-materialist and subjective-idealist perspectives is rooted deeply in the hegemony of ontological dualism, which systematically discourages any serious critical interrogation of capitalism's social relations of production and reproduction. Marxists must explore ways to break out of the blind alleys of this dualistic oscillation with a view to exposing these social relations as fundamental obstacles to human progress and the emancipation of humanity. Only on this condition can we rise to the challenge of Marx's famous edicts: to "educate the educators," and to *change*, and not merely interpret, the world.

Notes

1. For useful surveys, see Mepham and Ruben (1979), Norman and Sayers (1980), Moseley (1993), Laibman, Ollman, and Smith (1998), and Kincaid (2005).

2. In his 1873 postface to the second edition of *Capital*, Marx wrote: "My dialectical method is, in its foundations, not only different from the Hegelian, but exactly opposite to it. For Hegel, the process of thinking, which he even transforms into an independent subject, under the name of 'the Idea', is the creator of the real world, and the real world is only the external appearance of the idea. With me, the reverse is true: the ideal is nothing but the material world reflected in the mind of man, and translated into forms of thought" (1977: 102). This

statement has sometimes been cited to attribute to the mature Marx a problematic "reflection theory" of knowledge. In my view, it should be understood as an *ontological* proposition rather more than as an epistemological one.

3. Drawing on the work of Söhn-Rethel (1978a) in particular, I discuss the sources of dualistic thought at some length in Chapter 5 of this volume. See also Bukharin (2005: 214–23).

4. A comment on the way the concepts of mediation and reproduction are understood and used in this paper is required. "A" *mediates* "B" and "C" to the extent that it dominates and shapes "B" and "C" and regulates the relations between them. "A" can also mediate "B" (or "C") if it constitutes its form of appearance. *Reproduction* here refers to what Marx calls the production of "fresh life in procreation" as well as the domestic reproduction of labour-power, pre-eminently through familial forms.

5. Frisby and Sayer (1986) regard "society" as an absent concept in Weber's thought, while Ellen Wood argues that Weber's treatment of economic action suggests a teleological view of human history in which "there is only one, essentially capitalist, mode of economic activity, which may be present or absent in varying degrees" (1998: 391). Thus, Weber's much-vaunted principle of "multi-causality" conceals an underlying conception according to which capitalist economic action emerges naturally (much as Adam Smith suggests) to the extent that specifically "conventional" (cultural or political) obstacles to it are removed.

6. It must be acknowledged that Giddens' interpretation of historical materialism is in line with an influential stream of Marxist theory that defends the thesis of the "primacy of the productive forces." This deterministic thesis of "orthodox Marxism" was prominently championed by Cohen (1978) shortly before the publication of Giddens' critique. Not surprisingly, Cohen's interpretation of Marx's "theory of history" also displays a number of dualistic inflections, reflecting his commitment to functionalism and analytical-empiricist as opposed to dialectical methods. My own views on the "forces-relations" dialectic are found in Chapter 6 of this volume.

7. Thus, for example, what is missing from Weber's account of the genesis of "modern capitalism" is precisely the role of an emergent set of commercial social relations in unleashing a theological assault on the religious props of a declining feudal social order.

8. The thesis that Marx defended a dialectical-monistic ontology faces an important potential objection. In the whole of Marx's corpus, there is no explicit attempt to define a clear-cut "ontological position." Even so, this lacuna has not prevented a host of commentators from analyzing the ontology that is *implicit* in Marx's worldview. An outstanding example of an attempt to render explicit what is merely implied in Marx's own writing is István Mészáros' *Marx's Theory of Alienation* (1970), a work which is particularly insistent on establishing the anti-dualist and materialist-monist character of Marx's ontology.

9. This and all subsequent quoted passages from "Theses on Feuerbach" are taken from Marx (1989a: 7–11).

10. Among modern social theorists, the Natural-Social distinction had already been anticipated by Montesquieu, Adam Smith, and Jean-Jacques Rousseau. However, prior to Marx, the Social (for example, Smith's "conventional" or Rousseau's "artificial") had generally been seen either as a simple expression of the Natural or as a corruption of it resulting from the influence of "bad ideas" (or some combination of the two). The Natural-Social distinction in Marx must, of course, be viewed in light of an ontological position that rejects any such direct reduction of the Social to either the Natural or "the ideal."

11. Unfortunately, the "base-superstructure" metaphor of the 1859 Preface can also lend itself to a mechanically deterministic and dualistic interpretation of historical materialism.

12. In making these points, I do not mean to suggest that Tony Smith is himself committed to such idealist teleology.

13. As I hope to make clear, the proposed dialectical-ontological triad has little in common with the Fichtean triad of "thesis-antithesis-synthesis" that is sometimes attributed to Hegel and that was dismissed by Marx in a scathing comment about "wooden triochotomies."

14. "Generally, *Anlage* refers to a 'facility', 'arrangement', 'installation' or 'disposition'. [Also: 'natural tendency' or 'hereditary factors'.] Given this definition, *Anlagen* may serve as the generic category for the 'predispositions' inherent in human corporeal organization and thus as the ordering principle for a historical-materialist taxonomy of *Homo sapiens*" (Fracchia 2005: 46).

15. Certainly, there is much to be learned from the findings of modern genetics, which insists that genes "are both cause and consequence of our actions" (Ridley 2004: 6). While rejecting its non-dialectical, mechanical materialism, Marxists should be open to the possibility that "selfish-gene" evolutionary psychology may offer at least some insights into the construction of such a taxonomy. See, for instance, Dawkins (1976) and Dennett (1996), and, for necessary critiques, Rose and Rose (2000) and Callinicos (1996).

16. I am sympathetic to Brown's attempt to draw attention to the neglected work of Ilyenkov (1977, 1982), who was, among other things, a pioneer in recognizing the crucial importance of Spinoza's philosophy to materialist dialectics.

17. It seems reasonable to suppose that Marx had something like Spinoza's concept of "self-transformation through spatial action" in mind when he wrote his second thesis on Feuerbach: "The question whether objective truth can be attributed to human thinking is not a question of theory but is a practical question. Man must prove the truth—i.e. the reality and power, the this-sidedness of his thinking in practice. The dispute over the reality or non-reality of thinking that is isolated from practice is a purely *scholastic* question" (Marx 1989a: 8).

18. The centrality of language to many controversies in contemporary philosophy and social theory need hardly be emphasized here. Resources for a historical-materialist analysis of language are considerable. See McNally (2000), Palmer (1990), and Timpanaro (1980).

19. This is not the place to enter into a discussion of the disputes among Marxists surrounding value-form theory and systematic dialectics (see Kincaid 2005). Nevertheless, I would suggest that one of the more unfortunate consequences of these disputes has been the way they have diverted attention from the fundamental *substantive postulates* of Marx's own theory: in particular, his "abstract labour" concept of value and his account of capitalist crisis as centred on the contradiction between labour-displacing innovation (the material production process) and the imperative of capital to exploit living wage-labour (the valorization process).

CHAPTER 5

The Value Abstraction and the Dialectic of Social Development

The idea that human history evinces a pattern of development rooted in the propensity of human beings toward technical (labour-saving) forms of rationality is fundamental to Marx's materialist conception of history. Yet the "dialectic of forces and relations of production" as traditionally conceived in historical-materialist discourse has found only weak expressions in social formations dominated by precapitalist modes of production. In this chapter, the hypothesis is advanced that simple commodity production and exchange (and therefore rudimentary value relations) may be of decisive importance to the historic emergence of cognitive faculties capable of giving a systematic impulse to the development of science and technology, and therefore to a precapitalist forces-relations dialectic. This permits a new way of appreciating Marx's ranking of the Asiatic, ancient, feudal, and capitalist modes of production as "progressive epochs" in the development of human society, while illuminating the socio-historical provenance (and sources of variability) of the categories of human thought. More generally, the chapter offers a philosophical and historical framework for conceptualizing the historically limited contributions of value relations to human progress.

Contemporary debates surrounding Marx's "theory of history" centre on three overlapping yet distinguishable topics: the feudalism to capitalism transition (Hilton 1976; Brenner 1977; Gottlieb 1984; Laibman 1984); the problem of the specificity of Marx's "precapitalist modes of production" and the status of his concept of the "Asiatic mode of production" (Anderson 1979; Krader 1975; Vitkin 1981; Amin 1985); and the cluster of issues pertaining to the social ontology, philosophical anthropology, and scientific method informing Marx's own accounts of the materialist conception of history (Cohen 1978; Söhn-Rethel 1978a; Geras 1983; Sayer 1987).

In broad strokes, it is possible to survey the terms of current historical-materialist debate by citing a series of familiar and recurring theoretical oppositions: evolutionism versus anti-evolutionism; productive-forces determinism versus production-relations determinism; unilinearity versus multilinearity; objective laws of motion versus class struggle; technological determinism versus cultural (or superstructural) determinism; transhistorical prime movers rooted in invariant elements of human nature versus historically specific causal mechanisms rooted in ever-changing human propensities; "iron necessity" versus law-breaking contingency; and so forth. The very structure of historical-materialist debate suggested by this catalogue of binomial oppositions would seem to invite radical "deconstruction"—which is precisely what has been proposed by a growing roster of non-Marxist, ex-Marxist, and "post-Marxist" celebrants of postmodernism and/or poststructuralism (Derrida, Foucault, Baudrillard, Lyotard, Laclau and Mouffe, and so on). But to deconstruct such a structure of argument is a tricky exercise, and one that, in my view, should not be entrusted to intellectuals who call into question or reject such fundamentals of the Marxist worldview as the idea of objective truth or the possibility of progress while invoking an unbridled "subjectivism without a subject" (Anderson 1982: 54) as an antidote to the dogmatism, ethnocentrism, and productivism of capitalist "modernity." For instance, if Derrida (1982: 44) is not prepared to embrace a monistic social ontology in place of the ontological dualism implicit in the above-listed binomial oppositions (and it does seems to me that in the choice between monism and dualism one cannot meaningfully choose "*différance*"), it is perhaps better to return to Marx for some clues as to how we can make our way out of the theoretical maze and reorient ourselves in the struggle for a better future.

In this chapter, I want to show that a satisfactory way of conceptualizing the "forces-relations" dialectic of human social development *can* be established, despite the less-than-compelling derision for this notion emanating from the postmodernist camp, and despite the thoughtful reservations expressed by Anthony Giddens (1981) and Paul Sweezy (1981) concerning the pertinence of the concept to precapitalist social development. My starting point will be three basic premises that I take to be central to Marx's materialist conception of history.

The first of these is the *monistic* proposition that the reality confronted by human beings is an *ontologically unified* ensemble or totality, embracing natural, social, and ideal aspects. This premise is consistent with the traditional philosophical-materialist tenet that matter has ontological primacy as the "substance" of reality, but it breaks from this tradition in its insistence that material reality is subject not only to "natural law," but to the transformative influences of human practice as well (that is, the influences of human social relations and consciousness). In my view this is the fundamental theme of Marx's *Theses on Feuerbach*.

The second premise is that the true "subject" of human history is the "real living individuals" referred to by Marx and Engels in *The German Ideology* (1968); that is, human individuals whose actions are shaped by both natural *and* social imperatives and constraints. The historical subject, on this view, is most emphatically not a "transcendental logos," a reified "first principle," or an unchanging "human nature." Rather it is human beings seeking practical solutions to the natural, social and intellectual problems they confront ... precisely through natural, social, and intellectual means. The more complex the problems and the more varied the available means of recourse, the greater the creative response of human beings is likely to be.

The third premise is that human beings are driven to seek material security in the face of hostile natural and social forces. This is the basis for a certain duality within the elusive notion of "human rationality." Forms of "technical rationality" are distinguishable from forms of "sociological rationality" but not because of any ontological schism within reality of the type implied in the dualistic social ontologies of Weber, Habermas, or Giddens. They are distinguishable (and usefully distinguished within a dialectical social ontology) just because they can and do enter into complex and potentially contradictory relationships with one another. Yet their common basis should remain clear: purposive human activity as founded upon the socially mediated transformation of nature (both human and non-human). It seems to me that the tendency to privilege technical rationality in general over sociological rationality in general, or vice versa, may well be the unspoken theme behind recurring attempts to attribute deterministic primacy to either the productive forces or the relations of production in the development of society.

The desire to privilege the productive forces (and, *inter alia*, a form of technical-instrumental rationality) may well have been the inspiration of Marx's most "deterministic" historical-materialist text, the 1859 Preface to *A Contribution to the Critique of Political Economy*. It is just this text that happens to contain what is perhaps the most controversial and enigmatic passage in Marx's entire corpus, the one which reads: "In broad outline, the Asiatic, ancient, feudal and modern bourgeois modes of production may be designated as epochs marking progress in the economic development of society" (Marx 1859).

It will not be my purpose here to summarize or even identify the many debates that have devolved from the interpretation of this single passage. However, it should be noted that even a "soft" reading of it suggests that Marx is *ranking* these modes of production with respect to their potential to engender "progress" (even though he is almost certainly not positing a "hard" theory of stages through which all societies "must" pass). Moreover, it will be my purpose to defend the central idea implied in the passage—Marx's pivotal notion of a "universal human history" marked by a determinate (if not inexorable) developmental logic. The key that Marx provides to understanding this universal history is precisely the forces-relations dialectic as this unfolds in both precapitalist and capitalist eras.

A caveat is necessary here. The skepticism of Sweezy and Giddens, among others, concerning the reality of a precapitalist forces-relations dialectic contains an important grain of truth: the objective laws governing the historical movement of capitalist society are much stronger than those influencing the economic development of precapitalist social formations. This is so because only capitalism is under the sway of a fully reified "law of value"—a law that becomes fully determinative only under conditions of market competition (Amin 1985: 204). Capitalism's "economic law of motion," moreover, is defined by the contradictory relationship of elements internal to its social production relations—relations that are at once equalitarian, exploitative, and competitive (Rubin 1973). This distinguishes capitalism from precapitalist societies quite decisively, for it is precisely the interplay of social production relations (and perhaps forms of rationality) belonging to differentiated modes of production in precapitalist eras that appears to furnish a developmental dynamic conducive to the growth of the productive forces. This is one aspect of David Laibman's important argument concerning the role of simple commodity production during the feudal era in stimulating the development of the "intensive" (labour-saving) capabilities of the productive forces and thereby creating an "intensive surplus which enables commodity production to assume a new role, eventually moving to the center of the [production relations]" (1984: 275).

I concur with Laibman in regarding simple commodity production as a critical (and much-underestimated) element in the forces-relations dialectic of precapitalist history. Indeed, the argument that I present below should be seen as complementary to his stress on the importance of an individually appropriated "intensive surplus" to the development of the productive forces of Western European feudal societies. But I go beyond Laibman in suggesting that it is not only the competitive relations (and individual acquisitiveness) embryonic in simple commodity production that propel the growth of labour-saving technology, but the "equalitarian" relations implicit in them as well. Indeed, it is precisely the equalitarian aspects of commodity value (impressively delineated by Rubin [1973] in his essay "Equality of Commodity Producers and Equality of Commodities") that I regard as fundamental to the specific contribution of the "value abstraction" to the extension of human productive capacities during precapitalist times.

Where I depart from Laibman (and, arguably, from the Marx of the 1859 Preface) is in my rejection of the assumption that human technical rationality *must prevail* over a "class-appropriative" rationality (or indeed over other forms of "sociological rationality") in determining the course of history. No such presumption is, in my view, warranted on purely theoretical grounds. In the end what must determine the outcome of the clash of these two forms of rationality is the class struggle, and this can issue just as easily in the "mutual ruin" of the contending classes as in the inauguration of a more progressive epoch.

Marxism, of course, has no pretensions to being a "pure theory." It is defiantly a theoretically informed program and a programmatically informed theory—a *practical* project embracing a specific vision of human history and the struggle for a better future. This is why it can likely be said with confidence that even the "late Marx" of the 1870s and 1880s—who faced something of an intellectual crisis as he moved away from the Eurocentric standpoint of the 1859 Preface; who explored a far richer ethnography than he had previously ever imagined; and who even ruminated over the Russian peasant commune as a potential starting point for socialist development (Vitkin 1981; Shanin 1983)—never wavered from the idea that human history is possessed of a "meaning" to the extent that the rational human imperative to extend the productivity of labour can be said to hold sway in human history. The propensity of human beings toward labour-saving technical rationality of this sort was a fundamental premise of his philosophical anthropology—one that held out the promise of the eventual emergence of a mode of human existence in which, for the first time, human individuals would have the chance to develop their many-sided talents and capabilities unconstrained by either material hardship or social antagonism. All ethnocentrisms and postmodern relativisms aside, this is surely a vision of human emancipation worthy of all humanity—and it is certainly just as much a guiding thread of Marx's thought as any other that might be cited.

The Value Abstraction in Precapitalist History: Cognitive Faculties as Forces of Production

The idea that Marx was committed to a definite concept of human progress linked to the propensity of the human species toward technical rationality has been most prominently associated in recent years with the influential work of G. A. Cohen. In *Karl Marx's Theory of History: A Defence*, Cohen

undertook to champion what he characterized as an "old-fashioned historical materialism" according to which "history is, fundamentally, the growth
of human productive power, and forms of society rise and fall according as
they enable or impede that growth" (1978: x). Cohen readily admitted to a
"technological interpretation" of human history, but was circumspect with
respect to whether his account should be termed "technological determin-
ist." No doubt this was because his argument was not so much that technology dominates other aspects of human social life as that human beings
tend to *select* those social forms that are most propitious to the extension of
their productive powers given a certain level of development of technology
and technical-scientific knowledge. Human history possesses a "pattern"
because human beings can be expected, in the long run, to behave (collectively) in a technically rational fashion. Cohen's overall theoretic-meth-
odological framework might therefore be described as a "rational-choice
functionalism" or perhaps as a "functionalist praxeology."

The issue of Cohen's functionalism is not a central concern of the present discussion, although it is certainly prominent among the features that render his
account of historical materialism both novel and contentious. Of greater concern is the analytically rigorous fashion in which Cohen insists upon interpreting the "material-social" distinction in Marx's thought and in the 1859 Preface
in particular. For Cohen, the material aspects of human existence pertain
strictly to the "content" of human society (which is always a "natural content")
whereas the social aspects pertain just as strictly to the issue of "form" (defined
pre-eminently by social relationships of ownership and control of the means
of production). It is on this basis that he develops a somewhat non-traditional
understanding of the following famous passage from Marx's 1859 Preface:

> In the social production of their life, men enter into definite rela-
> tions that are indispensable and independent of their will, relations
> of production which correspond to a definite stage of development
> of the material productive forces. The sum total of these relations of
> production constitutes the economic structure of society, the real
> basis on which rises a legal and political superstructure, and to

which correspond definite forms of social consciousness. (Marx 1859, quoted in Cohen 1978: vii)

The real novelty of Cohen's interpretation of this passage has to do with the way he specifies (a) the distinction between the forces and the relations of production, and (b) the distinction between the "economic structure of society" and the "legal and political superstructure." According to Cohen, the forces of production belong to the material side of the material-social distinction, while the relations of production belong to the social side. Once this is recognized it becomes possible to specify with analytical precision those elements of reality that belong to the "material forces of production" and those that belong to the "social relations of production." At the same time, in Cohen's interpretation, the economic structure of society refers to the totality of social relations of production within a particular socio-economic formation and is not at all a synonym for "mode of production." That is to say, unlike Marx's concept of mode of production, the economic structure does not encompass the material forces of production. Rather the material forces of production (together with the "material relations of pro-duction" bearing on the physical organization of the labour process) belong to a material substratum existing below the economic structure.

If the material aspects of reality are conceptually excluded from the eco-nomic structure by Cohen, the ideal aspects of this same reality are just as resolutely excluded from his conception of the social superstructure. For Cohen this superstructure is composed exclusively of legal and political institutions that function to stabilize and reinforce the economic structure. Accordingly, the superstructure does not, strictly speaking, encompass ideas or consciousness and therefore does not refer to an "ideal" sphere or level of reality.

There is much in Cohen's restatement of the basic concepts of the 1859 Preface that is highly moot, but to some limited extent, at least, he has admirably captured a key aspect of Marx's social ontology, one overlooked by many other commentators. For Cohen has painstakingly demonstrated that the point of departure of Marx's historical sociology is not the "mate-rial-ideal" distinction that pervades the greater part of bourgeois social theory, but rather a "material-social" distinction, and that, related to this, ideas and consciousness for Marx are not part of an independent realm but are always embedded in the social and material conditions and practices through which human beings make their own history. Hence, it is not only necessary to insist that there are many cultural products that cannot and need not be included in Marx's "base-superstructure" metaphor; it is also necessary to underscore that "productively relevant" ideas and knowledge are themselves essential elements of the material forces of production. For tools, productive machinery, and even "skilled labour power" (the perishable expressions of the productive forces) cannot be said to exist independently of such knowledge.

I wish to extend this latter argument still further by suggesting that the practical technical knowledge embodied in the physical means of production is itself predicated upon the capacity of human beings to think in "problem-solving" ways. Moreover, the premise of any *systematic* development of the "productive powers of human beings" is the emergence of cognitive faculties favouring a technical-scientific form of rationality. Unlike Cohen, my claim is not that the human propensity toward technical rationality is explicable simply with reference to the human mammal's "excellent brain." The existence of such a brain is certainly a *condition* for the development of technical rationality, but the former's existence, even in the context of the "inclemencies of nature," fails to account for the *non-emergence* of technical rationality over vast stretches of human history. My claim is rather that social forms have decisively mediated the relation between the "excellent brain of human beings" and the human encounter with an inhospitable (non-human) nature, and that in fact it is only *certain* social forms that have encouraged the emergence of cognitive faculties capable of giving a systematic impetus to the development of labour productivity. These cognitive faculties may themselves be referred to as "mental elements" of the productive forces at a certain stage of the latter's development.

The cognitive faculties in question refer to the categories of abstract reason to which Immanuel Kant attributed a transcendental origin. Yet any such idealist (non-)explanation of the provenance of the abstract intellect must encounter the same objection as Cohen's explanation of the origin of human technical rationality in the (unmediated) interaction of "excellent brains" and the "inclemencies of nature." Kant's theory cannot account for the fact that over tens of thousands of years of human prehistory and over thousands of years of early civilization there is little evidence of the existence of an "abstract intellect" or of the influence of the "categories of pure reason" on human practice.

All of this suggests that Kant's categories must not only have a social provenance, as Durkheim following Marx suggested, but also a definite historical origin. And yet it was only with the publication of Alfred Söhn-Rethel's Marxist "critique of epistemology" in 1978 that a plausible historical-materialist account of the social and historical origins of the categories of reason was finally made. For Söhn-Rethel, the emergence of the cognitive faculties associated with classical Greek philosophy, mathematics, and modern natural science was directly connected with the emergence of the "real abstraction of exchange" attendant to the appearance of commodity production and money.

The implications of Söhn-Rethel's insight are clearly immense with respect to the possible place of simple commodity production/exchange in defining a precapitalist forces-relations dialectic. Moreover it is perfectly reasonable to hypothesize that the development of simple "value relations" (as sponsored by rudimentary forms of commodity production) might well have been the spark that ignited a veritable cognitive revolution without which the development of capitalism would have been impossible. It is this cognitive revolution, I contend, that marks a profound epoch-making transition within precapitalist history.

Within the classical Marxist tradition such a notion is most clearly foreshadowed in a passage from Engels' *Origin of the Family, Private Property and the State*:

> The appearance of private property in herds of cattle and articles of luxury [among the ancient Greeks] led to exchange between individuals, to the transformation of products into *commodities*. Here lies the root of the entire revolution that followed.... The Athenians were soon to learn ... how quickly after individual exchange is established and products are converted into commodities, the product

manifests its rule over the producer. With the production of commodities came the tilling of the soil by individual cultivators for their own account, soon followed by individual ownership of the land. Then came money, that universal commodity for which all others could be exchanged. But when men invented money they little suspected that they were creating a *new social power*, the one universal power to which the whole of society must bow. (Engels, 1970a: 279)

Most contemporary Marxists would agree that Engels rather overstates his case in this passage, according, as he does, a pre-eminence to this "new social power" that it was unable to really acquire until the emergence of modern capitalism. For money to appear as the "one universal power to which the whole of society must bow," commodity production had not only to exist; it had to be well on its way to being generalized—to becoming the *general* social form of production. This was not the case in either Greek or Roman antiquity, despite the considerable extension of trade and commodity production that occurred during this epoch.

Even so, Engels' argument should not be wholly dismissed, nor indeed should his related thesis that the law of value has its historical origins in the value relations established over thousands of years of simple commodity production (Engels 1981). To be sure, such precapitalist value relations must be seen as *rudimentary* antecedents of the capitalist law of value; and yet the existence of commodity production and exchange, even where it is decisively subordinated to other modes of production, still signifies the existence, if only in a rudimentary sense, of a trade-based division of labour and of a type of economic activity that is predicated upon the recognition of private-property rights. It need hardly be pointed out that such rights, which Söhn-Rethel quite properly defines in terms of the "laws of the separation of exchange and use," can have no meaning except where market-exchange has become a significant social form of the process of production (as distinct, say, from the communal, familial, or manorial forms that are so widespread in precapitalist formations). I wish to argue, however, that the impact of this social form and the new "social power" it represents may be greater in its sponsorship of new cognitive faculties than in its direct influence upon economic intercourse *per se*. Not only might simple commodity production sponsor a "law of value *sui generis*" that *directly* enters into the forces-relations dialectic of precapitalist history; it may well sponsor a modality of thought that is conducive to labour-saving technological innovation and the extension of the productive powers of humanity. The crucial historiographic issue must then become: to what extent have *particular* precapitalist societies (a) "permitted" the proliferation of simple commodity production/exchange, together with related social forms, and (b) "tolerated" the technical-scientific consciousness arising from a trade-based division of labour?

An argument can easily be made that, of all the precapitalist modes of production identified by Marx, only the feudal mode of production possessed the specific features and the endogenous dynamic that could give a systematic impulse to both of these developments. And it is for *this* reason that capitalism grew out of (Western European) feudalism and could not have grown out of either the ancient or Asiatic modes of production. Feudalism should be ranked higher among the "epochs marking progress in the economic development of society," not only because it encouraged the growth of a trade-based division of labour, but because it erected fewer obstacles to the technical-scientific progress made possible by the unleashing of the abstract intellect.

To buttress the credibility of this argument we need only draw upon a few well-established (and relatively uncontroversial) theoretical and historiographic points pertaining to the specificity of Western European feudalism in relation to other precapitalist modes. The first is that feudalism is distinguished from "despotic" or "slave" societies in its decentralized political structure—its "dispersal of political power" (Anderson 1979; Amin 1985: 206). The absence or weakness of a centralized political authority opens the door to a wide array of social forms, including those based upon the postulates of "equalitarian" commodity exchange and individual surplus appropriation.

This leads to the second point. It is just such social forms proliferating in the "pores" of feudal society that may be most responsible for the intensive development of the productive forces stressed by Laibman. The same point extends to Robert Brenner's (1977) important distinction between "absolute" and "relative" surpluses in the transition from feudalism to capitalism. "Pure" feudal relations are likely only to engender an absolute surplus; but feudal societies have a weak ability to maintain their "purity"—and their ruling elements also appear to have little *will* to do so. Hence, the stage is set for simple commodity production and long-distance trade to stimulate the intensive (labour-saving) productive forces that make possible the appropriation of a growing relative or "intensive" surplus.

The final point concerns the fact that "productively relevant" knowledge tends to be less centralized and is more likely to actually be applied to production under feudal conditions than in other precapitalist, class-antagonistic contexts. This is not only because the incentive to use such knowledge is greater in feudal societies; it is also because "despotic states" promote a radical division of intellectual and manual labour as between state functionaries and the direct producers. Non-feudal "state-classes" are notorious "hoarders" of knowledge, which they use primarily to reinforce and perpetuate the conditions of their own rule. Such elites are also apt to erect and sustain formidable ideological obstacles to the spread of technical-scientific forms of rationality.

An adequate specification of any "precapitalist forces-relations dialectic" requires recognition of both the pivotal role played by simple commodity production in developing the forces of production and the limits imposed on this role by other, more dominant, precapitalist forms. Fragile as it might have been in precapitalist eras, and incapable as it might have been of imposing its own norms and laws upon societies ruled by despots, slave-owners, or feudal lords, simple commodity production was nevertheless successful in sponsoring an extremely "subversive" form of human consciousness— a mode of thinking and problem solving that itself must be ranked with land, labour-power, and productively relevant knowledge as a major force of production. Its development, in tandem with the development of the other forces of production, could only eventuate in a challenge to the feudal relations that had (indirectly) nurtured it, particularly when the feudal mode of production itself entered, for numerous reasons, into protracted crisis.

It should be underscored that the "cognitive revolution" postulated here had an extremely uneven and historically discontinuous development. It began in antiquity, but could not possibly have triumphed in the ancient societies. It was unleashed to some limited extent wherever a trade-based division of labour took root, but was repeatedly suppressed by social forms as varied as the despotic state and the European guilds. Its ultimate triumph (in Western Europe) was predicated on the emergence of a particular "balance" of social forms, as well as favourable geographical and historical circumstances, all of which could very easily suggest that this cognitive revolution and the growth of the forces of production that propelled capitalist development had a somewhat fortuitous character. This I take to be true. Yet this in no way contradicts the thesis, which I believe to be central to Marx's historical vision, that *human history possesses a pattern of development to the extent that it is guided by the human propensity toward technical rationality.* There is no hint of a unilinear theory of human history here, still less of any speculative "historico-philosophical theory" of the type berated in *The German Ideology.* There is also no evolutionary inevitablism implicit in such a formulation. All that can be said is that history has unfolded in such a way as to unleash the productive power of technical rationality, that capitalism has emerged as the dominant mode of production on a planetary scale, and that this has created the potential for a worldwide development toward the sort of socialist society envisaged by Marx and Engels.

This interpretation of Marx's materialist conception of history is free, I believe, of any idealist teleology, of the sort that would claim that human history is unfolding according to some transcendental logic toward a preordained goal (communism), via a series of set "stages." But it does insist upon the possibility that human history may assume a determinate developmental pattern if the balance of social forms comes to favour the full flowering of technical rationality. The reality that Marx was faced with, and that we continue to be faced with, is that in the course of human history such a development *did* occur. And it is only by virtue of this that we can now entertain ideas about the contemporary results and future prospects of a "universal human history" that has materialized before the eyes of humanity in just the past few centuries.

While Marx certainly never discussed these issues in precisely these terms, the argument set forth here is, I think, fully consistent with the fundamental concepts and premises of his historical materialism, particularly as these have been elucidated in recent years in relation to the basic principles of his social ontology and epistemology.

Cohen, Sayer, and Söhn-Rethel on Historical Materialism

The argument presented above departs from Cohen's more traditional account of historical materialism in its stress upon contingency in the historical interplay of social forms and productive forces. At the same time it is predicated upon a more radical break from the dualistic ontology from which Cohen only partially distances Marx. Central to Cohen's account is the role of human technical rationality in promoting the development of the material forces of production and in selecting the social relations of production historically suited to technological progress. Yet this propensity toward technical rationality is never adequately explicated by Cohen; indeed, it appears to exist *independently* of the material-social relation that Cohen quite rightly has identified as the key concept of Marx's historical materialism. It appears to spring from a socially-unmediated relation of human beings to "nature" that Cohen tends to identify with the "material" or "natural" content of society and that is externally related to the social forms assumed and discarded by concrete societies. Thus, in defending the notion that Marx's theory of history highlights the material-social distinction and not a material-ideal opposition, Cohen has disclosed a necessary but not a sufficient basis for reasserting Marx's dialectical social ontology as against the claims of philosophical dualism. Indeed, in his handling of the form-content relation, Cohen has actually succumbed to the typically Kantian (and dualist) habit of regarding this as an external relation, and in so doing has readmitted an ontological opposition between "consciousness" (human rationality as embedded in "material content") and "social being" (as rooted in the "form" of society). It need only be assumed that content has ontological priority over form to conclude that human technical rationality must ultimately prevail over all forms of consciousness that are rooted in "mere" social relations. Here, indeed, is where Cohen's interpretation of Marx finally sanctions a rather crude, and historically indefensible, technological determinism, one quite incapable of accounting for the historical viability and persistence of class-appropriative forms of rationality that have often proven *inimical* to technical rationality.

Cohen's incomplete break with a dualistic social ontology has theoretical consequences that have been most fully explored by Derek Sayer in *The Violence of Abstraction: The Analytic Foundations of Historical Materialism* (1987), a work that represents a substantial advance over Cohen's in its grasp of Marx's historical sociology. Proceeding from an "*internal* relations" perspective of the type elaborated by Ollman (1976), Sayer suggests that, for Marx, neither the material-social distinction nor the form-content distinction has a hard and fast character. Indeed, Marx's dialectical social ontology enjoins us from drawing the sort of "analytically precise" boundaries between such concepts as the forces of production and the relations of production that Cohen draws: "we can no longer assume that terms like forces and relations of production, or base and superstructure, refer unambiguously or consistently to different, and mutually exclusive, bits of empirical reality as they would in an atomistic ontology.... On the view argued here, the empirical referents of Marx's concepts may neither be mutually exclusive, nor consistent across space and time" (Sayer 1987: 22). The upshot is that productive forces should not be treated as a "set of things," but as "attributes of human beings in association, their collective capacities" (27), while the relations of production should be conceptualized as "any and all social relations which are demonstrably entailed in a given mode of production, or 'way in which [people] produce their means of subsistence' [Marx]" (75). Such an approach makes it possible to see not only the internal relationship of social form and material content but also the social content of "things" and the "material forms" assumed by social relations: an analytical agenda splendidly pursued by Marx in his analyses of commodity and capital fetishism.

Sayer's critique of "traditional historical materialism" (including Cohen's) has the considerable virtue of emphasizing Marx and Engels' seminal historical-materialist proposition that "the production of life ... appears as a *double* relationship: on the one hand as a natural, on the other as a social relationship" (1947: 18). Thus, the *same* activities must be seen as having social and material (or natural) dimensions. This means that the forces of production have a social dimension as well as a material one, just as it means that the relations of production have both material and social expressions. It is only on this basis that one can explain Marx's repeated reference to such unmistakably *social* phenomena as the community, money, trade, and state activity as "productive forces" (29). Equally, it is only on this basis that it becomes possible to give an adequate general definition of the concept of relations of production as one which encompasses, in different times and places, "material relations of production" and "superstructural relations," as well as Cohen's "relations of ownership" or "relations of effective power over persons and productive forces" (1978: 34, 63).

This already suggests a second major area of Sayer's critique of Cohen and of traditional historical materialism; for if a hard and fast distinction cannot be made between the material and the social, it is no less true that the distinction between the mode of production and the superstructure is necessarily a fluid one. This is particularly so in precapitalist societies where the organic unity of the human community admits no distinction between "economy" and "polity" as discrete spheres. In a very real sense, the notion of a political and legal superstructure arising on the basis of the economic structure could only be articulated from the standpoint of capitalist society, and the transferability of this metaphor to precapitalist formations is therefore highly problematic. Yet Marx's notion of the superstructure involves something more than this. Despite the wording of the 1859 Preface, which Cohen takes all too literally, the superstructure is for Marx not so much an *institutional* sphere as "the 'ideal' form in which the totality of 'material' relations which make up the 'base' itself are manifested to consciousness" (Sayer 1987: 84). Marx's abundant references to "ideal" and "ideological" superstructures in many of his other works make this clear. According to Sayer, the base-superstructure metaphor of the Preface recapitulates Marx's long-standing philosophical position that "the ideal is nothing else than the material world reflected by the human mind, and translated into forms of thought" (Marx 1977: 102, quoted in Sayer, 1987: 86).

Cohen's failure to grasp this aspect of Marx's philosophical perspective is of crucial importance: for it leads him in the direction of a dualistic epistemology in which ideological forms of consciousness are associated with "social forms," while technical-scientific forms of consciousness are imbricated in the "material content" of society (the socially unmediated relation of "excellent brains" and non-human nature). Against this, Sayer argues that human consciousness, on Marx's view, must always be a projection of the "double relationship" in which human beings are inescapably implicated: a material world governed by both natural and social relations. This in no way vitiates the necessary distinction between science and ideology, as elements of consciousness. But it should sensitize us to the fuller meaning and contradictory implications of Marx's postulate that "social being determines consciousness."

At the same time, Sayer's interpretation of Marx's concepts closes the door to the proposition that the forces of production must enjoy "primacy" over the relations of production in determining the course of history. Once the form-content relation is treated as an internal one, it is no longer meaningful to ponder the sort of question to which Cohen admits he has "no good answer": namely, "how productive forces select economic structures which promote their development" (Cohen 1983: 124). Once forms are regarded as immanent in contents, this problem of "selection" quite simply disappears. More problematically, however, Sayer suggests that so too does the problem of "causality," at least insofar as we are speaking of the inter-relationship of relations and forces. After a compelling critique of Cohen's primacy thesis, Sayer proceeds to dismantle the converse proposition that social relations of production dominate the productive forces: "simply to reverse the line of causality between forces and relations obscures the important extent to which, for Marx, the growth of human productive power does remain the fundamental dynamic of historical progress" (Sayer 1987: 35). Yet the point of Sayer's argument is not that an internal relations perspective absolves Marx or any theorist of the responsibility to specify the "causal links" existing between phenomena; indeed, Sayer is quite explicit in associating Marx's method and ontology with a "realist" position that requires that "giving a causal explanation *necessarily* involves 'elaborating' a theory of causal mechanisms" (125). His point is simply that it is mistaken to establish a "line of causality" between forces and relations understood as discrete and externally related "categories." For Sayer, the causal mechanisms identified by Marx "lie ultimately in the actions of real individuals" and consequently "the causal explanation of social phenomena must ... be historical" rather than functional (125). In a related vein, Sayer argues:

> Contrary to Cohen, Marx's concepts of forces and relations of pro-
> duction ... do not then denote "items" which are "more basic than
> actions" (Cohen, 1983: 123).... These "items" are actions—forms of
> human relationship—and the whole point of Marx's critique is to
> unmask them as such. Behind the authorless theatre of fetishism lie
> "real living individuals," for Marx the true and the only subjects of
> history. (1987: 136)

For Sayer the problem with "traditional" historical materialism is that it has fetishized and reified Marx's categories of forces and relations of production in the process of theoretically reducing them to lists of empirical items. The all-too-predictable result has been the positing of "more or less implausible connections at the level of general theory" for which the indicated antidote is "a minimum of *a priori* theory, and the use of empirically-open general categories which are analytically capable of letting the real world in" (147).

Sayer's critique of Cohen is compelling and his proposed agenda for historical-materialist inquiry attractive. Yet there is something not altogether satisfying about his plea for a more "empirical" (if not empiricist) redefinition of the historical-materialist project. A clue to the deficiency is to be found in his repeated insistence that the starting point of analysis must be "the real, living individuals" invoked by Marx in *The German Ideology*. What Sayer gives insufficient weight to is the ability of concrete, historically existing individuals through their activities to create those "reified structures" and "economic laws" that come to dominate and constrain their existence. Human activity does indeed construct "the theatre of fetishism," but once constructed this theatre has a way of transforming its builders into scripted actors who sustain the theatre's operations. It may be true that the operations of the law of value are "ultimately" rooted in "the actions of real individuals." All the same, an adequate causal explanation of these operations must nevertheless consider the real existence of such "holistic" structural entities as "abstract labour" and "the world of commodities," entities that arise as *collective* expressions of a multitude of individual actions. Oddly, much of Sayer's argument leads away from this and lends itself to a methodologically individualist interpretation of Marx—one that is irreconcilable with his own insistence upon Marx's opposition to "atomist" ontologies.

A further problem with Sayer is that there is very little in his account of historical materialism that would enable us to understand what he means when he says that "for Marx, the growth of human productive power does remain the fundamental dynamic of historical progress" (1987: 35). If human productive power can refer to social relations as well as "material objectifications," what "objective" criteria can be deployed to assess whether "growth" and therefore "historical progress" is occurring? In this connection, it should be noted that in some earlier works Sayer expressed his solidarity with the ultra-voluntarist Maoist notion that even the poorest of societies (in material/technological terms) can "build socialism" provided the requisite social forms are in place (see Corrigan, Ramsay, & Sayer 1979). This may also explain his interest in "late" Marx's sympathy for Russian populism and for the proposition that the Russian peasant commune could be a base for socialist construction (Sayer & Corrigan 1983). Yet there is no theoretical warrant to proceed from the recognition that the social phenomenon of "co-operation" (as embodied in a detailed technical division of labour) ranks as one of the forces of production in the development of capitalism to the idea that social forms and mental attitudes are all that matter in the construction of socialism. As Sayer acknowledges (implicitly against Mao):

The productive power of social labour may indeed, in the course of human development, increasingly become embodied in things— like machines—and undeniably it is through such embodiment that it is most enhanced. This is what is so revolutionary about modern industry; for Marx it represented a qualitative break, a veritable quantum leap in the unfolding of human productive potential comparable only perhaps with the Neolithic revolution. Human beings are, distinctively, creatures who purposefully objectify their collective capacities in the material world they create through transforming nature, and this is fundamental to Marx's sociology. (1987: 27)

Yet human beings are also creatures who may purposefully seek to shelter themselves, as individuals, from the worst inclemencies of nature by turning their excellent brains to the enterprise of subjugating and exploiting their fellow humans. This is perhaps why the transformation of nature and the growth of human productive potential have been so painfully slow and discontinuous over the course of human history. For throughout this history, technical forms of rationality have had to wage a long battle against sociological forms of "appropriative rationality" rooted in *antagonistic* social postulates—postulates that find expression in class structures and state forms.

This leads to a third critical observation concerning Sayer. Unlike Cohen, who is openly dismissive of Marx's law of value, Sayer regards Marx's value theory as a critically important component of his historical-materialist analysis of capitalist society. But as has been the fashion in Marxist circles in recent years, Sayer fails to address the extent to which value relations might be said to have impacted on precapitalist societies. Not surprisingly, in view of this, he also fails to address the issue of the impact of "real abstractions" on precapitalist history. This is a crucial omission, for it must result in a failure to appreciate the cognitive revolution sponsored by simple commodity production and exchange.

It is here that a closer examination of Söhn-Rethel's argument becomes mandatory. As discussed earlier, Söhn-Rethel's fundamental thesis is that it is the historical appearance of a real abstraction—the commodity or value abstraction—that makes possible the development of those conceptual abstractions associated with classical philosophy, mathematics, and modern natural science. In substantiating this thesis, Söhn-Rethel begins by pointing to the "striking similarity" between the value abstraction and the thought abstractions of science:

> The economic concept of value [resulting from the commodity abstraction] is characterized by a complete absence of quality, a differentiation purely by quantity and by applicability to every kind of commodity and service which can occur on the market. These qualities of the economic value abstraction indeed display a striking similarity with fundamental categories of quantifying natural science without, admittedly, the slightest inner relationship between these heterogeneous spheres being as yet recognizable. While the concepts of natural science are thought abstractions, the economic concept of value is a real one. It exists nowhere other than in the human mind but it does not spring from it. Rather it is purely social in character, arising from the spatio-temporal sphere of human interrelations. It is not people who originate these abstractions but their actions. "They do this without being aware of it" [Marx]. (1978a: 20)

It is important to be clear on what Söhn-Rethel is saying here. The economic concept of value is a "real abstraction" rather than a "thought abstraction" because it derives from a real social process: that of commodity exchange (that is, from activities rather than thoughts). The "reality" of the commodity abstraction, however, defies the standard philosophical criterion for what is real (as opposed to ideal): an empirically-specifiable content. It is precisely the empirical emptiness of this abstraction that renders it "abstract," just as its provenance in the socio-temporal sphere of actual human interactions, as founded upon definite social norms, renders it "real." The existence of such a real abstraction within the human mind suggests a *social* origin for the non-empirical concepts whose basis traditional philosophical materialism has never adequately explained, and whose undeniable importance has been key to the (only comparative) "success" of philosophical idealism in accounting for the *duality* of the sources of knowledge ("pure reason" as well as sense perception). Söhn-Rethel elaborates as follows:

The entire exchange abstraction is founded upon social postulate and not upon fact. It is a postulate that the use of commodities must remain suspended until the exchange has taken place; it is a postulate that no physical change should occur in the commodities and this still applies even if the facts belie it; it is a postulate that the commodities in the exchange relation should count as equal despite their factual difference.... None of these form-concepts imply statements of fact. They are all norms which commodity exchange has to obey to be possible and to enable anarchical society to survive by the rules of reification. (1978a: 68)

The thrust of Söhn-Rethel's argument is thus to establish that an "inner relationship" does exist between the value abstraction and the thought abstractions of mathematics, philosophy, and natural science, and that, in fact, "the real abstraction operating in exchange *engenders* the ideal abstraction basic to Greek philosophy and to modern science" (1978a: 28, emphasis added). For if any of the elements of the real abstraction of exchange are correctly identified within the human mind, the result must be the formation of concepts (thought abstractions) that are "as non-empirical as the exchange abstraction itself" (67). Söhn-Rethel's detailed theoretical analysis of the formal elements of the exchange abstraction, as suggested by Marx's theory of value, serves to demonstrate that not only analogy but "true identity" exists between the formal elements of this abstraction and the formal cognitive constituents of those forms of thought that issued in the development of modern science. In particular the concepts of "abstract quantity," "abstract time and space," "abstract movement," and "strict causality" are all notions that have real counterparts in elements of the act of exchange (Söhn-Rethel 1978a: 47–55). Kant's categories *a priori*, then, are not transcendental properties of the human intellect, but historically-produced concepts originating in specific types of social interaction and founded upon a real abstraction. Yet it remains importantly true that "once the elements of the real abstraction have assumed conceptual form, their character, rooted in social postulates, evolves into the dialectic of logical argument attached to the concepts" (71). The "autonomy" of this "dialectic of logical argument" from social being follows from the fact that the exchange abstraction is an abstraction associated with the *actions* of people and not with their thinking. It is an abstraction of which people are not consciously aware, but which is nevertheless reproduced in human consciousness in the form of the "abstract intellect."

It is in this rather special sense that "value" (and its material expression as money) may have come to exert itself as a significant social power long before the advent of capitalism. To be sure, so long as exchange does not play a dominant part in giving social form to production, the forms of thought deriving from the value abstraction must wage an uphill battle against forms of thought rooted in different (and often hostile) social postulates: the more or less conscious, yet pre-scientific, forms of socio-economic regulation that are founded on custom, tradition, and social privilege. All the same, this in no way obviates the thesis that the value abstraction *causally* influences the growth of scientific and technical knowledge, and in this specific way enters into the forces-relations dialectic as this unfolds in pre-capitalist history.

Value Relations and Social Progress

The view that ideas and the categories of thought are rooted in social relations and the activities of "real, living individuals" originates with Marx. In *The German Ideology* he wrote that ideas and categories are but "the abstract ideal expressions of ... social relations" (1989d: 189), and in a letter to Engels (March 25, 1868) he remarked that "the logical categories are coming damn well out of 'our intercourse' after all" (Marx & Engels 1965: 202). The young Lukács was to further pursue the connection between the "commodity-structure" and the abstract intellect of bourgeois society in his essay "Reification and the Consciousness of the Proletariat." But it was left to Söhn-Rethel to provide ontological depth to the analysis of how commodity exchange engenders the categories of thought associated with *technical rationality* and how these could develop even in commodity-producing societies where the fully reified capitalist law of value did not yet hold sway.

According to Söhn-Rethel, the relationship between use and exchange as *contrasting* kinds of activity contains the real key to the abstraction of exchange; moreover, this is a relationship that resides at the very heart of the "formal structure of exchange." In defining this structure, Söhn-Rethel refers to the following passage from Marx's *Capital*:

> So long as the laws of exchange are observed in every single act of exchange—taken in isolation—the mode of appropriation [of the surplus] can be completely revolutionized without in any way affecting the property rights which correspond to commodity production. The same rights remain in force both at the outset, when the product belongs to its producer, who, exchanging equivalent for equivalent, can enrich himself only by his own labour, and in the period of capitalism, when the social wealth becomes to an ever-increasing degree the property of those who are in a position to appropriate the unpaid labour of others over and over again. (Marx 1977: 733)

This passage is noteworthy because it suggests that for Marx the "laws of exchange" remain invariant *across* socio-economic epochs distinguished by different modes of exploitation. (Note that the notion of "laws of exchange" is by no means synonymous with the law of value.) Moreover, commodity production is characterized by specific property rights that remain *formally invariant* as between simple and capitalist commodity production. For Söhn-Rethel it is precisely the characteristics of commodity exchange as these are articulated on the basis of these rights that are central to the analysis of the value abstraction:

> The point is that use and exchange are not only different and contrasting by description, but are mutually exclusive in time. They must take place separately at different times. This is because exchange serves only a change of ownership, a change, that is, in terms of a purely *social status* of the commodities as owned property. In order to make this change possible on a basis of negotiated agreement the physical condition of the commodities, their *material status*,

must remain unchanged. Commodity exchange cannot take place as a recognized social institution unless this separation of exchange from use is stringently observed. (1978a: 23–24)

All of this suggests that commodity exchange involves a socially specific type of "restriction of use." Where such restrictions are associated with "exploitation based on unilateral appropriation as opposed to the reciprocity of exchange," we are dealing with instances of what Marx calls "direct lordship and bondage." In such instances the restriction of use is a result of conscious design and deliberate intent, but not of "objective necessity." Things stand altogether differently with the restriction of use associated with commodity exchange; and it is this difference that is key to appreciating both the cognitive revolution associated with the exchange abstraction and the significance of the first tentative stages in the transition from "personal-dependency relations" to "objective-dependency relations" as promoted by simple commodity production (Marx 1973: 157–164). It was precisely his belief that the latter relations were absent from Oriental life that prompted the young Marx to regard it as a purely natural and "barbarian" form of human existence, one outside of history, just as it was his later recognition that *some* objective-dependency relations subsisted under the "Asiatic mode of production" that led him to include it in his sequence of "historical epochs" (Vitkin 1981).

This point returns us to the issue of Marx's appreciation of "progress" in human history. At the beginning of this chapter I suggested that Marx's vision of human progress was ultimately shaped by his belief in the realizability of a form of human society that is free of both material insecurity and social antagonism. Yet the realization of such a society is dependent upon a definite development of the forces and relations of production made possible only by capitalism. In a world-historical sense capitalism is indeed the *necessary* prelude to socialism, in part because it lays the basis for a world economy, but also because its encouragement of technical rationality creates the indispensable material premises of socialism and communism. The historical contribution of the capitalist mode of production has been to "bring together" technical rationality and appropriative rationality by giving technical rationality an appropriative form. This was mainly accomplished through the commodification of labour-power and the subordination of natural science to the demands of surplus value production and realization (that is, through the "formal" and then the "real" subsumption of labour under capital, the latter serving to extend the division of intellectual and manual labour into the very heart of the production process). The corollary to this, however, is that technical rationality has served the development of the productive forces under capitalism *only* to the degree that it has served the appropriation of surplus labour. It is precisely the object of Marx's *Capital* to disclose the limits of the convergence under capitalism of these historically antagonistic principles: labour-saving technological progress, on the one hand, and surplus labour appropriation, on the other. Indeed, the contradiction between these principles within capitalism is at the very heart of Marx's "law of the falling tendency of the rate of profit"—a law that Marx considered to be "in every respect the most important law of modern political economy and the most essential for understanding the most difficult relations" (Marx 1973: 748; see Chapter 2).

But if all this is so, how are we to explain Marx's revised estimation of the Asiatic mode of production and his fascination with the Russian peasant commune as a possible basis for socialist development in the last years of his life? A definitive answer is, I believe, beyond our reach. But it would seem that Marx in the 1870s and the 1880s moved toward a position that recognized that capitalism had created a "world history" to which the "primary social formations" of the East (including the Russian commune) could now contribute. Marx never embraced the notion that socialism could be achieved "within Russia alone" thanks to the collectivist social relations inherited from the peasant commune. But he was prepared to entertain the notion that the task of building *world* socialism might be jointly shouldered by formerly capitalist and Asiatic (or semi-Asiatic) societies alike. Thus, while a socialist revolution might well begin in semi-Asiatic Russia, the construction of socialism would still depend upon the enormous technological resources and productive capacities bequeathed by advanced capitalism: "The *contemporaneity* of Western [capitalist] production, which dominates the world market, enables Russia to build into the commune all the positive achievements of the capitalist system, without having to pass under its harsh tribute" (Marx 1983: 110). This, along with many of Marx's other formulations in the various drafts of his letter to Vera Zasulich, suggests a position far closer to Trotsky's "law of uneven and combined development" and his theory of permanent revolution than to either Stalin's or Mao's versions of socialist economic autarchy (that is, the doctrine of building "socialism in one country").

Finally, a few words should be said in defense of technical rationality and the social progress that it has made possible. When all is said and done, Marx's concept of "human productive powers" (the forces of production) can only refer to the capacities of human beings to transform the world that we inhabit in such a way as to reduce the burden of toil, increase the margin of material security, and attenuate the degree of social antagonism that we collectively confront. Technical rationality has contributed mightily to the development of these powers, and therefore to the potential for human well-being. To free it from its subordination to the logic of appropriation inherent in capitalist social relations, however, requires the promotion of a *socialist rationality* grounded in a vigorous commitment to *human progress*—to the realization of a society in which "human individuality" can develop unhampered by material hardship or social antagonism. Such a concept of human progress still stands as the loftiest of goals to which human beings can aspire. Yet its realizability and even its desirability must be persistently denied by forms of consciousness no less deeply rooted in the "exchange abstraction" than is technical rationality. Ironically the division of exchange and use as contrasting types of activity, together with the division of intellectual and manual labour that has been profoundly ramified by the generalization of commodity relations, must promote an abstract intellect prone to a profoundly *dualistic* worldview, one which habitually views the relations between fact and value, "is" and "ought," freedom and necessity, theory and practice, and so forth as "external" and eternally problematic. For many who share such a worldview, the epistemological and cultural relativism that is promoted by postmodernist thought may well appear to be the most humane as well as comfortable of intellectual options. But for those who reject it, together with its social basis, it must appear as the last line of intellectual defense of a social order that has exhausted its progressive historical mission.

An Unresolved Issue

A possible implication of my argument is that these cognitive faculties have not only *stimulated* technical rationality but have in large part been *constitutive* of this form of thought. Yet such a conclusion must be qualified by the observation that, prior to the cognitive revolution associated with the historical appearance of the commodity abstraction, labour-saving technological innovation was not at all unknown (the invention of projectiles, the wheel, and the plough are among the more obvious examples). This suggests that technical rationality may not be *identical* with the "abstract intellect" referred to by Söhn-Rethel, who, incidentally, regards the non-empirical concepts drawn from the real abstraction as constituting the "paradigm of mechanistic thinking" (1978a: 72). At the same time it suggests that technical rationality, as promoted by the particular cognitive faculties associated with the commodity abstraction, may well be subject to further historical transformations sponsored by the development of new social forms. In other words, Kant's "categories of pure reason" are by no means the last word in defining the formal constituents of the abstract intellect. As Marx averred, "the categories are no more eternal than the relations they express. They are historical and transitory products" (1989c: 11). Indeed, even the scientific critique of these relations, as Marx's own work testifies, may well generate new theoretical categories and perspectives of relevance to the social and the natural sciences alike (for example, the categories of "totality" and "real contradiction"). In light of these considerations it may well be fruitful to explore the question of the socio-historical provenance of quantum theory, scientific realism, and the "chaos" paradigm as substantial recent examples of an ongoing dialectical process of cognitive revolution.

CHAPTER 6

The "Intentional Primacy" of the Relations of Production: Further Reflections on the Dialectic of Social Development

In a stimulating contribution to the discussion of social evolution and Marx's theory of history in *Science & Society*, Alan Carling (1993) attempts to sustain three essential theses: (1) that the forces of production enjoy primacy over the social relations of production due to their capacity to confer a competitive edge upon social relations characterized by superior "forcehood" (a "Competitive Primacy Thesis"); (2) that the process of "social selection" embodied in the Competitive Primacy Thesis is vital to the explication of the tendency of the productive forces to develop beyond the subsistence level guaranteed by processes of "natural selection" of the productive forces (as determined by a "Natural Primacy Thesis"); and (3) that the transition from feudalism to capitalism may be seen as "almost inevitable" given the tendency of the feudal mode of production to engender crises capable of giving rise, at least occasionally and in particular locales, to a capitalist "solution" (a "Feudal Fission Thesis") and given capitalism's capacity, once established, to effectively compete with and ultimately prevail over other regimes of social production (as allowed by the Competitive Primacy Thesis).

In making these claims, Carling has sought, *inter alia*, to dispatch the thesis of "Intentional Primacy" of the productive forces, which he attributes to both G. A. Cohen (1978; Cohen & Kymlicka 1988) and David Laibman (1984), and to invoke the failure of what he calls the "Soviet social experiment" as an illustration of the superiority of "competitive" over "intentional" primacy as the basis of a general theory of historical development.

In what follows I wish to briefly interrogate each of Carling's principal theses in light of the argument in my own contribution to the debate (in Chapter 5), as well as to dispute the lessons that he draws from the Soviet experience.

Briefly, my own argument is that to attribute primacy to the productive forces in a precapitalist dialectic of forces and relations of production is to attribute priority to technical over "appropriative" forms of rationality in societies where these forms are tendentially divorced and opposed to each other. But precapitalist modes of production do not exhibit a dynamic toward technological revolution except to the extent that they permit, tolerate, or sponsor the development of simple forms of commodity production and exchange capable of unleashing an "abstract intellect" oriented toward technical rationality and encouraging technical innovations under the whip of competitive market pressures. In general, most class-divided precapitalist societies are characterized not by any consistent imperative to improve the productive forces through technical innovation but rather by the predominance of an appropriative rationality centred on the reproduction of the prevailing social production relations. Capitalist societies, by contrast, are characterized by the interpenetration of technical and appropriative forms of rationality, an interpenetration that itself is subject to certain historical limits. Ultimately, what made European feudalism the best possible precapitalist womb for the gestation of modern capitalism was its weak resistance to and sometime encouragement of social forms (essentially a trade-based division of labour) propitious to technical rationality and the proliferation/generalization of commodity production. Feudalism and feudalism alone among precapitalist modes was characterized by social relations of production that gave a systematic impetus to (simple) commodity production and therefore to an "intensive" development of the productive forces of the sort described by Laibman (1984).

The central contrast between the above argument and that of Carling is that, whereas Carling upholds the universal validity of the primacy of the productive forces, I suggest the possibility of the (effective) primacy of the social relations of production over vast stretches of human history. Where the two arguments converge is in their mutual rejection of the Intentional Primacy Thesis, according to which the "priority of the forces over the relations is ... given by the fact that the intention to improve the forces governs the intention to change the relations" (Carling 1993: 38). As Carling avers, the latter thesis posits "a primacy *of one intention over another* in the consciousness of a relevant actor"—actors whose motivations are inevitably decisively shaped by their relative powers and locations within the class struggle. But it is precisely due to the "sociality" of such actors' intentions that the notion of "intentional primacy" may be applicable *with respect to the social relations of production*—a hypothesis that is not entertained by Carling.

An alternative "Intentional Primacy Thesis" might therefore be formulated along the following lines: *the priority of the relations over the forces in certain societies and epochs is given by the fact that the intention to preserve (at least some aspects of) the production relations governs the intention to either change or not change the forces, as well as the intention to change or not change aspects of the production relations that bear upon changes in the forces.* Due to the overarching significance of appropriation (surplus extraction/exploitation) to all class-divided societies, I would suggest that insofar as "intentions" enter into the forces/relations dialectic, "Intentional Primacy" *generally* belongs to the social productions relations (SPRs) and only episodically to the productive forces. In other words, the conscious *intentions* of (most) living human agents—insofar as these find concrete expression—are usually to subordinate the development of the productive forces to the maintenance and perpetuation of the prevailing production relations. In this sense, the Intentional Primacy of the SPRs is a feature not only of precapitalist but also of capitalist societies, and stands as a significant brake on social progress.

Exceptions to this state of affairs may obtain where (a) subaltern classes successfully impose their "intention" to free the productive forces (ultimately human productive capacities *tout court*) from the fetters of out-moded SPRs (for example, through the proletarian socialist revolution), or (b) an established ruling class perceives greater benefits for itself through a development of productive forces made possible only by a transforma-tion of production relations from one class-antagonistic and exploitative mode to another (for example, feudal lords seeking to improve and simul-taneously monopolize the forces of production by transforming feudal agriculture into capitalist agriculture—precisely the scenario suggested by Laibman [1984: 278–279]).

It is apparent that any proposed new Intentional Primacy Thesis is contra-dictory to the Intentional Primacy Thesis that Carling attributes to Cohen and (rather less convincingly) to Laibman. But is the Intentional Primacy of the SPRs inconsistent with Carling's own notion of the *Competitive Primacy* of the productive forces? Not at all! To argue that what generally governs the conscious intentions of human agents—especially those agents in a position to successfully impose their intentions—is the will to preserve and perpetuate the prevailing SPRs (even at the expense of improvements in the productive forces) is not to deny that "superior forcehood confers a competitive edge on its associated production relations which is tenden-tially decisive" (Carling 1993: 46). For the simple *appearance* of potentially superior production relations is not in itself sufficient to guarantee the sur-vival or historical success of these relations, nor is "example" enough to compel abandonment of outmoded relations, when the example of supe-rior relations is unable to find expression in superior forcehood. Superior relations must be "allowed" to develop superior forces in the context of *competition* (economic, military, and political) with inferior relations if the Intentional Primacy of the SPRs is to be overcome.

This is precisely the significance of Carling's example of "medieval Catalonia, whose nascent capitalism, arguably, was extinguished by a pow-erful Castilian state whose economic base Catalonia would have easily out-stripped if its native capitalism had been allowed to flourish" (1993: 49). Significantly, however, this example renders problematic Carling's adden-dum to the Competitive Primacy Thesis according to which "the [competi-tive] edge [in forcehood] tends to ensure that technically superior relations prevail in competition with technically inferior counterparts" (46), for this simply *assumes* that superior forcehood will be matched to superior rather than to outmoded relations. The point is that it is entirely conceivable that, as a result of processes of uneven and combined development, it will be feudal Castille rather than (proto-)capitalist Catalonia that will be in possession of superior forces (in both an extensive and intensive sense) and therefore enjoy a competitive edge.

Nevertheless, much of what Carling says in defense of the Competitive Primacy Thesis seems unexceptionable. Indeed he has done an admirable job in showing how this thesis, when joined to the Feudal Fission Thesis, provides a satisfactory overall theory of the origins and subsequent success of capitalist over feudal SPRs. As Carling points out, the Feudal Fission Thesis explains how European feudalism sponsored a proliferation of social forms while regularly exhibiting a cycle of population boom and slump. This repeated "throwing of the feudal die" in the context of political decentralization was bound to eventually create conditions in which capitalism would not only take root but rapidly come to dominate a whole region (in the event, England). And having created a national economy obeying its laws of motion (and insulated, at least for a time, from undue external interference), capitalism was positioned to develop productive forces that would ensure its competitive supremacy, at first economically (in world markets) and later militarily and ideologically.[1]

The competitive primacy of the productive forces is thus a major factor—perhaps the main factor—in explaining processes of "social selection" that discriminate as between competing social relations of production in a post-subsistence context. But as Carling emphasizes, the process of the "social selection" of relations involves far more than a rational calculation of which relations are most technically fecund. Indeed, "under competitive primacy, agents are socially located and acting to defend and/or extend their existing regimes of production" (49)—a point entirely consistent with my proposed thesis of the Intentional Primacy of the SPRs. Suggestively, Carling argues that "if one system prevails over another because of its superior forces, no one need be aware that this is the reason for its success: victory might be ascribed instead to superior leadership, superior national character or superior religion" (50). I would add that Carling is far too quick to attribute such a success to superior SPRs. Indeed, much of his discussion echoes the conviction of anti-Communist triumphalists that the victory of Western capitalism over the Soviet bloc in the Cold War is attributable to the "superiority" of the former's social production relations: "why has the Soviet experiment failed, if not from its failure to compete economically and militarily with a system of production relations that has proved itself technically superior?" (63). Indeed, if superior forcehood is *always* matched to superior relations, then the outcome of the Cold War can only represent a clear-cut confirmation that Soviet-style "socialism" was not *in any sense* an advance beyond Western capitalism.

Much of Carling's brief for the Competitive Primacy Thesis over the Intentional Primacy (of the productive forces) Thesis rests upon one particular—and very debatable—assessment of the lessons of the Soviet collapse:

> It would be difficult to imagine an historical attempt to change relations of production in order to take advantage of the consequent improvements in the productive forces which began with a clearer conception of the end in view, and a greater commitment of political will, or a greater concentration of political power to achieve that end. Yet the [Soviet social] experiment failed, and it has done so in large measure because it proved beyond the power of the Soviet regime—and of the Marxist theory on which it relied—to predict and then install the kinds of social relations of production which could in fact as well as in theory provide a sustained impetus to improve the forces of production. (40)

This passage strikes me as fundamentally wrong in so many ways that it is difficult to know where to begin a much-needed critical dissection. Was "the Soviet regime" consistently "Marxist," and is it appropriate to speak of a *single* regime? Were Soviet SPRs fully socialist in character? If it is true that the "Soviet experiment" failed due to "its failure to compete economically and militarily" with a social system that has proved itself to be technically superior, why did this "experiment" not collapse *much earlier* than it did? Is the notion of a Soviet "experiment" in building "socialism in one country" not a fundamentally un-Marxist concession to both bourgeois and Stalinist ideology? And is it not true that successive Stalinist regimes studiously ignored the fundamental Marxist teaching that socialist SPRs must involve a real democracy of the associated producers and consumers and that socialism must incorporate within itself the international division of labour developed by world capitalism as one of its greatest productive forces?

Carling concludes his article by stating that the "collapse of the Soviet Marxist regime ... acts as a critical test between two versions of Marxist theory"—one committed to the idea of the Intentional Primacy of the productive forces, the other to Competitive Primacy. There is truth in this, but it must be more carefully specified. The collapse of the Soviet regime demonstrates the folly of the bureaucratic, and very un-Marxist, pipe dream of "building socialism" in one relatively backward country through administrative *diktat*—a reactionary utopia to which the Intentional Primacy (of the productive forces) Thesis has a clear affinity. At the same time, the notion of Competitive Primacy accurately indicates what was required of the (originally Marxist) Soviet regime in the years immediately after the October Revolution: to deprive world capitalism of its most important "productive force" (the international division of labour) by actively promoting a world revolution.[2]

The ascent to power of an oppressive oligarchy committed above all else to preserving bourgeois norms of distribution (a surviving aspect of capitalist SPRs in the Soviet transitional economy), to bureaucratic parasitism, and to achieving a *modus vivendi* with world imperialism ultimately accounts for the failure of Soviet "socialism" to develop either the production relations or the productive forces required for successful "competition" with capitalism. The fact that it was even in the running for as long as it was, however, suggests the tremendous potential of *certain* of its production relations—notably collectivized property and centralized planning—to unleash, extend, and improve the productive forces. Ironically, if not surprisingly, it is just these aspects of Soviet social relations that are now being held up to ridicule by capitalist ideologues as accounting for the "failure" of the Soviet "social experiment." Unfortunately and unnecessarily, Carling has lent his Competitive Primacy Thesis to the task of reinforcing this ideological message—when, joined to a conception of the Intentional Primacy of the SPRs, it has the potential to illuminate some of the more important lessons of the demise of Stalinist "real socialism."

Notes

1. The question is posed: does this make capitalism "almost inevitable"? The answer is: only if something like European feudalism can also be shown to be a necessary or "almost inevitable" product of social evolution. To the extent that this remains problematic, as indeed it does despite the best efforts of Laibman and others, the possibility of a "general theory of history" remains moot.

2. The view that the international division of labour is itself a critically important "force of production" is a little-understood but essential aspect of Trotsky's critique of the Stalinist doctrine of "socialism in one country." In *The Permanent Revolution*, he wrote: "Marxism takes its point of departure from world economy, not as a sum of national parts but as a mighty and independent reality which has been created by the international division of labour and the world market, and which in our epoch imperiously dominates the national markets. The productive forces of capitalist society have long ago outgrown the national boundaries.... In respect of the techniques of production, socialist society must represent a higher stage than capitalism. To aim at building a *nationally isolated* socialist society means, in spite of all passing successes, to pull the productive forces backward even as compared with capitalism. To attempt ... to realize a shut-off proportionality of all the branches of economy within a national framework means to pursue a reactionary utopia" (Trotsky 1969: 146).

CHAPTER 7

Marxism versus "Progressive Poststructuralism"

Marxist political economists have seldom addressed the poststructuralist challenge to social theory that has become such a prominent feature of the Western intellectual landscape since the 1970s. In large part this has to do with the fact that most Marxists concerned with studying the dynamics and crisis tendencies of the capitalist economy have seen little to gain from engaging with a host of "post" approaches that seem most united in their rejection of "economic reductionism," when they are not divided as to whether one can speak, at all or anymore, of something called capitalism. For better or worse, this situation has begun to change. As "progressive" poststructuralists have become more attentive to economic issues, Marxist political economy is now seen by many as a useful ally in the struggle against the global offensive of neoliberalism. Moreover, for many postmodernists and poststructuralists, the collapse of Stalinism has effectively eliminated Marxism's status as a threatening would-be "grand narrative," engendering a crisis within Marxist thought that appears to render it vulnerable to fundamental deconstruction and radical renovation along the lines urged by postmodernism/poststructuralism.[1] In response, some Marxist political economists, eager to forge "alliances" with non-Marxist "progressives" in a deeply reactionary political and intellectual climate, have welcomed with some alacrity these overtures from the "left wing" of the postmodernist camp.

187

It was with at least some of this in mind that I resolved in 1992–93 to address, both directly and indirectly, certain aspects of the postmodernist/poststructuralist challenge to Marxist thought in a book principally concerned with Marx's theories of value and crisis.[2] It was my view, and it remains so, that Marx's theory of value provides some important keys to resolving a number of long-standing problems that postmodernist thought has exploited in order to advance a mode of theorizing and a politics that is fundamentally counterposed to Marxian socialism. Indeed, it was for this reason that I (somewhat reluctantly) agreed, at the urging of my publisher, to include a reference to postmodernism in the book's subtitle.

Invisible Leviathan: The Marxist Critique of Market Despotism beyond Postmodernism was published in late 1994, and, perhaps not surprisingly, the most sustained and serious critical attention that it has received was from a theorist of poststructuralist, deconstructivist persuasion in an article in *Rethinking Marxism*. Noel Castree's "*Invisible Leviathan*: Speculations on Marx, Spivak and the Question of Value" (1996/97) is an important—and, I think, symptomatic—contribution to an emerging poststructuralist literature seeking engagement with Marxian political economy. His novel strategy of juxtaposing my "ocular" appreciation of Marx's value theory with Gayatri C. Spivak's more "textual" reading succeeds splendidly in framing areas of both agreement and disagreement between his version of "progressive poststructuralism" and the "modern Marxism" that he sees my work as representing.

Castree avows a certain sympathy for my theoretical project in *Invisible Leviathan*, characterizing his work as an "appreciative critique," and I thank him for the many generous things he says about my book as he goes about trying to build a bridge between poststructuralism and Marxist thought— a bridge that he hopes will further the project of an "ambivalent modern/ postmodern Marxism." In particular, I welcome his tribute to the "vital contribution" that he thinks my book can make in "[making] seen the otherwise invisible relations constituting global capitalism" as well as his apparent agreement with me that the transcendence of the despotic power of the capitalist leviathan requires "a strong and well-organized working class" armed with just this "vision."

That said, what is most striking about Castree's critique from my own perspective is the remarkably *limited* nature of its engagement with the theoretical and political implications of my defense of Marx's theory of labour-value, as well as the ease with which he dismisses (without answering) the explicit and implicit criticisms that I sketched of postmodernist and poststructuralist thought. Indeed, qualifying his endorsement of the book are a series of sharp criticisms laced with strongly negative characterizations of my "modern," "no-nonsense brand of Marxism." Among other things, Castree taxes me with an "omniscient, exorbitant opticality" and a "dogmatic monistic position" that "abjures moderation." Moreover, while affirming that my critique is effective against prevailing free-market ideologies, he avers that it is likely to "set back the cause of Marxism on the left"—apparently because he sees it recapitulating "Marxism's indifference towards and/or effacement of 'otherness' and 'difference."

Ironically, while reproving my "reductive" and "restricted" accounts of the value form, Castree seems only too willing to *reduce unproblematically* what he variously calls "modern Marxism" or "classical Marxism" to the caricature fashioned by decades of Stalinist hegemony on the putatively Marxist left. Yet, if Castree had read my book in its entirety, he should have known better than to assimilate my Marxism to a debased orthodoxy that is indeed vulnerable to many of the criticisms lodged by certain postmodern and poststructuralist critics. Insensitivity to "difference"—an obdurate indifference to and even backwardness regarding issues of gender, race, ethnicity, sexual orientation, and national or colonial oppression—*did* indeed characterize the politics of an international Communist movement that succumbed to the noxious Stalinist program of "building socialism in one country." And those politics *did* engender a form of Marxist theory that effaced "otherness" in multiple ways—not least by denying the interest of "other workers" in prosecuting effective struggles against capitalism on their own national terrains, irrespective of Moscow's efforts to promote "peaceful coexistence"!

Even so, it is important to affirm that not *all* proponents of classical Marxism succumbed to Stalinism and that many have contributed in important ways to extending the "classical" tradition's early, halting attempts to articulate its class-struggle, proletarian socialism with struggles against patriarchal relations, colonialism, racism, homophobia, xenophobia, and other forms of "special oppression." Yet Castree fails to affirm this; indeed, he never so much as alludes to the profound *differences* that exist within "modern Marxism," studiously ignoring my own forthright criticisms of Stalinized Marxism. The reason for this silence is, perhaps, not so difficult to fathom. My preference for Trotsky's Marxism over the Stalinist carica-ture may well be of little moment to a theorist whose case for an "ambiva-lent modern/postmodern Marxism" actually *depends*, at least implicitly, on rejecting authentic Marxism's program of "world revolution" and counter-posing to it a celebration of "difference," "otherness" and "heterogeneity" as these phenomena manifest themselves either within capitalism or in envi-ronments not yet fully absorbed into it.

To be sure, any claim on my part that I *do* take seriously the dimensions of "difference" that he highlights may strike Castree as disingenuous, and this could be for entirely understandable reasons. First, not all Marxists identifying with the Trotskyist tradition have understood the importance of addressing "extra-class" forms of social oppression. Second, my book touches on such issues only in passing. And third, while I oppose any "deferring" of difference in the name of a spurious "class unity," I remain committed (as Castree surely recognizes) to the Marxist proposition that a class-struggle politics is the *sine qua non* of any serious emancipatory project. Against those on the "postmodernist left" who champion a secto-ralist (that is to say, basically reformist) "politics of identity" in the name of opposition to "class reductionism," "economism," or "revolutionary ultima-tism," I continue to insist on the Marxist principle of working-class politi-cal independence and on the responsibility of those who have achieved a socialist consciousness to argue vigorously against any attempt to contain the emancipatory struggles of the oppressed within a capitalist framework.

To his credit, Castree acknowledges that he has risked "doing violence to the integrity" of my argument by limiting his attention to my "conception of the value form and its vital role in enabling [Smith's] disclosure of global 'Leviathan.'" The trade-off, he believes, is that this approach enables him to "open a valuable window" on the "'modern' cognitive and normative dimensions" of my argument. I interpret this to mean that, irrespective of what I argue in other parts of my book, Castree is intent on teasing out what he regards as the main deficiencies that "haunt" my "reductive reading of the value form" and on relating those deficiencies to what he sees as the principal weaknesses and elisions of an undifferentiated "modern Marxism."

While pleading innocent to Castree's charges of "Archimedean" arrogance, I would argue that Castree's own *elisions* in his critique of *Invisible Leviathan* serve to illustrate, albeit unintentionally, why authentic Marxism, despite its undoubted gaps and traditional blind spots, remains vastly superior to "progressive poststructuralism," both as a theoretical orientation and as a guide to an emancipatory political *practice*. Indeed, it is precisely around the question of practice that the deficiencies of Castree's "ambivalent modern/postmodern Marxism" are most clearly revealed. As I affirm in *Invisible Leviathan*, *program generates theory* (a point that seems little understood by postmodernist intellectuals), and *non-revolutionary* programs (be they Stalinism or postmodern "identity politics") are incapable of generating an adequate revolutionary theory. In this spirit, I urge the reader to keep in mind throughout this reply a heuristic question inspired by Marx's third and eleventh Theses on Feuerbach: Can what is *truly distinctive* to poststructuralist and/or postmodernist thought help anyone to become a better fighter for human emancipation?

A Summary of *Invisible Leviathan*

The main themes of *Invisible Leviathan*, as set out in its preface, are twofold: first, "that, while 'value relations' have played a role of paramount importance in the development of human society, the point has been reached where these relations need to be superseded by a new set of social arrangements that must, at a minimum, provide for a qualitative increase in the degree to which human social and economic affairs are governed by *conscious* decision-making at the level of the human collectivity as a whole"; and second, the "defense of Marx's *dialectical reason* against both the 'subjective reason' invoked by the currently fashionable school of so-called Analytical Marxism and the 'cynical reason' promoted by poststructuralism and conservative postmodernism" (Smith 1994a: ix–x).

With respect to the first theme, I argue that the core propositions of Marx's theory of labour-value are fundamental to his theory of capitalist crisis (in particular his law of the tendency of the rate of profit to fall) and to his vision of capitalism as a mode of production in which social wealth is necessarily measured in terms of abstract human labour time (the phenomenal form of which is money). But the measurement of social wealth in this way has a *social and historical foundation* in the determinate social relations of capitalism, not a natural or eternal one. Accordingly, it becomes possible to conceive (or "envision") a mode of production (socialism/communism) that can dispense with the measurement of social wealth in terms of labour time, and that can thereby redirect the labour-saving technologies developed by capitalism to the quantitative and qualitative expansion of that free, disposable time that will enable *all* human beings to develop their many-sided capacities and talents to the fullest. What stands in the way of the realization of such a society is precisely the "invisible leviathan"—the structure of socio-economic relations that form the basis of the capitalist law of value.

Why must social wealth be measured in terms of labour time in an era when "living labour" is a less and less significant "technical" input to material production? In a nutshell, because material production under capitalism is subordinate to the production of *surplus value*—that is, to the appropriation of surplus labour by those monopolizing the ownership of the means of production. The mechanism of this appropriation under capitalism must be understood as a contradictory ensemble of social relations encompassing exploitation, equalitarian exchange, market competition, and co-operation (objective socialization)—an ensemble of relations that imparts a distinctive social content to the capitalist law of value.

To sustain these theses, I undertook an exposition and defense of the two propositions that I regard as fundamental to Marx's law of labour-value: that living labour is the sole source of new value, and that value exists as a definite quantitative magnitude at the level of the capitalist division of labour as a whole (a magnitude that acts as a parametric determinant on profits, wages, and the realizability of prices set by capitalists seeking "reasonable" profit margins). I argue, not at all originally, that Marx's theory of the value form is fundamental to his value theory as a whole; that the significance of the value-form theory is missed by Marx's neoclassical critics as well as by his Ricardian-Marxist and post-Sraffian "sympathizers"; but also that many contemporary "value-form theorists" (whom I label "neo-orthodox value theorists") impoverish Marx's theory and gut it of its most profound programmatic implications by abandoning the task of articulating his value-form and value-magnitude analyses with each other. Only the inchoate "fundamentalist" school of value theory, I argue, remains true to Marx's fundamental value-theoretic agenda of sustaining the core propositions defined above. What is most "original" in my account is thus my attempt to define the distinctive features of "fundamentalist value theory."

Whereas neo-orthodox value theorists reject the notion of "embodied labour" as the measure of a commodity's value and emphasize Marx's thesis that "money as the measure of value is the *necessary* form of appearance of the measure of value which is imminent in commodities, namely labour-time" (Marx 1977: 188), fundamentalist value theorists criticize the neo-orthodox tendency to *dissociate* Marx's value-form and value-magnitude analyses, insisting in particular upon a conceptualization of Marx's category of "abstract labour" (for Marx, the metaphoric "substance" of value) as the reflection in thought of the structure of relations and processes through which commodities are produced for the purpose of sale and the realization of profit (Smith 1994a: 109; Chapter 3 of this volume). Abstract labour (carrying with it all the implications of Marx's "socially necessary and socially equalized labour-time") emerges as the category that links and mediates the microeconomic focus of the value-form analysis (money, price) and the macroeconomic concerns of the value-magnitude analysis (aggregate value flows, the "transformation problem," and so on). Thus, abstract labour must be understood not merely as "an undifferentiated capacity" (the general, "transhistorical" sense that Marx sometimes brings to the concept), but as a "non-particular entity" (Fischer 1982) that exists as a structural universal specific to capitalism and whose expression

193

is money, the "universal commodity." Accordingly, the *ontological reversals* that Marx specifies in his account of the value form (use-value appearing as value, concrete labour as abstract labour, and private labour as social labour) should extend as well to the relation between commodities as sensuously concrete *particulars* (to which are attached individual prices) and the *universal structure* of capitalist value relations (abstract socially necessary labour time, whose necessary form of appearance is money). It is on this basis, I argue, that the core propositions of Marx's theory of value can be sustained in a satisfactory way. This is extremely important because, deprived of these core propositions, Marx's account of capitalism's historical "law of motion" (in particular, its crisis tendencies) loses much of its theoretical cogency and programmatic force.

How does all this relate to my defense of Marx's "dialectical reason"? Apart from the fact that Marx's account of the value form relies on a number of concepts and methods inspired by Hegel's dialectical logic, I wished to stress Marx's commitment to a "dialectical social ontology" that is resolutely opposed to the idealism and dualism that mark bourgeois social theory. In particular, I tried to disclose the internal connectedness of the social relations of production to specific forms of consciousness, and the ways in which such forms animate the dialectic of forces and relations of production that is at the heart of Marx's vision of human social development.

For Marx, I argue, the key to historical-materialist inquiry is the distinction between the Natural and the Social, the relation of the two being decisively mediated by "consciousness" understood both as ideas in people's heads and as an active relation of people to their circumstances.[3] Value relations, including the rudimentary value relations that first emerged with the advent of simple (precapitalist) forms of commodity production, encourage within the human mind a mode of abstract thinking highly conducive both to Kant's "categories of pure reason" (which correspond closely to the formal elements of the "exchange abstraction"; see Söhn-Rethel 1978a) and to a "dualistic" worldview. As such, value relations, via the real abstraction of exchange, are a major factor in propelling the forces-relations dialectic (by stimulating the development of natural science, mathematics, and with them, productivity-enhancing technological innovation) *and* in fostering ideological modes of thought (by encouraging the sort of dualistic out-look that effaces the necessary role of historically specific social relations of production in mediating the "material/natural" and the "ideal/cultural" aspects of a unified—that is, non-bifurcated—reality).

All this has important implications for an understanding of postmodern-ism and poststructuralism, currents of thought that thrive on the alleged *indeterminacy* of the relationship between "the material" (for example, production) and "the cultural" (for example, the system of signs), and that problematize the notion of "objective reality" even as they "decentre the subject" and celebrate a riot of contending subjectivities. As I argue in *Invisible Leviathan*:

> None of this [argument against poststructuralism] should be con-strued as suggesting that the analysis of language, communication, or power/domination is "alien" to historical materialism. The issue is not whether these shibboleths of poststructuralism should be explored, but whether they should be explored *in connection with* an analysis of the social relations of production and the determinate socio-historical forms of human labour, or whether they should be accorded a kind of ontological *privilege,* such that they become a rationale for *ignoring* the issue of the social relations of production. Again, it is quite appar-ent that the tendency of bourgeois thought is to accord a theoretical privilege to anything that sublates the issue of the social relations of production. To this extent, poststructuralism serves a highly useful purpose from the bourgeois standpoint as a major intellectual *diver-sion* from the theoretical and programmatic results of Marx's devas-tating critique of capitalist social relations. (Smith 1994a: 235)

Is this a fair characterization of Castree's poststructuralist critique of *Invisible Leviathan*? Given his declared "anti-capitalist" sympathies, it may seem uncharitable to affirm that it is. Yet, the silences in Castree's critique may speak more powerfully on this score than his rhetoric. For the effect of Castree's critique is precisely to *divert* attention from the dominant themes

of my book; to problematize, on epistemological grounds, its main theoretical results; to ignore its empirical findings with respect to the law of the
tendency of the rate of profit to fall; and to recommend a "textual" reading of Marx's value theory that focuses one-sidedly on the "value-form"
account while relativizing its truth claims and evading its programmatic
implications. Moreover, in one of the central statements of his critique,
Castree argues that "what value 'represents' in Marx—as a real abstraction
which is a representation of something else (use-value, concrete labour)
and as a concept fashioned by Marx to re-present/make visible that representation—is, in effect, everything, the entire heteroclite world of living
labour, and therefore nothing." A purer statement of a *dualistic* misread-
ing of Marx would be difficult to imagine: for Castree affirms here that
value "represents" [*sic*] living labour (that is, the "material/concrete") and
is also a conceptual representation of that representation. Missing entirely
from this statement, which issues in the conclusion that value is a "cata-
chresis" (something lacking a literal referent), is Marx's idea that value is
fundamentally *a social relation of production* and that, as such, it plays a
decisive role in the *dialectical mediation* of the "material/concrete" and the
"ideal/conceptual." Castree thus recapitulates the dualist sublation of the
social relations of production that I was at pains to protest. All of this is
undertaken, we are told, in order to sensitize Marxists to the "limits" and
"limitations" of Marx's value theory, to make this theory "more politically
useful," and to help us all to avoid the "dangers" and "nightmares" to which
a purely "ocular" appreciation of the theory might expose us. Yet the real
effect of Castree's dualist reconstruction/misrepresentation of Marx's theory of value is to render extremely unclear whether value, which is "everything and therefore nothing," can or should be considered *socio-historically
transcendable*.

A Reply to Castree on Three Points

I have alluded to the presence of three overlapping, yet somewhat distinguishable, types of criticism associated with Castree's overall critique:

(1) a criticism regarding my alleged attempt to "grasp the social whole"; (2) a criticism of my "reductive," "restrictive" and "purely ocular" conception of value; and (3) a criticism of my "deferral of difference"—which he eventually links to my failure to adequately "subjectivize" value and to decentre the origin of value. Each of these calls for some additional comment.

GRASPING THE SOCIAL WHOLE

According to Castree, "Smith's is an omniscient, exorbitant opticality which seeks to grasp the social whole [sic] in all its dimensions through a particularly reductive reading of the value form." Furthermore, *Invisible Leviathan* represents a misguided attempt to "suture social life as such primarily around value relations."

To begin with, I want to *agree* with Castree that the economy, like social life itself, is, in Spivak's words, "woven by many, many strands that are discontinuous, that come from way off, that carry their histories within them, and that are not within our control" (Castree 1996/97: 69). If I am guilty of a too-violent abstraction of the global economy from the many other "strands" with which it is entangled (a procedure of abstraction that is perhaps unavoidable in a work of less than encyclopedic proportions), I do at least acknowledge that "commodities *share* the real world with human beings whose social relations and consciousness reflect the influence not only of commodity exchange but of an entire cultural continuum, not to mention cross-cultural antagonisms" (1994a: 206). This may not satisfy Castree, but it does register my view that there is more to social life than value relations and that such relations are reciprocally influenced by these other dimensions. Indeed, this is why I proceed to affirm that "it is precisely in the area of determining the value of individual labour-powers that these relatively autonomous cultural influences can be most profoundly felt—trampling underfoot all attempts to 'objectively' compare the 'value' of different work tasks" (206). Further, this is why I register the following caveat in the last chapter of *Invisible Leviathan*: "Marx's concept of value is inseparable from his analytic focus on the social relations of production as the mediating link between 'natural laws' and 'human agency' under capitalism. The limits of this focus also suggest the limits of a value-theoretical perspective in the analysis of capitalism and of human agency within capitalist societies" (1994a: 232).

A full response to Castree's epistemological criticisms of my alleged attempt to "grasp the social whole" would involve a lengthy discussion of my commitment to "scientific realism." I will limit myself here to the observation that Castree studiously—and highly symptomatically—ignores the emphasis that I repeatedly place on *practice* (as conditioned by determinate social relations) in the mediation of theory and reality. In my view, the theoretical reclamation of reality is *not* ensured simply by the "labour of thought," the notion that Castree rather unfairly attributes to me. Rather, the *only* way to maintain the "tension" of which Castree speaks "between theory as an accurate and 'true' representation of the real and theory as non-identical with the real" is through interventions aimed at changing the world (Smith 1994a: 135).

"PURE OCULARITY" AND THE ONTOLOGY OF VALUE

Castree claims that I have a "purely ocular" approach to value and that, unlike Spivak, I overlook entirely the "textual" aspects of value theory, including what "Marx's texts close off in their valuable attempt to envision capitalism."

To begin with, I agree that it is important, in company with Spivak, to address not only "value" (as a real "internal relation" of capitalism) but also "the question of value," that is to say, "what it is to talk of value in the first place, of what makes it visible and invisible." This was the burden of the third chapter of *Invisible Leviathan* entitled "Science, Ideology and Economic Value," where I canvas a number of competing conceptions of "economic value" and specify the particularities and unique aims of Marx's value theory. I return to this theme in Chapter 3 in a discussion of what differentiates the classical and Marxian labour-value formations. There I note: "The *relevance* of [Marx's] investigation ... can only be grasped by those who are prepared to see that commodity production is but one (perishable and transcendable) socio-historical form of production" (61). In brief, this is what Marx's theory of value (and value form) "makes visible."

USE-VALUE, DIFFERENCE, AND SUBJECTIVITY

According to Castree, Smith and Marx share a "continuist reading" that "posits use-value/labour power as a definite and clearly identifiable origin for the value chain to get going (use value, particularly the use value of labour power) and an end (capital and capitalism), wherein the end is simply a different form of the origin and where the whole chain is closed." Lacking the space for the sort of detailed response that this cluster of arguments demands, I will simply pose a few deliberately "leading" questions to Castree and then respond to the *political* upshot of his critique on this terrain.

First, how does Castree, following Spivak, understand the notion of a "chain" of "value determinations"? Does he regard Marx's account of the emergence of the value form as a "linear" account or a "dialectical" one? If the latter, on what basis does he suggest that a dialectical development of the value form *fails* to recognize the discontinuities and indeterminacies inherent in the *real contradictions* of the commodity and value forms? Second, what does he mean when he suggests that capital (as "the end" of the value chain) is "simply" a "different form" of use-value or labour-power (its starting point)? Where, if at all, do the *social relations of production* enter into the "value chain" in his reading? And to what extent, if any, is his understanding of the "value chain" compatible with the sort of "abstract labour theory of value" that I advance in *Invisible Leviathan*?

Castree's truly peculiar notion that "value forms" originate in "labour power" (not to mention his habit of *conflating* the categories of value and capital) bespeak not only imprecision, but a systematic confusion of the Marxian theses that I sought to clarify and defend, in particular the thesis that *the source of new value is living labour that is subject to processes of abstraction grounded in capitalist commodity production and framed by market exchange as the social form of the capitalist division of living labour.* The political "payoff" for Castree's theoretical legerdemain in this regard is, nonetheless, a revealing one: "an encouragement to envisage a form of Marxism and of anti-capitalist struggle in which the reality of international economic exploitation is *affirmed* but the classical constituency of economic insurgency, class, is *deconstructed.*" The burden of this argument is unmistakably to support the "disruption" of a "class-struggle politics" that has "traditionally" effaced any differences that might undermine the notion of a collective working-class actor.

I will limit myself to three points in response. The first is that there is *nothing* in the theoretical constitution of Marxism that prevents its adherents from recognizing the "heterogeneity" marking the working class; indeed, it was this heterogeneity that I had in mind when I spoke of the need for "transitional and democratic demands pertaining to the specific problems confronting women, minority, and immigrant workers" to be integrated into the program of class-struggle socialism "if it is to build a 'bridge' wide enough and strong enough to accommodate the working class as a whole" (1994a: 214). The second point is that the theoretical affirmation that value is a relation between people and that living labour is therefore the source of new value (a social relation reflecting and "representing" a societal division of labour, and *not* concrete labour as such) can by no stretch of the imagination be seen as motivated by a desire to efface "difference." And, finally, the general category of "the working class" remains indispensable to social theory inasmuch as it posits what is by no means obvious to those whose starting point is the subjectivities and manifold differences distinguishing individual workers: namely, that structural determinants of class and class interest do exist and that consequently, "the working class, despite its divisions and its relative dearth of resources, is united by powerful common interests that periodically assert themselves in the most unexpected of ways and that demand the formulation of a common working-class program based on socialist principles and goals" (1994a: 210). If Castree is dissatisfied with these points, it is incumbent upon him to explain why, as well as to flesh out the forms and content of the "anti-capitalist struggle" that he thinks his particular theoretical perspectives mandate. As it stands, his critique presents very little in the way of an alternative practice, while the poststructuralist theoretical perspectives to which he subscribes seem to provide grounds mainly for "ambivalence," if not paralysis, in the sphere of action.

The Symptomatic Nature of the Debate

The upshot of Castree's argument is disarmingly plain. Even as they seek to show just how nightmarish and dangerous capitalism really is, Marxists should remain ever vigilant against taking their truth claims too seriously. There are, Castree reminds us, "serious risks and responsibilities involved in the production of truth." Accordingly, Marxists should welcome the efforts of poststructuralists to "prise open" those truth claims and to disclose the aporias inhabiting "Marxists' normative-utopian prescriptions" so that these prescriptions will not become "others' nightmares."

Against this poststructuralist counsel, I would insist that a truly productive re-examination of Marxism's leading ideas must proceed not along the lines of textual deconstructions of *Capital* but along the lines of a careful assessment of how and why ostensibly Marxist practice (particularly in its dominant social-democratic and Stalinist forms) deviated so profoundly from the fundamentals of Marxist theory and in the process served to stunt and deform the latter's further development. Such a re-examination must start not with the (idealist) assumption that humanity's "nightmares" are caused by "prescriptions" (ideas), but from the premise that they are the products of powerful material and social forces—forces that cannot be fought successfully by those mired in skepticism regarding the "truth-claims" inspiring their own struggles.

Castree's intervention notwithstanding, I remain convinced that the idealism, dualism, and "cynical reason" that mark poststructuralist discourse make it a quite unsuitable prospective "ally" for the renewal of an emancipatory socialist project. Indeed, what is *distinctive* in poststructuralist thought (its particular strategies for unsettling truth claims and breeding skepticism about the possibilities for emancipatory social change) stamp it, at best, as a guardian of the status quo (against neoliberal "counter-revolutions," it should be said, no less than against Marxian socialism). By abjuring the need for strong truth claims that can challenge the notion that capitalism is the "best of all possible worlds," poststructuralism assists willy-nilly in the perpetuation of a global system that every year sacrifices millions of lives to starvation, and that over the course of a single decade claims more human lives than all the revolutions that have occurred in the modern era. To my mind, this shows the "serious risks and responsibilities" involved in *not* eschewing the cultivated "ambivalence" of postmodernist intellectualizing, in *not* telling the truth about the pernicious capitalist system, and in *not* fighting vigorously for its replacement by a higher order of social organization.

Notes

1. I am aware, of course, that postmodernism and poststructuralism should not be treated as homologous intellectual trends. However, considerable overlap exists between them, and I will assume here that poststructuralism denotes an intellectual practice that may be seen as largely subsumed under the broader postmodernist tent.

2. In a generally favourable review of *Invisible Leviathan*, Alfredo Saad Filho points out that "very little space is given to the Marxian critique of postmodernism, in spite of the title" (1996: 157). My intention, however, was hardly to develop a full-blown critique of postmodernism, but to demonstrate the continuing relevance of Marx's critique of capitalism "beyond" the assumptions, preoccupations, and shibboleths of postmodernist thinking. An extended *explicit* engagement with postmodernist theory was not at all necessary to such an undertaking.

3. In the totality encompassing the ideal, the natural, and the social aspects of human existence, each term takes its turn as the mediator of the other two terms, and each dialectical "syllogism" sheds light on definite aspects of the human condition. However, there is no doubt that Marx gives greatest attention to the dialectical opposition of the Natural and the Social (with the ideal, or consciousness, as mediator) for the purpose of grasping problems of social transformation. For an illuminating account of how Hegel's theory of the syllogism can be applied to a systematic dialectical ordering of the categories of Marx's theory, see Tony Smith (1990, 1993a).

PART III
Trotsky's Marxism

CHAPTER 8

Revisiting Trotsky: Reflections on the Stalinist Debacle and Trotskyism as Alternative

I

In his autobiography, Leon Trotsky (1879–1940) offers an illuminating and highly instructive account of the reaction among many young supporters of the United Left Opposition within the Communist Party of the Soviet Union (CPSU) to the decapitation of the Chinese Communist Party and the bloody suppression of the Second Chinese Revolution of 1925–27. Joseph Stalin's policy of subordinating the Chinese party to the bourgeois-nationalist Guomindang had produced an unprecedented calamity for the Chinese working class and the young Communist International, fully confirming the correctness of Trotsky's criticism of the class-collaborationist strategy of an "anti-imperialist united front." Surely, it was thought by many members of the Left Opposition, these events could only hasten oppositionist triumph within the party and the Communist International. Trotsky, however, was far less sanguine:

> During the first days after the *coup d'etat* by Chiang Kai-Shek, I was obliged to pour many a bucket of cold water over the hot heads of my young friends—and over some not so young. I tried to show them that the opposition could not rise on the defeat of the Chinese revolution. The fact that our forecast had proved correct might attract one thousand, five thousand, or even ten thousand new supporters to us. But for the millions, the significant thing was not our forecast, but the fact of the crushing of the Chinese proletariat. After the defeat of the German revolution in 1923, after the breakdown of the English general strike in 1926, the new disaster in China would only intensify the disappointment of the masses in the international revolution. And it was this same disappointment that served as the chief psychologic support for Stalin's policy of national-reformism. (1970a: 530)

My recollection of this passage haunted me insistently as I followed the unfolding of the "August revolution" of 1991 and its aftermath in the Soviet Union. The victory of Boris Yeltsin's counter-coup against the CPSU and the Soviet state seemed certain to be a decisive watershed in the protracted process of counter-revolution that the Soviet Union had experienced since the rise to power in 1924 of what Trotsky had called "Stalin's bonapartistic clique." For Yeltsin was openly proclaiming his intention to construct a regime fully committed to free-market capitalism and the return of Russia to "normal civilization." It seemed to me, as it did, unfortunately, to too few others, that Yeltsin's ascendancy represented a victory of world capitalism not only over decrepit Stalinism but over the most fundamental interests of the Soviet masses, and that the installation of his pro-capitalist regime marked the end of the Stalinist project of "building socialism in one country." In the absence of popular resistance to Yeltsin's counter-coup, the main battalions of the old state apparatus, with the notable exception of the banned CPSU, were quickly reconstituting themselves as loyal components of a nascent capitalist state.

My background as a Trotskyist during the 1970s predisposed me to measure these events against the analysis and forecasts that Trotsky had made between 1924 and 1940 concerning the nature and likely fate of the Stalinist bureaucratic oligarchy and the state over which it presided. In general, it appeared to me that Trotsky's fundamental analysis of Stalinism had been strikingly confirmed, and that his forecasts, though flawed by an unfulfilled historical optimism, had proved far more accurate than those proffered by competing political and intellectual currents.

According to Trotsky, Stalinism was to be understood pre-eminently as the social phenomenon of bureaucratic-oligarchic rule on the basis of collectivized property forms, together with the body of ideas that served to legitimate and perpetuate that rule. Moreover, the Soviet state was a bureaucratically degenerated workers' state presiding over a socio-economic formation combining elements of a capitalist class society and of a socialist society of the type that Marx referred to as the lower stage of communism:

The Soviet Union is a contradictory society halfway between capitalism and socialism, in which: a) the productive forces are still far
from adequate to give the state property a socialist character; b) the
tendency toward primitive accumulation created by want breaks out
through the innumerable pores of the planned economy; c) norms
of distribution preserving a bourgeois character lie at the basis of a
new differentiation of society; d) the economic growth, while slowly
bettering the situation of the toilers, promotes a swift formation of
privileged strata; e) exploiting the social antagonisms, a bureaucracy
has converted itself into an uncontrolled caste alien to socialism;
[and] f) the social revolution, betrayed by the ruling party, still
exists in property relations and in the consciousness of the toiling
masses.... (Trotsky 1970b: 255)

The Soviet "transitional" formation, Trotsky predicted, would either
move forward to socialism or revert back to capitalism. The condition for
progress toward socialism would be the international extension of the revolution to the citadels of world capitalism and the establishment of a vibrant
socialist democracy based on the direct rule of workers' councils. Capitalist
restoration, on the other hand, would be the likely outcome of a prolonged
isolation of the Soviet workers' state under the pressure of capitalist imperialism—an outcome that would certainly be favoured by increasing numbers among the privileged bureaucratic stratum (the *nomenklatura*) as they
sought to enlarge and transform their privileges into transmissible private
property. As Trotsky noted in 1937, "Privileges have only half their worth,
if they cannot be transmitted to one's children. But the right of testament is
inseparable from the right of property. It is not enough to be the director of
a trust; it is necessary to be a stockholder. The victory of the bureaucracy in
this decisive sphere would mean its conversion into a new possessing class"
(1970b: 254).

I knew that the confirmation of Trotsky's negative prognosis would
be unlikely to stir widespread interest in Trotskyism as an alternative to
Stalinism; but I was optimist enough to believe that many non-Trotskyist

socialist militants and left intellectuals might finally appreciate the importance of weighing Trotsky's observations as they drew their own conclusions about the debacle of Stalinism. In this hour of capitalist victory over
the distorted material embodiment of the socialist idea and of pervasive
disorientation on the radical left concerning the way forward in the struggle for world socialism, what, indeed, could be more appropriate—and
urgently necessary—than to revisit the ideas of the man who defended
this idea more vigorously than perhaps any other in the twentieth century?
Who better to consult than the Chairman of the St. Petersburg Soviet during the Russian Revolution of 1905; the main organizer of the Bolshevik
insurrection of 1917 and the co-founder with Vladimir Lenin of the Soviet
state and the Communist International; the architect of the Red Army and
the mastermind of the Soviet victory in the Civil War of 1918–21; the man
with whom an ailing Lenin had sought a bloc against the growing power
of Stalin; the leader of the Left Opposition within the CPSU and the most
powerful critic of Stalin's bureaucratic dictatorship; the theorist of "permanent revolution," who, exiled from his own country in 1929, carried
out a tireless struggle against the disastrous policies of the Kremlin-loyal
Communist parties; the foremost champion of the principles of socialist democracy during the 1930s; and the founder, in 1938, of the Fourth
International. Leon Trotsky's voice was silenced in 1940; a Stalinist assassin
saw to that. Yet his writings remained surprisingly fresh, and his analysis
to the point. To many of the questions troubling socialists in the 1990s,
Trotsky had provided highly relevant "answers" over 50 years previously.
Remarkably, they remained some of the best responses that could be given
to the current ideological offensive of world capitalism against the fundamental ideas of socialism.

Alas, apart from a handful of putatively Trotskyist publications, little
interest was exhibited in revisiting Trotsky's ideas at this critical historical
juncture, and very few of the post-mortems on "actually-existing socialism" produced by leftist academics over the next few years were to pay
much attention to his classic analysis of what had gone wrong with the
Russian socialist revolution.[1] As had been the pattern for several decades,
Trotsky's ideas were substantially ignored—not only by erstwhile Stalinists

but by most of the "independent socialist left" as well. As the capitalist mass media wallowed in anti-communist triumphalism, Trotsky's powerful analysis was largely abandoned to warring Trotskyist groups to "champion" in myriad and often mutually conflicting ways.

None of this should have been particularly surprising in light of Trotsky's poignant admonition to his followers in 1927 that a defeat of the "international revolution" could only strengthen the psychological bases of "national reformism." Even so, at a time when national reformism, whether in its Stalinist or social-democratic versions, appeared itself to have reached an historic dead end, one could only wonder at the attitude of all those self-styled "unrepentant socialists" who remained closed to Trotsky's analysis out of visceral and habitual anti-Trotskyist prejudice. The damage done by Stalinism to the socialist project seemed here to reveal its terrible comprehensiveness. For not only had the Stalinism-socialism identity succeeded in repelling millions from the very idea of socialism, but, tragically, the politics, practices, and ideological legacy of Stalinism were continuing to exercise a perfidious influence on "progressive politics" in new and ostensibly "anti-Stalinist" forms. For if a common denominator existed along a broad spectrum of left politics—from the post-Stalinist "left reformism" of erstwhile Communist parties to the "post-Marxist" identity politics of "new social movement" enthusiasts—it seemed to manifest itself most strikingly as a persistent determination to ignore Trotsky and the theoretical and political heritage he represented.

The hostility or indifference that characterizes the attitudes of many on the putatively socialist left toward Trotsky's fundamental ideas is both perverse and profoundly unfortunate, for these ideas are not merely the opinions of one controversial figure in the history of Marxist socialism. Rather, they constitute a largely successful crystallization of over 100 years of proletarian socialist theory and practice. The question of coming to terms with Trotsky's ideas is therefore by no means simply a matter of identifying with the personality "Trotsky" against the personality "Stalin." Instead, it is a matter of *recovering* the revolutionary, internationalist, and democratic traditions of classical Marxism, of *reclaiming* a rich body of theoretical and political "capital" that is entirely indispensable to the socialist left as it seeks to regain the initiative in world politics and prepares itself for the decisive struggles against capital that lie ahead.

II

In the long view of history, the twentieth century may well be remembered as a time when "socialist construction" was attempted under conditions virtually guaranteed to ensure its failure and the (temporary) ideological rearmament of world capitalism in the midst of its global-structural crisis. The recipe: create conditions in which it is all but impossible for the more backward sectors of the world to achieve economic and social development *except* by breaking away from the world capitalist system and "socializing" their economies; encircle the countries that take this "socialist road," blackmail them, invade them, force them into arms races they manifestly cannot afford, deny them access to technological innovations through trade embargoes, and do everything possible to force upon their leaderships the conclusion that reintegration into the capitalist-dominated world is their best option short of thermonuclear "star wars." Having crippled them, hold them up as examples of "Communism" and as the "inevitable" product of class-struggle socialism and anti-imperialism, and then very simply declare that, however good socialism looks "in theory," it can't hold a candle to capitalism "in practice."

The agents of world capitalism hardly concocted the twentieth century experience out of a recipe book. Nor did they welcome the socialist revolution of October 1917. But they did make the best of a highly worrisome situation. Containment was the strategy, and containment, in the long run, produced the desired results. Even the creation of *deformed workers' states*—in Eastern Europe under the auspices of Soviet military power and in Asia through Stalinist-led social revolutions in which the principal insurrectionary forces were peasant armies—failed to put in place a socialist international division of labour. Indeed, the proliferation of bureaucratized workers' states merely multiplied the national-reformist "experiments" in building "socialism in one country," while seeming to confirm the incompatibility of any feasible socialism with the classical Marxist commitment to working-class self-emancipation and socialist democracy. Thus, long before the Soviet "experiment" in socialist construction began to falter seriously, the strategy of containment had already helped to distill a highly potent ideological concoction: the Stalinism-communism identity. A political tradition and movement that had always been in the forefront of the struggle for democratic rights, civil liberties, and a delegatory "direct democracy" became identified with a police state, the Gulag, and mass murder. However impressive the economic and military successes of the Soviet Union were, its deserved reputation as a "closed" and often savagely repressive society stood as a major obstacle to winning over decisive numbers in the West to a program of socialist transformation. At the same time, the survival of capitalism in the West ensured the continual reproduction of the conditions that sustained Stalinism and undermined any prospect for a "healthier" transition to socialism in the existing degenerated and deformed workers' states.

The argument is frequently made against those who would try to distinguish the heritage of authentic Marxism from its Stalinist caricature that any such exercise is quixotic and "counter-factual" at best and irresponsible at worst. Only blind faith, it is said, could lead anyone to believe that a non-Stalinist version of socialism is possible. But if Marxists have "faith" in anything, it is simply the capacity of human beings to use their rational faculties to fashion a better world for themselves and future generations—not a perfect world, but a world that will at least dispense with such supposedly "eternal" principles of capitalist civilization as the "necessity" of economic competition and exploitation (that is, of winners and losers within the global division of labour), that will equalize the conditions of human individuals in such a way that "the free development of each [will be] the condition for the free development of all" (Marx & Engels 1998: 41), and that will develop the fruits of human reason and scientific discovery for the common good of humanity.

It is precisely *prejudice* and not scientific reason that the publicity agents of capitalism invoke to sustain the Stalinism-communism identity—in particular, the pervasive prejudice that one's own society represents the best of all possible worlds and that "actually existing capitalism" is the pinnacle of human social development. This is a prejudice that socialists have always felt obliged to combat. Even so, they have often done so in a confused fashion. For as much as pro-Moscow Communists or Maoists sanctified the "models" to which they declared fealty, they were also sustained by the belief that different "national roads" to socialism would inevitably produce "new models" free of the more unattractive features of the Soviet or Chinese regimes. And as much as "democratic socialists" sought to repudiate the "totalitarian Communism" of the Soviet bloc, Yugoslavia, Cuba, and China, they also drew strength from the knowledge that these societies had put the lie to the capitalist claims that "planned economies don't work" and "competitive markets alone can promote economic rationality and development." The disappearance of the Stalinist models of central planning could not fail to weaken the resistance of Western socialists to the old prejudices, and those socialists who had always been most inclined to a "worship of the accomplished fact" suffered the greatest immune deficiency. As the ideologists of capitalism congratulated themselves for having "just said no" to what Raymond Aron long ago described as "the opiate of the intellectuals," Western socialists and Marxist intellectuals could not help but wonder whether the continuing plausibility of Marxist socialism in their own minds attested more to their steadfastness in defense of a worthy political and intellectual legacy or to a chemical imbalance in their grey matter induced by repeated and habitual ingestion of its seductive concepts.

Still, facts are stubborn things, and the fact is that too many erstwhile socialist activists and intellectuals have too easily returned to the liberal-democratic fold for anyone to take seriously the idea that Marxism ever possessed much narcotic effect. Indeed it has only been the continuing theoretical and moral superiority of the Marxist socialist position over the pro-capitalist one—amply confirmed by the disastrous results of the vaunted "free market reforms" in the former Soviet bloc—that has prevented the more honest and politically prepared socialist intellectuals from succumbing to the enormous ideological pressures bearing down upon them in the wake of the "collapse of Communism." Peering into the hideously scarred face of "actually existing socialism" as the Ceaucescus, the Giereks, and the Gorbachevs were toppled, all socialists were inevitably visited with mixed feelings; but few were grasping at fideistic straws when they insisted that none of this proved very much about the relative merits of capitalism and socialism. After years of mismanagement by corrupt bureaucracies that repeatedly contributed to the derailing of socialist movements throughout the world in the name of "peaceful coexistence" with the capitalist bully-boys, a weak and decrepit caricature of socialism had been laid prostrate by a capitalist world order commanding many times its resources—and quite consciously betrayed by a "priviligentsia" masquerading as "democrats" (Singer 1991).

Was this the irrefutable "proof" of capitalism's superiority over socialism? Only those with the weakest of ideological immune systems could agree, especially as US President George Bush crowed that "Communism didn't just fall—it was pushed!" As for those who had learned something from Trotsky, the outcome of what Isaac Deutscher once called the Great Contest between the Soviet bloc and the West could only serve to confirm once again that in the battle of ideas, as in so many other conflicts, "might makes right"—if only for those who are inclined to support the mighty. Trotsky's writings provide us with an invaluable conceptual apparatus with which to answer the self-serving "balance sheet on communism" that "the mighty" and their sycophants are doing their best to promulgate. The appropriate starting point is Trotsky's "law of uneven and combined development"— perhaps his greatest single theoretical contribution to historical materialism. In his magisterial *History of the Russian Revolution*, Trotsky writes:

> A backward country assimilates the material and intellectual conquests of the advanced countries. But this does not mean that it follows them slavishly, reproduces all the stages of their past.... [Capitalism] prepares and in a certain sense realizes the universality and permanence of man's development. By this a repetition of the forms of development by different nations is ruled out.... The possibility of skipping over intermediate steps is of course by no means absolute. Its degree is determined by the economic and cultural capacities of the country.... Unevenness, the most general law of the historic

process, reveals itself most sharply and complexly in the destiny of the backward countries. Under the whip of external necessity their backward culture is compelled to make leaps. From the universal law of unevenness thus derives another law which ... we may call the law of *combined development*—by which we mean a drawing together of the different stages of the journey, a combining of separate steps, an amalgam of archaic with more contemporary forms. Without this law, to be taken of course in its whole material content, it is impossible to understand the history of Russia.... (1967, Vol. 1: 22–23)

The law of uneven and combined development is predicated on the proposition that capitalism has created *a global totality* and *a world history* outside of which it is entirely impossible to comprehend the dynamics, course, and limits of revolutionary processes in countries that Lenin defined as "the weak links in the imperialist chain." This law—adumbrated but not fully formulated by Marx in his writings on the Russian peasant commune (Smith 1994: 33–34)—is not only the conceptual basis of Trotsky's famous theory of "permanent revolution"; it is clearly also the real foundation of Trotsky's characterization of the Soviet Union as a *transitional* formation, "midway" between capitalism and socialism. While it is perfectly true that Marx never produced a theory of "transitional social formations" (a fact cited by some of Trotsky's critics to dispute his analysis of the Soviet Union), it seems quite reasonable to suppose that Marx would have embraced "the law of uneven and combined development" and the theory of transitional social formations as crucial additions to historical-materialist theory.

To accept the law of uneven and combined development means to accept Trotsky's insight that transitional formations standing between capitalism and socialism in less developed countries will necessarily fall well short of the "norms" established by Marxist theory for the "healthy" development of socialism. As Trotsky noted: "The backward nation ... not infrequently debases the achievements borrowed from outside in the process of adapting them to its own more primitive culture" (1967: 23). The attempt to implement the Marxist program of social transformation in backward Russia— an attempt dictated not by the "power lust" of Bolshevik intellectuals, but by the dynamics of a revolutionary process framed by definite historical and global realities—could not have failed to produce severe deformations of that program, deformations that anti-communists in the West were sure to seize upon and exploit to their own ends.

Of course, the demonization of the post-capitalist states by the West had far less to do with any presumed deviations from Marxist norms ("human rights abuses," etc.) than with their remarkable success over an extended period of time in charting a course of development that allowed them some real independence from capitalist imperialism, that permitted some of them to modernize and industrialize while most of the capitalist periphery stagnated or regressed, and that even allowed a challenge by the Soviet Union to the global military hegemony of the United States during the Cold War era. From this standpoint, Trotsky's analysis poses anew a key question: *what precisely* was it that enabled the bureaucratized workers' states to register the successes they did? Was it the socialist elements of the planned economy? Or was it the totalitarian methods of the Stalinist oligarchies? Marxist dialectics allow no tidy compartmentalization of the economic and the political, of the proto-socialist and the despotic, as discrete elements of this "transitional" synthesis. Yet some discrimination is both possible and mandatory. The wilfully ignorant and meanly tendentious inclination of the capitalist propaganda mills is to insist that what allowed the USSR to emerge as the fearsome "threat" that it was to the West was precisely its totalitarianism and *not* its elements of socialist economic rationality. Thus, the most draconian and repressive features of the Stalinist state are held up as its "real" source of strength—as if the purges of the CPSU and the Red Army in the 1930s had "steeled" the Soviet state on the eve of World War II; or the forced collectivization of agriculture and the concomitant deaths of millions of peasants had "strengthened" the Soviet economy; or the "proletarian science" policy that brought an end to free academic inquiry and scientific research had "enhanced" the Soviets' ability to compete with the West in technological innovation!

All of this contrasts in the starkest way with the picture painted by Trotsky, for whom the Stalinist bureaucracy was at best a blunted and unreliable instrument of "primitive socialist accumulation" and central planning[2]: "[The] privations of the masses in the USSR, the omnipotence of the privileged caste, which ... lifted itself above the nation and its misery, finally, the rampant club-law of the bureaucrats are not consequences of the socialist method of economy but of the isolation and backwardness of the USSR caught in the ring of capitalist encirclement. The wonder is that under such exceptionally unfavorable conditions planned economy has managed to demonstrate its insuperable benefits" (1963: 41). On this view, what gains the Soviet Union was able to make in productivity, in the creation of a modern industrial infrastructure, and in general social development were accomplished entirely in spite of the bureaucratism, the repression, and the totalitarian regime of "fear, lies and flattery" that characterized Stalinist rule. To liberate the full potential of socialist planning, the Stalinist oligarchy would have to be removed by a popular political revolution that would return the governance of the state and the economy to democratically constituted workers councils and establish a revolutionary and internationalist regime that would seek an integration of the Soviet economy into an international socialist division of labour as rapidly as possible. This was the inescapable programmatic upshot of Trotsky's theory—and strategic perspective—of permanent revolution:

[The theory] pointed out that the democratic tasks of the backward bourgeois nations lead directly, in our epoch, to the dictatorship of the proletariat and that the dictatorship of the proletariat puts socialist tasks on the order of the day.... The socialist revolution begins on national foundations—but it cannot be completed within these foundations. The maintenance of the proletarian revolution within a national framework can only be a provisional state of affairs, even though, as the experience of the Soviet Union shows, one of long duration....

In respect of the techniques of production, socialist society must represent a higher stage than capitalism. To aim at building a *nationally isolated* socialist society means, in spite of all passing successes, to pull the productive forces backward even as compared with capitalism. To attempt ... to realize a shut-off proportionality of all the branches of economy within a national framework, means to pursue a reactionary utopia. (1969: 132–33, 146)

The contrasts between Trotsky's Marxist assessment of Stalinism and the "politically correct" bromides of pro-capitalist ideologists concerning the alleged incompatibility of socialist planning and "democracy" are rooted not in different bodies of empirical information, but in different *programs*. Recognizing in the Stalinist *nomenklatura* a kindred love of privilege and power, the world bourgeoisie could only have hoped that this social stratum would one day "wise up," cut a deal with them, and dismantle the "socialist beginnings" in favour of a socio-economic order propitious to a truly obscene (that is, typically capitalist) accumulation and concentration of wealth in private hands. Little wonder then that their ideologists should have identified as most "dynamic" and "viable" in the Soviet system precisely what Trotsky regarded as most regressive and emblematic of that system's partial yet incomplete break with class society: the unrelenting hostility of the bureaucratic elite to the independent power and activity of the working class, both domestically and internationally.

III

It is not new to note that the identification of socialism and communism with Stalinism has injured the attractive power and credibility of the Marxist-socialist project. Nor is it surprising that this identification has been so successfully implanted in the consciousness of masses of people around the world. We are presented here with a truly striking instance of Winston Churchill's observation that a lie can be half way around the world before the truth gets its boots on (he should have known!). Those who would dispute this identity—this lie—have had to contend with the formidable propaganda capacities of *both* the capitalist world and the Stalinist states. But like all effective propaganda, the Stalinism-communism identity could have had no credibility without having had some basis in reality. And indeed, as Trotsky insisted, Stalinist "real socialism" was always a peculiar *synthesis* of socialist, capitalist, and even precapitalist elements—a social formation in which some, though by no means all, of the programmatic canons of Marxist socialism had found an expression, however distorted. The collectivization of the means of production, the displacement of market forces by central planning in the articulation of the social division of labour, and the state monopoly of foreign trade had long been seen by Marxists as necessary, if not completely sufficient, conditions for the transition to socialism; and, despite the proletariat's political expropriation by an oligarchy acting in its name, the presence of these socialist elements within the Soviet system had clearly conferred upon it a dynamic and character altogether different from those of capitalism. As Trotsky noted during the period of the second Five Year Plan:

> In the most *favorable* circumstances—that is in the absence of inner disturbances and external catastrophes—it would require several more five-year periods before the Soviet Union could fully assimilate those economic and educative achievements upon which the first-born nations of capitalist civilization have expended centuries. The application of *socialist* methods for the solution of *pre-socialist* problems—that is the very essence of the present economic and cultural work of the Soviet Union. (1970b: 56–57)

Unfortunately, many socialists failed to acknowledge this in their haste to dissociate the program of Marxist socialism from the actual experiences of "socialist construction" in the Stalinist-ruled workers' states. To be sure, the impulses behind characterizing these states as "state capitalist" or "bureaucratic collectivist" involved a variety of theoretical and political motivations, including the desire to absolve the Marxist, and sometimes the Leninist, tradition of all responsibility for the odious and patently anti-socialist practices of Stalinism: the strangulation of workers democracy, the physical liquidation of real or imagined opponents of the ruling coterie, the suppression of free political and intellectual debate, the encouragement of patriarchal relations and national chauvinism, and so on. In addition, however, such theoretical characterizations almost always went hand in hand with a *programmatic refusal* to defend these states against imperialist attacks or internal attempts at restoring (real) capitalism. They served, in other words, to relieve their proponents from the onerous duty of swimming against some very powerful currents in defense of what most of their "fellow citizens" considered The Enemy.[3]

In a world bitterly polarized between "democratic capitalism" and Stalinist "real socialism," there is no doubt that Trotsky's programmatic admonition of 1939 was an enormously difficult one to champion: "[The] question of the overthrowing of the Soviet bureaucracy is for us subordinate to the question of preserving state property in the means of production in the USSR; [the] question of preserving state property in the means of production in the USSR is subordinate for us to the question of the world proletarian revolution" (1970c: 21). Yet it was precisely this position that Trotsky's most faithful followers continued to defend against great odds and, no doubt, at some considerable cost to their potential political influence. From this "orthodox Trotskyist" perspective, the degenerated and deformed workers' states embodied real gains for the working class of the world, gains that were well worth defending. Trotsky had made the essential point only a few months prior to his assassination by an agent of Stalin's GPU: "It is the duty of revolutionists to defend tooth and nail every position gained by the working class, whether it involves democratic rights, wage scales, or so colossal a conquest of mankind as the nationalization of the means of production and planned economy. Those who are incapable of defending conquests already gained can never fight for new ones" (1973a: 166).

In hindsight it should now be clear that the Stalinist bureaucratic oligarchy was no "new ruling class" presiding over a class-antagonistic mode of production (whether state capitalism or bureaucratic collectivism). Rather, as Trotsky insisted, it was a parasitic, brittle, and sociologically superfluous stratum that owed its power and privileges—indeed, its very existence—to the survival on a world scale of that most aggressive and resilient of class-antagonistic modes of production: capitalism.[4] Indeed, this oligarchy was little more than an unstable "tumour" balancing between the proletarian-socialist forms of the Soviet economy and the pressures of world capitalism: a layer that was destined to fragment over the most fundamental of questions. It was to take about 50 years for Trotsky's forecast to be confirmed in relation to the Soviet Union—although its confirmation had been foreshadowed by other events, notably the decomposition of the Hungarian Stalinist regime under the impact of the workers' political revolution of 1956. As it entered into terminal crisis in the late 1980s, the Soviet bureaucracy *did not behave* like a "ruling class" in crisis; and it did not seek to defend a recognizable set of "common interests," as any ruling class worth its salt would have done. Instead, the bureaucracy *did* fragment, though not along the lines or to the extent that it might have had the Soviet working class entered the political stage as an independent actor, bearing its own program of socialist renewal.

Facing powerful currents of capitalist restoration, and a politically disoriented working class that had yet to articulate an independent program, the bureaucracy split into three principal camps: unreconstructed Stalinists who longed for a return to the "normalcy" of the Brezhnev era; reform-minded Stalinists who sought a relaxation of the CPSU's political and ideological monopoly (*glasnost*) and an economy restructured along "market-socialist" lines (*perestroika*); and an increasingly self-conscious layer of technocrats and "out-bureaucrats" (like Yeltsin) who took up the project of full capitalist restoration and reconciliation with Western imperialism.[5] As the political fortunes of these camps rose or fell, individual members of the *nomenklatura* vacillated and often moved swiftly between them; few seemed guided by firm principles. But no one can be certain that a large segment of the *nomenklatura* would not have sided with the working class had Trotsky's scenario of a "workers' political revolution" been realized: "A real civil war could not develop between the Stalinist bureaucracy and the resurgent proletariat but between the proletariat and the active forces of the counter-revolution. In the event of an open clash between the two mass camps, there cannot even be talk of the bureaucracy playing an independent role. Its polar flanks would be flung to the different sides of the barricade" (1972a: 118). However, owing to the passivity of the Soviet working class, itself the product of 65 years of Stalinist rule, an "open clash between the two mass camps" failed to develop, and the forces of capitalist counter-revolution scored an extraordinarily easy, and almost bloodless, victory.

IV

The damage done to the socialist project has not been confined to the association of the socialist ideal with the ugly realities of Stalinism. As noted earlier, the ideological legacy of Stalinism continues to weigh heavily on much that passes for "progressive politics" today. The irony is that it is most often the pseudo-orthodox trappings of the Stalinist legacy—the debased catchphrases of "Marxist-Leninist doctrine" as long promulgated by the Stalinist apparatuses—are held responsible for the Stalinist debacle rather than the departures from Marxism and Leninism that so clearly marked its practice. Insofar as Trotskyism claims the mantle of authentic Bolshevism, revolutionary Marxism, and the October socialist revolution, many on the self-styled socialist left consider it only a step or two removed from the more odious practices of the Stalinists. After all, Bolshevik-Leninism is supposed to have led, with inexorable "logic," to Stalinism. Altogether ignored are Trotsky's convincing efforts, in the last years of his life, to demolish this canard, which he quite perceptively saw as serving the interests of the Stalinists and the capitalists alike:

> The state built up by the Bolsheviks [reflected] not only the thought and will of Bolshevism but also the cultural level of the country, the social composition of the population, the pressure of a barbaric past and no less barbaric world imperialism. To represent the process of degeneration of the Soviet state as the evolution of pure Bolshevism is to ignore social reality in the name of one of its elements, isolated by pure logic.... [C]ertainly, Stalinism "grew out" of Bolshevism, not logically, however, but dialectically; not as a revolutionary affirmation but as a Thermidorian negation. (1970e: 3, 15)

For many on the "anti-Stalinist" left, fidelity to the concepts of "dictatorship of the proletariat," "vanguard party," "democratic centralism," "workers' revolution," "centrally planned economy," and so on disqualifies Trotskyism as an alternative to Stalinism worthy of consideration. Indeed, many leftists now applaud the open repudiation of these concepts by ex-Stalinists seeking to redefine and reposition themselves as born-again social democrats who have supposedly learned their lesson about the evils of Leninism. Trotsky's argument that Leninism, no less than Marxism, is a body of ideas to which the Stalinists laid a *false* claim seldom receives the consideration that it deserves. And yet, ironically, those on the left who would collapse Stalinism and Trotskyism into the same Leninist chowder often seem completely unaware of the Stalinist provenance and/or filiations of many of their own ideas and practices. The examples are legion, but a few deserve particular mention:

1. The idea that the organization of "broad coalitions of progressives" is fundamental to socialist strategy today is one whose lineage can be traced back to the Popular Front policy of Stalin's Comintern in the 1930s and 1940s; indeed it remains the foundation of the policy of Stalinist and post-Stalinist parties to this day. Such coalition-building, as it is usually conceived, has little in common with the Leninist tactic of the united front, and is explicitly counterposed to a perspective of *class struggle* on behalf of a *socialist program*. The principal purpose of such coalitionism—whether it takes the form of a "propaganda bloc" against free trade, a coalition government between social democrats and bourgeois liberals, or a "popular front" in which ostensible communists garnish the class-collaborationist fare with a hammer and sickle—is to tie working-class and socialist forces to a supposedly "progressive program" that stops well short of a full attack on capital. Given that the historical results of this strategy of coalitionism have been nothing less than disastrous, one can only wonder why so few non-Trotskyist socialists are willing to consider the long-standing Trotskyist critique of it.

2. The "sectoralism" that pervades the thinking of "new social movement" activists and theorists can easily be seen as a *generalization* of the "economism" against which Lenin fought in the workers' movement and to which the Stalinists eventually returned Communist trade union work. The narrow "workerism" and "economism" of Communist-led or Communist-influenced labour movements have

long provided a powerful rationale for writing off the workers movement as the leading force in the struggle against all manifestations of
social oppression. Similarly, Lenin's idea of building a revolutionary
workers party as the "tribune of the oppressed" has been discredited
as a result of the Stalinists' frequent unwillingness to champion in a
serious way the struggles of women, racial and national minorities, or
other oppressed groups. The false association of "Leninist orthodoxy"
with Stalinist practice has thereby prepared the way for the narrowly
sectoralist ideology that only women can fight women's oppression,
that only Blacks can fight Black oppression, that only gays can fight
gay oppression, etc. The common denominator, however, of all such
sectoralisms—trade union economism, middle-class feminism, Black
nationalism, gay and lesbian "identity politics"—is *bourgeois reformism:* the conviction that the just demands of the oppressed and the
exploited can be met within the framework of capitalism. Thus, the
Stalinist *abandonment* of Lenin's principles has enormously abetted
the sectoralism and reformism that characterize the "new social movements" of the present day, as well as the more explicitly class-collaborationist policies of the mass reformist parties of the working class.

3. The idea of "market socialism" has numerous roots, but among them
are the experiments in economic reform carried out by Stalinist
regimes firmly committed to the doctrine of building socialism in one
country and preserving their anti-working class political monopolies,
but willing to experiment with market mechanisms capable of "disciplining" their working classes and compensating for the rigidities
of bureaucratic planning. Domination of the debate over the political
economy of socialism by Stalinists, reform Stalinists, and traditional
market socialists opposed to central planning has served to divert
attention from Trotsky's fruitful idea that "only the interaction of three
elements, of state planning, of the market, and of Soviet democracy can
provide ... correct leadership in the transitional epoch" (1973b: 275).[6]

Several years ago, Ellen Meiksins Wood (1986) traced the striking parallels between the ideology of post-Marxists like Laclau and Mouffe and the

"true socialists" against whom Marx inveighed in the 1840s. Trotsky also noted how those anxious to embrace "new ideas" frequently revive very old ones: "Reactionary epochs like ours not only disintegrate and weaken the working class and its vanguard but also lower the general ideological level of the movement and throw political thinking back to stages long since passed through" (1970e: 9). Stalinism was itself a "throwback" at the ideological level—and its enormous influence within the world's labour, socialist, and anti-colonialist movements was necessarily regressive. Far from advancing a Marxist program of working-class political independence, Stalinism revived the class-collaborationist politics of right-wing social democracy (Millerandism). Far from constructing democratic-centralist vanguard parties on Lenin's model, the Stalinists returned to a "party of the whole class" model differing from Kautsky's only in its spurious internationalism and more ruthless bureaucratic centralism. Far from promoting socialist revolution in the colonial and semi-colonial countries, the Stalinists restored the "stages theory" of the Mensheviks and a policy of subordinating the workers' movement to the "progressive national bourgeoisie" in the struggle against imperialism. And far from advancing a strategy of world revolution, the Stalinists revived utopian-socialist notions of capital-labour harmony, of "peaceful coexistence" between the socialist and capitalist "camps," and of "unique national roads to socialism."

Stalinism has indeed contributed mightily to the lowering of the "general ideological level." How could it have been otherwise? As Trotsky noted incisively, "the bureaucracy which became a reactionary force in the USSR cannot play a revolutionary role on the world arena" (1973c: 106). And further:

Having strangled independence and initiative in the lower ranks of the people at home, [the Soviet bureaucracy] naturally cannot provide critical thought and revolutionary daring on the world arena. Moreover, as a ruling and privileged stratum, it values infinitely more the help and friendship of those who are kin to them in social type in the West—bourgeois radicals, reformist parliamentarians, trade union bureaucrats—than of the rank-and-file workers who are separated from it by social chasms.... The fact is that in its capacity as leader of the Communist International, the nationally limited and conservative, ignorant and irresponsible Soviet bureaucracy has brought nothing but misfortunes to the workers' movement of the world. As though in historic justice, the present international position of the Soviet Union is determined to a far higher degree by the consequences of the defeat of the world proletariat, than by the successes of an isolated Socialist construction. (1970b: 191)

The ideological convergence that we are now witnessing among rightward moving ex-Stalinists, social democrats, and "new social movement" activists has been prepared by years of accommodation by the left (not excluding elements of the putatively Trotskyist left) to the "realities" of the global power of capital and by the defeats resulting from these accommodations. Not surprisingly, the convergence has been around a set of propositions, some of which I noted above, that are very distant from the ideas and program of Marxist socialism. In this connection, Trotsky's remarks of 1937 are perhaps more germane today than ever:

In [reactionary times] the task of the vanguard is above all not to let itself be carried along by the backward flow: it must swim against the current. If an unfavorable relation of forces prevents it from holding the positions that it has won, it must at least retain its ideological positions, because in them is expressed the dearly-paid experience of the past. Fools will consider this policy "sectarian". Actually, it is the only means of preparing for a new tremendous surge forward with the coming historical tide. (1970d: 9)

V

It is inevitable that among those who continue to identify with Marxist socialism important differences of opinion will persist as to what the lessons of the past indicate about the current tasks of socialists. We all wish to prepare for the "coming historical tide" as best we can. But our political educations and life experiences play a huge role in determining how we define the hard-won "ideological positions" that we wish to preserve as we swim against the current. Some of us carry heavier backpacks than others. Some of us have a richer theoretical and historical understanding of the socialist movement than others. And some of us, owing to personal circumstances, risk more than others do by associating ourselves with certain ideas. These differences, among many others, determine a real heterogeneity of consciousness among Marxist socialists, and this heterogeneity must produce a myriad of programmatic, strategic, organizational, and tactical differences.

I was mindful of this as I read Ralph Miliband's *Socialism for a Sceptical Age* (1994), the final and in some ways crowning work of a dedicated socialist scholar from whom many socialists, including myself, have learned a great deal. Sadly, in spite of Miliband's creditable attempt to restate the enduring value of the socialist idea and, on this basis, contribute to a theoretical rearming of the socialist left, the book is a frequently misleading contribution to the necessary rearmament—one that fails to confront some of the most vexing problems of socialist strategy or to assimilate fully the lessons of past defeats. The deficiencies of Miliband's political vision and strategic proposals are nowhere more in evidence than in his short critical discussion of Trotskyism.

Miliband was no crude anti-Trotskyist. Rather he was an honourable representative of a proud breed of self-styled "independent socialists." As such, he attempts a balanced assessment of Trotskyism that, not surprisingly, yields the conclusion that what is best in Trotskyism can be reconciled with his own "left reformist" stance and what is worst can be rejected as irrelevant sectarianism. Hence, Miliband allows that "the propositions which are at the core of Trotskyism ... do not warrant the instant dismissal which they are commonly given; in fact, they present a significant challenge to anyone seriously concerned with the advance of socialism."[7] According to Miliband these propositions are fourfold.

The first is "the expectation that, sooner or later, the contradictions of capitalism will become so acute as to create a revolutionary situation leading to the overthrow of the existing regime by the working class under the leader-ship of a revolutionary party able to seize the opportunity presented by the situation." This is closely related to the third core proposition that Miliband attributes to Trotskyism, namely that "a radical transformation of the social order cannot be achieved by way of measures of reform alone, that the rul-ing class will not abandon its positions without unremitting and, if need be, violent resistance, and that a major confrontation between revolution-ary and reactionary forces is therefore inevitable." While Miliband agrees that only a very "utopian" socialist would fail to regard "a gradual, consti-tutional and peaceful transition to socialism" as an "extremely problem-atic enterprise," he argues that the Trotskyist "scenario" of "revolutionary upheaval led to victory by a 'vanguard' party is nowhere remotely on the cards." In his view, then, the efforts of socialists are more profitably directed toward the exploitation of those political opportunities for socialist edu-cation, mobilization, coalition-building, organization, electoral advance, and government formation that are provided by the constitutional guaran-tees of capitalist democracy. True, the bourgeoisie will not relinquish their power without a fight and will resist socialist change tenaciously; but the "real question is how well they would be able to do so, which itself greatly depends on what a socialist government and movement would do about it." Moreover, while capitalist crisis will certainly produce "violent eruptions," these should not be "confused with a 'revolutionary situation' in which, in countries with a capitalist democratic regime, a majority of the population, or even a substantial minority, would support the overthrow of the regime under the leadership of a revolutionary party." It is for these seemingly real-istic and sensible reasons that Miliband rejects the Trotskyists' "revolution-ary (or insurrectionary) position."

The political neophyte might be excused for assuming from Miliband's argument that the main focus of Trotskyist activity is the preparation of an armed insurrection against "capitalist democratic regimes." But this is not and never has been the case. Insurrectionary activity can only be envisaged during genuinely "revolutionary situations"—and these arise only periodi-cally and under exceptional circumstances. It is, however, important to be clear on what might produce such circumstances. "Capitalist crisis" or the intensified "contradictions of capitalism" have certainly underlaid all of the "revolutionary situations" that have materialized in advanced capitalist countries over the past century. War, too, as Lenin observed, can often be the "mother of revolution"—and capitalism has had an impressive record of fomenting wars, large and small. But, contrary to Miliband's implication, neither the absence of "capitalist democracy" nor the complete collapse of a capitalist economy has been a necessary ingredient for the eruption of revolutionary situations. If one surveys even a partial list of episodes that are usually adduced by Trotskyists as examples of "revolutionary" or "near-revolutionary" situations (Germany and Northern Italy after World War I; July 1927 in Austria; June 1936 in France; Spain in 1936–37; Italy and Greece after World War II; Indonesia in 1965; France in 1968; Chile in 1973; Portugal in 1974–75), it is apparent that many of these situations were *preceded by the type of broad-based popular mobilization and/or electoral success of working-class parties that Miliband posits as strategically essential to the transition to socialism.*

In the Trotskyists' view, all of these "lost" revolutionary opportunities attest to the need for a revolutionary party prepared to carry through the struggle against capitalism to the end.[8] All attest to the very great likelihood that when they are at last able to assume office, the reformist and "centrist" parties of the working class, often in coalition with openly bourgeois forces, will seek to limit mass mobilizations and prevent the organization from below of organs of dual power and militias of armed self-defense. And all attest to the rapidity with which the reformist leaders of the working class can turn against their mass base, and in the process accelerate the growth of "Far Left" organizations. In other words, the actual historical record of serious confrontations between the capitalist order and rising mass movements toward socialism suggests quite clearly that those parties of the working class committed to a "gradualist" and "constitutionalist" approach will end up in the camp of the *counter-revolution.* This was the case for the Russian Mensheviks in 1917; for the German Social Democrats in 1918–19; for the French Socialists and Communists in 1936 facing the general strike of June of that year; for the Spanish Socialists and Communists, who suppressed the Catalonian working class in 1937 in the name of "anti-fascist unity"; for the Italian Communists, who between 1944 and 1948 sought to disarm a revolutionary-minded working class and re-stabilize Italian capitalism through their participation in a coalition government of national unity; and for the Chilean Socialist and Communist parties, who, faced with a rising threat from the Right against the Popular Unity government in 1973, sought accommodations with the Christian Democrats and the armed forces while discouraging and openly repressing the independent organization of the masses. Miliband suggests that the need for insurrection would be removed by the simple resolve of "a socialist government" backed by a mass movement to stand firm against capitalist "resistance." But he is unable to cite a single instance where this has actually happened.

It is precisely in light of this historical record that the lessons of the October Revolution in Russia reassert their relevance—and it is the conviction of the Trotskyists that they have most adequately assimilated those precious lessons that sets them apart on the radical left. Miliband does not really address this claim, yet it is a vitally important one for all socialists to carefully assess. For ultimately the question concerns whether, in the context of episodes like the Russian Revolution of 1917, the Spanish Revolution of 1936, or the Portuguese Revolution of 1975, one will take one's stand with those seeking to limit the mass movement to "constitutionalist" avenues or with those seeking to lead the working class forward to the conquest of state power. To be a Trotskyist means to affirm well in advance of such revolutionary situations which side one will take in the midst of a decisive confrontation (a situation of "dual power"); and it is to proclaim the need to construct a party that will know how to resolve the confrontation decisively in favour of workers' power. Such a Trotskyist party will certainly distinguish itself from other leftist organizations in non-revolutionary conjunctures as well; but it will do so precisely as an organization of militants participating in broader movements of struggle against exploitation, oppression, and social injustice, articulating these struggles with a program of socialist transformation (as Trotsky's *Transitional Program* attempted), and, through it all, cultivating a "spirit of revolution" that has, at its core, a fundamental disrespect for the constitutional limitations, legal framework, and repressive agencies of the capitalist state.

This leads us directly to the second core proposition that Miliband attributes to Trotskyists. The proposition is derived directly from *The Civil War in France,* where Marx states that "the working class cannot simply lay hold of the ready-made state machinery, and wield it for its own purposes" (1974), but rather, in Miliband's words, "it must 'smash' that machinery and replace it with a state of an entirely new type, subject to genuine popular power, and well on the way to virtual disintegration." Arguing against this proposition, Miliband defends the view that the state can and must be transformed in "democratic directions," and that "means have to be found to combine state power and popular power." But in doing so he confuses two issues. One need not disagree with Miliband's point that the *immediate* result of a victorious socialist revolution is unlikely to be a workers' state well on its way to "withering away" to affirm that the conditions for a revolutionary victory *must* include the "smashing" of the *old* state machine. Certainly Trotskyists understand only too well that the Bolsheviks were obliged to rely on some of the structures and personnel of the old Czarist state in the process of constructing what Lenin candidly defined as "a workers' state with bureaucratic deformations," and that, owing to unfavourable internal and external conditions, the need for a rather coercive workers' state can persist over a protracted period. But Trotskyists are nonetheless quick to point out that a *sine qua non* of a socialist revolution is the "smashing" of what Marx and Engels always saw as the essential core of the state: its "armed body of men." No revolutionary transformation can succeed so long as the repressive apparatus put in place to defend the specific interests of the old ruling class remains intact. A *new* army, militia, police force, and judiciary must be established if the process of socialist reconstruction is to proceed on the basis of laws and statutes promulgated by the new class power.

Miliband's difference with the Trotskyist (and classical Marxist) position on the question of the state has an obvious connection with his aversion to "insurrectionary politics." The difference reduces itself once again to whether one proclaims, in advance, that a vital task of the socialist movement as it moves decisively to transform society is to confront the capitalist state's monopoly of arms—precisely by organizing workers' militias and revolutionary councils of rank-and-file soldiers, sailors, and air force personnel with the eventual purpose of splitting the armed forces and reconstituting them under a new (pro-socialist) leadership. To affirm the indispensability of setting the base of the armed forces against its top is to concede perforce to the indispensability of an "insurrection" at some decisive point in the confrontation between labour and capital, between the mass movement and the state.

There is a little-known episode that speaks volumes about the consequences of a socialist strategy that eschews "insurrection" and respects the boundaries of capitalist constitutional arrangements. Following an abortive coup attempt by officers of the Chilean armed forces in the summer of 1973, a series of arrests occurred in the naval installations at Valparaiso and Talcahuano. More than one hundred people were jailed on charges of "seditious activity"—the activity of organizing rank-and-file sailors to *resist* the preparations of the officer corps for a new *coup d'état* against Salvador Allende's "constitutionally elected" Popular Unity (UP) government. The "plotters" were brutally tortured and held incommunicado, and yet the UP government, knowing full well the nature of the charges brought against the accused "mutineers," refused to lift a finger in their defense. Twenty-nine of those arrested signed a smuggled-out letter that asked: "Is it a crime to defend the government, the Constitution, legality and the people? Or, on the other hand, is it legal not to respect the law, to overthrow the government and wipe out the lives of thousands of people? We will let the workers answer that." Unfortunately, the brutal answer of the military, on behalf of the bourgeoisie, came first. On September 11, Allende's regime was overthrown by the military and the independent organizations of the working class and peasantry were brutally crushed. The question that every "independent socialist" wary of "insurrectionary politics" must answer is this: in such a situation, should socialists acquiesce (as Allende's UP clearly did) in the repression of those courageously organizing against the forces of counter-revolution, or should they be in the forefront of popular efforts to thwart the counter-revolution and indeed to "smash" their main agencies, even if this means breaking decisively with the traditional leaderships of the working class? Surely those supporting the first option can only be

231

calling themselves socialists "as a result of a misunderstanding," as Trotsky once remarked of the American social democrat Norman Thomas.

The final core proposition that Miliband attributes to Trotskyism is "the notion that 'socialism in one country' is a nonsense and that revolution must be conceived on a global scale, with revolution in one country or in one continent detonating revolutionary upheavals elsewhere." This is an unfortunate way of posing the question of "permanent revolution" versus "socialism in one country"—one that betrays an inadequate understanding of Trotsky's position as well as the influence of Stalinist and social-democratic critiques of Trotskyism's supposed "ultra-left adventurism." Moreover, Miliband's response to the Trotskyist case against "socialism in one country" is an astonishingly simplistic one: "As for 'socialism in one country', it is quite true that no such thing can be 'achieved'. But once the notion of socialism as an achieved state has been rejected, and socialism is seen as an objective involving a permanent striving, the point loses much of its strength: it is possible for a socialist government to *advance* the process, without waiting for world revolution." The implication of this argument is that Trotsky was opposed to "advancing" the process of socialist construction in the Soviet Union until after the "world revolution"! This is an enormous injustice to Trotsky and entirely misses the point of his critique of "national reformism." The burden of Trotsky's position, as noted earlier in this chapter, was that the *subordination* of the world revolution to the project of building "socialism in one country" can only corrode the revolutionary fibre of ostensibly communist movements that come to regard their *main* task as promoting "good relations" between their "own" bourgeoisies and the "socialist countries." In the long run this has the effect of strengthening world capitalism as well as the forces of capitalist restoration in the "socialist world." Thus Trotsky argued: "In an isolated proletarian dictatorship, the internal and external contradictions grow inevitably along with the successes achieved. If it remains isolated, the proletarian state must finally fall victim to these contradictions. The way out for it lies only in the victory of the proletariat of the advanced countries" (1969: 133). Policies that *discourage* the international extension of socialism are therefore not only "anti-internationalist" and theoretically misguided as to the essential prerequisites of a socialism that would truly transcend capitalism; they are also profoundly inimical to the project of "advancing" socialist construction on a national foundation. As Trotsky argued in the text that launched the International Left Opposition to Stalinism:

> The theory of socialism in one country inexorably leads to an under-estimation of the difficulties which must be overcome and to an exaggeration of the achievements gained.... We must tell [the Soviet people] that we will enter on the path of *real* socialist construction only when the proletariat of the most advanced countries will have captured power; that it is necessary to work unremittingly for this, using both levers—the short lever of our internal economic efforts and the long lever of the international proletarian struggle. (1970f: 66)

When Miliband suggests that Trotsky's critique of "socialism in one country" loses much of its force once it is recognized that socialism is more a "permanent striving" than an "achieved state," he provides us with an important clue as to why he is unable to grasp Trotsky's critique in its *strategic* dimension. For Miliband, with this formulation, comes remarkably close to Eduard Bernstein's classically "revisionist" notion that "the movement is everything, the final goal nothing." Could it be that Miliband is unable to grasp Trotsky's point because the Stalinist doctrine of building socialism in one country had the ultimate effect of bringing the international Communist movement to strategic and programmatic positions closer to his own? To be sure, Miliband's "left reformism" owes more to the influence of classical social-democratic conceptions than to Stalinist ones, and Miliband was certainly never an uncritical defender of the Stalinist regimes. But if the Stalinist doctrine of "socialism in one country" encouraged Moscow-loyal Communist parties to eventually reject an "insurrectionary politics" in favour of "left reformism," as Trotsky had predicted it must (1970f: 71–73), then, from the perspective defended by Miliband, perhaps this was at least partly to the good!

What Miliband fails to consider is that the reason the "Trotskyist scenario" of working-class revolution does not appear "remotely on the cards" today is precisely due to the long-term impact of Stalinist "national reformism" on the workers' movement of the world—not least those segments of the international working class who were most open to a revolutionary perspective for overcoming capitalism. It is the programmatic and strategic *results* of the doctrine of "socialism in one country" that now permit Miliband to make an argument against revolutionary Marxism, couched not in terms of defending the "socialist motherland," but in terms of pragmatic "political realities." And this is also what allows him finally to agree with "most people on the left" that there is truth to the charges that Trotskyism is "an accumulation of slogans, with no bearing on reality" and that its adherents are "sectarian, opportunistic, and living in a self-made ghetto." The fact that these same charges are now being brought against the socialist left as a whole, however, should give all "independent socialists" reason to pause as they consider Miliband's further claim that "the very marginality to which [insurrectionary socialism] is doomed is one factor among others which will continue to attract some people, for whom anything less marginal is itself a matter of deep suspicion."

VI

"Actually existing Trotskyism," it must be conceded, has not withstood well the long decades of its marginality within the international labour and socialist movements. Over and over again, Trotskyists have been able to point to how events have confirmed the veracity of Trotsky's indictment of both Stalinism and social democracy. But defeat after defeat under the banners of national reformism—parliamentary "democratic socialism," the popular front, the anti-imperialist united front, socialism in one country—have failed to lead significant sections of the international labour and socialist movements to break in the direction of Trotskyism. The myriads of competing Trotskyist tendencies are marked to varying degrees by sectarianism, messianism, opportunism, and cultism. But neither these deformations nor the obvious marginality of the ostensibly

Trotskyist left within the global political culture can be properly gauged without taking into account the extremely adverse historical conditions under which four generations of Trotskyists have laboured. It is easy—far too easy—for "independent socialists" (especially those who style themselves simultaneously as anti-Leninist and as "left critics of social democracy") to ridicule the efforts of Trotskyists to build vanguard parties and to construct, reconstruct, or reinvent the Fourth International as the "world party of socialist revolution." But while such independent socialists have also laboured under adverse conditions, it should, in fairness, be acknowledged that they have precious little—and, in any case, incomparably less than the Trotskyists—to show for their efforts to "pressure to the left" the Communist and social-democratic parties and/or to construct "broad and non-sectarian" socialist movements, despite the fact that their activities since the 1930s have been impeded to a much lesser extent by the repressive machinations of Stalinist, fascist, and bourgeois-democratic states.

It is time for Trotskyists and independent socialists alike to show some humility. The Trotskyists stand on a proud tradition, but actually existing Trotskyism is politically and organizationally in too much disarray for many to take seriously the competing claims that any one of the existing Trotskyist organizations possesses a monopoly of Marxist wisdom. Grandiose posturing is a sure way to continued isolation. Like the Trotskyists, some independent socialists can take pride in a record of steadfast defense of the fundamental ideas of the socialist tradition; but if they are to play a positive role in the revival of the socialist left, they must shed the prejudices against Trotskyism they have acquired through long years of work in and adaptation to Stalinist and social-democratic milieus.

As an unaffiliated socialist with a profound respect for the Trotskyist heritage and a fair knowledge of the movement's history, I am always surprised when independent socialists, of Ralph Miliband's genre, suggest that the most important factor in determining the "marginality" of Trotskyism has been the Trotskyists' commitment to "insurrectionary socialism."[9] Hundreds of thousands of militants have passed through various ostensibly

Trotskyist organizations around the world since World War II, and very few of them were won to the movement because they expected to immediately organize an insurrection. It may be true that some socialist intellectuals have remained outside the Trotskyists' ranks owing to reservations about the "Bolshevik model of revolution." But on the other side of the ledger, it must be acknowledged that large numbers of militants were drawn into the mass Stalinist parties under the misapprehension that these parties were committed to replicating that very model, if not immediately, then at some indefinite point in the future. There are good reasons, therefore, to doubt Miliband's claim that "Trotskyism has done very poorly almost everywhere" owing to a refusal by Trotskyists to repudiate the insurrectionary model of the October Revolution or to deny the enduring relevance of its lessons for socialist strategy.

Equally curious is the bewilderment that many independent socialists like to express about the fractious character of contemporary Trotskyism. Miliband's comment is altogether typical: "Trotskyist parties and groups have generally been very small in numbers, and extremely prone to splits, with bitter accusations and counter-accusations of deviation and betrayal leveled by the warring factions against each other. What Freud, in a different context, once called 'the narcissism of small differences' certainly applies to them."

There is, without question, an element of truth in these observations. For easily-understood historical reasons the Trotskyist groups have remained relatively small, though not entirely without real influence in certain times and places, and small groups do seem to be especially prone to splits. But is it really true that Trotskyists are prone to splitting over "small differences"? Were the differences that resulted in the split and organizational destruction of the Fourth International in the early 1950s of a trifling character; that is, different assessments of the prospects for pressuring the Stalinist, social-democratic, and anti-colonialist movements to the left and transforming them into "adequate" instruments of social revolution? The followers of Michel Pablo and Ernest Mandel's International Secretariat at that time were advancing a perspective that brought "Trotskyism" perilously close to Miliband's "left reformism." The followers of James P. Cannon and Pierre Lambert's International Committee, on

the other side, were continuing to insist upon the need to build independent Trotskyist parties as the *indispensable instruments* of working-class
revolution. Was this a "small difference"? When Ted Grant's followers in
the Militant Group decided to burrow within the British Labour Party for
several decades while Gerry Healy's Socialist Labour League tried to build
an independent party capable of regrouping left-moving ex-Stalinists and
trade unionists, was this a "small difference"? When Tony Cliff decided
that "orthodox Trotskyism," with its new theory of "deformed workers'
states," had reached a position that was no longer compatible with the
Marxist idea of socialism as proletarian self-emancipation, and subsequently refused to defend China and North Korea as "workers' states" in
the midst of the Korean War, was his difference with Mandel and Cannon
and Healy and Grant a "small" one? More recently, when the followers of
Mandel called for critical support to the Islamic Revolution in Iran while
the Spartacists raised the slogan "Down with the Shah, Down with the
Mullahs, For Workers Revolution," was this a "small difference"? When
many ostensible Trotskyists hailed Lech Walesa's Solidarność as the vanguard of a workers' political revolution while others condemned it as a
tool of capitalist counter-revolution, was this a "small difference"? And
when Mandel's United Secretariat argued that their duty was to stand with
Boris Yeltsin in defense of "democracy" during the events of August 1991
while the International Bolshevik Tendency argued that a military bloc
with the Stalinist "Emergency Committee" against capitalist counter-revolution was urgently necessary, is it reasonable to argue that such a difference should be "containable" within a common organization?

It is not difficult to see why these questions were, and are, "split issues."
Many of them would have placed the factional antagonists on opposite
sides of the barricades! Only "independent socialists" working within the
amorphous milieus of nationally limited Social-Democratic parties could
possibly entertain the idea that such profound programmatic, strategic,
and tactical differences need *not* lead to acrimonious disputes and deep
splits. Let them try to build a "broad socialist organization" beyond the pale
of the "official political arm" of the labour movement and see if they could
contain under a common roof even a small fraction of the differences that

have rent the world of ostensible Trotskyism over the past 50 years. It is only too obvious that they could not.

So what is to be done? A modest proposal is all that can be offered here, but it is surely one that no socialist can reject in good faith. Those of us who remain seriously committed to *socialism*—not to "advanced democracy," not to "a family of the Left," and not to "capitalism with a human face in one country"—must learn to work and argue with each other in the context of genuine "united fronts." We must learn, as Lenin and Trotsky's early Communist International urged, to "march separately but strike together." We must learn to accept with good grace the criticism of groups either larger or smaller than our own as a condition not only for joint action but also for the clarification of political differences and the eventual regroupment and unification of socialist forces on principled, and, one hopes, more adequate foundations. Only in this way can a healthy socialist praxis begin to mature in this post-Stalinist era. Beyond this, we must all seek *a political practice that is appropriate to our political understanding,* without gratuitously vilifying those whose understanding has led them in different directions. We must seek, in other words, to avoid both opportunism and sectarianism—the opportunism that tempts us to keep our ideas under wraps until the dawning of a better day, and the sectarianism that deludes us into thinking that the organizational interests or political shibboleths of a single group can or ought to supersede the needs of the broader movement. In this spirit, the socialist Left as a whole could do worse than to reflect upon and take to heart the "rules" that Trotsky elaborated for his "world party of socialist revolution" at its founding conference in 1938:

> To face reality squarely; not to seek the line of least resistance; to call things by their right names; to speak the truth to the masses, no matter how bitter it may be; not to fear obstacles; to be true in little things as in big ones; to base one's program on the logic of the class struggle; to be bold when the hour of action arrives—these are the rules of the Fourth International. (1973c: 108)

Notes

1. My own attempt in 1991–92 to publish a contrived "conversation" with Trotsky on the collapse of Stalinism, based largely on his writings from 1924–40, met with a notable lack of success. Evidently, few editors agreed with me that it was "a matter of elementary historical justice" that Trotsky be given a forum at that critical juncture. In the summer of 2011, to mark the twentieth anniversary of Yeltsin's pro-capitalist coup, I circulated an updated PDF version of this piece under the title "Leon Trotsky Speaks: Burying Stalinism and Defending Socialism." Although I granted permission to any and all interested websites to freely post this document (provided only that it be reproduced in its entirety), only two websites, as far as I am aware, chose to do so: www.bolshevik.org and www.socialistviewpoint.org/sepoct_11/sepoct_11_52.html. The International Bolshevik Tendency has since published it as a printed pamphlet in its "Marxist Studies" series.

2. The idea of "primitive socialist accumulation" was elaborated by Preobrazhensky (1965), a co-leader with Trotsky of the Left Opposition. For additional insight into the economic ideas of the Left Opposition, see Filtzer (1978), Mandel (1994, 1995), Trotsky (1973b), and Rakovsky (1981).

3. The theory of "bureaucratic collectivism" has been defended by Shachtman (1962), among others. Left groups embracing this characterization have either adopted a neutral, "third-camp" position in the struggle between "bureaucratic collectivism" and "democratic capitalism" or ended up supporting the latter as a "lesser evil." Trotsky was evidently open to revising his characterization of the Soviet Union in the direction of "bureaucratic collectivism" if the Soviet bureaucracy succeeded in holding on to power after World War II *and* "if the world proletariat should actually prove incapable of fulfilling the mission placed upon it by the course of development" (1970c: 9). In a subsequent manifesto, however, he added: "It is not a question of a single uprising. It is a question of an entire revolutionary epoch.... It is necessary to prepare for long years, if not decades of wars, uprisings, brief interludes of truces, new wars, and new uprisings." To concede that the Soviet bureaucracy had successfully transformed itself into a new exploiting class of a *post-capitalist* mode of production was to concede

perforce that "the socialist programme, based on the internal contradictions of capitalist society, ended as a Utopia" (1970c: 9). For somewhat differing interpretations of Trotsky's views on these matters, see Callinicos (1990: 29–30), Mandel (1995: 8–10), and Bolshevik Tendency (1989: 14). Theorists of Soviet "state capitalism" avoided the pessimistic implications of the theory of bureaucratic collectivism by insisting that Soviet society evinced all or some of "the internal contradictions of capitalist society"—although there is notorious disagreement among "state capitalist" theorists as to how Marx's analysis of capitalism should be applied to Soviet-type societies (see Cliff 1974, Dunayevskaya 1964, James 1956, Nicolaus 1975, and Resnick and Wolff 1994 for a variety of theorizations; see also Farl 1973, Kemp 1973, SYL 1977, and Howard and King 1992 for useful surveys). Trotsky's only substantial critical engagement with a theorist of state capitalism is to be found in his 1933 article "The Class Nature of the Soviet State," where he addresses the arguments of Hugo Urbahns, a pioneer of the "state capitalist" characterization of the USSR (Trotsky 1972a). The most prolific writer in defending and developing Trotsky's position as against the various state-capitalist analyses is Ernest Mandel (1974, 1985), who also participated in an important debate with supporters of the Cliff school of state capitalist theory (Mandel, Kidron and Harman, n.d.). Other notable contributions to the critique of state capitalist theories of the USSR are Bolshevik Tendency (1989), Laibman (1978), Kemp (1973), SYL (1977), and Szymanski (1979).

Resnick and Wolff (1994) defend the proposition that "value categories" played a role in Soviet state capitalism inasmuch as "a state agency may use Marxian value categories to define values of outputs" (15). The question of whether or not Soviet workers' surplus product assumed a value form is rightly perceived by them as crucial to their contention that the Soviet system constituted a form of capitalism, albeit one distinct from "private capitalism." However, their analysis proceeds from the dubious "empirical" observation that "values were assigned to outputs in the Soviet economy and those values had social consequences" (16). In response to a similar argument advanced by the League for a Revolutionary Party, Bolshevik Tendency defenders of Trotsky's position point out that the fact that Soviet planners said that they were operating according to the law of value proves only that "these Stalinist bureaucrats [did] not themselves understand the law of value" (Bolshevik Tendency 1989: 10; see also Smith 1994: 138–139). The central difficulty with all arguments that the USSR constituted a "state capitalist" formation is that it is impossible to demonstrate the existence of "generalized commodity production" and the operation of the capitalist law of value in an economy where means of production and labour-power are not freely exchanged in a market; where wages and labour-power do not assume the form of variable capital; and where no structural imperative exists to measure social wealth in terms of abstract human labour time.

4. "The rule of the proletariat, already maimed by the backwardness and poverty of the country, is doubly and triply deformed under the pressure of world imperialism. The organ of the rule of the proletariat—the state—becomes an organ for the pressure from imperialism (diplomacy, army, foreign trade, ideas and customs). The struggle for domination, considered on an historical scale, is not between the proletariat and the bureaucracy, but between the proletariat and the world bourgeoisie" (Trotsky 1970d: 94).

5. David Kotz observes: "A study of the hundred wealthiest and most influential business people in Russia by sociologist Olga Kryshtanovskaya (1994) found that 62% of them came from the party-state elite. Almost all of these 62 had entered private business during 1987–90, before the breakup of the old system was yet visible. Kryshtanovskaya also found that 75% of the leadership circle around Russian President Boris Yeltsin, who led the pro-capitalist coalition to power, came from the former party-state elite" (1995: 4).

6. See also Smith (1994: 215–219), McNally (1994), Spartacist (1988), and Mandel (1994, 1995).

7. This and all subsequent quotes are taken from Miliband (1994: 153–156).

8. An excellent source of Trotskyist analysis of the course of twentieth-century revolutions is the journal *Revolutionary History* (published in Britain by Socialist Platform Ltd.), to which a number of Trotskyist groups contribute. For a classic polemic explicating the dialectic of "class, party and leadership" with specific reference to the Spanish revolution, see Trotsky (1973d).

9. See also Panitch (1989: 7–12) and a critique of the Miliband-Panitch position in Chapter 10 of this volume.

CHAPTER 9

The Revolutionary Betrayed: Trotsky and the Crisis of Trotskyism

In his memoirs, Leopold Trepper, the one-time head of the Soviet Union's "Red Orchestra" spy network in Nazi-occupied Western Europe, paid the following tribute to the Trotskyist Left Opposition to Stalin's regime—a regime Trepper had served throughout World War II despite his growing sense that it had betrayed the principles of the October socialist revolution:

> The Trotskyites can lay claim to this honor. Following the example of their leader, who was rewarded for his obstinacy with the end of an ice-axe, they fought Stalinism to the death, and they were the only ones who did. By the time of the great purges, they could only shout their rebellion in the freezing wastelands where they had been dragged in order to be exterminated. In the camps, their conduct was admirable. But their voices were lost in the tundra.

> Today, the Trotskyites have a right to accuse those who once howled along with the wolves. Let them not forget, however, that they had the enormous advantage over us of having a *coherent political system* capable of replacing Stalinism. They had something to cling to in the midst of their profound distress at seeing the revolution betrayed. (1977, emphasis added)

Trepper's memoirs and his belated tribute to Trotskyism testify eloquently to the accuracy of Leon Trotsky's claim of 1938 that the Soviet bureaucracy was by no means a homogeneous monolith united behind a single political project, but a sociologically brittle and politically unstable phenomenon that owed its temporary unity to a peculiar combination of venality, fear, inertia, and, for at least some of its members, continuing commitment to the original ideas of the October Revolution. Referring to the defections of the Soviet diplomat Butenko to fascist Italy and the top-ranking GPU (secret service) agent Ignace Reiss to the movement for a Fourth International, Trotsky noted:

> The public utterances of former foreign representatives of the Kremlin, who refused to return to Moscow, irrefutably confirm in their own way that all shades of political thought are to be found among the bureaucracy: from genuine Bolshevism (Ignace Reiss) to complete fascism (F. Butenko)....
>
> If tomorrow the bourgeois-fascist grouping, the "faction of Butenko," so to speak, should attempt the conquest of power [in the Soviet Union], the "faction of Reiss" inevitably would align itself on the opposite side of the barricades. Although it would find itself temporarily the ally of Stalin, it would nevertheless defend not the Bonapartist clique but the social base of the USSR, i.e., the property wrenched away from the capitalists and transformed into state property. (1973c: 102–104)

The Trotskyist "political system" referred to by Trepper contained, as one of its key programmatic elements, implacable opposition to Stalinism combined with unconditional defense of the Soviet Union from external imperialist attack and internal capitalist counter-revolution. Indeed, this was the touchstone of what later came to be known as "orthodox Trotskyism." In a pithy, yet definitive, programmatic statement of 1939, Trotsky declared:

> [The] question of the overthrowing of the Soviet bureaucracy is for us subordinate to the question of preserving state property in the

means of production in the USSR; [the] question of preserving state property in the means of production in the USSR is subordinate for us to the question of the world proletarian revolution. (1970c: 21)

It is hard to imagine a principled political position more difficult than this to champion in a world bitterly polarized between Stalinist "real social-ism" and "democratic capitalism," and this alone goes far to explain the Trotskyist movement's persistent marginality within the international labour movement since World War II. Trotsky's last major political fight was waged precisely over the "Russian question"—and it was waged against some of his own erstwhile followers who insisted that the USSR was no longer a workers' state (however degenerated) and that it therefore no lon-ger merited unconditional defense. Since then, putatively Trotskyist groups have been continually wracked by schisms over whether and how Trotsky's fundamental programmatic positions with respect to the Soviet Union (unconditional defense against capitalism combined with a struggle for anti-bureaucratic "political revolution") should be upheld and applied to a succession of concrete political events, including: the "revolutions from above" in Soviet-dominated Eastern Europe; the peasant-based revolutions of Yugoslavia, China, Vietnam, Korea, and Cuba; the worker-led insurgen-cies in Hungary and Poland in 1956; the Chinese Cultural Revolution; the Soviet military intervention in Afghanistan; the Solidarność movement in 1980s Poland; the "pro-democracy" movements in Eastern Europe and China at the end of the 1980s; and the final crisis of Stalinism in the Soviet bloc between 1989 and 1991, followed up by the consolidation of openly capitalist-restorationist regimes.

There is no doubt that these schisms decisively weakened the ability of the Trotskyist movement to present itself as a coherent political-organi-zational alternative to the Stalinist and social-democratic apparatuses dominating the international labour movement. To be sure, the vari-ous ostensibly Trotskyist tendencies—whether they define themselves as "orthodox Trotskyist" or as "neo-Trotskyist" in some sense—have devel-oped profound differences over a range of other programmatic, strategic, and tactical questions. And yet the "Russian question" has always loomed largest. Indeed, the disarray among ostensible Trotskyists in the face of the victory of capitalist counter-revolution in the Soviet Union in 1991 goes far to explain why, despite the apparent *vindication* of Trotsky's analysis of Stalinism that this event signified, little interest has been displayed by a crisis-ridden Marxist left in revisiting the Trotskyist "political system" that Trepper identified as the only "coherent" socialist alternative to Stalinism.

It is in light of these considerations that two books, *Trotsky as Alternative* by Ernest Mandel (1995) and *Trotskyism in the United States: Historical Essays and Reconsiderations* by George Breitman, Paul Le Blanc, and Alan Wald (1996), need to be evaluated. The former was the last work published in English by Mandel before his death in 1995, while the latter is a volume of essays written by former members of the Socialist Workers Party (SWP) of the United States—the "historic" party of American Trotskyism that formally renounced Trotskyism in favour of an erratic Castroism in the early 1980s. Despite certain differences, all four of these authors agree that the United Secretariat-led "Fourth International"—the product of a reunification of the SWP and Mandel's International Secretariat in 1963—constitutes the "mainstream" and legitimate continuator of the Trotskyist tradition. I should make clear that this is a premise that I do not share. Although the United Secretariat is certainly the largest putatively Trotskyist formation in the world, substantial grounds exist for arguing that all of its major contending tendencies and factions (from the 1960s to the present day) have departed from Trotsky's own Marxism in fundamental ways. Indeed, one important element in today's "crisis of Trotskyism"—its inability to present itself as a coherent political-organizational alternative to social-democratic and Stalinist movements that have long since demonstrated their incapacity to lead a serious struggle for world socialism—derives from the reputation that the United Secretariat formation has enjoyed as the pre-eminent "mainstream" Trotskyists on the world political arena. The story told by Paul Le Blanc in his two contributions to *Trotskyism in the United States* provides many clues as to why such a reputation is undeserved, even though Le Blanc himself fails to draw any of the necessary conclusions.

The appropriate starting point, however, is with Mandel's attempt to restate the case for Trotsky's politics in an era of Stalinist collapse. An influential Marxist economist and certainly the best-known ostensibly Trotskyist political figure of the second half of the twentieth century, Ernest Mandel brings an authority and reputation to his argument that few others could match. Mandel's familiarity with Trotsky's voluminous writings, together with his acumen in illuminating both the historical and contemporary relevance of many of Trotsky's ideas, is impressive. And it must be acknowledged that, in many ways, Mandel does a fine job of honouring the intellectual and political legacy of the man to whom he pays the following tribute: "Of all the important socialists of the twentieth century, it was Trotsky who recognized most clearly the main tendencies of development and the principal contradictions of the epoch, and it was Trotsky also who gave the clearest formulation to an appropriate emancipatory strategy for the international labour movement" (1995: 1).

Mandel begins by pointing to the centrality of Trotsky's "law of uneven and combined development" within the totality of his theoretical and political views. This "magnificent theoretical achievement," avers Mandel, "brings to light the articulation of all the major elements (economic, political, class, psychological, ideological and organizational) of a historical mechanism at work" (1995: 1). Indeed, it constitutes the indispensable foundation of Trotsky's theory and strategic perspective of "permanent revolution," his analysis of the principal contradictions and crisis tendencies of the imperialist epoch of capitalist development, his conviction that the wage-earning working class is the only consistently revolutionary class in the modern world, his understanding of the uneven and discontinuous development and spread of revolutionary consciousness within the international working class, and his analysis of the bureaucratic tendencies at work within the labour movements of the capitalist world and within the Stalinist-led Soviet degenerated workers' state.

The law of uneven and combined development goes well beyond the more familiar Marxist law of "uneven development" by grasping that the very unevenness of global development—in its variegated technological, economic, social, political, and ideological dimensions—cannot fail to produce specific and original (local) combinations of features that coexist within a global totality that has been unified and rendered permeable by the growth and extension of world capitalism. This means that the more backward countries are by no means condemned to pass through the same "stages of development" as the more advanced ones. As they seek to solve the problems of national unification, industrial modernization, agrarian revolution, democratization, and secularization, they have access to at least some of the technological, socio-economic, political, and educative achievements of societies that have already wrestled successfully with them. At the same time, precisely because they address these problems at a time when the global system of capitalist production relations has reached a stage of structural crisis, such countries are obliged to look beyond the horizon of capitalism for their successful resolution. The tasks of the bourgeois-democratic revolution become combined with the tasks of "socialist construction"; the leadership of the revolutionary process in *all* countries devolves to the working class; and the strategic perspective of revolutionary Marxism in an age of "permanent revolution" becomes more dependent than ever on the victory of the socialist revolution on a *world* scale.

Just as Trotsky's law of uneven and combined development establishes *why*, in the epoch of imperialism, the struggles and historical tasks associated with the classical "bourgeois-democratic" revolutions tend to merge with those of the proletarian-socialist revolution, it also points to why any attempt to limit the revolutionary process to a single country or group of countries—in the name of "building socialism in one country" or "securing peaceful coexistence between the socialist and capitalist camps"—leads perforce to the creation of a deformed caricature of socialism and ultimately to the re-establishment of capitalism.

Trotsky's analysis of Stalinism, then, is inextricably bound up with his larger analysis of the contradictions, crisis tendencies, perils, and revolutionary potentialities of an epoch of transition from capitalism to socialism *on a world scale*. From the standpoint of the early twenty-first century, when the "world revolution" seems not only to be in retreat but to have disappeared from the horizon almost entirely, such an analysis may appear to be hopelessly outdated and even quixotic. Yet it is precisely Trotsky's specific analysis of Stalinism—and of the severe *damage* that Stalinism as the "gravedigger of revolutions" has done to the global socialist project—that may furnish the conceptual resources to explain *how* we have arrived at the present global conjuncture of capitalist triumphalism, and *why*, now that Stalinism has lost its pre-eminence on the anti-capitalist left, there are grounds for hope that the Marxist-socialist project, like the fabled Phoenix, will eventually re-emerge from its own ashes stronger than ever. In all events, *only* Trotsky's analytical perspectives appear fully consistent with a rational socialist optimism that looks to the revival of a proletarian socialist movement inspired by the internationalist, revolutionary, and democratic principles of authentic Marxism. In this connection we might note that Trotsky's fundamental ideas seem altogether more consistent with Antonio Gramsci's prescription for "pessimism of the intellect and an optimism of the will" than any of the essentially national-reformist projects currently claiming Gramsci's legacy.

If all this is true, the stakes involved in a proper evaluation of Trotsky's legacy are very high. Yet, on a number of points central to that legacy, Mandel's discussion must be judged as profoundly flawed. This is nowhere clearer than in his discussions of Stalinism and the problem of "substitutionism." Mandel affirms, correctly, that the key to Trotsky's theoretical analysis of Stalinism was his recognition that the Stalinist bureaucracy represented "a specific social layer with its own particular material interests." But by identifying Stalinism simply with the political rule and material interests of the *Soviet* bureaucracy, Mandel is unable to grasp the significance of anti-capitalist social revolutions led by Stalinist parties that refused to subordinate their policies to the dictates of the Kremlin oligarchy. For Mandel, such parties—the Yugoslav, the Vietnamese, and the Chinese in particular—had "broken from Stalinism in practice," precisely by creating new, albeit bureaucratically deformed, workers' states. But, contrary to Mandel, Stalinism is not inherently a "national" phenomenon (the peculiar result of the degeneration of the Russian Revolution), but a *social* one (as Mandel elsewhere seems to grasp): the phenomenon of bureaucratic rule on the basis of property forms that correspond to the historic interests of the working class. As such, Stalinism possesses a *dual character*. On the one hand, it is implacably hostile to the direct political rule of the working class; on the other, it defends—albeit inadequately and inconsistently—the proletarian-socialist forms of collectivized property, planned economy, and state monopoly of foreign trade. Hence, the specific "material interests" of a Stalinist bureaucracy are rooted in its political domination of a post-capitalist "transitional" socio-economic formation featuring many of the structural prerequisites of a socialist society, but also lacking many of the latter's most indispensable elements: above all, a real democracy of the associated producers, an international division of labour, and an adequate development of the productive forces. These considerations define the Stalinist bureaucracy as a privileged, parasitic layer within a workers' state rather than as a new ruling class presiding over a class-exploitative mode of production. Yet they also define it as a mortal enemy of the global socialist project and of the full and healthy development of socialist relations, institutions, and practices.

In light of this understanding of Stalinism, what the Yugoslav, Chinese, and Vietnamese revolutions signified is that, in a world polarized between capitalist imperialism and the Soviet bloc, it was quite possible, under specific conditions, for Stalinist parties—that is, parties committed to the Soviet model of "real socialism"—to lead peasant-based social revolutions and to create bureaucratically deformed workers' states qualitatively similar to those that issued from the bureaucratic degeneration of the October socialist revolution and from the Soviet-sponsored "revolutions from above" in Eastern Europe. Even so, the victory of these revolutions in no way suggested that the role of the Fourth International had become any the less historically indispensable. For *none* of these degenerated and deformed workers' states could play a positive role in promoting a *world proletarian revolution* and none could be expected to build a nationally delimited "socialism" truly worthy of the name. A workers' political revolution remained urgently necessary in these bureaucratized workers' states to create revolutionary, internationalist regimes based upon the direct rule of workers' councils; and proletarian-led socialist revolutions remained necessary elsewhere in the world to create the conditions for world socialism.

In hindsight, it is relatively easy to say that, in *both* the societies ruled by Stalinists and in the capitalist-dominated world, the Fourth International's mission of organizing the working class for its "self-emancipation" should have remained clear, despite the unexpected "revolutionary capacities" displayed by the insurrectionary (but also profoundly anti-proletarian) Stalinists of China and Yugoslavia. Unfortunately, these peasant-based, Stalinist-led revolutions engendered a profound disorientation within the postwar Fourth International. One of its central leaders, Michel Pablo (Raptis), spoke of the likelihood of deformed workers' states existing for "an entire historical period of several centuries," and urged the national sections of the Fourth International to transform themselves into little more than ginger groups within the mass Stalinist, social-democratic, and anti-colonialist movements. Pablo's proposals—and accompanying organizational machinations—precipitated the 1953 split in the Fourth International, a split from which world Trotskyism has yet to recover.

While Mandel pays tribute to Trotsky's opposition to "substitutionism" within the workers' movement (in particular, the tendency of bureaucratic apparatuses to substitute themselves for the self-activity of the working-class masses), he evinces very little self-consciousness about his own long-standing support, extending back to his collaboration with Pablo, for a politics constantly in search of "substitutes" for the class-conscious working class under revolutionary Marxist leadership. This "substitution-ist" politics—and its astonishingly opportunist range—is largely concealed in *Trotsky as Alternative*, but it nevertheless reveals itself at a number of points: in Mandel's contention that Mao Zedong "tried to fight" the "hardened party, military and state bureaucracy" in the course of the Chinese Cultural Revolution (rather than simply fight for the triumph of his own bureaucratic faction); in his soft-pedalling of Trotsky's critique of popular-front coalitionism[1]; and in his call for a "reformed" United Nations. But it finds its most striking expression in Mandel's fulsome support (left unmentioned in *Trotsky as Alternative*) for the Solidarność "trade union" in Poland despite the explicitly anti-socialist character of that organization's leadership and stated program from 1981 on.

Throughout the 1980s, Mandel's objectivist and substitutionist methodology led him to conclude that the "objective dynamics" of working-class struggles against Stalinist regimes *guaranteed* their progressive character, leading him to abandon in practice any defense of the Polish deformed workers' state against a movement, backed by the Pope and Ronald Reagan, bent on the restoration of capitalism. This political capitulation to Cold War anti-communism, along with many of his other political positions, confirm that Mandel was far better at defending Trotsky's ideas in the abstract than applying them correctly to concrete contemporary developments. Indeed, Mandel's substitutionism and indiscriminate anti-Stalinism placed him in the camp of that "political fatalism" that he counterposes (abstractly but correctly) to the revolutionary Marxism of Trotsky—"a Marxist who was severely critical of the political fatalism of the Second International and who attributed to the subjective factor in history a decisive role in the drama of our century" (1995: 166). All this points to an unmistakable conclusion: that Mandel, in the political vernacular of classical Leninism, was an inveterate "centrist"—a revolutionary in words but an opportunist in deeds.

In his splendid essay "Centrism and the Fourth International" (1934), Trotsky noted that "[in] the choice of his international allies, the centrist is even less discriminating than in his own country" (Trotsky 1972b: 233). This observation is a good starting point for considering the significance of the reunification of the US Socialist Workers Party (SWP) and Mandel's rump Fourth International in 1963, Mandel's 20-year toleration of an SWP leadership that was moving rapidly to the right, and the SWP's decision in the 1980s to formally break from all pretenses of Trotskyism while concurrently calling for a new revolutionary International centred on the Cuban Communist Party. There is no shortage of irony in these historical developments. The SWP, at the time of the 1953 split, was the largest and most experienced national section of the Fourth International (aside from the Ceylonese section, which was both politically and organizationally marginal to world Trotskyism). Against Mandel and Pablo, the SWP leadership waged a principled—if not altogether adequate—defense of "orthodox Trotskyism." Between 1959 and 1963, however, it became clear that the SWP and Mandel's International Secretariat had developed convergent perspectives on the Cuban Revolution. Despite continuing disagreement over the issues that had led to the 1953 split, the newfound agreement on Cuba was deemed to be substantial and significant enough to warrant reunification of the SWP (and several of its international camp-followers) with Mandel's International Secretariat.

Inasmuch as the agreement on Cuba basically consisted in uncritical cheerleading for the Castro-Guevara leadership, an unwillingness to characterize Cuba as a *deformed* workers' state, and a consequent refusal to call for a working-class political revolution to institute a regime of workers' democracy, one can say that the SWP had substantially embraced key elements of the "Pabloist" perspective it had opposed in 1953. The *irony* is that, having embraced the substitutionist methodology of Pablo and Mandel, the SWP soon moved far to the right of the Mandelite majority of the United Secretariat. This was evidenced in the liberal-pacifist ("popular-frontist") character of its leadership of a major wing of the Vietnam anti-war movement and in its support of Black Nationalism and related abstentionism from the struggle for racial integration, as well as in many other aspects of its politics. The SWP's formal break with Trotskyism and the United Secretariat in 1983 was thus long presaged by an increasingly *reformist* orientation that appears to have been inspired by its "discovery" (in Cuba) of "adequate substitutes" for Trotskyist parties and proletarian leadership (as incarnated in the peasant-guerrilla bands led by the "unconscious Trotskyists" Castro and Guevara).

One will look in vain for an adequate analysis of these questions in the Breitman-Le Blanc-Wald collection. And yet the irony—and tragedy—of the SWP's political trajectory from 1959 to 1983 are what most haunt the reader of *Trotskyism in the United States*. In six essays, each fascinating in its own way, the three contributors to this volume provide historical and biographical sketches that capture something of the original spirit of American Trotskyism (especially its "heroic" years of the 1930s and 1940s when James P. Cannon was its pre-eminent leader) even while failing to identify the (rather obvious) source of the SWP's turn to Castroism in the 1980s in its uncritical appreciation of the Cuban Revolution in the early 1960s.

Given the centrality of the Cuban question to the SWP's trajectory from 1960 on, it would seem appropriate to give some serious attention to the arguments of those within the SWP who opposed the leadership's political adaptation to Castro's regime as well as the reunification of 1963. The failure of the authors to do this is, however, hardly accidental.[2] Their uncritical support for the United Secretariat position on Cuba apparently precludes any serious investigation of the "anti-Pabloist" positions of the Revolutionary Tendency (RT) of the early 1960s, as does their factional hostility to the groups that trace their lineage to the RT (in particular, the "Spartacist" International Communist League [Fourth Internationalist] and the International Bolshevik Tendency). No doubt this is why Le Blanc, in his two substantial historical and interpretive essays, chooses to focus instead on the bad *organizational* precedent established by the expulsion of the RT in 1963 and the way in which the 1965 SWP organizational resolution that justified it was used by the "leadership team" around Jack Barnes to consolidate its bureaucratic grip on the SWP in the 1970s. Barnes' proto-Stalinist interpretation of this resolution—and of Leninist organizational norms in general—is obviously of considerable importance to any analysis of how the democratic internal life of the SWP was strangled and how the SWP leadership was able to so easily dispose of two waves of left oppositionists: the Mandelite opposition of the mid-1970s (the Internationalist Tendency to which Wald adhered) and the "Trotsky-loyalist" opposition of the early 1980s (which included Breitman and Le Blanc, along with most of the SWP's old guard). The problem is that, by stressing "organizational" questions above all others, Le Blanc leaves the reader with the impression that the *politics* of the SWP remained basically consistent with "orthodox Trotskyism" up to the point that Barnes finally decided that his grip on the party was strong enough to permit him to formally dump the "old Trotskyism."

Even for those relatively unfamiliar with Trotskyist ideas, this thesis should ring rather hollow. To explain the SWP's *formal* disavowal of Trotskyism in the 1980s, it is surely necessary to trace its *de facto* break with both the political and organizational principles of Trotskyism that began around 1960. But to do this one must be prepared to analyze critically the substitutionism that continues to inform the politics of the international organization that was led for decades by Ernest Mandel. This is something that none of the authors of *Trotskyism in the United States* is prepared to do, and this failure is finally what renders the book not only disappointing but a real disservice to the best traditions of American Trotskyism.

Notes

1. Mandel devotes less than three pages to Trotsky's critique of the politics of the "popular front," and a part of this woefully inadequate discussion is devoted to criticizing unnamed "sectarians" who are viewed as less tactically flexible in their approach to popular-front coalitions than is Mandel's United Secretariat. Mandel long insisted that a policy of "critical support" to the workers' parties participating in an electoral coalition with bourgeois parties is a legitimate application of Leninist-Trotskyist tactics. But this position reveals a failure to see that what is at stake in an openly class-collaborationist coalition is not a "tactic," but a *strategic* question linked to the principle of the political independence of the working class. As Trotsky noted: "In reality, the People's Front is the *main question of proletarian class strategy* for this epoch" (1970g: 43). Trotsky argued that it was the Bolsheviks' *refusal* to extend any political support, however critical, to the Russian "people's front" of 1917—including to its Menshevik "proletarian" contingent—that was crucial to their successful leadership of the October Revolution.

2. One of the contributors, George Breitman, was obviously not in a position to do so, since his piece was written as a series of talks to a national education conference of the SWP in 1974. Its inclusion in this collection is motivated principally by the fact that Breitman (a long-time cadre of the SWP) was among the victims of the purge of "veteran Trotskyists" engineered by the SWP leadership in the early 1980s. Together with Le Blanc, Breitman helped form the Fourth Internationalist Tendency, which regrouped some of the *several hundred* expelled from the SWP for no other reason than their continuing rhetorical fidelity to Trotskyism and the Fourth International. Breitman's article is not altogether lacking in interest, however, since it captures unwittingly much of the substitutionist methodology that contributed to the SWP's degeneration.

PART IV
Class, Labour, and Socialist Strategy

CHAPTER 10

Socialist Strategy, Yesterday and Today: Notes on Classical Marxism and the Contemporary Radical Left

Co-authored with Joshua D. Dumont

A ttempting to repair the damage associated with the global economic slump that began in 2008, capital and capitalist states have ushered in a period of savage attacks on the living standards and security of working people throughout the world. The gradual erosion of the hard-won gains of the working class in the capitalist core that began after the onset of the profitability crisis of the 1970s, and which facilitated a partial recovery from that crisis, is now being eclipsed by concerted efforts to transfer unprecedented amounts of wealth directly into the hands of the super-rich, allegedly with a view to "stabilizing" the system. Our point of departure in this essay is the proposition that *this class strategy of capital can only be met with an effective counter-offensive through a major revival and reassertion of the fundamental programmatic tenets of Marxist socialism.*

As a body of ideas and as a movement toward a society beyond capitalism, Marxist socialism stands for the dissolution of capitalist private property, collective ownership of the means of production and distribution, a democratically planned economy, and the replacement of antagonistic social relations of exploitation, competition, and domination with relations of equality, co-operation, and solidarity: a classless, communist society. From the Marxist perspective, socialism is not merely an ethical ideal: it is the only fully rational response to the intensifying contradictions of the capitalist world order. Socialism aims at eliminating the deeply entrenched material inequalities—between classes, "races," nations, and genders—that have been fostered and perpetuated by a succession of class-antagonistic modes of production, inequalities that have reached truly monstrous proportions in the world capitalist system. Its goal is not the "formal equality" sanctified by liberalism—a merely juridical and legal equality, which effaces and ignores the persistent differences that distinguish human beings in their concrete circumstances. Rather, its goal is to achieve a global society in which, in the words of *The Communist Manifesto*, "the free development of each is the condition for the free development of all."

The fundamental contradictions of capitalism, as identified and analyzed by Marx, remain every bit as germane today as they were in the past: (i) the contradiction between the growing power, sophistication, and labour-displacing bias of productive technology and the social imperative of the capitalist mode of production to subordinate wealth creation (the satisfaction of human needs) to profit making (the creation of surplus value via the exploitation of living labour); (ii) the contradiction between the increasing "objective socialization" of production and the private appropriation of wealth; (iii) the contradiction between the internationalization (and "globalization") of production and human intercourse and the persistence of the capitalist nation-state as the pre-eminent political unit for promoting and safeguarding the interests of nationally based "social capitals" and managing the recurrent crisis tendencies of capitalism; and (iv) the contradiction between the imperative of the capitalist law of value to measure wealth in terms of "abstract social labour" (as manifested in money) and the humanistic-ecological requirement to define and measure wealth in terms of the joint contributions of nature and human labour, that is, in a way that takes full account of the metabolic exchanges between nature and society as mediated by human labour. These contradictions, and the systemic irrationality and crises to which they give rise, can be positively transcended only through a global socialist transformation carried out by the international working class.

On the face of it, the conditions for a renaissance of socialist theory and practice, and the widespread promulgation of the Marxist theses enunciated above, should be highly favourable. And yet at no time since the fall of the Paris Commune of 1871 has the socialist project been worse off. Proponents of socialism are relatively isolated and few in number—a faint echo of a time when tens and even hundreds of millions of people eagerly anticipated and struggled to bring about a world without capitalism. What's more, many self-styled socialists seem wilfully ignorant of the crucial strategic questions and debates of the past—not to mention the close resemblance of their own political positions to ideological trends within the international labour movement that have long proved to be dead ends. Vladimir Lenin's aphorism that there can be no revolutionary movement without revolutionary theory is taken seriously by few; and yet the need for the conscious activity of the working-class movement to be guided by Marxist theory is greater than ever.

In this chapter we pursue two basic aims. First, we review some of the more important theoretical features and strategic dimensions of "classical Marxism" as a distinct body of thought originally formulated by Karl Marx and Friedrich Engels and subsequently developed by several major figures of the revolutionary socialist movement. Second, we critically survey some of the main strategic themes and theoretical propositions typical of many academics and activists identified with what we will call "the contemporary radical left."

Classical Marxism

Marx's most important contribution to socialist theory was his insight that the working class is the sole historical actor with the consistent objective interest, structural location, and social power to replace capitalism with socialism, and that this class must organize itself as an *independent political force* to achieve that goal. Already in 1843 Marx had concluded that the modern wage-earning working class is the central and indispensable agent of human emancipation. The proletariat, for Marx, is a class with "radical chains"—a class that is

the dissolution of all classes, a sphere which has a universal character because of its universal suffering and which lays claim to no
particular right because the wrong it suffers is not a *particular wrong*
but *wrong in general*; a sphere of society which can no longer lay
claim to a *historical* title, but merely to a *human* one ... and finally a
sphere which cannot emancipate itself without emancipating itself
from—and thereby emancipating—all the other spheres of society,
which is, in a word, the *total loss* of humanity and which can therefore redeem itself only through the *total redemption of humanity....*
When the proletariat demands the *negation of private property*, it
is only elevating to a *principle for society* what society has already
made a principle *for the proletariat*. (1975: 256)

Marx argued that the proletariat, as the class upon whose labour and
oppression the entire social edifice rested, could only liberate itself by abolishing private property as a social institution and creating a classless society.
The mechanism by which the working class, in the course of its labouring
activity under capitalism, is perpetuated as a property-less class was first
grasped by Marx in his *Estranged Labour* manuscript of 1844, where he
observes that "[l]abour not only produces commodities; it also produces
itself and the workers as a *commodity* and it does so in the same proportion
in which it produces commodities in general" (1975: 324). This insight into
the *alienation* of labour was deepened with the formulation of Marx's theories of labour-value and surplus value, and it was extended in his magnum
opus, *Capital*, where he echoes his earlier discovery: "The capitalist process
of production, therefore, seen as a total, connected process, i.e. a process of
reproduction, produces not only commodities, not only surplus-value, but
it also produces and reproduces the capital-relation itself; on the one hand
the capitalist, on the other the wage-labourer" (1977: 724).

The proletariat is not only "negatively" predisposed to reject private
property; it is "positively" inclined toward the socialization of productive
property inasmuch as it operates the means of production *co-operatively*
(albeit under the domination and discipline of capital). Indeed, the capitalist
division of labour encompasses an ever-increasing degree of co-operation,

which is paradoxically constrained by an ever-increasing concentration of capital into fewer and fewer hands. In the course of its struggle, the working class is pushed toward resolving this contradiction through the establishment of a democratic, producer-run, and collectivized economy. From this perspective, the emergence—in different times and places, and as moments in the real history of the class struggle—of strikes, picket lines, workplace occupations, factory councils, forms of workers' control, and, at the highest level of struggle, soviet-type bodies as the institutional foundation of workers' power, is neither an accident nor the mere result of "communist agitation." Rather it is *socially determined* by the structure and contradictions of capitalist production itself.

Recognizing the (largely unconscious) striving for communism that is implicit even in the most "economistic" of labour strikes is key to a specifically Marxist understanding of class struggle. As Marx noted in a letter to Joseph Weydemeyer in 1852:

> As to myself, no credit is due to me for discovering either the *existence of classes* in modern society or the struggle between them. Long before me bourgeois historians had described the historical development of this class struggle and bourgeois economists the economic anatomy of the classes. What I did that was new was to demonstrate: 1) that the *existence of classes* is merely linked to *particular historical phases in the development of production*, 2) that class struggle necessarily leads to the *dictatorship of the proletariat*, 3) that this dictatorship itself only constitutes the transition to the *abolition of all classes* and to a *classless society*. (Marx & Engels 1965: 64)

The capstone to Marx's insistence upon the centrality of the proletariat to the struggle for socialism is the principle that the working class (even in situations where it is expedient for it to temporarily ally itself with other forces) must jealously guard its organizational and political *independence*—as incarnated, ultimately, in a revolutionary workers' party. The enduring programmatic thread of such a party, Marx believed, had to be a commitment to guiding the working-class struggle at every step toward a transcendence of "bourgeois right." Addressing the Communist League in March 1850, Marx and Engels advanced this fundamental principle in the following terms:

> It is our interest and our task to make the revolution permanent until all the more or less propertied classes have been driven from their ruling positions, until the proletariat has conquered state power and until the association of the proletarians has progressed sufficiently far—not only in one country but in all the leading countries of the world—that competition between the proletarians of these countries ceases and at least the decisive forces of production are concentrated in the hands of the workers. Our concern cannot simply be to modify private property, but to abolish it, not to hush up class antagonisms but to abolish classes, not to improve the existing society but to found a new one. (1973: 323–24)

In the twentieth century, several revolutionary socialists made critically important extensions and refinements to this Marxist program of working-class self-emancipation. As it is clearly impossible to summarize in a short essay all of these contributions, we will concentrate on some of the central ideas of three outstanding Marxists—Rosa Luxemburg, V. I. Lenin, and Leon Trotsky—with a view to identifying what is *distinctive* about revolutionary Marxism in relation to other nominally socialist approaches.

In her pivotal 1900 polemic *Social Reform or Revolution*, Rosa Luxemburg (1971) elaborated an uncompromising critique of the "revisionist" current that had emerged in the Second International in the 1890s. Revisionism had drawn upon pre-existing tensions and tendencies within the Social Democracy to formulate for the first time an explicitly reformist strategy, summed up in Eduard Bernstein's famous formula: "The final goal, whatever it may be, is nothing to me; the movement is everything." Bernstein's strategic conception boiled down essentially to the proposition that the Social Democratic party should not be fighting for socialist revolution but should instead advance the struggle for socialism by building up the strength of the working class through incremental social reforms wrested from capital and the state. An evolutionary, and not a revolutionary, road to socialism was thereby proposed.

In a vigorous defense of the revolutionary socialist perspective, Luxemburg maintained that reformist socialism is, in fact, not a genuine socialism at all:

> He who pronounces himself in favor of the method of legal reforms *in place of and as opposed to* the conquest of political power and social revolution does not really choose a more tranquil, surer and slower road to the *same* goal. He chooses a *different* goal. Instead of taking a stand for the establishment of a new social order, he takes a stand for surface modifications of the old order. (1971: 115–16)

At the heart of revisionist theory, Luxemburg argued, is a corruption of Marxism. Marx's understanding of the class struggle, for instance, is formally acknowledged, as is the need for socialism. But whereas Marxism sees the dictatorship of the proletariat as the mighty oak contained within the acorn of class struggle and works to cultivate it, revisionism seeks to mitigate class antagonisms and to "*attenuate* the capitalist contradictions" (89) through social reform: "As soon as immediate practical results become the principal aim, the clear-cut, irreconcilable class standpoint, which has meaning only in so far as it proposes to take power, will be found more and more an obstacle" (87). In opposition to the revisionist view, Luxemburg insisted that the existing state is a "class state"—the political-repressive organization of the ruling class—and that "the natural limits of social reforms lie with the interest of capital" (76). Rather than limiting themselves to a fight for reforms, Marxists had to orient the struggle toward the destruction of the capitalist state: "Only the hammer blow of revolution, that is, *the conquest of political power by the proletariat*, can break down [the 'wall between capitalist and socialist society']" (84–85). Here Luxemburg echoes Marx's famous declaration that "the working class cannot simply lay hold of the ready-made state machinery, and wield it for its own purposes" (Marx 1974: 206) and anticipates Lenin's insistence in *The State and Revolution* (1969) that the proletariat must establish its own unique organs of class rule and "smash" the capitalist state.

Luxemburg's position was undeniably revolutionary, but it must be placed in its proper historical context. As a socialist leader writing at the turn of the twentieth century, her framework remained that of classical Social Democracy, which had traditionally bifurcated the party's program into immediate "minimum" demands for social reform and the distant "maximum" goal of socialism (codified most clearly in the Erfurt Program of 1891). Luxemburg charged the revisionists with *counterposing* the minimum and maximum programs, whereas, in her view, the "struggle for reform is [the party's] *means*; the social revolution, its *goal*" (1971: 52). Her pamphlet seethes with revolutionary vigour, but the critique is constrained by the limits imposed by the historical period in which she was writing.

Two key developments would soon pose the need for significant changes and extensions to the programmatic and strategic corpus of classical Marxism: the consolidation (and crisis) of an imperialist stage of capitalist development (expressed most sharply by World War I) and the Russian Revolution of 1917. Lenin and Trotsky, the two principal leaders of that revolution—the *only* successful working-class revolution in history—are also the two most important theoreticians of twentieth-century revolutionary Marxism.

Lenin's most important theoretical contribution was to draw out and systematize the politico-organizational lessons of the experience of the Second International in the wake of the support the national leaderships of most Social Democratic parties gave to their own governments at the start of World War I. In two central texts ("The Collapse of the Second International" [1915a] and "Socialism and War" [1915b]), Lenin argued that the political basis for "social imperialism" or "social chauvinism" was the *opportunist* trend in the Second International, which found definite, albeit varying, expressions in most Social Democratic parties before the war. Ultimately, the social basis for opportunism is the petty-bourgeoisie and, most importantly, a relatively privileged and conservative layer of the working class—"a petty-bourgeois upper stratum or aristocracy (and bureaucracy) of the working class" (1915a: 243)—supported by the surpluses associated with imperialist plunder. Lenin observed: "An entire social stratum, consisting of parliamentarians, journalists, labour officials, privileged office personnel, and certain strata of the proletariat, has sprung up and has become *amalgamated* with its own national bourgeoisie, which has proved fully capable of appreciating and 'adapting' it" (250).

Before the war, the opportunist trend was seen as ultimately harmless, marginalized insofar as the proletarian character of the party remained predominant. Yet the "all encompassing" breadth of the Social Democracy (formulated by Karl Kautsky as "a party of the whole class") involved a problematic "unity" between revolutionaries and reformists and led, in reality, to the growing influence of the latter at the expense of the former, at least in the mass parties of Western and Central Europe.

On the eve of World War I, with disputes in the Russian Social Democracy uppermost in his mind, Lenin was already insisting that "unity is a great thing and a great slogan. But what the workers' cause needs is the *unity of Marxists*, not unity between Marxists, and opponents and distorters of Marxism" (1914: 231). A year later, he was arguing that Karl Kautsky's conception of *"unity* with the opportunists *actually* means subordinating the working class to their 'own' national bourgeoisie" (1915b: 311). This marked the beginning of Lenin's transformation from a revolutionary Social Democrat into the founder of a new, revolutionary-communist International.

By 1915, Lenin had concluded that the need for "a *new* form of organisation and struggle," as definitively demonstrated by the betrayal of the Social Democracy, flowed from the demands of a new historical epoch:

> The crisis created by the Great War has torn away all coverings, swept away conventions, exposed an abscess that has long come to a head, and revealed opportunism in its true role of ally of the bourgeoisie. The complete organisational severance of this element from the workers' parties has become imperative. The epoch of imperialism cannot permit the existence, in a single party, of the revolutionary proletariat's vanguard and the semi-petty-bourgeois aristocracy of the working class. (1915a: 254, 257)

On this basis, Lenin re-evaluated the experience of the Russian Social Democratic Labour Party, which had been split *de facto* into two separate parties for several years: the Mensheviks and the Bolsheviks. Using the Bolshevik Party as a model, Lenin (1915b: 329) proposed to construct a new international socialist organization that would regroup the revolutionary vanguard of the working class as a Third International. The Hungarian philosopher Georg Lukács, an early convert to Lenin's project, observed that this "vanguard party" perspective involved a basic reassertion of the role of the "subjective factor" in history:

> Lenin's concept of organization therefore means a *double break with mechanical fatalism*; both with the concept of proletarian class-consciousness as a mechanical product of its class situation, and with the idea that the revolution itself was only the mechanical working out of fatalistically explosive economic forces which—given the sufficient "maturity" of objective revolutionary conditions—would somehow "automatically" lead the proletariat to victory. (1972: 31)

It is Lenin's clarification of the role of the working-class vanguard as the key subjective agent in revolutionary transformation that accounts for his dogged insistence on *programmatic clarity*. Differences over principled and strategic questions are not secondary matters to be set aside in the name of "unity"; rather, revolutionaries must place "program first."

If Lenin's concept of the vanguard party provided a solution to the problems created by a broad socialist party of "the whole class"—a solution predicated on the imperative for revolutionaries to organize themselves separately from the bureaucrats, revisionists, and opportunists who seek an armistice with the bourgeoisie in the class war—it was Leon Trotsky's contribution to raise revolutionary Marxist strategy decisively out of the morass of the "minimum-maximum" programmatic dichotomy. In 1938, Trotsky, distilling and clarifying the methods and experiences of the Russian Bolshevik Party and the early Communist International, codified the idea of a "transitional program" in the founding manifesto of his fledgling Fourth International:

> The Fourth International does not discard the program of the old "minimal" demands to the degree to which these have preserved

at least part of their vital forcefulness. Indefatigably, it defends the democratic rights and social conquests of the workers. But it carries on this day-to-day work within the framework of the correct actual, that is, revolutionary perspective. Insofar as the old, partial "minimal" demands of the masses clash with the destructive and degrading tendencies of decadent capitalism—and this occurs at each step—the Fourth International advances a system of *transitional demands*, the essence of which is contained in the fact that ever more openly and decisively they will be directed against the very bases of the bourgeois regime. The old "minimal program" is superseded by the *transitional program*, the task of which lies in systematic mobilization of the masses for the proletarian revolution. (1998: 36–37)

Among the demands included in Trotsky's transitional program were the call for a sliding scale of wages and hours, workers' control of industry, opening the books of the employers, militant picket lines, workers' self-defense guards and labour-based militias, factory councils, soviets, the expropriation (without compensation) of industry and the banks, and, as a crowning demand toward which all other transitional demands point, a workers' government. Trotsky proposed that the selection and presentation of demands by the revolutionary vanguard would have to be tailored to the specific needs and level of consciousness of the workers in a given context of struggle. Yet he also insisted that putting forward socialist solutions in terms readily understandable to workers did not mean *adapting* one's program to their consciousness—it meant building a "bridge" between "today's conditions and from today's consciousness of wide layers of the working class and unalterably leading to one final conclusion: the conquest of power by the proletariat" (36). Crucially, Trotsky's conception of a transitional program does *not* project "reforms" that gradually erode the power of the bourgeoisie; rather, it was an attempt to provide a flexible and open-ended basis of struggle around a system of demands that, taken as a whole, cannot be satisfied so long as the capitalist state and the institution of private property in the means of production remain intact. The essential idea is that concrete struggle on *this* basis will be key to educating workers on the need to seize power and build socialism.

A strategy involving a transitional program was not only employed by the Bolshevik Party from April to October 1917 (the slogan of "All Power to the Soviets" constituting its most famous element)—it had been the essential approach of Marx and Engels in *The Communist Manifesto*. Shortly before her death, Luxemburg explicitly rejected the minimum-maximum division and argued that it was necessary "to place our program upon the foundations laid out by Marx and Engels in 1848": "Our program [of the newly-founded Communist Party of Germany] is deliberately opposed to the leading principle of the Erfurt program; it is deliberately opposed to the separation of the immediate and so-called minimal demands formulated for the political and economic struggle, from the socialist goal regarded as the maximal program" (1970: 408, 413).

Following the Russian Revolution of 1917, the strategic orientation embodied in the transitional programmatic approach was taken up for only a comparatively brief period by the national sections of the early Communist International and the trade-union currents allied with them. After the defeat of the German Revolution in 1923, and the consolidation of Stalinist, bureaucratic domination over the Soviet state and the International, the policies of these communist parties were decisively subordinated to the short-term twists and turns of Soviet foreign policy. The goal of world revolution was replaced by the program of building "socialism in one country" and promoting "peaceful coexistence" between the capitalist world and the USSR. In its new role, Trotsky argued, the Stalinized Communist International became the "gravedigger" of revolutions. It fell to Trotsky's small band of followers, at first within the International Left Opposition and later the Fourth International, to defend and carry forward the programmatic legacy of revolutionary Marxism.

The Contemporary Radical Left: A Critical Survey

One of the defining political events of our era—and one that has unquestionably weighed heavily on all elements of the contemporary radical left—was the collapse of Stalinism and the restoration of capitalism in what was once the Soviet bloc. The identification of Stalinism with revolutionary Marxism (that is to say, Leninism) since the 1920s—an identity assiduously promoted by the Stalinist regimes, the ideological apparatuses of world capitalism, and much of the radical left—has done incalculable damage to the socialist/communist project. In part, this damage resulted from widespread acceptance of the fundamentally false notion that the crimes of Stalinism (famines, frame-up trials, despotic rule, forced labour camps, etc.) were the necessary and unavoidable product of a revolutionary transformation from capitalism to socialism, and that therefore socialist revolution exacts too high a price in human suffering. At least equally important, however, was the profoundly conservatizing and sometimes outright counter-revolutionary influence that the Stalinist regimes exerted on the majority of forces that had defined themselves as anti-capitalist and identified with Russia's socialist revolution of 1917.

Stalinism is not fundamentally an ideology, still less the "logical" continuation of Marxism or of Lenin's Bolshevism. Rather it is the social phenomenon of bureaucratic rule on the basis of proletarian-socialist property forms. It is associated with what Trotsky and his followers defined as "degenerated and deformed workers' states"—post-capitalist regimes that constitute *qualitatively distorted* expressions of the "dictatorship of the proletariat" (see Chapters 8 and 9). In each of the bureaucratized workers' states, the working class had either been politically expropriated by a privileged oligarchy (as was the case in the Soviet Union due to the isolation of the young workers' republic and the exceptionally adverse material circumstances it faced) or it had never exercised its direct political rule in the first place, owing to the pre-eminent role of the Soviet military or of non-proletarian popular forces in their establishment (as was the case in Eastern Europe, Yugoslavia, China, North Korea, Vietnam, and Cuba). While there has been some controversy concerning the nature and extent of bureaucratic rule—particularly in Cuba—it is safe to say that most of those who continue to claim Trotsky's political mantle believe that any significant advance toward socialism in such countries must involve an anti-bureaucratic political revolution and the establishment of a *revolutionary workers' state* committed to socialist democracy and world revolution.

Within the international labour movement, the authority and prestige enjoyed by Stalinist regimes (particularly those headed by Joseph Stalin and his successors, and to a lesser extent that of Mao Zedong) were linked to their historic association with successful anti-capitalist social revolutions. Yet the evidence is considerable that this authority was repeatedly used to discourage proletarian-revolutionary policies on the international arena and to transform Communist-led workers' movements in the capitalist world into guardians of the "socialist motherland" and instruments of the foreign policy of the Soviet or Chinese governments. The revolutionary energy of the most advanced and socialist-minded layers of the working class was dissipated as the bureaucratic, national-reformist projects of building "socialism in one country" collided with the imperatives of the international workers' movement to advance along the road of socialist revolution. Eventually, as they asserted their independence from Moscow, many of the larger Communist parties came to resemble mass social-democratic parties—a process that was evident in the "Eurocommunist" turn of the 1970s and accelerated following the collapse of the Soviet Union in 1991. Repeated defeats—often resulting from policies predicated on the false notion that "progressive reform" of capitalism was all that was needed to promote "peaceful coexistence" and to improve the conditions of the working masses in the capitalist-dominated world—led to a fatal weakening of working-class leadership, organization, and consciousness on a global scale. The deliberate derailing by the Stalinist and social-democratic parties of a succession of potentially revolutionary working-class upsurges helped stabilize world capitalism, and thus indirectly strengthened the forces of capitalist restoration in the "Communist world."

It would have been a miracle if the global regression in class and socialist consciousness that resulted from these many defeats had not taken a heavy toll on those who continue to regard themselves as socialists or communists; that is to say, if it had not produced a significant demoralization and disorientation in the ranks of the putatively socialist left. No such miracle transpired. The upshot has been the ascendancy on what is euphemistically called "the Left" of a spectrum of ideas that, notwithstanding their diversity, have tended to converge in opposition to Marxist "scientific socialism" and its proletarian-revolutionary perspective. The entry of the world capitalist economy in 2008 into its most severe crisis since the Great Depression and the "business as usual" (essentially left-reformist) response of most of the radical left only underscores the vast distance that separates the thinking of these leftists from the urgent task of constructing a new, socialist leadership for the international labour movement.

Today's radical leftists may still cling to an abstract socialist ideal, but they often do so with a diminished capacity to think with clarity and resolve about the elementary requirements of an effective strategy to overcome capitalism and replace it with a socialist order. Debates about the very real life-and-death issues that have historically divided socialists—debates that were engaged inadequately but with some seriousness by would-be socialists in the 1960s and 1970s—have not been settled so much as swept to the side, replaced by arid calls for unity, tired and simplistic denunciations of sectarianism, theoretical "innovations" that rehearse the ideas of anarchism, utopianism, and evolutionary socialism, vague platitudes about the need to build new "capacities" in the struggle against exploitation and oppression, and a political practice far more oriented to the progressive reform of capitalism than to its supersession.

The contemporary radical left in most advanced capitalist countries is thus both theoretically and politically distant from the core principles of classical revolutionary Marxism.[1] Even many individuals and groups that continue to formally identify in some manner with the latter tradition have rejected its applicability to the present period, thus facilitating varying degrees of rapprochement with avowedly "left-reformist" socialists. Indeed, the basic ideas of Lenin, Luxemburg, and Trotsky are, when encountered today, often characterized as dogmatic and hopelessly sectarian by the contemporary radical left. Those who continue to espouse them are sometimes described as "dinosaur Marxists" seeking to build "sects" rather than vibrant socialist movements.[2]

Four distinct but also interrelated theoretical/strategic propositions seem to be shared in one form or another by much of the radical left. First, not only workers but "broad sectors of society" must be drawn into the struggle for socialism, since contemporary capitalism is marked by a diversity of forms of oppression. *Second,* while a socialist political organization is necessary to resist the depredations of neoliberalism and pose a challenge to the rule of capital, such an organization will have to be of a fundamentally new character and quite unlike any major project of the past (particularly those that identified with Leninism). *Third,* concern for programmatic clarity and/or "purity" is inherently sectarian and must be set aside if any real progress toward building a mass movement is to be made. *Fourth,* socialist organizing may be characterized as revolutionary to the extent it achieves tangible progress in developing the "capacities" of those who are oppressed by capitalism to "alter the relationship of forces." These four propositions are accepted either as categorically correct and universally applicable or as conjuncturally necessary and expedient (the latter tending to be the rationale for self-identified Leninists participating in and building such formations as Greece's SYRIZA, France's New Anti-Capitalist Party, Portugal's Left Bloc, and Canada's Socialist Project or Québec Solidaire).

While most contemporary radical leftists continue to argue that the working class is a vitally important component of any anti-capitalist movement worthy of the name, many other sections of the population (who may or may not also be workers) are considered to be indispensable strategic "allies" in the struggle for socialism. This conception goes well beyond, and indeed negates, the traditional Leninist notion that the revolutionary workers' party must act as a "tribune of the people" (that is, the most ardent opponent of all forms of oppression). Instead it involves the problematic notion that because capitalism is at the root of the oppression of women, indigenous peoples, homosexuals, immigrants, people of colour, youth, the disabled, and so on, the struggles of these groups to better their conditions are implicitly anti-capitalist in some general sense and possess an anti-capitalist "logic" or "dynamic." Socialist transformation, from this point of view, will grow out of a multiplicity of struggles, which need to be "linked up" in a project of mutual solidarity. While socialists should help "clarify" the anti-capitalist content of various social struggles, what is *not* proposed is to have a pro-socialist workers' movement *leading* the oppressed.

If the working class is not the sole social agent with both the material interest and capacity to bring about socialism, then proletarian vanguardism in a general sense must be rejected. More specifically, the idea of a vanguard within the working class is rejected in favour of anti-vanguardism or (what amounts to the same thing) multi-vanguardism. On the organizational front, this translates into an argument for a very broad and "inclusive" socialist organization (sometimes, but not always, a party-type formation).

It follows from these propositions that the strategic orientation and programmatic clarity associated with Leninism are anathema to effective socialist organizing. In the view of the contemporary radical left, differences that once divided activists are now outdated or reduced in significance in light of recent historical developments. In some measure this reflects the opinion of some of those who still identify with revolutionary socialism that perspectives they once considered left-reformist have taken on an objectively revolutionary significance in the context of the need to "rebuild the left" in what is viewed as a qualitatively new era. Thus Alex Callinicos, the leading theoretician of the Socialist Workers Party (Britain's largest "far-left" formation and one which still formally identifies with Leninism and Trotskyism), has put forward an argument that is essentially congruent with the contemporary radical left's rejection of Leninist vanguardism:

The political experience of the 20th century shows very clearly that in the advanced capitalist countries it is impossible to build a mass revolutionary party without breaking the hold of social democracy over the organised working class. In the era of the Russian Revolution it was possible for many European communist parties to begin to do this by splitting social democratic parties and winning substantial numbers of previously reformist workers directly to the revolutionary programme of the Communist International. October 1917 exercised an enormous attractive power on everyone around the world who wanted to fight the bosses and imperialism.

Alas, thanks to the experience of Stalinism, the opposite is true today. Social liberalism is repelling many working class people today, but, in the first instance, what they seek is a more genuine version of the reformism that their traditional parties once promised them. Therefore, if the formations of the radical left are to be habitable to these refugees from social democracy, their programmes must not foreclose the debate between reform and revolution by simply incorporating the distinctive strategic conceptions developed by revolutionary Marxists. (Callinicos 2008)

The concrete approach to practical work associated with Callinicos' perspective is one that is concerned not to "alienate" the broad sectors of society engaged in actually existing struggles against oppression. Rather than fighting for a *transitional programmatic* approach within social movements dominated by reformist perspectives, the job of socialists, from this point of view, is to deepen and radicalize these movements by drawing out connections and advancing more militant demands. The rationale for this approach is in part informed by the belief that the major obstacle to socialist transformation is not, as Trotsky argued in *The Transitional Program*, a "historical crisis of the leadership of the proletariat" (1998: 33), but rather that the masses no longer possess a generally pro-socialist disposition and revolutionary yearning. The solution for the present stage of history, it follows, is to "build capacities" and develop socialist consciousness by getting people involved in struggles that make real advances within the framework of capitalism—baby steps that will teach them how to walk and one day to run.[3] In the final analysis, this perspective is an *objectivist* one that relies on the "spontaneous" dynamic of "struggle" to change consciousness—precisely the sort of perspective criticized by Lenin in his polemic against "economism" in *What is to be Done?*

In the Canadian context, a good exemplar of the contemporary radical left is the Socialist Project, a loose organization that brings together leftist academics and pro-socialist activists involved in organized labour and a variety of social movements. In an article entitled "What should we do to help build a New Left?" appearing in *Relay* (a Socialist Project journal), Greg Albo and Herman Rosenfeld offer a succinct and revealing analysis of what they consider to be the root causes of the recent malaise of socialist organizing:

The defeat of the Left and the workers' movement dates from the end of the post-war boom and the militant attempts through the 1970s to develop alternatives in multiple forms—a radicalized social democracy, reform communism, liberation struggles carrying the banner of socialism, workers' control and participatory democracy movements, and still others. The ascendancy of neoliberalism to revitalize capitalist power as a response to these developments still haunts us. This also has deeper roots in the often ossified ways that Marxism was translated into the political, cultural and economic realities of developed capitalist society. (2009: 4)

It is perhaps highly significant that no mention is made in this account of the perfidious policies of Stalinism and Social Democracy (including their more "left" variants), nor of the activities of many self-styled revolutionary organizations that failed to present a coherent alternative to these misleaderships. The implication is that the defeat of the workers' movement and "the Left" (that amorphous entity that is often evoked but seldom defined) must be attributed to two other factors: the "ascendancy of neoliberalism" (in other words, *the success of capital's class strategy*—an explanation that really amounts to a tautology), and the "ossified ways that Marxism was translated" in the context of advanced capitalist societies ("ways" that remain as ill-defined by Albo and Rosenfeld as their conception of what constituted "Marxism" in the 1970s).

Advancing their own perspective on how "a new revolutionary politics" might be developed, Albo and Rosenfeld (2009) cite favourably some passages from veteran Latin American leftist Marta Harnecker's 2007 book, *Rebuilding the Left*:

Our efforts should be realistically focused on changing the current balance of power so that what appears to be impossible today becomes possible tomorrow.... [I]n order to respond to the new challenges set by the twenty-first century we need a political organisation which, as it advances a national programme which enables broad sectors of society to rally round the same battle standard, also

277

helps those sectors to transform themselves into the active subjects building the new society for which the battle is being waged.

While not defining what this "new society" will actually look like, Albo and Rosenfeld argue that "we need to push beyond the present disorganization and divisions of the Left to what Harnecker refers to as 'the creation of an alternative social bloc.'" What this means exactly remains unclear, but it should be noted that the neo-Gramscian notion of an "alternative social bloc" has often been adduced by radical leftists who argue for new forms of "popular frontism"—a class-collaborationist strategy (of impeccably Stalinist vintage) for "changing the current balance of power," moving the struggle forward through discrete "stages," and postponing indefinitely the fight for working-class independence and a socialist program.

In his 2008 book *Renewing Socialism*, Leo Panitch rounds out the radical-left perspective with a critique of what he calls "insurrectionary socialism," by which he means the revolutionary Marxist tradition of Lenin, Luxemburg, and Trotsky. While critical of contemporary Social Democracy, Panitch argues that its earlier rejection of Leninism was basically sound: "the premise that underlay the social-democratic position—that an insurrectionary strategy was impossible in the West—must be recognized as having been fundamentally correct" (2008: 22). Instead of working toward the *overthrow* of the bourgeois state, "the first task of a democratic socialism, in remaking the state, no less than movement building, is to actively facilitate the creation of democratic capacities" (8).

It must be said that the leading representatives of classical revolutionary Marxism would have strenuously objected to the notion that they were exponents of an "insurrectionary" *strategy*. Insurrection is in one sense no more a "strategy" than is a general strike or participation in an election (whether for parliament or a soviet-type assembly). Rather, it is essentially a military-technical operation, a tactic of great importance that is appropriate to the penultimate phase of the struggle for power by the working class. As Smith pointed out in a response to Ralph Miliband's (1994) left-reformist critique of Trotskyism's so-called insurrectionary position: "Insurrectionary activity can be envisaged only during genuinely 'revolutionary situations'—and these arise only periodically, and under exceptional circumstances" (1996–97: 57; see Chapter 8 of this volume).[4] Moreover, a genuinely revolutionary situation in which the seizure of power by the working class is an immediate possibility is precisely one in which a revolutionary Marxist vanguard is not only present but is capable of vying in a serious way for the leadership of the mass movement. To dismiss the possibility of a successful insurrection in the absence of a mass revolutionary party is entirely sensible; to reject it when such a party is "on the ground" (as was the case in Germany in 1923, for example) would be to effectively side with the counter-revolution ("democratic" or otherwise). Rather than preoccupying themselves with theoretical abstractions violently wrenched from actual historical circumstances, partisans of the radical left need to think carefully and concretely about the implications of such an "anti-insurrectionary" stance. Above all, they need to decide whether—in the context of events like the October Revolution of 1917, the German Revolution of 1923, the Spanish Revolution of 1936–37, or the Portuguese Revolution of 1975—they would stand with those "seeking to limit the mass movement to 'constitutionalist' avenues or with those seeking to lead the working class forward to the conquest of state power" (1996–97: 58; see Chapter 8 of this volume).[5]

Conclusion

Even the rather cursory comparison that we have offered here reveals the vast gulf that separates the contemporary radical left from classical Marxism. At the risk of generalization and oversimplification, we would submit that the contemporary radical left recapitulates many of the themes and ideas of Bernsteinian revisionism and even pre-Marxist, "utopian" socialism: the rejection of working-class centrality and independence; the advocacy of broad, and even cross-class, political formations that are programmatically vague enough to appeal to self-styled socialists looking to "get rich quick" as well as to radical activists involved in more narrowly focused campaigns (such as immigration law reform, gay and lesbian rights, etc.); and, finally, the promotion of a new variant of the "minimum-maximum" approach premised on the view that "the movement" is everything and the socialist program "nothing."

The strategic perspective of the contemporary radical left falls well short of even the best traditions of classical Social Democracy. When Karl Kautsky codified the minimum-maximum approach in the 1891 Erfurt Program of the German Social Democrats, the latter were still resolutely committed to the political independence of the working class, even as they recognized that, in their epoch, considerable scope for progressive reform remained possible within the framework of capitalism. Moreover, the Erfurtian Social Democrats of the 1890s (and beyond) were serious about building what Kautsky described as a "party of the whole class" on an explicitly socialist programmatic basis and recognized, as both Kautsky and Lenin did, that "socialist consciousness" cannot arise spontaneously within the labour movement (or any other social movement), but that socialist ideas, initially at least, must be brought into the struggles of the oppressed "from the outside"—by those who have assimilated the main theoretical discoveries of Marxism and the principal lessons of working-class history (Lenin 1970a).

By contrast, the "mini-maxi" radicals of today are far more tentative in their advocacy of *class-against-class* politics and much more hesitant to speak explicitly about socialism in their day-to-day practice. While quick to denounce "sectarianism" (by which they really mean an active defense of Marxist-socialist principle), they are often just as quick to immerse themselves in projects that are reminiscent of the failed strategies of the past (notwithstanding their pretensions to "new thinking"). The inclination toward *opportunism* is pronounced, finding expression in an increasing focus on electoralism and softness toward class collaboration, while eschewing any serious perspective of building class-struggle oppositions in the trade unions to *politically* combat the bureaucratic misleaders of the labour movement.[6] Rather than seeking to rediscover the precious programmatic and strategic heritage of Marxism—which, as we have sought to show, involves a synthesis of the theory of working-class self-emancipation, the vanguard party principle, and a transitional programmatic approach to the struggle for workers' power—much of the radical left is retreating, in the name of a false realism, to strategic conceptions that have much more in common with social-democratic revisionism and even Stalinism.

The idea that one can more "realistically" advance the socialist project by abandoning (or hiding) the revolutionary Marxist tradition is a foolish and opportunist illusion that reflects the pressures of the reactionary ideological climate prevailing today in the West. Key to the revival of Marxism will be the reassertion of a genuine *internationalism*. In fighting for the ideas of Marx, Luxemburg, Lenin, and Trotsky, revolutionary socialists must not be concerned merely with building "national" organizations (which will inevitably face widely differing local conditions) but an *international working-class party* that will incorporate its understanding of the uneven development of global class struggle into its strategic perspective. "Realistically," the establishment of a revolutionary workers' state in even one country in the world would do incomparably more to transform mass consciousness on a global scale than any amount of opportunist manoeuvring conducted on national and local levels by the contemporary radical left.

We recognize that our argument will be seen by many as a paean to "sectarianism"—which most radical leftists mistakenly view as the main current obstacle to building a mass and effective socialist movement. But sectarianism can be understood in different ways, and we consider the label substantially inapplicable to Marxists who uphold the need to work within the mass organizations of the working class (in particular the trade unions), who are prepared to engage in united-front activity with other groups around issues of common concern, who do not refuse "on principle" to use electoral campaigns as a platform for socialist ideas, and who are willing to debate their leftist opponents in ways that do not preclude mutual understanding and principled collaboration. The conception that the defense of revolutionary Marxist ideas is *inherently* sectarian is a liberal and reactionary notion, one that should not be countenanced by any sincere socialist.

That said, we are in no way oblivious to the genuinely sectarian, cultist, and bureaucratic tendencies that have prevailed in many of the groups that have laid claim to revolutionary Marxism. In part these tendencies and deformations can be attributed to the *isolation* of the groups afflicted by them—an isolation imposed by the concrete historical conditions in which they have functioned. But it must be acknowledged that many of these groups have also laboured under their own "crisis of leadership" and that formal adherence to the principles of Lenin's democratic centralism and ostensible fidelity to Trotsky's *Transitional Program* provide no guarantee against the emergence of bureaucratic centralism and sectarian or cultist degeneration. The fight against such tendencies must be consciously incorporated into the program and practices of a revolutionary socialist formation, even as it is recognized that no organizational or strategic formula can provide an ironclad "guarantee" against either opportunism or sectarianism. The experience of the Bolshevik Party prior to the Russian Revolution remains, in this connection, a tremendous source of inspiration and optimism: for here was a party of *cadres*, of professional revolutionaries, that successfully resisted all such tendencies, and, precisely because it did so, was able to lead a workers' revolution to victory.

The desire of many radical leftists to break out of isolation and to "make a difference" in a world gone mad is both understandable and healthy. But if they are to make a positive contribution to the building of a real socialist movement, they must abandon the prejudice that the fight for a principled socialist program and a revolutionary, internationalist workers' party is an impediment rather than a vital prerequisite for transforming the actually existing struggles of workers and all the oppressed into an all-out battle to fundamentally change the world.

Notes

1. Our focus in this chapter is on the radical left of the developed capitalist world. Even so, we believe that much of what we will say about it applies with equal force to its counterparts in Asia, Africa, and Latin America.
2. In making these claims, many radical leftists are perfectly aware that they are playing to the prejudices and ignorance of elements newly attracted to socialist ideas. Instead of educating the uninitiated to the profound differences between anarchism and Marxism, Stalinism and Leninism, Maoism

and Trotskyism, etc., they often pander to their naïve view that what is needed on "the Left" is greater "unity." But how can a Trotskyist committed to the independence of the working class achieve unity with a Stalinist committed to supporting "lesser-evil" bourgeois politicians? How can a Leninist committed to smashing the capitalist state achieve unity with a social democrat who seeks to "democratize" it?

3. It should be noted that this general approach is not really "new" to much of the ostensibly revolutionary left. Even in the 1970s, when socialist consciousness was much more widespread in the working class, many groups claiming to be Leninist and Trotskyist found other reasons to reject a strategy based on a transitional program.

4. Due to an error in copy-editing, this quotation was originally and inaccurately attributed to Miliband (1994) in Smith and Dumont (2011), from which the present chapter was taken.

5. As in the previous case, this quotation was originally and inaccurately attributed to Miliband (1994) in Smith and Dumont (2011), from which the present chapter was taken.

6. The case for building such anti-bureaucratic, class-struggle alternatives in the unions is made in complementary ways by Knox (1998), Butovsky and Smith (2007; see Chapter 13 of this volume), and Smith and Butovsky (2013).

CHAPTER 11

Rethinking "The Middle Class": Ideological Constructions and Contradictory Structural Locations

An economy that grows from the middle out.... That's what we need.
—Barack Obama, 2013

Along with the suppression of any reference to "the working class" or, still worse, to "the proletariat," a key element in the political algebra of liberal-democratic capitalist societies has long been the sanctification of "the middle class" as the "majority" class of such societies. Indeed, the idea of the middle class is usefully seen as an ideologically malleable "x"—the content or specific value of which is both ineffable and continually redefinable at the level of individual subjectivity. Winning political strategies seem always to presuppose successful conjunctural assessments of the aspirations, values, and subjectively perceived interests of those segments of the populace who, at any particular time, choose to identify themselves with this always ill-defined yet purportedly majoritarian class.

Conventional politicians and the corporate mass media actively abet the image of a preponderantly middle-class society for the very good reason that such imagery is crucial to liberal-democratic ideological hegemony (and therewith the political stability of capitalist society). Even so, this imagery should by no means be regarded as a mere "illusion"—as simply a "false understanding" of social reality consciously perpetrated by elites in a determined effort to dupe the masses. For, as we shall see, the notion that the "middle class" encompasses the *majority* has a real and substantial social-psychological basis in the lived experiences of most members of liberal-democratic societies. That said, the idea that "most of us are middle class" must be seen as a quintessentially *ideological* construction, if by ideology we understand a way of thinking and of seeing things *that reduces the social to the natural, that is partial and one-sided, and that serves dominant class interests.*

The Middle Class and Contradictory Structural Locations

The widespread invocation of "the middle-class," particularly when conjoined to the notion of a "middle-class majority," serves a quintessentially ideological function insofar as it *conceals* fundamental aspects of capitalist social reality and its attendant class structure. It is troubling, therefore, when otherwise critical sociologists become complicit in legitimating the idea of "the middle class" in its most vulgar and taken-for-granted conventional usages. A case in point is Dennis Forcese in his textbook *The Canadian Class Structure*. Forcese is here criticizing the widespread notion that Canadian society is a largely "classless" one:

> What classlessness has meant is peculiar to the middle class. Middle-class Canadians tell researchers that they perceive themselves as living in a homogeneous middle-class society. We are taught to think in such a fashion by our parents, peers, the media, and the schools.... The myth of a middle-class society of equal opportunity is thereby perpetuated. As one author sums it up, "Canadians see their society as 'classless' because the vast majority of persons with whom they interact are, just as they themselves are, members of the middle class. It is precisely because we perceive our [class] structure in this way that we ignore both the extremes, that is, the poor and the rich. The larger the middle class, the less visible the extremes" [Hofley 1971]. (Forcese 1986: 24)

Despite their evident and welcome concern with establishing the social-scientific salience of poverty and concentrated wealth in Canadian society, Forcese and Hofley come close here to replacing the myth of "classlessness" with the similar and no less pernicious myth of a "middle-class society." Furthermore, neither sociologist seems to recognize that to define the extremes of society as "the rich" and "the poor" is essentially *arbitrary*; that this is a purely distributional and impressionistic notion of what constitutes the poles of the capitalist class structure; and that such a conceptualization obscures the decisive *capital/labour* antagonism that is at the heart of the dynamic and developmental tendencies of a capitalist class society.

Writing from a Marxist perspective, Bill Livant has deplored the consequences of beginning the analysis of class structure with the assumption that middle-class predominance is the defining reality of an advanced capitalist society. "We know," he writes, "that the middle cannot be found in itself. We know that the middle is a contradiction; if we start with the middle as the basis of our description we won't be able to see it. In short, we won't have any idea what 'the middle' is in the middle of" (1979: 287). Livant then makes the important point that, when we speak of extremes in relation to which a "middle" is defined, we need to refer to those extremes having the greatest significance—the greatest practical relevance. While he defines these as "the many" and "the few," a more precise Marxist specification, with regard to capitalist societies, would be "those who must sell their labour-power for a wage" (wage-labourers/the proletariat) and "those who appropriate the labour of others by virtue of their ownership of means of production" (capitalists/the bourgeoisie). In relation to these (objectively definable) classes, a "middle" can be conceptualized that combines, in contradictory ways and in varying permutations, certain aspects or elements of each "extreme."

The strength of Marxist class theory is its commitment to a conception of class that is both *relational* and based on *objective criteria* (pre-eminently structural locations with respect to the means of production) rather than on arbitrary, subjective notions. And yet ostensibly Marxist theories of class are also quite varied. Significant differences exist between such theorists as Erik Olin Wright, Guglielmo Carchedi, and Robert Weil, to name just a few.

Wright (1978) dispenses with the concept of the middle class entirely, preferring to invoke the category of the petty-bourgeoisie as a survival of precapitalist, independent (or simple) commodity production: a "pure" class-in-*itself* whose members are characterized by ownership of means of production, self-employment, and non-exploitation of wage-labour. For Wright, objectively "contradictory class locations" exist between this traditional petty-bourgeoisie and the capitalist class (small employers who command the labour of others); between this petty-bourgeoisie and the working class (salaried employees who direct their own labour, but not the labour of others); and between the working class and the bourgeoisie (managers, supervisors, and foremen, who embody some of the characteristics of both capital and wage-labour). Taken together, these contradictory class locations encompass most of the elements that Carchedi refers to as "the new middle class"—a class whose "structural interests are contradictory since this class partly performs the function of labour (i.e., it carries out the labour process) and partly performs the function of capital (i.e., it carries out the work of control and surveillance within the production process)" (Carchedi 1988: 119, 1977).

Weil (1995) provides a compelling argument for the proposition that the traditional petty-bourgeoisie, together with Wright's "contradictory class locations," should be conceptualized as elements straddling the capital-labour divide, and that the petty-bourgeoisie is thus itself in a contradictory structural location. On this view, the petty-bourgeoisie is not simply a survival of a mythic self-sustaining mode of production known as "independent commodity production" but an *integral component* of the capitalist mode of production. The petty-bourgeoisie, although originating in precapitalist forms of production, has long been and is today "capitalistic" in character. It encompasses within itself the role of capital (ownership of means of production/the imperative to exploit labour) and the role of wage-labour (the imperative to work for a living). As Weil suggests, "[F]or Marx the idea of 'self-employment' involves both being a 'wage-earner' for oneself and gaining a 'rentier' profit from capital as well. It arises precisely because even 'self-employed' small owners, the 'pure' petty-bourgeoisie, are capitalistic" (1995: 13).

Weil makes the important point that what is fundamental to an authenti-
cally Marxist understanding of "class" in general, and the "middle class" in
capitalist society in particular, is Marx's law of labour-value, which holds
that the sole source of all new value, including the surplus value realized as
profit, is living labour. He writes:

> For [Marx], commodity and labour value are both aspects of a single
> "unity," bearing the nature of each other even when "formally" apart.
> It was this that enabled him to see that even the "pure" petty-bour-
> geoisie simultaneously realize the full value of their labour and at the
> same time treat it capitalistically as wages and profit. (1995: 15)

Against Wright, who regards the traditional, self-employed petty-bourgeois
proprietor as simply "neither exploiter nor exploited," Weil counterposes
Marx's dialectical insight that the petty-bourgeois is "neither exploiter nor
exploited" *and* "both exploiter and exploited." Under capitalist conditions, the
"pure" petty-bourgeois, no less than the capitalist, is compelled to appropriate
surplus labour; and where petty-bourgeois producers are not in a position to
appropriate the surplus labour of others (usually that of family members), they
are obliged to appropriate their *own* surplus labour. Thus, petty-bourgeois pro-
prietors treat their income as effectively divided between "wages" and "profit,"
with the combined sum constituting the total value yielded by their own labour
(Weil 1995: 11). In a remarkable passage cited by Weil, Marx writes:

> [T]he producer in fact creates his own surplus-value [on the assump-
> tion that he sells his commodity at its value], in other words, only
> his own labour is materialized in the whole product. But, that he is
> able to appropriate *for himself* the whole product of his own labour,
> and that the excess of the value of his product over the average price
> for instance of his day's labour is not appropriated by a third person,
> a *master*, he owes not to his labour—which does not distinguish him
> from other labourers—but to his ownership of the means of produc-
> tion. It is therefore only through his ownership of these that he takes
> possession of his own surplus-labour, and thus bears to himself as

wage-labourer the relation of being his own capitalist. (Marx 1963a: 408–409)

By bringing together Marx's insight concerning the inherently contradictory character of the petty-bourgeoisie as a class and Carchedi's insight into the contradictory functions of the many waged or salaried employees whom he subsumes under the rubric of "the new middle class," we are better positioned to define an authentic, albeit relatively small, "intermediate" class that is situated, in contradictory fashion, between capital and wage-labour. Some elements of this *highly heterogeneous* class are objectively very close to a working-class structural location while others stand closer to the capitalist class.

The existence of such an intermediate class (as an ensemble of contradictory class locations) is not in dispute here, nor is the scientific value of its analysis. But the discursive association of this class (which constitutes a distinct *minority* within contemporary capitalism) with hegemonic conceptions of which class constitutes "the majority" within advanced capitalist societies represents an illegitimate adaptation to the *ideological* presuppositions embedded in popular discourse on class. The persistence of this association within the social-scientific literature constitutes a compelling reason for insisting that the term "the middle class" is *inherently obscurantist and ideological,* and that it therefore ought to be banished from any discourse on class that aspires to scientific rigour.

The Social Psychology of Subjective Perceptions of "The Middle Class"

To be sure, the social-scientific analysis of class must still address, as *one* of its concerns, the *source* of the popular notion that "most people are middle class." The habit of identifying the middle class with *middle income groups* that comprise the majority of the population but that are most often *components of the working class* is obviously one that has many sponsors, including those same agencies of socialization that Forcese cites as perpetrators of the myths of classlessness and equal opportunity. Schools, churches, political parties, governments, and corporate mass media are all faithful purveyors of ideas and images of society that emphasize social harmony, a symmetry of merit and reward, and the naturalness of "class peace."

In addition to these transmission belts of the dominant ideology, however, it is necessary to give due weight to certain social-psychological factors rooted in "reference group" dynamics. In this connection, Kelley and Evans make the following interesting observation:

> People's subjective images of class and class conflict reflect a mixture of both materialist forces and the vivid subjective images of equality and consensus among family, friends, and co-workers. These reference group processes distort perceptions of class. They make most people think they are middle class, thereby weakening the link between objective class and subjective perceptions of class and class conflict, fostering consensual rather than conflictual views of class relations, and attenuating the links between class and politics. (1995: 157)

By materialist forces, Kelley and Evans understand those objective aspects of class position that are defined by ownership and control of the means of production (traditional Marxist criteria) as well as educational attainment, occupational status, and income level (criteria associated with the "socioeconomic status" approach of sociological functionalism). While it is certainly problematic to treat occupational status as an objective "materialist" indicator of class, and simply wrong to attribute to Marx "the materialist thesis that politics reflects people's objective class positions" (157), Kelley and Evans argue, with some justification, that reference group dynamics can have a more powerful effect on people's perceptions of their class position than "materialist forces." One might quibble with the assumption that reference group processes are not themselves "materialist forces," but, leaving that question aside, Kelley and Evans are quite right to observe that people often "perceive the world as an enlarged version of their reference group" (158). For this reason

[people] assess their class locations in light of the educational levels, occupations, and incomes of the people around them. Because
family, friends and coworkers are usually similar ... most people
see themselves as average and unexceptional. Moreover, even very
high-status people place many others above themselves, and very
low-status people see others even lower.... Hence, most people locate
themselves near the middle of the class hierarchy. (1995: 158)

In the mid-1990s, surveys of popular perceptions of class in six Western
countries confirmed that subjective class identification is overwhelmingly
with the "middle classes" in a standardized 10-class schema. In Australia,
Austria, Germany, Switzerland, the United States, and Great Britain, "the
modal class position is near the middle of the 10-class scheme, with a
majority perceiving themselves to be in class 4, 5, or 6." This leads Kelley
and Evans to conclude that there is "no evidence of a numerically dominant lower class, as traditional materialist theories posit. Instead, reference
group forces restrict the subjective arena to a narrow range in the middle of
the class hierarchy" (166).

Kelley and Evans are undoubtedly correct to adduce reference group
dynamics as a powerful factor inhibiting the development of the working
class as a "class for itself" while also fostering the notion among working-
class people that they are rather typical members of a middle-class society.
But the existence of powerful forces deflecting the development of proletarian class consciousness would hardly be a revelation to Karl Marx and
his successors. Furthermore, there is no evidence that the Marxist tradition of class theory has ever maintained that something called "the lower
class" is "numerically dominant"—either in "objective" or "subjective"
terms. Rather, Marx's view was that the development of capitalist society
would bring about the inexorable *proletarianization* of the majority of its
population. It was a *working-class majority* that Marx anticipated, not a
"lower-class majority." What's more, the key political and pedagogical task
from Marx's perspective was hardly to combat workers' conceptions of
themselves as average members of the "middle-income strata" of society,
still less to convince the working-class majority that they belong to "the

lower class," but rather to impart to them an understanding that (a) capitalism operates primarily in the interests of the capitalist class and at the expense of those who must work for a living, and (b) capitalism can and should be replaced by a new socialist order that can serve the interests of the vast majority—a majority that would most certainly encompass the bottom 8 to 9 "classes" of the 10-class scheme referred to by Kelley and Evans. Such an understanding is the essence of Marx's concept of proletarian class consciousness.

Contrary to Kelley and Evans' implication, Marx never held that such a political class consciousness could arise *spontaneously* under the impact of "materialist forces." If it could, there would be no need for political organization, agitation, and education to help the working class overcome the many subjective factors and persistent ideological notions that impede an objective, scientific understanding of capitalist social reality—obstacles to class consciousness that have engaged the theoretical and practical interest of Marxists as diverse as Kautsky and Lenin, Gramsci and Trotsky.

To be sure, capitalist development since Marx's day has produced a bewilderingly complex occupational structure that *appears* to contradict Marx's prediction of an inexorable process of proletarianization and simple class polarization. The rapid growth of the industrial proletariat during the era of capitalist industrialization was succeeded in the cradles of Western capitalism by the decline of the "blue-collar" industrial workforce. Until recently, the twentieth century saw a proliferation of white-collar employments, many of them "bureaucratic positions" predicated on the separation of head and hand. More and more wage-labourers, in the developed capitalist countries, began to perform what Marx would have called *unproductive labour,* that is, labour that may be "socially necessary" to the reproduction of the capitalist system, but which is not directly implicated in the production of goods and services in the *commodity* form: the form of the product of labour that yields a profit to capital (Smith 1993, 2010; Sato 2012). The secular expansion of the state in most capitalist countries (up to the 1980s at least) also produced a growing number of (unproductive) wage-labourers who were not in the employ of private capital, but who nevertheless served the *social capital* by reproducing the institutional conditions and attenuating the systemic contradictions of the capitalist order.

Another significant development in the most advanced societies has been the emergence of a new layer of salary-earners employed in the digital-technology industries that some theorists assert have fundamentally transfigured contemporary capitalism. Hardt and Negri's writings (discussed in Chapter 4) have inspired a new school of thought according to which an age of "cognitive capitalism" has arrived (Boutang 2011)—a stage of capitalist development in which manual wage-labour has been eclipsed as the main source of surplus value by the "cognitive labour" of highly skilled workers overseeing the production and development of enormously profitable digital devices whose "market value" depends much more on the technical information they embody than on the labour required for their production. These well-paid "middle-class knowledge workers" are held to be central to contemporary capitalism not so much because of their numerical weight (which is insubstantial) but by dint of the increasingly crucial role they allegedly play in the valorization of capital. And yet, as both Carchedi (2011b) and Starosta (2012) have persuasively argued (albeit in somewhat different ways), the theorists of "cognitive capitalism" have by no means succeeded in refuting the idea that the exploitation of the mass of wage-earners remains the fundamental source of surplus value or in establishing that the production of "wealth" in contemporary capitalism has somehow been liberated from the dictates of the law of value. Indeed, the deepening valorization crisis and accompanying financialization of global capitalism over the last 30 years would seem to testify to the manifest *failure* of digital technology to even stabilize much less reinvigorate the global economy. From the standpoint of the global, macroeconomic requirements of capital, this new technology may well be much more a part of the problem than a solution to the malaise of twenty-first-century capitalism.

The upshot is that none of the labour-force trends discussed above belie Marx's fundamental prognostications regarding the developmental tendencies of the capitalist class structure. On the contrary, Marx's theoretical framework remains essential to *explaining* the proliferation of socially necessary unproductive labour, the bureaucratization of industry and the state, the decline of the blue-collar industrial workforce, the emergence of a new layer of "knowledge workers" involved in information and digital technologies, and the growing global "surplus population" of precariously employed or self-employed labourers. For what is critical to the explication of these trends is precisely an adequate analysis of the laws of capital accumulation, the real subordination of labour to capital, the crisis tendencies of advanced capitalism, and the processes of objective socialization that prefigure, albeit in a highly distorted form, some of the contours of the future socialist society—an analysis vigorously pursued by Marx in *Capital* and the *Grundrisse*.

Notwithstanding Kelley and Evans' entirely unfounded assertion of the "numerical decline of the working class" (1995: 175), Marx's main predictions have been strikingly confirmed concerning the future evolution of the capitalist class structure. Marx was entirely right to foresee an increasing tendency for the direct producers to be separated (alienated) from their means of production and to be transformed into wage-labourers. In a related vein, he was correct to forecast the gradual disappearance of independent commodity producers—the traditional petty-bourgeoisie of small farmers, fishermen, artisans, and so on—as well as small shopkeepers in the sphere of circulation. What's more, he was able to foresee accurately—and to specify the "law of motion" of the capitalist economy that promotes—the process of concentration and centralization of capital that permits the greater part of the productive resources of society to come under the control of a relatively small number of capitalist enterprises (what nowadays are called monopolistic or oligopolistic transnational corporations), while a growing mass of humanity is consigned to a life of misery. In all of these forecasts Marx has been proven remarkably prescient—and far more so than any of his contemporaries. Above all, his prediction of a deepening division within capitalist society between capitalist employers and those who must sell their labour-power (intellectual or manual, skilled or unskilled) in order to live has been completely borne out.

What *is* questionable, however, for Marxist and non-Marxist theorists alike, is the notion that the obligation to sell one's labour-power can be seen as a *sufficient* criterion for a specifically "working-class" location on the class map. If it is, then clearly the great mass of working people in advanced capitalist societies (between 80% and 90% in Western Europe, the US, Canada, Japan, and Australia) have already been inducted into the ranks of "the working class," even if many fail to realize it. And yet, from a Marxist perspective, while there is an attractive simplicity to such an image of developed capitalist societies, there are also some major problems with it. For example, how meaningful is it to include within the same class category an assembly-line worker at an auto plant and a police officer whose job may be to escort scabs across the auto workers' picket lines in the midst of a strike? Members of the police force may well be wage-labourers, but they also happen to be "hired guns" on behalf of bourgeois property: the enforcers of laws that pre-eminently serve the interests of capital. Consider another example. Within the production process, some wage-labourers may carry out supervisory functions that are of crucial significance to maintaining capitalist domination over the labour process. Such wage-labourers (call them scientific managers) may carry out a range of work tasks that are technically *necessary* to production, but their supervisory tasks also define them, in good measure, as "troubleshooters" for capital. (Recall the notorious boast of nineteeth-century American railroad magnate Jay Gould to the effect that he could hire half the working class to kill the other half!)

The point is simple: the obligation to sell one's labour-power to make a living is certainly a necessary condition for a working-class designation, but *the nature of the work they perform* will serve to situate many wage- and salary-earners in ambiguous spaces somewhere "between" the working class and the capitalist class. Moreover, such elements constitute, quite clearly, a significant "buffer" between the two principal classes of advanced capitalist society.

But how large is that buffer, how independent can it become from capitalist control, and how significant an obstacle is it to the development of the class struggle that Marx saw as crucial to the transition to socialism? These are the questions that must ultimately shape the most important debates regarding "the middle class." As in all such debates, our first task must be to sort out its ideological determinants from its scientific ones.

Ideological Constructions of the Middle Class

I have already indicated that there are powerful forces at work promoting the notion of the centrality or overarching significance of the middle class in advanced capitalist societies. I want now to indicate the senses in which the conventional (popular and often putatively "social-scientific") notion of "the middle class" is an *ideological* construction, and I want to do this in connection with two fundamental propositions.

Proposition One: Within non-Marxist social theory, the notion of a pre-ponderantly middle-class society functions to discourage a focus on the class struggle and the structural antagonism between labour and capital.

The ideological strength of non-Marxist approaches to class analysis lies in their *flexibility* in the service of the notion of the "middle-class society." If the conventionally understood middle class begins to disappear according to one set of definitional criteria, it can be readily reconstituted on a new set. For functionalists, this is easily done by changing the relevant distributional criteria (income levels, socio-economic status indices, etc.) defining upper, middle, and lower "classes." For those following in the tradition of Max Weber, classical sociology's greatest anti-Marx, the problem is one of redefining the unique "market capacities" that are designated to conceptualize the middle class: levels of authority or control on the job; relative positions within a bureaucratic hierarchy; and skills and educational credentials (Weber 1978; Giddens 1973). The fundamental *arbitrariness* of both functionalist and Weberian approaches to defining class boundaries appears well suited to the bourgeois ideological imperative to give pride of place to *subjective* considerations in the conceptualization of class. In this way, non-Marxist social theory adapts to and encourages those ideological and social-psychological forces that dominate popular discourse on class and that encourage the notion of "the middle-class society," *regardless of objective trends with respect to income inequality and regardless of the persistent realities of structured social inequality under capitalism.*

From the end of World War II until the 1970s, most advanced capitalist societies saw a small but real attenuation of income inequalities, one that conferred some credence on the notion that "the middle class" was both expanding and becoming more prosperous. If the middle class is defined as an ensemble of *middle-income categories*, as it usually is in popular discourse, then socio-economic trends for some three decades lent powerful support to the notion of an emerging "middle-class society." Even today, income distribution graphs for most Western countries still appear as bell-shaped curves. However, with the advent of neoliberalism, humps have been growing at the extremes of the income scales of these countries at a rapid rate. In the United States in particular, the statistical evidence for the decline of the "middle-income" middle class is considerable. The majority of the population may still be clustered around the median income, but that is cold comfort for the 80% of the workforce whose real wages were at least 18% lower at the turn of the twenty-first century than they had been in the early 1970s (Head 1996).

Non-Marxist class theories are not entirely subjectivist in orientation, however. Within the context of a dualistic and non-dialectical social ontology, considerable weight is often given to material factors that are deemed to have a "natural" basis. Hence, the *technological determinism* that informs both functionalist theory and Weberian class theory encourages the notion that class is largely an epiphenomenon—a mere "effect"—of the technical division of labour, which itself is influenced by the changing characteristics of "the market" (cf. Campbell 1977). In contrast to Marxist theory, class relations are not seen as *fundamental*, as a central determinant of changes in the technical division of labour (for example, the transition from "Fordism" to lean production) or in market structures (for example, the expansion of the reserve army of the unemployed). Accordingly, the forces that are reshaping and restructuring the world economy in this era of neoliberal globalization are not conceived to be essentially *class-based*, and their effects on the class structure (whether this is defined in "occupational" or "market capacity" terms) are conceived as simple givens that flow inexorably from the march of science/technology, on the one hand, and the disciplining rigours of the "free market," on the other.

The upshot is that the symbiotic articulation of subjectivist and technological-determinist perspectives on class permits bourgeois social theory to continually redefine the middle class in ways that encompass the majority, even when this putative "middle-class majority" is suffering a significant decline in living standards owing to factors that are purported to be *independent* of any inherent structural antagonism between capital and labour.

Proposition Two: Ideological constructions of the middle class are not unique to apologists for capitalism or theoretical antagonists of Marxism. Many Marxists also abuse the term, and they frequently do so for reasons having less to do with "science" than with justifying a particular political strategy or programmatic orientation.

The history of political parties and social movements identifying in some measure with Marxian socialism is replete with efforts to deny the "necessity" or the "practicality" of Marx's own strategic and programmatic vision of workers' revolution. The impulse toward the adoption of a *reformist* orientation has been a powerful one, in the first place among Social Democrats linked to bureaucratized labour movements in advanced capitalist societies, but also among Communists (read, Stalinists) following the lead of ostensibly Marxist states wishing to appease powerful capitalist enemies. The German Social Democrat Eduard Bernstein sought to justify his "revisionist" doctrine of evolutionary socialism, in part, by documenting empirically the growth of the German petty-bourgeoisie in the last years of the nineteenth century and therewith the predictive failure of Marx's analysis. Stalin's Communist International proclaimed the need for the class-collaborationist policy known as the Popular Front in the 1930s, supposedly as the best means of drawing "the middle classes" into the struggle against fascism. The shift from an ultra-left sectarian policy (which in Germany had precluded even a "united front in action" with Social Democratic workers against the Nazis) to a policy of government coalitionism with openly pro-capitalist forces (however insignificant, as in Spain) was justified by Stalin with the claim that the "middle class" was too significant a social force—and potential ally in the struggle against fascism—to be ignored. In the end, the policy of the Popular Front was no less a failure than that which had paved the way for Hitler's victory in Germany. In France, the left-leaning Blum popular front was succeeded by the right-leaning Daladier popular front, which in turn gave way to the fascist Vichy regime. In Spain, the policy of collaborating with what Trotsky aptly called the "shadow of the bourgeoisie" (a few lawyers) resulted in the disarming and the demoralization of the Spanish workers, who had sought to extend the struggle against Franco into a struggle against capitalism (Trotsky 1973e; Morrow 1963). In the end, the Stalinists' accommodation of capitalist interests, including opposition to independence for Spanish Morocco, failed to prevent the military victory of Franco's armies, which just happened to include a large number of Moroccan conscripts (Broué & Témime 1972: 266–67).

Ellen Wood (1986) has documented the politico-ideological determinants of some other, more recent trends in ostensibly Marxist class theory. The influential works of Nicos Poulantzas (1973, 1975, 1978) are a case in point. Wood argues that Poulantzas's excessively narrow definition of the working class (one that excludes unproductive wage-labourers as well as all wage-labourers with any degree of control over the labour of others or with any role in the dissemination of bourgeois ideology) and his concomitant view that the "new petty-bourgeoisie" is the most rapidly growing class within advanced capitalist societies must be seen, above all, as a theoretical justification for a long-standing class-collaborationist politics that culminated in his support for the Eurocommunist project of the mass Communist parties of the 1970s. Italian CP leader Enrico Berlinguer's call for an "historic compromise" between the working class and the bourgeoisie was a far cry from Marx's "workers of the world unite"—but it was given the mantle of realism by Poulantzas's treatises proving, through definitional sleights of hand, the ineluctable numerical decline and decomposition of the working class. The political logic of this unity of neo-Marxist theory and Eurocommunist reformism and class collaboration played out in the 1990s with the transformation of the bulk of the Italian CP into the overtly pro-capitalist Democratic Left Party (now the Democratic Party) and of its rump "left-wing" split-off (Communist Refoundation) into a minor player in a series of class-collaborationist "centre-left" coalitions.

The Concept of Ideology

To support the above propositions regarding the ideological construction of "the middle class," I want now to indicate the senses that I bring to the concept of ideology.

Sense One: *Forms of consciousness, and structures of knowledge and belief, are socially constructed.* Jorge Larrain (1979) refers to this as the *positive* conception of ideology. The emphasis in such a conception is on how the *lived experiences* of people both shape and limit their consciousness. With respect to the popular ideological construction of the middle class, the impact of reference group processes is an excellent example of such lived experiences. So is the psychological propensity of many working people to believe that the next best thing to *being* a bourgeois is to *think* like one (a credo that finds striking expression in "celebrity culture" and in the ethos of professional sports). A key point to be made in this connection is that the "social being" that Marx says "determines consciousness" includes much more than objective class relations, as Marx himself certainly realized. It includes a myriad of structures and processes (from commodity fetishism to intimate personal relationships) that influence people to adopt forms of consciousness that may be inimical to their interests. Ideology is, in this limited sense, a "false" consciousness; but it is also "authentic" inasmuch as it is rooted in the realities of a determinate form of society and reflects its contradictions. As Sean Sayers aptly puts the matter:

> *Where do incorrect ideas come from?* They come from *reality*—like all ideas. In particular, ideological representations derive from and reflect reality. They take idealized and distorted forms, moreover, because of the contradictions and conflicts which are part and parcel of real life. *Their power is the power of reality.* (1985: 106)

Closely related to this is a concept of ideology as the "common sense" view—the "practical wisdom" and "common knowledge" of everyday life (Althusser 1971). An ideological construct on this understanding is one that is based on an uncritical acceptance of what seems practically necessary and expedient from the standpoint of the prevailing social relations (for example, the supposed "imperative" to reduce government deficits by cutting social programs, with nary a thought given to the revolutionary alternative of *cancelling* the national debt through the socialization of the means of production, distribution, and exchange).

The notions of a "middle-class society" or of an "ascendant middle class" are ideological constructs in the sense that they focus attention on the experiences of class that are most visible and immediately available to the great majority of people, as well as on the means available to them *as individuals* to achieve some measure of personal success and upward social mobility within actually existing capitalist society. Furthermore, these notions reinforce quite powerfully the view that it is "education"—or more precisely, the acquisition of educational credentials—that is most likely to make a real difference to people's "life-chances." While there is some limited truth to this, such a view also involves a good deal of exaggeration, deception, and simple wishful thinking, while also serving to divert attention from the need for collective working-class action to bring about an egalitarian socialist society.

Sense Two: *Ideology always works to favour the interests of some, while disadvantaging others,* or what Larrain calls *the negative conception of ideology.* In this conception, ideology facilitates the *domination* and/or *exploitation* of some groups over/by others. This is close to Joseph McCarney's (1980) interpretation of Marx's concept of ideology as thought that serves class interests, as well as Terry Eagleton's definition of ideology as "processes whereby interests of a certain kind become masked, rationalized, naturalized, universalized, [and] legitimated in the name of certain forms of political power" (1991: 202).

The notions of a middle-class society or an ascendant middle class are ideological in this sense because they serve to conceal the social antagonisms at the basis of capitalist society, while representing the structured social inequality of capitalism as *natural*—the product of a fixed human nature on the one hand and the imperatives of technological development and market forces on the other. Once again, by emphasizing the importance of educational credentials to personal success, such a conception directs attention to the occupational structure as the locus, and even the ultimate source, of class differentiation (thereby also deflecting attention from those elements within the class structure, namely the capitalist class, whose *dominant* class position is defined not by occupation but by *ownership*).

In a similar vein, the image of an expansive middle-class society buttresses a whole range of ideological notions that are crucial to legitimating the forms of political power associated with contemporary liberal democracy. These notions include the priority of "citizenship" in the construction of political identities and the illusion that being "taxpayers" confers real political power on the "middle-class majority"—who are also rather dubiously purported to be the main source of tax revenues.[1]

Sense Three: *Ideology exists in a contradictory relationship to a scientific approach to the understanding of social reality.* At a minimum, science involves a commitment to disclosing the non-obvious, non-"commonsensical" dimensions of reality, and to analyzing empirical data in a way that is informed by theoretical perspectives that *account* for such hidden, but nevertheless very real and determining, aspects of social being. Conventional conceptions of the middle class—whether embedded in popular or in ostensibly social-scientific discourse—fall well short of these minimal criteria for a scientific approach. Among other things, they privilege consciousness (or more precisely, subjectivity) over social being, while simultaneously underestimating the degree to which consciousness can be deflected from truth by misleading appearances and by reducing historically determinate social relations of production (the capital-wage-labour relation, the law of value, etc.) to the status of "natural laws."

A satisfactory approach to the scientific conceptualization of class must take account of both objective and subjective factors in class formation, while insisting upon the "internal" relationship of these factors (Ollman 1993). Furthermore, it must impose a theoretical order on raw empirical facts by identifying those empirical features that are most decisive to the development of classes as entities that "make a difference" (in Livant's sense)—entities that are capable of defining and/or altering the course of social development in *significant* ways.

The Collapse of "Post-Capitalism" and the Future of the Professional-Managerial Middle Class

In light of these last considerations, I want to suggest that the concept of an ascendant and increasingly "independent" middle class (so integral to conventional, liberal-democratic images of modern capitalism) is now on particularly shaky ground. In popular liberal-democratic discourse, the middle class is seen as a class that owes its pre-eminence not only to its (expanding) numerical weight, but also to the power conferred upon it by its privileged role in social reproduction. Ultimately, the "middle class" can be seen as the defining reality of contemporary society only to the extent that it sheds its "contradictions"—its role in *mediating* between capital and labour—and asserts itself as a hegemonic class force; that is, to the degree that it succeeds in *transforming* capitalist society into a "post-capitalist" society founded upon the traditional petty-bourgeois values of "classless-ness" (or class harmony), meritocracy, and what Marx called "bourgeois right" ("from each according to his ability, to each according to his contri-bution" [Marx 1970: 18–19]).

Since the World War II, there have been numerous attempts in the social-scientific literature to establish the centrality of the "middle class" to "post-capitalist," "post-industrial" or "postmodern" society. In the early postwar period, middle-class dominance was celebrated as a triumph of techno-cratic and meritocratic principles over the inherited privileges of private property ownership. A "managerial revolution" and "new industrial state" were supposedly allaying the spectre of class struggle between socially irre-sponsible capitalists and socialist-minded workers (Berle & Means 1932; Parsons 1953; Galbraith 1968).

New times, however, bring new ideas—and new twists on old ideological themes. Since the early 1980s, neoconservatives have revisited and popu-larized a new take on the thesis of "managerial" or "technocratic" revolu-tion—by deploring the usurpation of power by "liberal elites" and blaming "bureaucrats" and "technocrats" for the malaise of contemporary capitalist society (Ehrenreich 1989). If the idea of a managerial revolution was once deployed to support the notion of a convergence between capitalist and socialist "industrial systems" (Mayer 1970), the collapse of "actually exist-ing socialism" has dealt a decisive blow to this idea. What's more, the very partial "decommodification" of social life that was imposed on Western capitalism by the postwar strength of national labour movements and the "threat" of Soviet-style "real socialism" is now regarded as a tumour on the underbelly of a crisis-ridden capitalism. In this context, contradictory class locations have begun to shrink for increasing numbers of workers, both in the private and public sectors. It is an old-fashioned capitalism that is once again on the rise, and the champions of this neoliberal capitalism believe fervently that it can—and must—manage with a substantially smaller buffer between capital and labour than it did during the more economically buoyant, but also more politically perilous, days of the Cold War. Far from being an ascendant class, what Barbara and John Ehrenreich (1978) once called "the professional-managerial class" has fallen victim to the sharpening contradictions of a capitalist order in crisis, as well as the ideological triumphalism of a bourgeoisie now convinced that it has finally exorcised "the spectre of communism."

It is worthwhile noting that the provenance of many of the theoretical perspectives that have supported the notion of an "invading middle-class, post-capitalist society" were theses originally developed by erstwhile followers of Leon Trotsky who sought to justify their rejection of Trotsky's analysis of the Soviet Union under Stalinist rule. Bruno Rizzi initiated the theoretical trend with his book *The Bureaucratization of the World* (1939), which argued against Trotsky that the Stalinist bureaucratic oligarchy was not simply a "parasite" or "tumour" on the Soviet workers' state, but a new ruling class presiding over a veritable new mode of production: bureaucratic collectivism. Stalinist Russia was described as the most advanced expression of a global bureaucratization process that was also finding expression in Nazi Germany and in Roosevelt's New Deal America. The grandfather of American neoconservatism, James Burnham (erstwhile Trotskyist theoretician and long-time *National Review* editor), developed some of Rizzi's themes in his highly influential war-time book *The Managerial Revolution* (1941). Burnham argued that a rising managerial middle class would inherit the postwar world, and that Soviet bureaucratism was simply an extreme prefiguration of this trend. Neither Rizzi nor Burnham remained for long in the orbit of ostensibly socialist politics after repudiating Trotsky's analysis and programmatic perspective. Others did, and for a time gave a more "progressive" spin to the theory of bureaucratic collectivism (and, hence, of a rising bureaucratic class).

Max Shachtman led a split from American Trotskyism that for many years continued to identify with revolutionary socialism (and even Trotskyism), while refusing to accept the orthodox Trotskyist position of "unconditional defense of the Soviet degenerated workers' state." Adopting a "third camp" stance, the Shachtmanites denounced Soviet bureaucratic collectivism as a new form of class society and eventually evolved toward a "State Department socialism," supporting "American democracy" against "Soviet totalitarianism." Many intellectuals in the orbit of Shachtmanism went on to have a strong influence in wider circles of American academic life (for example, the social democrat Irving Howe and the neoconservative Irving Kristol). In France, former Trotskyists, regrouped for a time around the journal Socialisme ou Barbarie, also insisted that the Soviet bureaucracy constituted a new ruling class. It was from this milieu that Jean-Francois Lyotard, a leading light of postmodernist theory, emerged.

As already noted, events since 1989 have not supported the theses of managerial revolution, bureaucratic collectivism, or an ascendant professional-managerial middle class—all of which have some roots in the *rejection* of Trotsky's analysis of Stalinism. Yet it can be argued that Trotsky's analysis, grounded in the theoretical categories of classical Marxism, has proven to be remarkably resilient in the face of the collapse of Stalinist "real socialism" (see Chapter 8 of this volume). To be sure, Trotsky's "optimistic" scenario of working-class political revolution against the Stalinist oligarchy was not realized in the Soviet Union (although it showed some promise of occurring in Hungary in 1956 and Czechoslovakia in 1968). But his thesis that this oligarchy was not in fact a new ruling class but a heterogeneous parasitic layer, destined to fragmentation and vulnerable to the siren calls of capitalist restoration, now seems vindicated. If the collapse of the Soviet Union and the fragmentation of the former *nomenclatura* prove anything, it is surely that many of Trotsky's critics were wrong in forecasting the consolidation of the Soviet bureaucracy as a stable ruling class riding the crest of a post-capitalist, managerial revolution that was supposedly invading East and West alike.

Conclusion

If the middle class cannot credibly be seen as an *ascendant* professional-managerial class, poised to restructure fundamentally the social relations of modern (or postmodern) societies, and if it likewise cannot be conceived as a "majority class" that combines within itself the contradictory functions of capital and labour, then "the middle class" can really only be regarded as a purely obscurantist and ideological category. The idea of "the middle class" almost inevitably invites a conceptualization of class structure consisting of upper, middle, and lower categories—categories that lend themselves to arbitrary definition and profound ideological mystification. To be sure, intermediate classes or "class locations" situated between capital and labour do exist, and these certainly include professional-managerial elements as well as the traditional, self-employed petty-bourgeoisie (from farmers to accountants). But the discursive confusion and conflation of these "in between" or "buffer" elements with the middle class of popular imagination—a confusion that seems unavoidable—should oblige social theorists to end their habit of referring to these contradictory class locations as "the middle class"—"new" or otherwise. To continue the habit is to invite the cuckoo of ideology to remain safely ensconced in the nest of science.

Notes

1. I have argued elsewhere that the component of "gross wages" withheld from workers and remitted to the capitalist state as taxes on labour income can easily be conceptualized as a *de facto* tax on capital, not labour. Moreover, all taxes paid for out of take-home ("after-tax") wages, including sales and property taxes, can be understood in the same way. In this view, taxes ostensibly "paid" by wage-earners actually form elements of the constant-capital flow—a mechanism for the transfer of value from private capitals to the capitalist state, enabling the latter to acquit its specific social-reproductive

functions on behalf of the social capital (see Smith 1994: 247, notes 14 and 15). Among other things, the idea that "labour's income" includes taxes that are then "paid by labour to the government" serves to ideologically integrate the working class into capitalist politics by encouraging the notion that wage-workers, no less than capitalists, are "citizen taxpayers" to whom the state is answerable. (With regard to this point, see Chapter 12 of this volume.) The reality is different: as most working people know only too well, their "real" income is what is left over "after taxes"—the "net income" that enables them to purchase their means of subsistence. And it is the vicissitudes of that net income that matters most to working people as they struggle with capital and the state to maintain or improve their living standards.

CHAPTER 12

"As Radical as Reality"

The streets of our country are in turmoil. The universities are filled with students rebelling and rioting. Communists are seeking to destroy our country. Russia is threatening us with her might. And the republic is in danger. Yes! Danger from within and without. We need law and order! Without law and order our nation cannot survive.

—A Harvard law student addressing parents and alumni in the 1960s. After the prolonged applause died down, the student quietly informed his audience: "These words were spoken in 1932 by Adolf Hitler." (Zinn 1990: 108–109)

"Radicalism"—of both left-wing and right-wing varieties—is the target of routine and almost ritualistic condemnation by those who fancy themselves to be part of the political centre—the so-called "mainstream." Whether conservative, liberal, or social-democratic in their political sympathies, mainstream critics of radicalism (a concept often mistakenly confused with "extremism") pride themselves on their moderation, pragmatism, and good sense in resisting the slogans and nostrums of political creeds they consider irrational and even down-right evil. For such "centrists," radicalism of any sort is a pathological and wholly illegitimate departure from a Golden Mean that has been carefully and diligently cultivated by generations of men and women possessed of sober political judgment and unimpeachable moral rectitude. Radicals are, in this definition, "fringe" elements who wish to overturn the Golden Mean and plunge society into unnecessary conflict and turmoil—whether between classes, races, ethnic and religious groups, or whole nations.

In mainstream political discourse, to characterize an individual or group as radical, and especially as "extremist," is to cast aspersions on both the goals and the methods of the individual or group in question. Radicals are often accused of embracing the morally suspect notion that "the end justifies the means," the implication being that they are prepared to use *any* means, however violent, underhanded, or undemocratic, to further their goals. It seldom occurs to the mainstream-centrist critic that the means of achieving a particular goal are usually intimately related to its very nature—and that therefore not just *any* means will do in realizing a particular end. It is also rarely acknowledged that mainstream politicians routinely practice the principle that "the end justifies the means." Indeed, if it was not with reference to the goal of ending World War II in the Pacific (and terrifying the US's war-time Soviet ally), then how exactly *did* American President Harry Truman justify his decision to drop atomic bombs on the civilian populations of Hiroshima and Nagasaki in August 1945?

According to mainstream-centrists, both the "radical left" and the "radical right" seek to effect dangerously fundamental changes—and their programs, while seemingly very different and mutually antagonistic, are equally deplorable. But this is really a tendentious claim, and one motivated by a basic satisfaction with the *status quo*. What's more, the very notion of a "radical right" is actually an oxymoron—a contradiction in terms—because, far from seeking fundamental social change, the extreme right's goal is always to preserve the existing capitalist social order, albeit through recourse to the most odious of methods.[1]

A generation ago, during the Cold War, the American political scientist William Ebenstein gave expression to the mainstream-centrist worldview with an illustration that depicts the political spectrum as a great circle. At the apex (or North Pole) of this circle is liberal-democratic capitalism, which implicitly constitutes the Golden Mean. As we move to the right or to the left away from the Golden Mean, we encounter various forms of

right-wing and left-wing "authoritarianism"; but as we continue the journey south around the circle we finally encounter fascism and communism,
which, while ostensibly on the far right and far left of the spectrum, are
actually variants of "totalitarianism." In other words, as we move to the
"radical left" or the "radical right" we paradoxically arrive at the same
unpleasant place: a political system characterized by Draconian state
repression, a complete disregard for civil liberties, and hostility toward
both "democracy" and the "free market." (Entirely absent from the political
universe depicted by Ebenstein was an array of political currents, marginal
to twentieth-century *Realpolitik*, from "libertarian capitalism" on the right
to anarchism, Trotskyism, and council communism on the left.)

The self-righteousness of those who identify with the liberal-democratic
and pro-capitalist Golden Mean, while inveighing against "radicalism" and
equating fascism and communism as twin evils, is one of the most chemi-
cally pure prejudices of our era. Furthermore, the apostles of this Golden
Mean are, at bottom, fervent defenders of the global *status quo*. While they
may sometimes advocate a few changes here and there in the ways that
the global political economy is structured, they are actually far more concerned with maintaining its "stability." But is such a stance morally balanced, moderate, or rational?

Let's recall a few facts about the present world order. Ten million or
more people die each and every year from starvation. Many millions
more die from easily preventable diseases. Over any given decade of the
past century, more people died from starvation, malnutrition, and illnesses caused by a lack of public sanitation than from all the wars and
revolutions of the modern era. The Global North, with 20% of world
population, uses up 80% of world resources and has an average per capita
income that is 15 times higher than that of the Global South. During the
five decades following the World War II, world income increased sev-
enfold in terms of real Gross Domestic Product, and income per person
more than tripled. But this gain was spread so unequally that by the 1990s
the share of world income for the richest 20% of the global population
had reached 85%, while the share for the poorest 20% had declined to
1.4% (Sklar 1995).

The global *status quo* is one in which more than three billion people (about one half of humanity) subsist on less than $2 (US) per day; in which 200 transnational corporations, employing fewer than one half of 1% of the global labour force, account for 28% of global output; in which military expenditures represent an average of around 20% of governmental expenditures worldwide; and in which well over one billion people are unemployed or underemployed. Moreover, historical statistics indicate that the trend on a global scale has been toward increasing inequality over the past century; that the existence of nominally socialist countries moderated but did not reverse that trend; and that the collapse of the former Soviet bloc and its reabsorption into the capitalist world has accelerated the dynamic toward increasing global inequality.

By what perverse logic do centrist defenders of the capitalist world order presume to lecture so-called "left-wing radicals" that they abjure moderation when they insist that these global realities are unacceptable and that fundamental, transformative change is desperately needed? How is it possible for defenders of such *extreme inequality* to posture as "moderates"? Is it not perfectly clear to all those prepared to look that the real "extremists" are those who consider the extreme inequalities and irrationalities of the global political-economic order as "normal," "natural" and even "just"?

To begin to think clearly about some of these questions we should recall the historic meaning of the "left-right" distinction. It goes back to the French Revolution. To be on "the left" means that one is troubled, to one degree or another, by the material inequalities between people in society, whereas to be on "the right" means that one supports the institutional arrangements that sustain and perpetuate those inequalities. Of course, many mainstream-centrists would now have us believe that the left-right distinction is no longer an important one—that since there is now supposedly "no alternative" to capitalism, the critique of class-based inequality has become passé and irrelevant. Sensible people have no choice but to turn their energies toward making the existing capitalist system operate as smoothly and humanely as possible. But this line of argument is simply the latest funeral oration for a political outlook that has resisted final burial time and time again: the *egalitarian* outlook that has long inspired the socialist tradition. True, the egalitarian-socialist project has suffered terrible setbacks in recent decades, but history demonstrates that it always finds a way of reviving itself.

Those who situate themselves in the political centre (or even more fashionably, if absurdly, in the "radical centre") regard themselves as sober-minded critics of a left-socialist radicalism that seeks to achieve social equality through the elimination of private property in the productive assets of society and therewith class divisions. At the same time, they also fancy themselves to be champions of a kind of "formal equality" between all members of society.[2] They are often in favour of eliminating overt discrimination against women, visible minorities, gays and lesbians, and immigrants. They denounce the racism, sexism, homophobia, and xenophobia of the extreme (sometimes fascist) right—and to this degree they seem to embrace many of the enlightened values professed by the left. But their tolerance for the *material* inequalities that are inevitably engendered by *class exploitation* means that they share a fundamental family resemblance with the right. Indeed, contrary to Ebenstein's schema, the political centre is really much closer to the "extreme right" than the "radical left"—for, like the extreme right, mainstream-centrists are in the business of defending the massive material inequalities that are the seedbed of all manner of social antagonisms, both domestically and globally.

Vladimir Ilyich Lenin, the principal leader of the Russian socialist revolution of 1917 and one of the founders of the Soviet state, was reported to have once said: "One can never be radical enough; that is, one must always try to be as radical as reality itself" (cited in Cockburn 1995: 225). Lenin believed that the existing state of the world was fundamentally flawed and argued passionately that bold, revolutionary action was urgently needed to transform it. His outlook and commitment was "radical" in that he sought to get to the root of the central problems confronting humanity and bring about the fundamental changes required to root out all forms of exploitation and social oppression.

Lenin has long been vilified in the West for having led the first and only successful workers' revolution in human history. A recent profile of him by an American critic illuminates all too well the utter hypocrisy and dishonesty of the mainstream-centrist critique of the radical left. Writing in a special issue of *Time* magazine devoted to "Leaders and Revolutionaries of the 20th Century," David Remnick quotes the following assessment of Lenin written by one-time Soviet dissident Andrei Sinyavsky: "The incomprehensibility of Lenin is precisely [his] all-consuming intellectuality—the fact that from his calculations, from his neat pen, flowed seas of blood, whereas by nature this was not an evil person. On the contrary, Vladimir Ilyich was a rather kind person whose cruelty was stipulated by science and incontrovertible historical laws. As were his love of power and his political intolerance" (1998: 56).

Remnick goes on to comment: "It is, perhaps, impossible to calculate just how many tens of millions of murders 'flowed' from Leninism....Very few of Stalin's policies were without roots in Leninism: it was Lenin who built the first camps; Lenin who set off artificial famine as a political weapon; Lenin who disbanded the last vestige of democratic government, the Constituent Assembly, and devised the Communist Party as the apex of a totalitarian structure; Lenin who first waged war on the intelligentsia and on religious believers, wiping out any traces of civil liberty and a free press" (59). Remnick provides little evidence to support these sweeping accusations. But as an example of Lenin's "cruelty" he does cite a 1918 letter by Lenin, recently unearthed from Soviet archives, in which he supposedly exhorts "Bolshevik leaders to attack peasant leaders who did not accept the revolution." Lenin wrote: "Comrades! ... Hang (hang without fail, so that people will see) no fewer than one hundred known kulaks, rich men, bloodsuckers.... Do it in such a way that for hundreds of versts around, the people will see, tremble, know, shout: 'They are strangling and will strangle to death the bloodsucker kulaks'.... Yours, Lenin."

As is common practice with anti-communist ideologues, Remnick doesn't bother to inform his readers that when Lenin penned those "cruel" words the young Soviet workers' republic was engulfed in a bitter civil war, and the rich peasants (whom Remnick prefers to call "peasant leaders who did not accept the revolution") were backing the White armies of the old order in their determined efforts to crush the Bolshevik government and undo the revolutionary victory of 1917. The impression given by Remnick is that by

1918 Lenin was already presiding over an "all-powerful" regime and that his call to hang one hundred kulaks was an act of gratuitous bloodthirstiness. He doesn't mention that the counter-revolutionary White armies, with the strong support of the most powerful capitalist countries in the world, were waging a campaign of mass terror in the countryside to dissuade poor peasants from supporting the Red Army and the Bolshevik government, or that most historians of the Russian Civil War concede that the "cruelty" of the counter-revolutionary forces far exceeded that of Lenin's followers.[3] The reader is also left in the dark concerning the fact that the Civil War raged for over three years, costing millions of lives and devastating a society already reeling from the blows of World War I. There is no acknowledgment that Lenin's commitment to a pluralistic socialist democracy was sorely tested by these conditions of civil war, or that, faced with far less dire circumstances, President Abraham Lincoln had suspended "freedom of the press" during the US Civil War of 1861–65. Remnick accuses Lenin of setting up "camps"— but what government on earth has failed to set up detention camps for prisoners of war and other perceived foes under comparable conditions of war? He accuses Lenin of creating the "totalitarian structure" later dominated by the truly murderous Joseph Stalin. But, unlike Stalin, Lenin regarded "one party rule" as a *temporary expedient* to save the Soviet republic during the first years of its existence and never as a "principle of Leninism."[4]

To equate Lenin and Stalin, as Remnick does, is to equate a revolutionary internationalist, whose "last struggle" was precisely to block the growing bureaucratization of the Communist party and the Soviet government, with the tyrant who was the personification of the nationalist, venal, and conservative bureaucracy that usurped power in the Soviet Union in the name of "building socialism in one country" (Lewin 1968; Lenin and Trotsky 1975). As early as the 1930s, Leon Trotsky, co-leader with Lenin of the Bolshevik revolution and implacable foe of the Stalinist regime, demolished the canard that Bolshevik-Leninism had led "logically" to Stalinism:

> The state built up by the Bolsheviks [reflected] not only the thought and will of Bolshevism but also the cultural level of the country, the social composition of the population, the pressure of a barbaric past

315

and no less barbaric world imperialism. To represent the process of degeneration of the Soviet state as the evolution of pure Bolshevism is to ignore social reality in the name of one of its elements, isolated by pure logic. ... [C]ertainly, Stalinism "grew out" of Bolshevism, not logically, however, but dialectically; not as a revolutionary affirmation but as a Thermidorian negation. (1970e: 3, 15)

Of course, such materialist arguments are not likely to sway such profound thinkers as Andrei Sinyavsky and David Remnick, for whom "seas of blood" flowed from Lenin's "pen." They would prefer to believe that the millions who died under Stalinism (in Mao's China, no less than in the Soviet Union) were the victims of a "bad idea"—Lenin's alleged attempt to "create a new model of human nature and behavior through social engineering of the most radical kind" (Remnick 1998: 57). Yet, as heinous as the Stalinist record of "socialist construction" really was, the fact remains that it involved both a break from many of Lenin's own most fundamental principles and a flawed but successful attempt to modernize and industrialize backward countries at breakneck speed in defiance of an aggressively hostile capitalist world. If the "primitive socialist accumulation" carried out by Stalin's and Mao's regimes cost millions of lives (many quite unnecessarily), the "primitive accumulation of capital" that permitted the industrialization of Great Britain and Western Europe produced a death toll that was at least ten times greater. Consider the millions of African slaves who died en route to the Americas or who were worked to death on New World plantations, and the tens of millions of Aboriginal peoples in the Americas, Polynesia, and Australasia who perished as a result of the spread of European colonialism. Consider the ten million Africans massacred by the Belgian colonists in the Congo in the 1890s, or the untold number of Chinese who died in the Opium Wars that Britain fought in order to open China's market to opium imports from India.

For all the undoubted horrors of the Stalinist experience of "socialist construction," the undeniable fact remains that the bureaucratized workers' states of Russia, China, Cuba, and Eastern Europe were able to achieve levels of "human development" unmatched in most of the capitalist-dominated world. Their "planned economies" produced astonishing advances, despite the bureaucratic mismanagement that plagued them. Analyzing the United Nations Human Development Index (HDI) data for 1987, shortly before the reabsorption of the Soviet bloc countries into world capitalism, the Canadian sociologist Francois Moreau calculated that the HDI for the capitalist world as a whole (including its industrialized core and third world periphery) was 629, while the HDI for the bureaucratized workers' states (or transitional societies, as he called them) of Eastern Europe, China, South-East Asia, and Cuba was 764. Moreau concluded: "What the UNDP analysis shows, no doubt without consciously intending to do so, is that transitional societies have actually achieved a higher level of 'human development' for a given level of economic development than capitalist countries" (1991: 141). Much of this progress was soon to be undone, as the forces of capitalist restoration triumphed throughout the former Soviet bloc. During the 1990s, the HDI index plummeted in many Eastern European countries, and most dramatically in the lands of the former Soviet Union.

A true measure of the "moderation" of the centrist critics of radical socialism is the equanimity with which they have witnessed the catastrophic decline of living standards in Russia and Ukraine as these countries returned to the fold of what Russian President Boris Yeltsin called "normal civilization." We do not find David Remnick and his ilk writing articles about how the mass of the former Soviet population has been sacrificed on the altar of capitalist restoration. On the contrary, we find them celebrating this "victory over communism," seemingly oblivious to its human costs. For them, apparently, the scales of human history have been re-balanced—the Golden Mean secured. And that is all that really matters.

Notes

1. The sponsorship of fascist movements in the 1920s and 1930s by some of the biggest capitalists in Germany and Italy is an inconvenient fact for those centrists (and right-wingers) who make the absurd claim that Hitler and Mussolini were proponents of a form of socialism. For more reliable assess-

ments of the actual nature of these movements, see Daniel Guerin (1973), Leon Trotsky (1972a), Alfred Söhn-Rethel (1978b), and Michael Parenti (1997).

2. It was this "formal equality" that Anatole France had in mind when he wrote famously of the "majestic egalitarianism of the law, which forbids rich and poor alike to sleep under bridges, to beg in the streets, and to steal bread."

3. W. Bruce Lincoln, hardly a pro-Bolshevik historian, writes: "[T]he enemies of Bolshevism committed some of the most brutal acts of persecution in the modern history of the Western world." He quotes White Army General Denikin: "The greater the terror, the greater our victories.... We must save Russia even if we have to set fire to half of it and shed the blood of three-fourths of all the Russians" (1989: 317, 85–86).

4. The idea that Lenin was, from the outset of the Russian Revolution, bent on achieving a political monopoly for the Communist (Bolshevik) party is belied by the fact that the Bolsheviks formed a coalition government with another party, the Left Social Revolutionaries (LSR), immediately follow-ing the October 1917 insurrection. This coalition dissolved when the LSRs refused to support the Treaty of Brest-Litovsk that ended Russia's war with Germany. Marxists, including those sympathetic to Bolshevism, do not always agree in their assessments concerning many of Lenin's policies be-tween 1918 and his death in 1924. See for example the debate in *Interna-tional Socialism*, nos. 52 (1991) and 55 (1992), involving John Rees, Robert Service, Robin Blackburn, and Sam Farber. But even Lenin's harsher Marx-ist critics acknowledge that the objective conditions confronting the fledg-ling Bolshevik regime necessitated a "repressive policy." The implicit stance of David Remnick and his ilk is that Lenin and the Bolsheviks should have simply committed suicide and abandoned their working-class base to the tender mercies of the Whites. The progenitor of this style of criticism of Leninism was the historian Leonard Schapiro, who did more to promote the idea that "Leninism led to Stalinism" than any other twentieth-century scholar. For a devastating critique of Schapiro's dishonest arguments, see "Leonard Schapiro: Lawyer for Counterrevolution" (Spartacist 1989). For a good scholarly account of the "first year of Soviet rule" from a non-Marxist perspective, see Rabinowitch (2007). See also the International Bolshevik Tendency document, *Conversation with an Anarchist* (2012).

CHAPTER 13

Beyond Social Unionism: Farm Workers in Ontario and Some Lessons from Labour History

Co-authored with Jonah Butovsky

I. Introduction

In the Canadian province of Ontario, the arrival of the new century saw a major upsurge of interest and activity surrounding the interrelated questions of farm labour unionization and the Seasonal Agricultural Workers Program (SAWP), a "guest worker program" that brings thousands of migrant farm labourers to the province each year. Scholarly studies (Basok 2003; Bauder & Preibiech 2002) and the 2003 documentary film *El Contrato* offered vivid portraits of the substandard living and working conditions of the migrant workers, as well as critical commentaries on the SAWP. In 2001, several major unions backed the Canadian office of the United Farm Workers of America in launching the Global Justice Care Van Project, whose findings were the basis of a much-publicized report and a series of public policy recommendations. In the years that followed, union officials followed up with court actions, reports, and position papers, and a Toronto-based group, Justicia for Migrant Workers (JMW), campaigned for far-reaching reform of the Canadian state's policies toward SAWP-enrolled workers.

Almost without exception, these initiatives adopted, explicitly or at least tacitly, a liberal-legalistic frame of reference. From academics to social movement activists to union officials, the assumption was widespread that "justice" for farm workers could be won through pressuring governments to enact new forms of protective legislation, extend trade union rights, and eliminate the more blatantly discriminatory features of the SAWP.[1] Court challenges, moral suasion, and public education constituted the tactical repertoire of this essentially legalistic and legislative strategy, one that accepted as a given the permanence of capitalist exploitation.[2]

In this essay, we start from a rather different set of premises. Our view is that the history of the labour movement, in North America as elsewhere, demonstrates that workers' rights have always been won through workers' own direct struggles against capital and the capitalist state, usually in defiance of prevailing legal frameworks. This is especially true for the most brutally exploited and previously unorganized sectors of the working class. Unfortunately, this elementary (Marxist) truth has been obscured in recent decades owing to the bureaucratic ossification of the organized-labour leadership and the persistent hegemony within it of a social-democratic, legalistic perspective that seeks assiduously to avoid and even derail militant, extra-legal forms of working-class struggle.

We believe that significant improvements in the conditions of both Canadian and migrant farm workers, including their attaining the same rights that are enjoyed by non-agricultural workers in Canada, depend upon a bold recovery and indeed a further development of the *class-struggle* strategy and tactics that were essential to the earlier advances of organized labour. Furthermore, such a perspective necessarily demands a struggle *within* the labour movement against the conservatism and sclerotic gradualism that now pervade it.

The case of farm labour is particularly revealing of the politico-ideological limits of "social unionism"—the most ostensibly progressive form of mainstream unionism in Canada since the advent of the neoliberal era in the early 1980s. Often contrasted to a business unionism that is wholly preoccupied with narrowly defined collective-bargaining issues, social unionism purports to address wider questions of social justice and welfare, including gender and racial oppression, as well as international labour solidarity and, more rarely, environmental issues. "Social unionism," writes Bryan Palmer (1992: 371), "preaches coalition-building, stressing that labour should unite with other progressive sectors to implement reform and better the lot of the weak and the underprivileged." Union officials who espouse social unionism are also likely to stress the need to organize the unorganized and to organize workers transnationally in response to the new realities of the North American Free Trade Agreement (NAFTA) and corporate globalization.[3]

Unfortunately there is a striking dissonance between the rhetoric of social unionism and the actual practices associated with it. For while social unionist officials can "talk the talk" (and often with great passion and urgency), they almost always fail to "walk the walk" (by mobilizing the independent power of the rank and file in militant struggle), relying instead on litigation and electoral activity in support of the New Democratic Party—activities that promise, at best, a glacial pace of social change.[4] Near-exclusive reliance on such policies amounts to a betrayal of the interests of the "underprivileged" workers that social unionists profess to champion; and this has been abundantly clear in the activity of the organized labour movement on behalf of farm labour, perhaps the most super-exploited sector of the Canadian labour force.

Compounding the problem has been the general reluctance of scholars in the field of Canadian labour studies to undertake a critical analysis of the contemporary labour movement from a Marxist, class-struggle perspective. This essay is offered as a modest contribution to such an analysis. Its purpose, it bears emphasizing, is not to provide new and original research findings on either farm labour or recent trends in organized labour, but to synthesize the findings of some of the best critical scholarship on these issues with a Marxist-socialist theoretical and historical-analytic perspective. By critically examining the response of the union officialdom to the farm labour issue, it seeks to illuminate the current impasse of organized labour and to outline some directions for its reorientation on the basis of a militant, class-struggle policy.

Our central concern is to show how some specific lessons drawn from past labour struggles can inform such a reorientation. We recognize that this enterprise is likely to arouse skepticism among those who are ill-disposed to accept the relevance of such "historical lessons," as well as among many who are keenly aware of the formidable barriers that exist to their assimilation by contemporary labour movement activists. But it is our view that the issue of relevance is ultimately inseparable from the capacity of militants to acquire and utilize forms of knowledge that an array of powerful forces seeks to suppress. A great many obstacles exist to the activation of this capacity; the silence of labour studies scholars, we think, should not be one of them.

Foremost among these obstacles is the *regression in class consciousness* that has resulted from the heavy defeats that capital has inflicted on labour on a world scale since the 1970s. Two issues, which in our judgment were critically important factors in these defeats, have received scant attention in the labour studies literature. The first is the long-standing dominance of conservative bureaucracies within the organized labour movement. The second is the "anti-hegemonic" and "anti-vanguardist" perspective that has developed among so many critical intellectuals and leftist social movement activists in recent decades. Each of these issues deserves some preliminary comment here to better situate our argument theoretically and politically.

The problem of bureaucratism has been a persistent one within organized labour movements of advanced capitalist societies for well over a century.[5] At bottom, the bureaucratization of the labour movement is a product of three factors: the need for a functional division of labour and a cadre of full-time leaders and staff members within trade unions once these organizations have established themselves as ongoing apparatuses commanding significant material resources; the ability of capital and the state to transform the full-time leaders of trade union organizations into "labour lieutenants" of the capitalist order, both through the cultivation of a labour aristocracy enjoying significant material privileges in relation to the mass of workers and through the institutionalization of a state-sanctioned collective-bargaining process that legally obliges union officials to contain workers' struggles within prescribed limits; and, finally, a "dialectic of partial conquests" (Mandel 1992) that predisposes the labour movement as a whole to reject or retreat from more radical goals in order to avoid any confrontations with capital and the state that might jeopardize previously won gains.

Together these factors tend to continually reproduce conditions conducive to "bourgeois trade union consciousness"—an outlook that limits workers' struggles to an incremental improvement in the terms and conditions of the sale of labour-power within the framework of capitalism. The corollary to this in the parliamentary-electoral arena is an "independent working-class political practice" whose ostensible purpose is to exert pressure on the capitalist state apparatus to safeguard workers' rights and to implement pro-labour policies (without encroaching upon the fundamental prerogatives of capital). This form of working-class political practice is usually referred to as *social-democratic reformism*. From a Marxist perspective, the essential problem with trade union "economism" and social-democratic reformism is their shared assumption that working-class interests can be reconciled with the requirements of the capitalist social order, and that this reconciliation can be effected on the basis of bourgeois institutions.[6]

Historical experience testifies resoundingly that a challenge to the dominance of social-democratic reformism and gradualism within the labour movement is highly unlikely to emerge from within the trade union bureaucracy itself, for this bureaucracy's materially privileged position is tied up with its perennial role as a mediator between capital and labour and its determined containment of workers' struggles within the capitalist framework. Instead, a counter-hegemonic, oppositional current must be organized in the rank and file of the labour movement to challenge it. Yet history also shows that a key subjective factor in the emergence and development of such a political class consciousness has always been the presence of an *organized* current—a vanguard—of socialist activists committed to educating the rank and file, bolstering its self-confidence, and galvanizing it in opposition to the bureaucratic leadership.[7]

The emergence (or re-emergence) of a counter-hegemonic, anti-bureaucratic opposition is long overdue in the Canadian labour movement, as it is in labour movements throughout the world. But two developments in particular have militated over the past period against any serious attempt to address the chronic crisis of leadership afflicting the working class: the huge propaganda victory scored by world capitalism that was associated with the demise of Stalinist "actually existing socialism" in the former Soviet bloc in the early 1990s, and the severe disorientation of leftist activists that attended and followed this fateful event. Reinforcing as well as reflecting these developments has been the abandonment of working-class socialism by a large majority of ostensibly left-critical intellectuals in favour of an *anti-hegemonic* politics, inspired by a postmodernist "politics of identity" and by new, reform-oriented social movements that have prioritized their own autonomy and goals over any attempt to articulate a *counter-hegemonic* basis for the mobilization of progressive forces.[8] This anti-hegemonic politics stands in explicit and conscious opposition to those trends within the socialist left (above all, Leninism/Trotskyism and revolutionary syndicalism) that have traditionally stressed both the necessary leading role of the labour movement in the struggle against exploitation and oppression, and the need to build an opposition to its existing leadership. Anti-vanguardism and reformist sectoralism have served, in other words, to *divert* left-critical intellectuals and radical activists from precisely the sort of political practice that, in the past, played such a vital role in enabling the labour movement to break free of its bureaucratic straitjacket, even if only episodically.

It has been in just this political and intellectual context that social unionism has flourished as a seeming compromise between a narrow "business unionism" and a purportedly outmoded, Marxist-inspired *class-struggle unionism*. While projecting a more modest role for organized labour in the struggle for social change (on the grounds that labour should be seen as merely one among several progressive constituencies), the social unionist bureaucrat has found common ground with "postmodern progressives" by accepting the idea that progressive change is necessarily limited to the incremental *reform* of capitalism.[9]

The common basis of social unionism and of all "new social movement" sectoralisms is precisely *reformism*—the faith that human needs (whether for material necessities, world peace, environmental sustainability, or human equality) can be met adequately within the capitalist system. Such a faith has little use for historical memory; indeed, it must devalue it. And it is for just this reason that the lessons of labour history must remain a closed book to bureaucratic conservatism and to postmodern sectoralism alike. Contrariwise, for those who uphold a politics of working-class emancipation and socialist transformation, these lessons constitute a crucial repository of hard-won knowledge that remains indispensable to defeating the now decades-old capitalist offensive against labour and to informing the latter's future struggles for a better world.

Our itinerary in this chapter is as follows. We begin with a general over-view of the situation of farm workers in Ontario, with special attention to the Niagara region. This is followed by a review of organized labour's response to the issue to date. By viewing this response in light of the con-crete historical experiences of farm worker mobilization in particular and industrial union organization in general during the last century, the pos-sibility emerges of formulating a winning strategy to organize the agricul-tural sector and win substantial improvements in the living and working conditions of all farm workers. This approach is sharply opposed to the devaluation of historical memory and experience common to bureaucratic conservatism, reformist sectoralism, and postmodernist fashions. We conclude by outlining some elements of a class-struggle approach to the problem of farm labour and with some general observations on the cur-rent malaise of organized labour and the need for a socialist intervention to renew it.

II. Farm Labour in Ontario, the SAWP, and the Response of Organized Labour

In North America, migrant farm labour tends to be associated in the public imagination with dusty sun-drenched Hispanic workers or the itinerant Joad family of John Steinbeck's *Grapes of Wrath*, set in the Depression-era United States. It is less commonly associated with Canada. Yet migrant agricultural wage-labour is a large and growing phenomenon within the Canadian economy, particularly in Southern Ontario.

The Commonwealth Caribbean and Mexican Seasonal Agricultural Workers Program was introduced by Canada's federal government in phases between 1966 and 1974 to address a chronic shortage of labour in the agricultural sector. During this period, the importation of migrant workers seemed to be the only way to maintain an adequate supply of cheap agricultural labour. Over the next three decades, however, the labour market in Southern Ontario underwent a significant change, and grow-ing numbers of Canadian wage-labourers entered the agricultural sector alongside the migrant workers. These changes reflected the transformation of Canadian agriculture as small family farms were progressively displaced by highly capitalized agribusiness operations.[10]

The Niagara region strikingly illustrates the growing concentration and capitalization of the agricultural sector. In the decades since the SAWP was introduced, Niagara has seen a shift from industrial manufacturing (cars, paper, and steel) to a predominantly service-sector economy. Today, farm operators and greenhouse growers in the region employ an expanding army of migrant workers, not because Canadian workers are being absorbed into a well-paying manufacturing sector, but because the use of migrant workers renders their operations significantly more profitable. Legislation proscribing unionization in the agricultural sector—once motivated by the precarious position of small family farms facing tight profit margins—is now a guarantor of a compliant labour force vulnerable to super-exploitation by agribusiness.

In the traditional farming communities of Niagara-on-the-Lake, Grimsby, Lincoln, and Pelham, family farms are being rapidly replaced by winemaking operations and greenhouses. Westbrook Flowers and Greenhouses Inc. in Lincoln, for instance, employs 600 workers in veritable "factories in the field"—albeit open-shop factories whose workers lack union-bargained wages and benefits. The Niagara Chamber of Commerce boasts over 250 greenhouses in operation with 18.2 million square feet "under glass or plastic" in the region.

Agricultural work in Ontario tends to be low-paying and relatively dangerous, and the historic discrimination against agricultural workers in law makes it exceedingly difficult to win improvements. The importation of migrant "guest workers" from Mexico and the Caribbean serves to depress wages and complicates union organizing by dividing workers along linguistic, racial, and national lines, as well as on the basis of citizenship.

Satzewich (1991), who was among the first to analyze migrant labour in Canada as an aspect of capitalist political economy, has observed that the importation of migrant labour has provided employers with a pool of "unfree" (effectively indentured) workers to perform work that would otherwise have to be performed by costlier "free" Canadian workers. Migrant workers are tied to particular employers, prevented from seeking alternative jobs, and denied many of the rights enjoyed by workers with citizenship or landed-immigrant status. Despite this, they remain eager to come to Canada due to a lack of economic opportunity in their home countries.

The role of racism in the super-exploitation of the migrant labour force has also been highlighted by Satzewich. Beginning in 1962, Canadian immigration policy underwent a formal deracialization, but the subsequent introduction of the SAWP was predicated on a *de facto* racialization of the migrant segment of the labour force and the deepening of divisions in the agricultural labour market. The fact that migrant workers arriving from the Caribbean and Mexico under the SAWP are almost exclusively Black and Hispanic has made it far easier for the Canadian state to deny them rights that are normally accorded to foreign workers recruited by Immigration Canada to meet specific labour market needs.[11] The denial or attenuation of basic rights and protections (employment insurance, health and safety regulations, the ability to organize against coercive practices, etc.) lowers labour costs, thereby facilitating the extraction of larger magnitudes of surplus labour from SAWP-enrolled migrant workers relative to non-racialized "free" wage-workers. In short, the racialization of unfree "guest labour" results in a regime of labour control that is both onerous and pernicious.

THE SEASONAL AGRICULTURAL WORKERS PROGRAM

As previously noted, the SAWP was introduced in the 1960s ostensibly to help satisfy a demand that was not being met by the Canadian labour force.[12] Agricultural labour shortages have existed since the turn of the twentieth century in Canada, but during a period of low unemployment and rising real wages within an expanding manufacturing sector, it was particularly difficult to recruit Canadian-born as well as landed-immigrant workers to low-paying and physically demanding agricultural jobs. Consequently, growers intensified their pressure on the federal government to open the door to migrant workers. Over the course of several decades, the SAWP expanded considerably, even though wages and benefits for agricultural work are not now substantially different from the low-paying, service-sector jobs that currently dominate the Ontario economy.

The SAWP is a component of the Non-Immigrant Employment Authorization Program run by Human Resources and Development Canada (HRDC) and Immigration Canada. A sister program is the Live-In Caregiver Program that brings "domestics" to Canada. Interestingly, the Caregiver Program permits workers to leave their positions after two years to pursue other jobs, thereby opening the prospect of eventual Canadian citizenship.[13] By contrast, migrant agricultural workers enrolled in SAWP are legally tied to their employer and must return home after a contractually stipulated period of no more than eight months. As Sharma (2001: 435) has suggested, a SAWP migrant farm worker is the "quintessential flexible employee"—a wage-labourer whose labour-power is deployed on a "just in time" basis and tailored to a post-Fordist strategy of accelerated capital accumulation. Indeed, the state-sponsored expansion of a migrant labour force that is vulnerable to super-exploitation has served Canadian capital well at a time when business and government have been seeking new and innovative methods (under the rubrics of lean production and flexible labour markets) to jack up the overall rate of exploitation and thereby raise levels of profitability on an economy-wide scale (Smith 2000; Yates 2003; T. Smith 2000).

In recent years, up to 20,000 migrant agricultural workers have come to Canada annually under the auspices of the SAWP. From 2000 to 2004, the (predominantly male) migrant agricultural labour force in Ontario increased from about 13,000 to 15,000, even as the total agricultural work force declined from 99,000 to 78,000. The proportion of migrant workers within the farm labour force jumped from 13% to 19% in just four years. In Ontario, half of the migrant workers are now from Mexico, with the other half coming from Barbados, Jamaica, Trinidad and Tobago, and other Caribbean countries.[14]

The SAWP stipulates that migrants' transportation costs to Canada are to be covered by the employer, but these costs are partially recouped later through deductions from workers' wages. SAWP-enrolled farm workers toil for nine to fifteen hours per day for little more than minimum wages. While the SAWP requires equality between wage rates for Canadian and migrant agricultural workers, and employers incur additional expenses

by providing the migrants with housing, the flexibility afforded by having employees "on call" at any time, as well as the migrants' "willingness"
to endure hard, physically debilitating labour, makes the SAWP especially
attractive to growers. Not surprisingly, the program's "equal pay for equal
work" directive is often violated in practice.

Workers enrolled in the SAWP contribute to the Canada Pension Plan
and the Employment Insurance Program, but are ineligible to collect from
either. Like all agricultural workers, they are excluded from several provisions of employment standards legislation and, in Ontario, from legislation
that permits unionization. These exclusions are especially significant given
that agricultural workers are exposed to unique hazards associated with
the use of heavy farm machinery and toxic pesticides. Migrant workers are
particularly vulnerable to such hazards because they risk repatriation at
the discretion of their employer if they resist—or even complain about—
unsafe working conditions.

While the conditions facing migrant agricultural workers are uniquely
onerous, they are also constitutive of more general conditions in what has
become a split labour market.[15] By topping up the agricultural labour pool,
the SAWP serves to keep wages for all farm workers low. In a structural,
if not in an immediate day-to-day sense, Canadian workers compete for
employment with racialized migrant workers. The resulting dynamics of
this split labour market discourage unionization in the agricultural sector
as a whole. The question is therefore posed: *Can agricultural workers in
Canada mount a serious struggle for union organization so long as the SAWP
remains in place?*

THE RESPONSE OF ORGANIZED LABOUR
Historically, the Canadian labour establishment has displayed little interest in the plight of farm workers. In part, this indifference has reflected the
equanimity with which the leaders of organized labour have accepted the
exclusion of farm labour from legislative protections of the right to trade
union organization. In part, it has reflected the growing bureaucratic conservatism and passivity of the trade unions since the high water mark of
private-sector union organization in the period immediately after World

War II. Recently, however, Canadian labour leaders have begun to protest the discriminatory treatment of migrant workers and to demand that agricultural workers be allowed to organize. To some extent, this change in attitude is attributable to the development of a social unionist sensibility. But it probably is also related to the fact that agribusiness constitutes a promising new target for recruitment at a time when union membership is declining among manufacturing, transportation, and primary resource workers.

The federal government's 1948 Industrial Relations and Disputes Investigations Act (IRDIA) obligated employers to recognize the right of workers to representation through duly certified trade unions. This legislation was a product of a number of historic (illegal) strikes waged during the 1930s and 1940s. In Ontario, a parallel piece of provincial legislation, the Collective Bargaining Act of 1943, predated the IRDIA and had been modelled on the American Wagner Act of 1935. Both the IRDIA and the Collective Bargaining Act excluded agricultural workers on the grounds that farm enterprises were unable to pay higher wages due to their low profit margins.

This exclusion has remained in effect in Ontario for more than 50 years, although it was suspended briefly in 1994 when Bob Rae's New Democratic Party (NDP) government passed its Agricultural Labour Relations Act (ALRA). The ALRA gave *non-seasonal* agricultural employees the right to unionize and allowed for the settlement of disputes through mediation and "final offer selection" arbitration. At the same time, however, the Act banned strikes on the grounds that they could damage perishable produce. This made the NDP's reform little more than a feeble half-measure, one that was easily reversed a year later when Mike Harris's victorious Conservatives rolled back the major labour reforms enacted by the NDP. The United Food and Commercial Workers (UFCW), which had organized a few hundred poultry and mushroom workers in Leamington, responded with a court challenge, arguing that the exemption of agricultural workers from the Labour Relations Act was discriminatory and therefore a violation of the Canadian Charter of Rights and Freedoms.

This challenge culminated in a 2001 Supreme Court of Canada decision (*Dunmore v. Ontario*) that directed the provincial government to extend the right of association to agricultural workers—but not the right to bargain or to strike. In response to the Supreme Court ruling, the Conservative government in 2002 introduced Bill 87, the Agricultural Employees Protection Act—a supremely cynical piece of legislation permitting farm workers to form toothless "associations," without requiring employers to recognize them. The upshot was that agribusiness remained entirely free from any legal obligation to bargain collectively with its employees (Panitch & Swartz 2003).

Despite this discouraging history, the labour officialdom has remained exclusively committed to a strategy of "judicial activism" and legislative lobbying. Since 2002, three new court challenges, all backed by the Ontario Federation of Labour (OFL), have been mounted on issues relating to Canadian and migrant agricultural workers. The first, supported by the UFCW, demanded the inclusion of agricultural workers under health and safety legislation in Ontario.[16] A second has been directed against the federal government's practice of deducting Employment Insurance premiums from migrant workers' pay cheques despite their ineligibility to receive benefits. Finally, a court challenge against the Ontario government's exclusion of agricultural workers from collective bargaining legislation has been launched by workers seeking UFCW representation at Rol-Land Farms in Kingsville, Ontario.

In 2001, OFL President Wayne Samuelson endorsed a series of recommendations made by the United Farm Workers of America (UFWA [Canadian Office]) to "address the sub-standard conditions ... migrant workers face."[17] The OFL highlighted the following demands raised in the UFWA report:

- The exclusion of farm workers from occupational health and safety legislation must be addressed. The Federal Government must either mandate the provinces to include this occupation within its legislation in order to be eligible for the SAW program or must itself include farm workers in the federal legislation for occupational health and safety.
- Provincial agricultural industries and employers should not be eligible for participation in the SAW programs until their respective

provincial governments institute protection for the migrant farm workers.

- The establishment of a national bipartite board to oversee the migrant farm worker program. The re-direction of the employment insurance premiums that migrant farm workers are obligated to pay to finance occupational health and safety training, community services, and an appeals process.
- The signing and ratification by the Canadian government of the United Nations' Convention on Migrant Workers' Rights.

While uncritically endorsing the UFWA report, the OFL leadership failed to propose any concrete means for implementing the proposals. Its implicit stance was to trust in the good will of the federal government to eliminate the discriminatory features of the SAWP and to apply pressure on provincial governments to extend legislative protections to agricultural workers. In any case, there was no demand to unionize the agricultural sector in defiance of existing legal prohibitions; no call to campaign for full citizenship rights for migrant farm workers; and no recognition that the SAWP is an important factor in perpetuating the deplorable conditions detailed in the UFWA report. Faced with overwhelming evidence of the super-exploitation of farm labour in general and the abuse of migrant workers in particular, the OFL leadership limited itself to plaintive calls for *government* action, followed up by support for the court challenges mentioned above.

Given its history in California, one might have expected the UFWA to propose direct action to terminate the SAWP as part of a union-organizing drive in the agricultural sector. Instead, it actually praised the SAWP while also calling for its reform:

All parties involved in the SAW agreements realize benefits from the migrant worker program. Consulates from the participating countries oversee their programs to ensure that their workers' rights are maintained. However conflicts may arise between the opposing needs of protecting migrant farm workers' rights and creating an environment that encourages continued employer participation....

The United Farm Workers of America—Canadian Office is not confident that the current structure of the SAW agreement, and the investigation and enforcement of the provisions contained therein are meeting current demands and needs. We do not believe the status quo of limited advocacy, community services, and training will meet the needs of an expanded program and increased workers.[18] (UFWA-CO 2001)

This position echoes the conservative and anti-labour conventional wisdom according to which the SAWP reflects permanent structural realities: a presumed necessity in the agricultural sector for indentured labour, given the reluctance of free wage-workers to seek employment there; and the convergence of agribusiness and state interests in both Canada and participating "developing countries." Ignored is the preponderance of domestic agricultural wage-workers labouring in the greenhouse industry in particular. At the same time, the UFWA position gives ground to traditional arguments by capital and the state, extending back to the earliest years of union organizing, that fixed economic barriers exist to improvements in hours of labour, working conditions, wages and collective bargaining, not only in agribusiness but in other sectors as well.

The attitude of the UFWA toward the SAWP attested to two things: a changed policy toward guest worker programs (in both the US and Canada) since the union's heyday in the 1970s, and a desire to accommodate the social unionist vision of its partners in the Global Justice Care Van Project, the history of which was noted in the report:

The United Farm Workers Union, Canadian Office was contacted early this spring with regard to a group of migrant farm workers in Leamington, Ontario. Concerns were raised over the repatriation of some twenty migrant farm workers who had expressed dissatisfaction with their living and working conditions. As a result of these early conversations with migrant workers in Leamington, the UFWA–Canadian Office proposed the Global Justice Care Van Project. The Care Van project allowed the UFWA to continue the discussions and undertake preliminary research and investigation of migrant farm worker issues. The Canadian Labour Congress, United Steel Workers of America, United Food and Commercial Workers and Canadian Auto Workers Unions contributed the necessary funding to finance the program as a measure of their commitment to worker global solidarity. (UFWA-CO 2001)

This solidarity, however, stopped well short of any attempt to organize the unorganized or to transgress the boundaries of the judicial process and legislative reform politics.[19]

III. Some Lessons from the History of the Labour Movement

Those who seek to advance the interests of farm workers in Ontario today would do well to study the important lessons of the struggles of the United Farm Workers (UFW) in California since the 1960s. The necessity for an *industrial* form of union organization makes the lessons of the earlier, historic battles that forged industrial unions like the United Auto Workers, the Teamsters, and the International Longshore and Warehouse Union equally important to recall.

We recognize that the agricultural labour market of California in the 1960s and 1970s differed in some important respects from that which exists in Ontario today. One major difference is that *domestic* farm workers in California in the 1960s were overwhelmingly Chicano and Filipino. Divisions within the farm labour force were not clearly along the lines of race or ethnicity, and so these were not major factors in defining the contours of the split labour market. In Ontario, today, where the migrant labour force is racialized, combating any and every manifestation of racism toward migrant workers is a necessary precondition for successful organizing. A second difference is that, after the Bracero Program ended in 1964, the most significant division within the farm labour force was between US domestic workers and undocumented migrant workers (so-called "wetbacks" or "illegals"), whose influx into the farms and orchards of California not only continued but expanded enormously from the 1950s up to the present day.

These differences should be kept in mind as we review the general lessons of the California experience and assess their relevance to the current situation of farm workers in Ontario. It should be said, however, that neither of these differences made the unionization of farm workers in 1960s California easier than it is today in Ontario. On the contrary, the growing army of undocumented Mexican workers in California has presented an unusually formidable problem that is not faced by those seeking to organize Ontario's agricultural workers.

Our purpose here is not to review in detail the history of the UFW, but rather to focus on what worked and what failed to work in the UFW's organizing efforts. Such a balance sheet requires that the policies of Cesar Chavez and his successors in the UFW leadership be subjected to a searching criticism—one which is entirely warranted, we think, in view of the dismal long-term results of the UFW's reliance on pacifism, consumer boycotts, and legislative initiatives by "friends-of-labour" Democrats following the UFW's initial successes with the strike weapon in the early phases of its organizing drive. In short, the UFW experience offers both positive and negative lessons for Canadian farm workers.[20]

Lesson One: The existence of a government-sponsored "guest worker program" that provides unfree migrant farm labour constitutes a major obstacle to successful organizing.

Most accounts of the UFW's history agree that the termination of the Bracero Program was a necessary, if not sufficient, condition for the dramatic successes achieved by the union in the 1960s. This program, which originated during World War II as an informal agreement between the US and Mexican governments to supply Mexican labour for American growers, was formalized in 1951 as Public Law 78:

Public Law 78 stated that no *bracero*—a temporary worker imported from Mexico—could replace a domestic worker. In reality this provision was rarely enforced. In fact the growers had wanted the Bracero Program to continue after the war precisely in order to replace domestic workers.

The small but energetic National Farm Labor Union, led by dynamic organizer Ernesto Galarza, found its efforts to create a lasting California farmworkers union in the 1940s and 50s stymied again and again by the growers' manipulation of *braceros*.

Over time, however, farmworkers, led by Cesar Chavez, were able to call upon allies in other unions, in churches and in community groups affiliated with the growing civil rights movement, to put enough pressure on politicians to end the *Bracero* Program by 1964. (Glass 2005)

The Bracero Program was undoubtedly an important factor in a set of objectively unfavourable circumstances that militated against the success of farm worker organization in the 1940s and 1950s. In his history of the Bracero Program and of the NFLU's attempted organizing drive, Ernesto Galarza noted:

Adverse effect brought the National Farm Labour Union to [California] in 1947. In the following five years the Union established locals in Kern, Imperial, Monterey, Fresno and other major production centers.... A strike was called against the DiGiorgio Fruit Corporation in October 1947, and another attempt was made against large commercial producers of cantaloupes in the Imperial Valley in 1951. In both instances the *bracero* was a most effective weapon in turning back unionization. (Galarza 1964: 216)

However, what is ignored in Galarza's account and in other histories depicting the *braceros* as strikebreakers is the fact that the first response of the *braceros* was to leave the fields in support of the National Farm Labor Union's strike of 1947. Only the threat of deportation forced them back to work, thereby sealing the defeat of the strike. The NFLU played into the hands of the growers and alienated the *bracero* workforce for years to come by calling for deportations in order to stop scabbing. The outcome of the 1947 strike and the history of farm worker organization in the 1950s and beyond might well have been very different had the NFLU and its allies in the American Federation of Labor opposed deportations and taken a strong stand on behalf of *bracero* rights.[21]

It is widely accepted that Chavez had little choice but to campaign for the exclusion of *braceros* in the early 1960s as part of his organizing drive. Yet, it is at least conceivable that the changed political climate fostered by the civil rights and other movements in the 1960s might have allowed for a union strategy aimed at organizing farm workers across the *bracero*-domestic divide. By linking the struggle to organize US farm labour with a campaign for full citizenship rights for all immigrant workers—both *braceros* and undocumented migrants—the UFW could have laid a solid basis for a powerful union movement. Such a strategy could have undercut later efforts on the part of the growers to use undocumented Mexican workers as scabs in the 1970s—efforts to which Chavez responded, to his discredit, by co-operating with the Immigration and Naturalization Service (INS) in operations to round up and deport "illegals."[22]

Chavez's organizing strategy depended crucially on winning the support of liberal-minded consumers, the Catholic Church, and "labour-friendly" (Democratic Party) capitalist politicians, elements unlikely to favour extending citizenship rights to Mexican migrants. To be sure, Chavez's nativist orientation appeared to work for a time. The elimination of the Bracero Program in 1964 helped pave the way for the UFW's organizing successes later in the decade. But in sacrificing the principle of class solidarity across national lines to avoid offending the political mainstream, Chavez's policy eventually undermined the union's position.

What lesson does this hold for Canadian farm labour? Clearly, the SAWP is similar to the Bracero Program in its essentials, involving the government-managed importation of unfree migrant labour and the creation of a two-tier agricultural labour market. The lesson of California is that to win free collective bargaining and significantly improve living and working conditions for agricultural workers in Canada, *the SAWP must be abolished*. But in taking this stand, the Canadian labour movement must also make clear that it defends the right of migrant farm workers who have come to depend on the SAWP for continued employment in Canada. Indeed, a case can be made that significant *reparations* are owed by the Canadian state to migrant workers for the injustices perpetrated upon them since the 1960s.

In view of these considerations, the Canadian labour movement should advance the demand *for the abolition of the SAWP and the extension of full citizenship rights to all workers enrolled in it, past and present.* The intent here is not to deny trans-migrant workers access to agricultural jobs in Canada but to oppose the state's use of discriminatory guest worker programs to split the labour market to the detriment of Canadian and migrant workers alike. Indeed, this demand should be part of a general policy of supporting full citizenship rights for all "foreign" workers, regardless of how they arrived in Canada.

Such a policy would resonate powerfully with migrant workers and could serve as a key plank in the drive to organize agricultural labour. Backed by the full power of the trade union movement as a whole, such a drive could unite Canadian and migrant workers in a common struggle against the split labour market and for significant improvements in wages and working conditions in the agricultural sector.[23]

Lesson Two: Reliance on legislative remedies and consumer sympathy rather than class struggle is a recipe for defeat.

To a considerable extent, the early success of the UFW in Southern California can be attributed to the spontaneous militancy of Chicano and Filipino farm workers who had a long history of conducting (extra-legal) strikes to win wage increases. The intervention of the Filipino-dominated Agricultural Workers Organizing Committee (AWOC) and of Chavez's National Farm Workers Association (NFWA) in 1965–66 made it possible for these largely uncoordinated and dispersed strikes to find a common focus around the demand for union recognition. A major breakthrough came in 1966 in Delano with the signing of union contracts by the area's two biggest grape growers, Schenley and DiGiorgio. Key to these victories was militant strike action in the fields, backed by roving pickets to disperse scab labour. Chavez's much-publicized 25-day march on the state legislature in Sacramento in March–April 1966, culminating in a 10,000-strong rally, as well as the UFW's appeal to consumers to boycott non-union grapes, played a supplementary role. The subsequent fusion of AWOC and NFWA into the United Farm Workers Organizing Committee led to affiliation with the AFL–CIO, which made available significant financial assistance to the ongoing organizing drive.

Following the victories over the wine growers, the UFW campaigned for a new consumer boycott of table grapes, one that became famous as *La Causa*. Support from high-profile politicians like Senator Robert Kennedy made the table grape boycott a *cause célèbre* in liberal circles, and this both encouraged and appeared to vindicate Chavez's strategy of appeals to consumers (and even to grocery chain executives!) rather than engaging in militant strike action. Yet, *La Causa* was by no means an unqualified success. Undercut by the Pentagon's purchase of huge quantities of scab produce as well as by non-co-operation from many AFL–CIO affiliates, the boycott lasted *five years*. While the pressure of the consumer boycott eventually forced the growers to sign contracts with the UFW, most of these proved short-lived. Despite its limited effectiveness, Chavez and liberal supporters of the UFW elevated the consumer boycott tactic to the level of a strategy, depicting it as key to the UFW's early successes and downplaying the vital role that strike action by the UFW rank and file and cross-union labour solidarity had played.

By 1970, the UFW had organized most of the grape growing industry, signing more than 50,000 dues-paying members, the most ever represented by a farm union in California (Ferris & Sandoval 1998). In addition to winning higher wages, the UFW had established a union-run hiring hall, a health clinic and health plan, a credit union, a community centre, and a co-operative gas station. The union hiring hall was a particularly significant concession wrung from the growers, as it brought an end to the rampant favouritism of labour contractors whose long-time practice had been to divide the farm workers against one another along ethnic and national lines.[24]

The forward march of UFW organization came to an abrupt halt, however, in the early 1970s. Beginning in 1970 the venal leadership of the Teamsters union signed sweetheart agreements with Salinas Valley lettuce growers to block what appeared to be the imminent victory of the UFW throughout California agriculture. This signalled the start of a grower-Teamster alliance against the UFW that nearly destroyed the Chavez-led union. By 1975, the Teamster bureaucrats, who presented themselves as a conservative alternative to the "militant" UFW, claimed 95% of farm workers' contracts in California.[25]

The battle between the UFW and the Teamsters union was an especially egregious and tragic episode in the history of the US labour movement, and responsibility for it rests squarely with the Fitzsimmons leadership of the Teamsters. To protect its contracts and dues base, the Teamster bureaucracy worked closely with the growers and the police to intimidate an agricultural labour force that looked overwhelmingly to the UFW for representation, frequently deploying thugs to disperse UFW pickets.[26]

As reprehensible as the Teamster bureaucracy's actions were, the response of the Chavez leadership to this attempted union busting was itself a departure from the best traditions of the labour movement. By the early 1970s, Chavez was relying increasingly on the consumer boycott "strategy," the success of which, he believed, depended on the UFW's ability to present itself as both a union and a "civil rights movement" committed to moral suasion and "turn-the-other-cheek" Christian pacifism. Chavez called on "friends-of-labour" Democrats to pass legislation to guarantee free elections for union representation in the agricultural sector. Rather than calling for militant strike action, mass picketing, self-defense by UFW pickets, and hot-cargoing of scab produce, Chavez appealed to the federal government to investigate Teamster corruption and launched court actions against the union. Objectively, this targeted not only the corrupt officials but also rank-and-file Teamsters, despite indications that a direct appeal to the latter for solidarity action could have struck a receptive chord and catalyzed opposition to the Fitzsimmons leadership from within.[27] At the same time, Chavez persisted in his antagonistic attitude toward "illegal" Mexican workers—supporting the anti-"wetback" Rodino-Kennedy Bill and co-operating with the INS border patrol in 1974–75. During the UFW's strike against grape and lettuce growers in 1973, he reacted to the killing of two strikers and other violent attacks by police and Teamster thugs by calling off the strike in favour of yet another consumer boycott.

The dividend reaped by this pacifist-legalist policy was California's Agricultural Labor Relations Act (ALRA), signed into law by California governor Jerry Brown in 1975. While making it easier for the UFW to turn back the Teamster-grower offensive, the legislation also imposed legal restrictions on union activity in the agricultural sector that were to hamstring the UFW in the years to come. The victory that Chavez proclaimed in 1975 looked largely hollow by 1979.[28]

The ALRA was the product of a compromise between the UFW, the Teamsters-growers alliance, and Governor Brown. It provided for union representation elections supervised by a five-member Agricultural Labor Relations Board (ALRB) appointed by the governor while also banning strikes to win bargaining representation. While permitting harvest-time strikes as part of the collective bargaining process, it also prohibited the union from appealing to workers in other unions to refuse to handle scab goods (hot-cargoing and "hard" secondary boycotts). The Act recognized the principle of industrial unionism by stipulating that all agricultural employees in any given farm establishment had to be organized into a single union, irrespective of craft or skill distinctions, and recognized the right of the union to organize consumer boycotts against scab produce (so long as it had not lost a representation election at the farm operation being targeted).

The ALRB-supervised elections in 1975 were won resoundingly by the UFW. In 1977, Chavez and Fitzsimmons signed a five-year agreement recognizing UFW jurisdiction over field workers while reaffirming long-standing Teamster jurisdiction of cannery, food-processing, and produce-trucking workers. Before long, the Chavez leadership's cautious tactics and its strict adherence to every restriction imposed by the ALRA emboldened the growers to resume their offensive. The ALRB was at first rendered dysfunctional by a multitude of "unfair labour practices" grievances (provoked by the growers) as well as by legal wrangling surrounding the interpretation of the ALRA. The board was subsequently transformed into an undisguised agency of the growers' interests as conservative appointees replaced liberals under the Republican administration of Governor George Deukmejian.

During the 1980s, a period of generalized labour retreat and decline in the US, the UFW's ranks were decimated. When Cesar Chavez died in 1993, UFW contracts covered a mere 5,000 workers. Although it made a partial comeback by the early 2000s, it remains a shadow of the union that burst on the scene in the mid-1960s and rapidly organized almost 70,000 farm workers—*at a time when these workers enjoyed no legislatively sanctioned right to unionize or to strike.*

Various factors can be adduced to explain the UFW's decline: unfriendly Republican-appointed ALRB members; the rising tide of undocumented workers from Mexico; and the declining clout of organized labour in the US in a deeply reactionary political climate. Yet the UFW's decline was not simply the result of an accumulation of unfavourable external factors but also a product of a *strategic orientation* to turn away from direct militant strike action and to rely instead on the good will of consumers and supposedly pro-labour legislators.

Canada has yet to witness any farm worker mobilization or organizing drive remotely comparable to what occurred in the fields and orchards of California in the 1960s. This is perhaps why the NDP's short-lived Ontario Agricultural Labour Relations Act was such a pale imitation of its California namesake. Where Jerry Brown's ALRA recognized the right to strike at harvest time, Bob Rae's ALRA forbade all strikes and provided only for mediation or binding arbitration. Yet, in the end, the California ALRA hardly secured the position of the UFW. The lesson is hard to miss: for Canadian unionists to pursue a strategy of pressuring governments to pass pro-labour legislation is to abdicate the fight for farm workers' rights before it even really begins.

Lesson Three: Militant action and labour solidarity are key to long-term gains.

Contrary to the mythology and iconography surrounding Cesar Chavez, the early successes of the UFW were due to the determined militancy of its rank and file to forge a union capable of winning major concessions from the farm bosses. Chavez's organizing skills and political perspective were much better suited to fashioning a union bureaucracy, albeit one adept at moralistic appeals to its membership and to a liberal-minded public, than to leading militant workers' struggles. In effect, Chavez rode a rising tide of worker militancy during a favourable political conjuncture for "social movement unionism" in the 1960s, only to channel it into the dead end of consumer boycotts, pro-Democratic Party politics, and nativist chauvinism toward immigrants by the 1970s.

The militant direct action carried out by rank-and-file UFW activists in the early organizing strikes of the 1960s belongs to the best traditions of industrial union organization in North America. They recall the examples of labour militancy that made possible the victory of the Teamster strikes in Minneapolis, the Auto-Lite strike in Toledo, the UAW sit-in strikes in Flint, the ILA-led general strike in San Francisco, and numerous other class battles that laid the foundation for the Congress of Industrial Organizations (CIO) in the 1930s and 1940s (Preis 1972; Bernstein 1969; Dobbs 1972, 1973; Dollinger & Dollinger 2000; Knox 1998; Palmer 1992). What many of these historic battles had in common was a leadership that was prepared to transgress the boundaries of legality, to arm the workers for self-defense, to call upon support from other unions in the form of secondary boycotts and respect for picket lines, and, above all, to refuse to subordinate workers' struggles to a policy of collaboration with the employers or with capital's political representatives, whether liberal or conservative.

The UFW experience, however, contains a precious and unique lesson that is more directly germane to the labour struggles of the twenty-first century than it was to any of the historic fights for industrial unionism in the manufacturing, mining, and transportation sectors: *The principle of labour solidarity is one that must be fought for, not only across craft or occupational or industrial lines, but across national lines as well.* In a context of increasing economic globalization, in which capital is already highly mobile and transnational in its reach and in which labour is increasingly so, organized labour must champion the rights of all workers, regardless of their nationality, and counter the unrelenting capitalist drive to divide them on the basis of "citizenship."

IV. Conclusion: The Capitalist Offensive and the Future of Unionism

In a recent study of the implications of legal and political contexts for union organizing strategies in the US, Tamara Kay has argued that there is little evidence to support the view that union strategies centred on reform of labour laws are effective in bringing about significant pro-labour social change. Citing the influential work of Gerald Rosenberg, Kay writes: "Litigation, even liberal litigation, is largely useless as a method of pursuing social reform, for not only does it produce few if any results, it also saps movements of resources and obscures other, more effective strategies" (Kay 1998; Rosenberg 1991). Kay's analysis of the experience of two unions, the UFW and the UNITE garment workers' union, led her to conclude that "[for] labor activists, the law does matter ... but it matters more as a constraint than as a resource."

Arguably, the Kay-Rosenberg thesis may be less germane to Canada than it is to the United States given the different situations confronting organized labour in the two countries. Clearly, the Canadian labour movement has not been subjected over the past decades to the magnitude of defeat (as reflected in declining union density) that has been inflicted on US trade unionism. Further, the labour movement has a political arm in Canada, the NDP, whose existence has made a difference for Canadian workers by fostering a political climate less hospitable to open union busting by capital and the state.

Even so, the (only relative) success of Canadian labour in defending past gains is a warrant neither for complacency nor for illusions that legal action and legislative reform offer a promising road forward for the labour movement. Canadian unionism is in slow decline and has suffered significant defeats in recent years, not least in the realm of labour law (Panitch & Swartz 2003; Smith & Butovsky 2013). For this situation to be reversed and for the labour movement to take the offensive through the organization of new sectors of the labour force (such as agricultural, retail, and service-sector workers), the gradualist, social-democratic vision that has long been hegemonic within the Canadian labour movement will need to be super-seded in favour of more militant policies and tactics (Palmer 1987; Smith & Butovsky 2013). This is not to say that court actions and legislative lobby-ing should be entirely abandoned; but an effective, forward-looking policy must *subordinate* such methods to a strategy centred on the mobilization of labour's ranks in direct mass action, up to and including general strike action.

Such a reorientation will depend upon the assimilation by ordinary workers of the crucial lessons of organized labour's history. But it will also require an adequate understanding of the structural roots of capital's current offensive against labour and the systemic obstacles to pro-labour reform. In this connection, the farm labour question throws into sharp relief many of the principal strategies that have been and continue to be employed by capital and the state to overcome the economic malaise and associated profitability crisis that has afflicted the Canadian economy for much of the past three decades. These strategies centre on increasing the rate of exploitation through measures that maximize *absolute surplus value*: intensifying the labour process; lengthening the working day; reduc-ing the value of labour-power by driving down real wages; and weakening the capacity of workers to resist intensified exploitation through an assault on trade union rights and freedoms.[29] The deliberate fostering of a split agricultural labour market in Ontario through the SAWP unmistakably serves this neoliberal strategy. At the same time, the SAWP may also be seen as a harbinger of how capital and the state will seek to address labour shortages in specific sectors through "managed migration" and the super-exploitation of foreign workers. As such, it poses a critical challenge to the organized labour movement as well as to activists broadly concerned with issues of immigration, race, and citizenship.

TOWARD A CLASS-STRUGGLE PROGRAM

An adequate response by the labour movement and its allies to the capital-ist offensive will require a fundamental strategic reorientation. The follow-ing points constitute a partial programmatic distillation of the lessons of labour history sketched in this chapter and constitute, we think, the necessary starting point for an effective counter-offensive:

- Opposition to existing and proposed guest worker programs.
- Championing full citizenship rights for all immigrant workers in Canada, regardless of the circumstances of their arrival.
- Opposition to the deportation of foreign-born workers, particularly those targeted for their political and labour-organizing activities.
- A campaign of reparations for workers enrolled in SAWP and other guest worker programs, past and present. Workers formerly enrolled in guest worker programs in Canada should also be extended citizenship rights.
- Organizing the unorganized. The Canadian labour movement must uphold the right of all workers employed in Canada to organize themselves into unions and to withhold their labour-power in the pursuit of their demands, notwithstanding legislative prohibitions.
- Labour solidarity across craft, industrial, national, ethnic, racial, and gender divides must be vigorously championed, including the organization of secondary boycotts (refusal to handle struck goods) and general strike action, notwithstanding legislative prohibitions.
- Self-defense against anti-labour attacks organized by capital and the state.
- No reliance on the political parties of the capitalist class or the agencies of the capitalist state (including its judicial and legislative branches).
- A policy of extending support only to candidates for office who champion the interests of labour and the oppressed, and of seeking to build a mass workers' party to advance those interests.

By themselves, these points form an insufficient basis for transforming the trade union movement into an agency of fundamental social change, but they do adumbrate a strategic orientation that could significantly strengthen organized labour's position in relation to the farm labour issue and beyond.

BEYOND SOCIAL UNIONISM AND BUREAUCRATIC CONSERVATISM

In the 1980s and 1990s, social unionism was very much about forging defensive alliances with "sectors" (women, minorities, the poor) that were being targeted along with the labour movement by neoliberal and neoconservative governments. It was decidedly not about unleashing the power of the labour movement to challenge a social system that was manifestly in crisis. More recently, however, social unionism has also come to mean participating in collaborative projects with other unions, community organizations, and advocacy groups with a view to refurbishing the image of organized labour and shoring up or extending its base. This was precisely the import of the participation of such traditional business unions as the UFCW in the Global Justice Care Van Project of the UFWA. The union bureaucracy, having recognized the impotence of the old formula of "business unionism plus the NDP," is hopeful that the inclusion of a third element—movement unionism—will stem the decline of organized labour.

Like Cesar Chavez, the trade union leadership in Canada has little appetite for direct strike action or worker militancy. Even as it defends its conciliatory policies by pointing to structural changes that have allegedly undercut labour's capacity to fight back against capital in a new era of corporate globalization, the labour bureaucracy fails to pursue a militant organizing drive even in those sectors of the economy, like agriculture or retail (Walmart), where capital is least able to credibly play its "global relocation" card. The strategy of the OFL, the UFCW, and the UFWA in relation to farm labour in Ontario is, of course, in no sense determined by the political economy of globalization. Rather, it is dictated by bureaucratic conservatism and fearfulness of mobilizing the full power of organized labour in defiance of the capitalist state and its laws.[30]

The question is thus posed: what are the prospects for a fundamental, class-struggle reorientation of the Canadian labour movement, one emanating not from its existing leadership but from its rank and file? In this connection, Smith has argued:

> [In] presiding over the decline of the very movement that provides its material basis, the trade union bureaucracy is undermining itself as well, and inviting the emergence of militant alternative leaderships that, consciously or unconsciously, will put the interests of working people ahead of respect for the economic, political, and juridical framework of capitalist society. It was the presence of such a breed of new labour leaders—typically socialists, Communists, and Trotskyists—during the labour upsurge of the 1930s and 1940s that ensured the success of North American industrial unionism and that forced even some of the more politically conservative union leaders to strike a militant pose. It remains to be seen if history will repeat itself in this respect. (Blackwell, Smith, & Sorenson 2003: 301)

However, a repetition, much less a positive surpassing of this historical experience, will not result from an accumulation of defeats by the labour movement, nor from the deepening material privation of the working class and its (existing and potential) allies. The intervention of organized socialist forces seeking to forge what Gramsci called a "collective will"—the *subjective factor* in the struggle for real social change—will be indispensable to this process. One of the key tasks of such forces today must be the articulation of a satisfactory programmatic and strategic foundation for the development of a truly counter-hegemonic opposition within the organized labour movement.

Elements of such a counter-hegemonic project have been sketched by leftist intellectuals in a number of recent works on the labour movement. What is disappointing about so many of these contributions, however, is the assumption that the problems confronting the movement can be addressed by combining a marginally more left-wing version of the prevailing reformist perspective with some organizational innovations. Panitch and Swartz, for example, rightly reject the "progressive competitiveness" strategy espoused by many Canadian labour leaders, pointing out its corporatist and formally class-collaborationist implications. However, instead of calling for an explicitly class-struggle socialist program, they recommend a campaign by labour for "democratic capital controls" and a restructuring of unions to encourage greater rank-and-file democracy, coalition-building, and international solidarity (2003: 223–42). In a similar vein, Dan Clawson (2003) argues that, historically, the union movement has grown through large leaps rather than gradually and that the next leap must involve a stronger and more positive orientation on the part of organized labour toward the new social movements.

The thrust of these proposals is toward a more democratic, internationalist, and cross-sectoral "movement unionism," all of which, in general terms, is unobjectionable and necessary. Yet, as we think is indicated by the experience of farm workers in Ontario and the UFW's record in California, such a refurbished social (movement) unionism is unlikely to gain much traction unless it has the perspective of mobilizing the working class to "stop the productive forces of advanced capitalist society in their tracks" as an essential component of the struggle to "transform social relations" (Palmer 1992: 415). Such a perspective will require, sooner rather than later, the compass of a class-struggle and internationalist socialist program—one that is not only attentive to the new conditions, opportunities, and challenges confronting organized labour, but has also assimilated fully the political, strategic, and tactical lessons of labour's past.[31]

Notes

1. Justicia for Migrant Workers is a partial exception inasmuch as the demands raised by this group of activists objectively called into question the continuance of the SAWP.

2. In a revealing comment, Basok writes: "With their working and living conditions improved, Mexican workers are likely to feel even more loyal to their *patrones* than they do already, and from that point of view these improvements would be an investment well spent" (2003: 151).

3. The critical discussion of social unionism in this essay targets the way in which union officials have *appropriated* the progressive themes and sensibilities associated with "rank-and-file social unionism" in order to deflect attention from the need for a class-struggle policy. Accordingly we do *not* discuss the more salutary aspects of social unionism as a manifestation of democratic, grassroots union activism. For a discussion of this latter dimension of social unionism, see Moody (1997) and Clawson (2003).

4. The New Democratic Party (NDP) is Canada's social-democratic party. It was launched in 1960 as the "political arm of the Canadian labour movement" through the collaborative efforts of the Canadian Labour Congress (CLC) and the Co-operative Commonwealth Federation (CCF).

5. For a survey of the literature on this question up to the 1970s, including the contributions of Marx, Engels, Lenin, Michels, Gramsci, Trotsky, and a number of mid-century academic sociologists, see Hyman (1975). See also Mandel (1992) and Dumont (2012).

6. Marxists deny this assumption on three main grounds: (1) ephemeral improvements in the material conditions of the working class under capitalism are unevenly distributed across the world system (such that working-class gains in some countries or regions are offset by losses in others); (2) such improvements are *conjuncturally reversible*, owing to the fact that the recurrent crises of the capitalist system must periodically compel capital to attack working-class interests in order to restore an adequate average rate of profit; and (3) the historical interest of the working class lies not in gradual improvements to its position as a social class, but in the realization of a classless society committed to human emancipation. The first consideration points to the need to combat national chauvinism and racism within the working class, to champion working-class internationalism, and to organize workers on an international level; the second points to the need to educate the labour movement that the contradictions and laws of motion of capitalism are such that global progress in the quality of life of working people is impossible under this system; and the third points to the need to construct a socialist workers' movement that regards the realization of world socialism as the only way to secure general human progress.

7. We hasten to add that such vanguard formations within the trade unions may or may not take the form of ostensibly Leninist vanguard parties,

and they may or may not be committed to an ostensibly "revolutionary" practice and program. Syndicalists, classical Leninists, Stalinists, Trotskyists, left social democrats, radical nationalists, and socialist-feminists have all played vanguard roles in particular times and places, demonstrating a capacity to spark and lead workers' struggles that have heightened class-consciousness and transgressed the boundaries of struggle normally imposed by the trade union bureaucracy. It should also be noted that in many countries the role normally played by Social Democracy in containing workers' struggles within a reformist framework was also assumed by the mass pro-Moscow Communist parties.

8. In a recent critique of postmodernist political fashions, John Sanbonmatsu has written: "If Gramsci today is largely remembered as the theorist of hegemony—the forging of political unity across cultural differences—Foucault might well be described as the theorist par excellence of *anti-hegemony*, what Aronowitz describes as a politics 'recognizing the permanence of *difference*', and in which 'movements for liberation ... will remain autonomous both in the course of struggle and in the process of creating a new society'" (2004: 131). Sanbonmatsu points out, correctly, that to "say that experience is only a 'discourse' is to remove any basis for substantive human knowledge of any kind, including knowledge that might be helpful to the oppressed" (113). In counterpoint to Sanbonmatsu, however, we regard Gramsci's ideas as congruent with an authentic (that is, non-Stalinist) Leninism—and in particular with Lenin's concept of the vanguard party as a "tribune of the people." For two instructive, and quite different, treatments of the Leninist theory, see Mandel (1971b) and Seymour (1997).

9. Thus, as Palmer argues: "Social unionism ... might be seen as simply a progressive facade behind which a wing of the labour hierarchy adroitly masks its traditional business unionist refusal to use and extend the class power of the unions to launch a struggle for social change" (1992: 372).

10. As the absolute number of farms has decreased, the average farm operation in Canada has grown dramatically since the 1960s, and particularly since the early 1990s. In Ontario, the number of farms appraised at less than $100,000 decreased by 58% between 1996 and 2001 (from 4,730 to 1,995), while the number of farms worth more than a million dollars increased by 38%, from 15,050 to 20,580, over the same period.

11. Of course, the phenomenon of racialization extends far beyond "guest workers." For a comprehensive analysis, see Galabuzi (2006).

12. As early as the 1930s, American workers were employed in the Ontario tobacco harvest, although the numbers were typically less than 3,000 per year. See Satzewich (1991: 108).

13. We do not mean to suggest that the Live-In Caregiver Program represents a benign or enlightened policy. See Grandia and Kerr (1998), and Baken and Stasiulus (1994).

14. See "Statistics," Foreign Agricultural Resource Management Service, at: http://www.farmsontario.ca (retrieved 24 August 2005).

15. It should be noted that while SAWP-enrolled migrant farm workers are severely disadvantaged compared to their Canadian counterparts, their legally precarious position has not entirely prevented them from engaging in limited forms of resistance to their super-exploited status. The National Film Board of Canada documentary *El Contrato* reveals some instances of this resistance—along with harsh responses by agribusiness and the state.

16. In July 2005, the newly elected Liberal provincial government agreed to this inclusion beginning on 1 July 2006. Chris Ramsaroop of JMW points out however that "migrant farm workers will still be unprotected because the basic legal conditions of their employment have not changed.... [We] continue to press the government to implement real changes that ensure that migrant farm workers can refuse unsafe work without fear of reprisals from the employer" (quoted in Nadeau 2006: 8–9).

17. Ontario Federation of Labour, *Report on Agricultural Workers* (2001).

18. Quoted in United Food and Commercial Workers Canada, *Status of Migrant Farm Workers in Canada, 2003* (2003).

19. The UFCW, to its credit, has organized five "support centres" for migrant farm workers in Southern Ontario over the past decade, but not, evidently, with a view to preparing a serious organizing drive. The union maintains that a *precondition* for any organizing drive among farm workers in general is a reform of the labour laws that currently prohibit unions in the agricultural sector.

20. Our appreciation of the history of the UFW has been shaped by a number of scholarly as well as partisan accounts. Martin (2003) provides an excellent, sympathetic overview written from the perspective of a liberal-minded

agricultural economist. However, he fails to place union strategy and tactics in the forefront of his analysis. Our understanding of the limitations of the UFW's methods of struggle under the Chavez leadership benefited greatly from journalistic reports and analyses produced by American left groups in the 1970s—particularly those published in the International Socialists' *Workers Power*, the Socialist Workers Party's *The Militant*, and the Spartacist League's *Workers Vanguard*. Correspondence with long-time California labour activist Howard Keylor provided several useful insights corroborating this understanding.

21. While agreeing with Galarza that *bracero* strikebreaking was important in blocking unionization during this period, Martin argues that the main factors were "a surplus of workers, which made the traditional union weapon of withholding work (strikes) ineffective; inappropriate leadership and tactics, such as organizing workers via employers or contractors; and confusion among workers as to the source of their low wages" (2003: 66).

22. Bert Corona, a long-time labour organizer and Chicano nationalist leader, clashed with Chavez over this fundamental issue, as did many on the socialist left. Corona was quoted years later as saying: "[I] believed that organizing undocumented farm workers was auxiliary to the union's efforts to organize the fields. We supported an open immigration policy as far as Mexico was concerned" (quoted in *Rural Migration News*, April 2001, and reprinted in Martin 2003: 53).

23. This struggle would need to be spearheaded by domestic agricultural workers and their allies in the Canadian labour movement. To the extent that the organizing drive addresses the migrant labour issue successfully, SAWP-enrolled workers could be brought into the struggle at a later stage.

24. The hiring regime sanctioned by the SAW Program in Canada has parallels with the labour contracting system in California. Union control of hiring would be an important element in advancing the interests of the Ontario agricultural labour force as a whole.

25. In the fight with the grower-Teamster alliance in lettuce, Chavez relied once again on the consumer boycott tactic, but it was largely ineffective. Martin notes that "the Teamsters wound up representing 70 percent of California lettuce workers and the UFW 15 percent" (2003: 70). Despite this setback, the UFW held its own and even extended its base in other

sectors of California agriculture over the next couple of years, reaching a "high-water mark in March 1973 when it claimed sixty-seven thousand members and 180 contracts covering forty thousand farm jobs," although some UFW members "were employed only a few weeks under UFW contracts" (70). In 1973, most table grape growers switched to the Teamsters with the expiry of the UFW's 1970–73 contracts. By the end of the year, the UFW was left with 12 contracts while the Teamsters had 305.

26. The attitude of the Teamster bureaucrats toward the UFW was captured in a newspaper interview with Einar Mohn, a West Coast Teamster official: "I'm not sure how effective a union can be when it is composed of Mexican-Americans and Mexican nationals with temporary visas. Maybe as agriculture becomes more sophisticated, more mechanized, with fewer transients, fewer green carders, and as jobs become more attractive to whites, then we can build a union that can have structure ... and have membership participation" (Los Angeles Times, 28 April 1973). According to a contemporary account in a revolutionary socialist publication: "Teamster bureaucrats are using hired professional thugs largely recruited from motorcycle gangs, paid $67 a day and armed with clubs and chains to beat pickets and force workers to stay in the fields" (Workers Vanguard, 22 June 1973).

27. In our view, court suits by one union against another are anathema to the fundamental principles of labour solidarity, which must include opposition to any and all intervention by the capitalist state in the internal affairs of the labour movement.

28. By the mid-1980s, Chavez was himself calling the ALRA/ALRB an obstacle to farm worker organization (Martin 2003: 172).

29. Such measures for increasing "absolute surplus value" differ from "relative surplus value" methods that involve displacing living labour from production through technological innovation, thereby producing what Marx called a rising "organic composition of capital" and a downward pressure on the average rate of profit. It should be noted that one of the effects of the SAWP is to encourage continued reliance on back-breaking human labour and therefore to discourage investment in labour-saving innovation in the agricultural sector.

30. Bryan Palmer correctly notes that "no successful struggle against capital and the state on our home ground, let alone internationally, can be successful with the working class inhibited by a leadership fearful to lead and antagonistic to the one force that has historically insured humanity's advance: civil disobedience" (2003: 489–90).

31. For further discussion, see Smith and Butovsky 2013, especially pp. 190–95.

CHAPTER 14

Twenty-First-Century Socialism: Utopian or Scientific?

Those inclined to reject the Marxist vision of socialism as "unrealistic" are often surprised to learn that Karl Marx and Frederick Engels waged a long and vigorous struggle against many ostensibly socialist ideas that they considered "utopian." They did so by critiquing not only the views of such early nineteenth-century figures as Henri de Saint-Simon, Charles Fourier, and Robert Owen (as well as the anarchist doctrines of Pierre-Joseph Proudhon and Mikhail Bakunin), but also the attempts of many contemporary thinkers to import utopian elements into Marx's own theories and thereby dilute the latter's "scientific" character. This struggle against utopianism found expression in some of Marx and Engels' best known works, among them *The German Ideology* (Marx 1989d), *The Poverty of Philosophy* (Marx 1963b), *The Communist Manifesto* (Marx & Engels 1998), *Capital* (Marx 1977), *The Critique of the Gotha Programme* (Marx 1970), and, above all, Engels' *Anti-Dühring*, a portion of which was later published under the title *Socialism: Utopian and Scientific* (Engels 1970b)—perhaps the most popular primer on Marxist theory ever written.

Marx and Engels objected to "utopian socialism" for three principal, closely related reasons. First, the utopian socialists sought to ground the case for socialism on abstract and transhistorical ethical considerations ("moral precepts written in the sky," as it were) rather than on a scientific analysis of the real laws of motion, contradictions, and limits of the capitalist mode of production, and the need for a rational human response to them. Second, the utopians saw socialism as a new "model" of human society—a blueprint for social and economic reorganization based on purportedly universal principles of human harmony and social justice—rather than viewing it as a practical project for overcoming the concrete obstacles to social progress and human well-being thrown up by the growing contradiction between the social relations of capitalism and the powerful productive forces they bring into being. Third, utopian socialists failed to recognize the necessity and centrality of *class struggle* in achieving a socialist society, proposing instead that people of good will, from a variety of classes (including the bourgeoisie), could be won to progressive, "socialist" goals through education, moral suasion, and the power of example.

Such utopian socialist themes continue to find stubborn expression in a range of *reformist* ideas (long dominant on the putatively socialist left and critiqued at various points in this book) that will need to be confronted and defeated if the Marxist Phoenix is to re-emerge and eventually triumph. Among the more important of these ideas are: the concept of a gradual and incremental transition to socialism through progressive economic reforms and the transformation of the existing capitalist state into a truly "popular" and "democratic" one; the need for political collaboration and compromise between socialists and "enlightened" non-socialist forces on the basis of progressive programs that stop short of a full assault on capital; the idea of "building socialism in one country" (including economically backward ones) and the related idea that there are "different national roads to socialism"; and, finally, the view that "class division" is *not* (or *not always*) the most significant form of exploitation or oppression within society, and that the struggle against it should be *deferred* until a more perfect "liberal democracy" has been achieved—one in which substantial progress has been made in overcoming gender, racial, and other inequalities within a still-capitalist framework.

The common denominator of such "utopian socialist" or "petty-bourgeois reformist" conceptions is the notion that capitalism remains a fertile ground for egalitarian and democratic reform, and that the easiest and most effective way to move toward socialism is by first establishing a more "equal" and democratic capitalist order—one that might even provide breathing space for nationally limited experiments in "building socialism" in certain (primarily "developing") countries. But as the arguments and analyses presented in this book have tried to show, such a notion is not merely unrealistic; it is *a dangerous illusion*, and one upon which histori- cal experience has rendered the harshest possible verdict. As I wrote in the midst of the severe financial crisis of autumn 2008:

> It was precisely in the service of his programmatic struggle against reformism and utopianism within the workers movement that Marx developed his scientific critique of bourgeois political economy as a guide to a revolutionary political practice....
>
> The time has come for a revival of Marx's scientific socialism.... [T]he time has come for a socialist message that declares loudly and clearly that our species can no longer afford an economic system based on class exploitation—a system whose social relations impe- riously necessitate the outmoded measurement of wealth in terms of "abstract social labour" and that must, as a consequence, deny humanity the full benefits of scientific rationality while plunging us recurrently into economic depression and war. (Smith 2010: 25–26)

As capital's crisis of valorization continues to deepen in the second decade of the twenty-first century, testifying to the decay of the capitalist profit system, this call to action has lost none of its force or relevance. And nor has it lost any of its *moral urgency*.

Science and Morality in the Struggle for Socialism

While making a vigorous case against utopian-socialist and left-reformist perspectives that so often rely on moralistic and "lesser-evil" sentiments, Marxists must nevertheless insist that a properly understood "scientific socialism" is in no sense detached from human morality and values. On the contrary, Marxist socialism conceives itself to be the harbinger of a *human science* devoted above all to the emancipation of the oppressed and the full flourishing of our species: *morally worthy goals* that require no "scientific" justification in themselves. For this reason among others, Marxism is utterly opposed to any *dualistic* separation of "facts" and "values" or "science" and "morality." Socialism will not be brought into existence by impersonal and inexorable laws of history, but by human agents endowed with both scientific reason and definite moral purpose.

In his best-selling book *The Moral Landscape: How Science Can Determine Human Values*, the renowned "new atheist" Sam Harris has aroused much controversy by arguing that human morality and values ought to be based on science instead of on faith or allegiance to long-standing cultural traditions. Harris writes:

> To summarize my central thesis: Morality and values depend on the existence of conscious minds—and specifically on the fact that such minds can experience various forms of well-being and suffering in this universe. Conscious minds and their states are natural phenomena, of course, fully constrained by the laws of Nature (whatever these turn out to be in the end). Therefore, there must be right and wrong answers to questions of morality and values that potentially fall within the purview of science. On this view, some people and cultures will be right (to a greater or lesser degree), and some will be wrong, with respect to what they deem important in life. (2011: 195)

From the Marxist standpoint (which the neuroscientist Harris almost entirely ignores), this argument contains glaring weaknesses as well as several obvious strengths. On the one hand, the preceding statement of his central thesis assumes the form of a formal-logical syllogism, one of the premises of which is that "conscious minds and their states are natural phenomena." In the Marxist view, however, these phenomena are both natural *and* social, inasmuch as they are profoundly shaped and mediated by variable social forms and practices (see Chapters 4 and 5 in this volume).

Accordingly, an adequate science of morality must be part of what Marx in his manuscripts of 1844 called a "science of man"—one that unites and synthesizes the best of the natural and social sciences:

> *One* basis for life and another basis for *science* is *a priori* a lie. The nature which develops in human history—the genesis of human society—is man's *real* nature; hence nature as it develops through industry, even though in an *estranged* form, is true anthropological nature.... Natural science will in time incorporate into itself the science of man, just as the science of man will incorporate into itself natural science: there will be *one* science. (Marx 1964: 143)

Apart from the insufficient attention that Harris gives to "the social" in his account of morality, his argument is badly compromised by an ethnocentrism and an ideological blindness that lead him to assume, at least tacitly, that his own (liberal-democratic, capitalist, American) culture stands higher on the "moral landscape" than most others. Thus, while he is quick to point out that we must not "hesitate to condemn the morality of the Taliban—not just personally, but *from the point of view of science*" (2011: 42), he seldom finds reason to condemn the "morality" or actions of the US imperialist state. Yet, from the standpoint of scientific socialism, the Taliban's backward, religiously inspired "morality" is, in the scheme of things, a relatively minor obstacle to "human well-being" compared to the blatant immorality of a predatory imperialist bourgeoisie composed of would-be Masters of the Universe. Harris and other liberal rationalists of his ilk would do well to reflect on whether what his own US ruling class deems "important in life" and "morally right"—namely the unlimited accumulation of private wealth in a world in which tens of millions die of hunger each year—is informed by the best "science" on offer.

On the other hand, Harris is able to score many good points against his more idealist, relativistic, and dualistic detractors. Thus, he argues: "Most scientists treat facts and values as though they were distinct and irreconcilable in principle. I have argued that they cannot be, as anything of value must be valuable *to* someone (whether actually or potentially)—and, therefore, its value should be attributable to facts about the well-being of conscious creatures" (180). And further, in response to one of his more vehement critics, he writes:

> Contrary to [Russell] Blackford's assertion, I'm not simply claiming that morality is "fully determined by an objective reality, independent of people's actual values and desires." I am claiming that people's actual values and desires are fully determined by an objective reality; and that we can conceptually get behind all of this—indeed, we must—in order to talk about what is actually good.... I am claiming that there must be frontiers of human well-being that await our discovery, and certain interests and preferences surely blind us to them. Yes, morality must be understood in terms of what we value—but it is also possible to value the wrong things. (205–206)

Harris is completely correct to insist that people's values and desires are determined by an "objective reality." But, again, he fails to register the fact that objective reality has *social* as well as natural dimensions, and that conscious Activity can also have a determining effect on it. Indeed, for objective reality to be transformed in ways that will truly promote human well-being and flourishing, the conscious Activity of human beings must be directed toward radical changes in the Social and not simply toward continued progress in the natural sciences.

Can and should science determine human values? My answer is an unequivocal yes. But Harris's question needs to be asked, above all, in relation to how science can be placed in the service of a project of social transformation (a "scientific socialism") that can adequately address the grave threats to the very survival of the human species that now loom. Crucially, the question also needs to be considered in a *strategic* context. What agencies can be mobilized to bring about this necessary social transformation?

These questions go to the heart of why Marx's critical analysis of capitalism and his programmatic-strategic insistence upon the political independence of the working class in the struggle for socialism must together occupy such a central and indispensable place in any serious consideration of the supreme moral question of our time: *How will humanity both survive and flourish?*

An illuminating way to approach this cluster of questions is to consider an opinion expressed by the Marxist philosopher Tony Smith in a short critical article on the theory and politics of postmodernism written two decades ago. Smith asserts that it is "true that there are a variety of general types of oppression (for example, by race, sex, class), and that from a moral standpoint each general type of oppression is equally wrong." Having conceded this point to the postmodernists, he then proposes that "the women's movement, the anti-racist movement and other movements struggling against oppression must have independent political organizations, independent leaderships and their own press. The goal of politics must include creating a space within which differences can flourish, and it will take a plurality of different social movements for us to ever get there" (1993b: 22–23).

At first blush, Smith's argument might seem to be simply an affirmation of a revered principle of socialist democracy: namely, different popular constituencies, as well as various factions within them, should have the *right* to advance their own interests and agendas as they struggle against a legacy of exploitation and oppression, both within capitalism and in the future socialist society. But Smith is actually saying something more than this, and, in doing so, he makes an unfortunate concession to what is often called the "politics of identity." For instead of strongly affirming the need for a socialist workers' party to become the "tribune" of the oppressed and to articulate its class-struggle program with the demands of other movements against oppression and injustice within capitalism, he is indicating that the efforts of women, racial minorities, and others to organize themselves "independently" of a Marxist-led workers' movement ought to be encouraged. In practice, this amounts to an endorsement of efforts to organize oppressed people on the basis of a non-socialist, usually *liberal-reformist* program, something that can only reinforce the political hegemony of the bourgeoisie. In the United States, Tony Smith's own country, it has meant the corralling of "struggles against oppression" within the precincts of the capitalist Democratic Party.

To be fair, Smith recognizes the one-sidedness of the postmodernists' "celebration of difference" and affirms the need for unity between the various "movements of the oppressed." Indeed, he even argues that "class struggle retains a certain priority," particularly in view of the fact that any serious attempt at social transformation must confront the "capitalist class's control of the economic surplus," which "gives *that* class a form of power that is unmatched in society" (23). All the same, he seems ambivalent about championing what is *objectively* needed to seriously challenge the class power of the bourgeoisie: a determined struggle by a Marxist vanguard to win the most advanced, *class-conscious* elements within organized labour and all the other "movements of the oppressed" to *a fully socialist program* and to the building of a workers' party that can function, in Lenin's words, as a "tribune of the people." In the absence of such a struggle, there can be no real prospect of defeating capitalism and abolishing its myriad iniquities. Nor can there be much prospect for the survival of the human species.

Would-be "progressives" have an ever-growing catalogue of good and noble causes from which to choose as they seek to "change the world." But the cause of "proletarian socialism" is altogether unique. For it is not only the most *comprehensive* of causes in terms of its potential to promote human well-being; it also happens to be the cause that is in most urgent need of many more committed militants—people who are willing to fight for Marxist-socialist ideas and battle against those reformist, sectoralist, and utopian ideas that help to contain the struggles of the oppressed within the capitalist framework.

In taking up this battle, the militants of Marxist socialism offer our best hope for creating a world in which the necessary and indispensable conditions of general emancipation and human flourishing can at last be realized.

In Praise of Revolutionary Leadership

There can be no more fitting way to conclude this book than to note that its publication coincides with the eightieth anniversary of one of the signal events in the history of the American labour movement and also world

Trotskyism: the Minneapolis Teamsters strikes of 1934, one of three city-wide labour upheavals that year that paved the way for "industrial union-ism" in North America and the formation of the Congress of Industrial Organizations (CIO).

The Minneapolis strikes were organized by Teamsters Local 574 under the leadership of supporters of the Communist League of America, a rela-tively small group of Trotskyists who had been expelled from the Stalinist Communist Party (CPUSA) a few years earlier. During the course of those strikes, martial law was declared, the National Guard was mobilized, and huge protest rallies involving tens of thousands were frequently held. Although the aims of the strikes were modest (for example, employer recognition of the new industrial form of union organization across the trucking industry, improved wages and working conditions), the methods and tactics of the strikers were highly resourceful and even revolution-ary in their implications, including: "flying pickets" dispatched as needed throughout the city, the publication of a daily newspaper, militant resis-tance to all efforts by authorities to repress the strikes, and the setting up of a hospital and commissary to attend to strikers' needs. The ultimate success of the Minneapolis strikes set the stage for the 11-state over-the-road orga-nizing campaign that transformed the Teamsters into the largest union in the United States, while also giving a tremendous impetus to the efforts of American Trotskyists to challenge Stalinist dominance over the most mili-tant segments of the labour movement—efforts that were later thwarted with the Roosevelt administration's prosecution of the Trotskyists under the anti-communist Smith Act.

As Bryan Palmer suggests in the following passage from his book *Revolutionary Teamsters*, the Minneapolis uprising of 1934 was an episode from which we can still draw many precious lessons and one that illustrates exceptionally well how the Marxist Phoenix can indeed still rise:

> The dialectic of leaders and led in Minneapolis, a fusion of revo-lutionary Trotskyists and insurgent workers, resulted in a union-mobilization within one of the most reactionary enclaves of the American Federation of Labor. All of this, especially the push for

militant industrial unionism, *anticipated* the CIO at its very best. This validated revolutionary leadership within the labor-movement and consolidated significant trade-union advances, inoculating, for a time, many workers against the infectious germ of anticommunism.

This was an accomplishment of considerable magnitude, and one not to be forgotten even as it was undermined in later years of concerted assault. It has many lessons for our own era. Among them are a sense of both the necessity *and* possibility of rebuilding the kind of revolutionary organization that can simultaneously nurture a creative leadership *and* encourage and develop the militant combativity of the working class. Struggles that secure gains in new causes have to be fought through, planned, and mobilized in order to be won. The desperate need of our particular times is to revive the kind of dialectic of leaders and led that was evident in Local 574's historic achievements in the 1930s. In this lies the possibility of victories. (Palmer 2013: 268)

The Marxist Phoenix hope can wing her way through the desert skies, and still defying fortune's spite, revive from ashes and rise.

REFERENCES

Albo, Greg, Sam Gindin, and Leo Panitch. 2010. *In and Out of Crisis*. Oakland: PM Press.

Albo, Greg, and Herman Rosenfeld. 2009. "What should we do to help build a New Left?" *Relay*, 28.

Althusser, Louis. 1969. *For Marx*. New York: Pantheon.

Althusser, Louis. 1971. "Ideology and Ideological State Apparatuses," in L. Althusser, *Lenin and Philosophy*. London: New Left Books.

Amazon. n.d. Summary for *Race Against the Machine* by E. Brynjolfsson and A. McAffee (2011). Retrieved from: http://www.amazon.com/race-against-machine-accelerating-productivity/dp/0984725113

Amin, Samir. 1985. "Modes of Production, History and Unequal Development." *Science & Society*, 49(2).

Anderson, Perry. 1979. *Lineages of the Absolutist State*. London: Verso.

Anderson, Perry. 1982. *In the Tracks of Historical Materialism*. London: Verso.

Arthur, Christopher J. 1998. "Systematic Dialectic." *Science & Society*, 62(3).

Baken, Abigail, and Daiva Stasiulis. 1994. "Foreign Domestic Policy in Canada and the Social Boundaries of Modern Citizenship." *Science & Society*, 58(1).

Bakir, Ergodan, and Al Campbell. 2010. "Neoliberalism, the Rate of Profit and the Rate of Accumulation." *Science & Society*, 74(3).

Basok, Tanya. 2003. *Tortillas and Tomatoes: Transmigrant Mexican Harvesters in Canada*. Montreal: McGill-Queen's University Press.

Bauder, Harold, and Kerry Prebiech. 2002. *Community Impacts of Foreign Farm Workers in Ontario: A Comparative Analysis*. Guelph.

Baudrillard, Jean. 1975. *The Mirror of Production*. St. Louis: Telos.

Bellofiore, Riccardo (ed.). 1998. *Marxian Economics: A Reappraisal—Essays on Volume III of Capital*, Volume 2: *Profits, Prices and Dynamics*. London: MacMillan.

Berle, Adolph, Jr., and Gardiner C. Means. 1932. *The Modern Corporation and Private Property*. New York: Macmillan.

Bernstein, Irving. 1969. *Turbulent Years, 1933–1941*. Boston: Houghton-Mifflin.

Blackwell, Judith, Murray E. G. Smith, and John Sorenson. 2003. *Culture of Prejudice: Arguments in Critical Social Science*. Peterborough: Broadview Press.

Bolshevik Tendency. 1989. "On the Nature of the USSR: BT Debates LRP." *1917*, 6.

Boutang, Yann Moulier. 2011. *Cognitive Capitalism*. Cambridge, UK: Polity.

Breitman, George, Paul Le Blanc, and Alan Wald. 1996. *Trotskyism in the United States: Historical Essays and Reconsiderations*. Amherst, NY: Prometheus Books.

Brenner, Robert. 1977. "The Origins of Capitalist Development: A Critique of Neo-Smithian Marxism." *New Left Review*, 104.

Brenner, Robert. 1998. "The Economics of Global Turbulence." *New Left Review*, 229.

Broué, Pierre, and Emile Témime. 1972. *The Revolution and the Civil War in Spain.* Cambridge, MA.: The MIT Press.

Brown, Andrew. 1999. "Developing Realistic Methodology: How New Dialectics Surpasses the Critical Realist Method for Social Science," Economics Discussion Paper No. 66. Retrieved from: http://www.raggedclaws.com/criticalrealism/archive/abrown_drm.html

Brynjolfsson, Erik, and Andrew McAfee. 2011. *Race Against the Machine: How the Digital Revolution is Accelerating Innovation, Driving Productivity, and Irreversibly Transforming Employment and the Economy.* Lexington, MA.: Digital Frontier Press.

Bukharin, Nikolai. 2005. *Philosophical Arabesques.* New York: Monthly Review Press.

Burnham, James. 1941. *The Managerial Revolution: What is Happening in the World.* New York: John Day.

Butovsky, Jonah, and Murray E. G. Smith. 2007. "Beyond Social Unionism: Farm Workers in Ontario and Some Lessons from Labour History." *Labour/Le Travail*, 57.

Callinicos, Alex. 1990. *Trotskyism.* Minneapolis: University of Minnesota Press.

Callinicos, Alex. 1996. "Darwin, Materialism and Evolution." *International Socialism*, 71.

Callinicos, Alex. 2008. "Where is the radical left going?" *International Socialism*, 120.

Camfield, David. 2007. "The Multitude and the Kangaroo: A Critique of Hardt and Negri's Theory of Immaterial Labour." *Historical Materialism*, 15(2).

Campbell, Ken. 1977. "The Marxist and Weberian Concepts of Class." Unpublished manuscript, Department of Sociology and Anthropology, Carleton University.

Campbell, Martha, and Geert Reuten (eds.). 2002. *The Culmination of Capital—Essays on Volume III of Marx's Capital.* Hampshire: Palgrave.

Carchedi, Guglielmo. 1977. *On the Economic Identification of Social Classes.* London: Routledge and Kegan Paul.

Carchedi, Guglielmo. 1988. "Class Politics, Class Consciousness, and the New Middle Class." *Insurgent Sociologist*, 14(3).

Carchedi, Guglielmo. 1991. *Frontiers of Political Economy.* London: Verso.

Carchedi, Guglielmo. 2011a. *Behind and Beyond the Crisis*. Unpublished manuscript. Retrieved from: http://gesd.free.fr/carchedib.pdf

Carchedi, Guglielmo. 2011b. *Behind the Crisis: Marx's Dialectics of Value and Knowledge*. Chicago: Haymarket.

Carling, Alan. 1993. "Analytical Marxism and Historical Materialism: The Debate on Social Evolution." *Science & Society*, 57(1).

Castree, Noel. 1996/97. "Invisible Leviathan: Speculations on Marx, Spivak, and the Question of Value." *Rethinking Marxism*, 9(2): 45–78.

Caudwell, Christopher. 1971. *Studies and Further Studies in a Dying Culture*. New York: Monthly Review Press.

Choonara, Joseph. 2009. "Marxist Accounts of the Current Crisis." *International Socialism Journal*, 123.

Clarke, Simon. 1982. *Marx, Marginalism and Modern Sociology*. London: Macmillan.

Clawson, Dan. 2003. *The Next Upsurge: Labor and the New Social Movements*. Ithaca: Cornell University Press.

Cliff, Tony. 1974. *State Capitalism in Russia*. London: Pluto.

Cockburn, Alexander. 1995. *The Golden Age Is In Us*. London: Verso.

Cohen, G. A. 1978. *Karl Marx's Theory of History: A Defence*. Oxford: Oxford University Press.

Cohen, G. A. 1981. "The Labour Theory of Value and the Concept of Exploitation," in I. Steedman (ed.), *The Value Controversy*. London: Verso.

Cohen, G. A. 1983. "Forces and Relations of Production," in Betty Matthews (ed.), *Marx: A Hundred Years On*. London: Lawrence and Wishart.

Cohen, G. A., and Will Kymlicka. 1988. "Human Nature and Social Change in the Marxist Conception of History." *The Journal of Philosophy*, 85(4).

Colletti, Lucio. 1972. *From Rousseau to Lenin*. London: New Left Books.

Colletti, Lucio. 1973. *Marxism and Hegel*. London: New Left Books.

Corrigan, Philip, Harvie Ramsay, and Derek Sayer. 1979. *For Mao*. London: Macmillan.

Dawkins, Richard. 1976. *The Selfish Gene*. Oxford: Oxford University Press.

Dennett, Daniel. 1996. *Darwin's Dangerous Idea*. New York: Simon and Schuster.

Derrida, Jacques. 1982. *Margins of Philosophy*. Chicago: University of Chicago Press.

Diamandis, Peter, and Steven Kotler. 2012. *Abundance: The Future Is Better Than You Think*. New York: Free Press.

Dobb, Maurice. 1973. *Theories of Value and Distribution since Adam Smith*. Cambridge, UK: Cambridge University Press.

Dobbs, Farrell. 1972. *Teamster Rebellion*. New York: Monad.

Dobbs, Farrell. 1973. *Teamster Power*. New York: Monad.

Dollinger, Sol, and Genora Dollinger. 2000. *Not Automatic: Women and the Left in the Forging of the Auto Workers Union*. New York: Monthly Review Press.

Dumenil, Gerard, and Dominique Levy. 2004. *Capital Resurgent: Roots of the Neoliberal Revolution*. Cambridge, MA: Harvard University Press.

Dumont, Joshua. 2012. Pension Reform & the Labor Movement in France, 1993–2003. PhD dissertation, York University, Toronto.

Dunayevskaya, Raya. 1964. *Marxism and Freedom*. New York: Twayne.

Eagleton, Terry. 1991. *Ideology: An Introduction*. London: Verso.

Ehrenreich, Barbara. 1989. *Fear of Falling: The Inner Life of the Middle Class*. New York: Harper-Collins.

Ehrenreich, Barbara, and John Ehrenreich. 1978. "The Professional-Managerial Class," in P. Walker (ed.), *Between Labor and Capital*. Montreal: Black Rose.

Elson, Diane. 1979. "The Value Theory of Labour," in D. Elson (ed.), *Value: The Representation of Labour in Capitalism*. London: CSE Books.

Elster, Jon. 1978. "The Labor Theory of Value: A Reinterpretation of Marxist Economics." *Marxist Perspectives*, 3.

Engels, Frederick. 1941 [1867]. "Review of Marx's Critique of Political Economy," in F. Engels, *Ludwig Feuerbach and the End of Classical German Philosophy*. New York: International Publishers.

Engels, Frederick. 1954. *Dialectics of Nature*. Moscow: Progress Publishers.

Engels, Frederick. 1969 [1894]. *Anti-Dühring*. Moscow: Progress Publishers.

Engels, Frederick. 1970a [1884]. *The Origin of the Family, Private Property and the State*, in K. Marx and F. Engels, *Selected Works, Volume 3*. Moscow: Progress Publishers.

Engels, Frederick. 1970b [1892]. *Socialism: Utopian and Scientific*, in K. Marx and F. Engels, *Selected Works*, Volume 3. Moscow: Progress Publishers.

Engels, Frederick. 1981 [1895]. Supplement and Addendum to Volume Three of *Capital*, in K. Marx, *Capital*, Volume 3. New York: Vintage.

Farl, Erich. 1973. "State Capitalism Revisited." *International*, 2(1).

Ferris, Susan, and Ricardo Sandoval (eds.). 1998. *The Fight in the Fields: Cesar Chavez and the Farmworkers Movement*. Orlando: Harvest (Harcourt Brace & Co.).

Filtzer, Donald. 1978. "Preobrazhensky and the Problem of the Soviet Transition." *Critique*, 9.

Fischer, Norman. 1982. "The Ontology of Abstract Labor." *Review of Radical Political Economics*, 14(2).

Foley, Duncan. 1986. *Understanding Capital: Marx's Economic Theory.* Cambridge, MA.: Harvard University Press.

Forcese, Dennis. 1986. *The Canadian Class Structure.* Toronto: McGraw-Hill Ryerson.

Foster, John Bellamy. 2000. *Marx's Ecology: Materialism and Nature.* New York: MR Press.

Fracchia, Joseph. 2005. "Beyond the Human-Nature Debate: Human Corporeal Organisation as the 'First Fact' of Historical Materialism." *Historical Materialism,* 13(1).

Freeman, Alan. 1998. "A General Refutation of Okishio's Theorem and a Proof of the Falling Rate of Profit," in R. Bellofiore (ed.), *Marxian Economics: A Reappraisal,* Volume 2. Basingstoke: McMillan.

Freeman, Alan. 2009. "What Makes the US Profit Rate Fall?" Unpublished manuscript. Retrieved from: http://mpra.ub.uni-muenchen.de/14147

Frisby, David, and Derek Sayer. 1986. *Society.* London: Tavistock.

Fukuyama, Francis. 1992. *The End of History and the Last Man.* New York: The Free Press.

Galabuzi, Grace-Edward. 2006. *Canada's Economic Apartheid: The Social Exclusion of Racialized Groups in the New Century.* Toronto: Canadian Scholars' Press Inc.

Galarza, Ernesto. 1964. *Merchants of Labor: The Mexican Bracero Story—An Account of the Managed Migration of Mexican Farm Workers in California.* San Jose: McNally & Loftin.

Galbraith, John Kenneth. 1968. *The New Industrial State.* New York: Houghton Mifflin.

Geras, Norman. 1983. *Marx and Human Nature: Refutation of a Legend.* London: Verso.

Giddens, Anthony. 1971. *Capitalism and Modern Social Theory.* Cambridge, UK: Cambridge University Press.

Giddens, Anthony. 1973. *The Class Structure of the Advanced Societies.* London: Hutchinson.

Giddens, Anthony. 1981. *A Contemporary Critique of Historical Materialism.* Berkeley and Los Angeles: University of California Press.

Glass, Fred. 2005. "A Long Time Coming: The United Farm Workers, from Golden Lands Working Hands." Retrieved from: http://sunsite.berkeley.edu/calheritage/UFW/documents/Farmworkers-lesson 9.pdf

Gottlieb, Roger. 1984. "Feudalism and Historical Materialism: A Critique and a Synthesis." *Science & Society,* 48(1).

Gould, Carol. 1978. *Marx's Social Ontology.* Cambridge, MA: The MIT Press.

Gramsci, Antonio. 1971. *Selections from the Prison Notebooks*. New York: International Publishers.

Grandia, Nona, and Joanna Kerr. 1998. "Frustrated and Displaced: Filipina Domestic Workers in Canada." *Gender and Development*, 6.

Guerin, Daniel. 1973. *Fascism and Big Business*. New York: Pathfinder.

Habermas, Jürgen. 1971. *Knowledge and Human Interests*. Boston: Beacon.

Hardt, Michael, and Antonio Negri. 2000. *Empire*. Cambridge, MA: Harvard University Press.

Hardt, Michael, and Antonio Negri. 2004. *Multitude: War and Democracy in the Age of Empire*. New York: Penguin.

Harris, Sam. 2011. *The Moral Landscape: How Science Can Determine Human Values*. New York: Free Press.

Head, Simon. 1996. "The New, Ruthless Economy." *The New York Review of Books*, XLIII, Feb. 29.

Hegel, G. W. F. 1969. *Science of Logic*. London: Allen and Unwin.

Hegel, G. W. F. 1975. *Hegel's Logic*. Oxford: Clarendon.

Hilferding, Rudolf. 1975. *Boehm-Bawerk's Criticism of Marx*, in P. Sweezy (ed.), *Karl Marx and the Close of His System* and *Böhm-Bawerk's Critique of Marx*. London: Merlin.

Hilton, R. H. (ed.). 1976. *The Transition from Feudalism to Capitalism*. London: New Left Books.

Himmelweit, Susan, and Simon Mohun. 1981. "Real Abstractions and Anomalous Assumptions," in I. Steedman (ed.), *The Value Controversy*. London: Verso.

Howard, M. C., and J. E. King. 1992. *A History of Marxian Economics: Volume II, 1929–1990*. Princeton: Princeton University Press.

Husson, Michel. 2010. "The Debate on the Rate of Profit." *International Viewpoint*, article 1894. Retrieved from: http://www.internationalviewpoint.org/spip.php?article1894

Hyman, Richard. 1975. *Marxism and the Sociology of Trade Unionism*. London: Pluto.

International Bolshevik Tendency. 2012. *Conversation with an Anarchist*. Toronto: Bolshevik Publications.

Ilyenkov, E. V. 1977. *Dialectical Logic*. Moscow: Progress Publishers.

Ilyenkov, E. V. 1982. *The Dialectics of the Abstract and the Concrete in Marx's "Capital."* Moscow: Progress Publishers.

Jackson, James K. 2011. "U.S. Direct Investment Abroad: Trends and Current Issues." Congressional Research Service. Retrieved from: http://www.crs.gov

James, C. L. R. 1956. *State Capitalism and World Revolution*. Detroit: Facing Reality.

Kay, Tamara. 1998. "Bypassing the State: The Effects of Legal and Political Contexts on Union Organizing Strategies." Paper presented to the International Sociology Association's 14th World Congress of Sociology, Montreal.

Kelley, Jonathan, and M. D. R. Evans. 1995. "Class and Class Conflict in Six Western Nations." *American Sociological Review*, 60.

Kemp, Tom. 1973. "Class, Caste and State in the Soviet Union," in *What is Revolutionary Leadership?* New York: Spartacist.

Kincaid, Jim. 2005. "Debating the Hegel-Marx Connection." *Historical Materialism*, 13(2).

Kitching, Gavin. 1988. *Karl Marx and the Philosophy of Praxis*. London and New York: Routledge.

Kliman, Andrew. 2010a. "Appearance and Essence: Neoliberalism, Financialization, and the Underlying Crisis of Capitalist Production." Retrieved from: http://www.marxisthumanistinitiative.org/

Kliman, Andrew. 2010b. *The Persistent Fall in Profitability Underlying the Current Crisis: New Temporalist Evidence*. New York: Marxist-Humanist Initiative.

Knox, Chris. 1998. "Revolutionary Work in the American Labor Movement: 1920s to 1950s," in L. Trotsky, *The Transitional Program*. London: Bolshevik Publications.

Kotz, David. 1995. "Lessons for a Future Socialism from the Soviet Collapse." *Review of Radical Political Economics*, 27(3).

Krader, Lawrence. 1975. *The Asiatic Mode of Production*. Assen: Van Gorcum.

Laibman, David. 1978. "The 'State Capitalist' and 'Bureaucratic-Exploitative' Interpretations of the Soviet Social Formation: A Critique." *Review of Radical Political Economics*, 10.

Laibman, David. 1984. "Modes of Production and Theories of Transition." *Science & Society*, 48(3).

Laibman David, Bertell Ollman, and Tony Smith (eds.). 1998. *Dialectics: The New Frontier.* Special Issue of *Science & Society*, 62(3).

Lapavitsas, Costas, and Iren Levina. 2010. "Financial Profit: Profit from Production and Profit upon Alienation." *Research on Money and Finance*, Discussion Paper No. 24.

Larrain, Jorge. 1979. *The Concept of Ideology.* London: Hutchinson.

Lefebvre, Henri. 1968. *Dialectical Materialism*. London: Jonathan Cape.

Lenin, Vladimir. 1914. "Unity," in V. Lenin, *Lenin Collected Works*, Volume 20. Retrieved from: http://www.marxists.org

Lenin, Vladimir. 1915a. "The Collapse of the Second International," in V. Lenin, *Lenin Collected Works*, Volume 21. Retrieved from: http://www.marxists.org

Lenin, Vladimir. 1915b. "Socialism and War: The Attitude of the R.S.D.L.P. towards the War," in V. Lenin, *Lenin Collected Works*, Volume 21. Retrieved from: http://www.marxists.org

Lenin, Vladimir. 1965 [1920]. *Left-Wing Communism, an Infantile Disorder*. Peking: Foreign Languages Press.

Lenin, Vladimir. 1969 [1917]. *The State and Revolution*. Moscow: Progress.

Lenin, Vladimir. 1970a [1902]. *What is to be Done?* London: Panther.

Lenin, Vladimir. 1970b [1917]. *Imperialism, the Highest Stage of Capitalism*. Peking: Foreign Languages Press.

Lenin, Vladimir, and Leon Trotsky. 1975. *Lenin's Fight against Stalinism*. Edited by Russell Block. New York: Pathfinder.

Leontieff, Wassily. 1982. "The Distribution of Work and Income." *Scientific American*, September.

Lewin, Moshe. 1968. *Lenin's Last Struggle*. New York: Random House.

Li, Minqi. 2008. *The Rise of China and the Demise of the Capitalist World Economy*. New York: Monthly Review Press.

Li, Minqi. 2010. "The End of the 'End of History': The Structural Crisis of Capitalism and the Fate of Humanity." *Science & Society*, 74(3).

Lincoln, W. Bruce. 1989. *Red Victory: A History of the Russian Civil War*. New York: Touchstone.

Livant, Bill. 1979. "A Tale of Two Medians," in J. A. Fry (ed.), *Economy, Class and Social Reality*. Toronto: Butterworths.

Lukács, Georg. 1971. *History and Class Consciousness*. London: Merlin.

Lukács, Georg. 1972. *Lenin: A Study in the Unity of His Thought*. London: New Left Books.

Luxemburg, Rosa. 1970 [1920]. "Speech to the Founding Convention of the German Communist Party," in M. Waters (ed.), *Rosa Luxemburg Speaks*. New York: Pathfinder.

Luxemburg, Rosa. 1971 [1900]. "Social Reform or Revolution," in D. Howard (ed.), *Selected Political Writings of Rosa Luxemburg*. New York and London: Monthly Review Press.

Macy, Michael W. 1988. "Value Theory and the 'Golden Eggs': Appropriating the Magic of Accumulation." *Sociological Theory*, 6.

Mage, Shane. 1963. *The "Law of the Falling Tendency of the Rate of Profit": Its Place in the Marxian Theoretical System and Relevance to the U.S. Economy*. PhD dissertation, Columbia University, New York.

Mandel, Ernest. 1971a. *The Formation of the Economic Thought of Karl Marx.* New York: Monthly Review Press.

Mandel, Ernest. 1971b. *The Leninist Theory of Organization.* London: International Marxist Group.

Mandel, Ernest. 1974. "Ten Theses on the Social and Economic Laws Governing the Society Transitional Between Capitalism and Socialism." *Critique*, 3.

Mandel, Ernest. 1985. "Marx and Engels on Commodity Production and Bureaucracy," in S. Resnick and R. Wolff (eds.), *Rethinking Marxism: Essays for Harry Magdoff and Paul Sweezy.* Brooklyn: Autonomedia.

Mandel, Ernest. 1992. *Power and Money: A Marxist Theory of Bureaucracy.* London: Verso.

Mandel, Ernest. 1994. "Trotsky's Economic Ideas and the Soviet Union Today," in S. Bloom (ed.), *Revolutionary Marxism and Social Reality in the 20th Century: Collected Essays of Ernest Mandel.* New Jersey: Humanities.

Mandel, Ernest. 1995. *Trotsky as Alternative.* London: Verso.

Mandel, Ernest, Michael Kidron, and Chris Harman. n.d. *Readings on State Capitalism.* London: International Marxist Group Publications.

Martin, Philip L. 2003. *Promise Unfulfilled: Unions, Immigration and the Farm Workers.* Ithaca and London: Ilr Press Books.

Marx, Karl. 1859. Preface to *A Contribution to the Critique of Political Economy.* Retrieved from: http://www.marxists.org

Marx, Karl. 1963a [1863]. *Theories of Surplus Value: Part I.* Moscow: Progress Publishers.

Marx, Karl. 1963b [1847]. *The Poverty of Philosophy.* New York: International Publishing.

Marx, Karl. 1964 [1844]. *Economic and Philosophical Manuscripts of 1844.* New York: International Publishers.

Marx, Karl. 1965 [1867]. *Capital Volume One.* Moscow: Progress Publishers.

Marx, Karl. 1970 [1875]. "Critique of the Gotha Programme," in K. Marx and F. Engels, *Selected Works,* Volume 3. Moscow: Progress Publishers.

Marx, Karl. 1973 [1857]. *Grundrisse.* Harmondsworth, Middlesex: Penguin.

Marx, Karl. 1974 [1871]. "The Civil War in France: Address of the General Council," in *Karl Marx: The First International and After.* Harmondsworth, Middlesex: Penguin.

Marx, Karl. 1975 [1843]. "Critique of Hegel's Philosophy of Right. Introduction," in *Karl Marx: Early Writings.* New York: Vintage.

Marx, Karl. 1977 [1867]. *Capital Volume One*. New York: Vintage.

Marx, Karl. 1978 [1865]. *Capital Volume Three*. Moscow: Progress Publishers.

Marx, Karl. 1981 [1865]. *Capital Volume Three*. New York: Vintage.

Marx, Karl. 1983 [1881]. "First Draft of a Reply to Vera Zasulich," in T. Shanin (ed.), *Late Marx and the Russian Road*. New York: Monthly Review Press.

Marx, Karl. 1989a [1845]. "Theses on Feuerbach," in D. Sayer (ed.), *Readings from Karl Marx*. London: Routledge.

Marx, Karl. 1989b [1881]. "Notes on Adolph Wagner," in D. Sayer (ed.), *Readings from Karl Marx*. London: Routledge.

Marx, Karl. 1989c [1846]. "Letter to Annenkov," in D. Sayer (ed.), *Readings from Karl Marx*. London: Routledge.

Marx, Karl. 1989d [1845–46]. "The German Ideology," in D. Sayer (ed.), *Readings from Karl Marx*. London: Routledge.

Marx, Karl, and Frederick Engels. 1947 [1845]. *The German Ideology*. New York: International Publishers.

Marx, Karl, and Frederick Engels. 1965. *Selected Correspondence*. Second Edition. Moscow: Progress Publishers.

Marx, Karl, and Frederick Engels. 1968 [1845]. *The German Ideology*. Moscow: Progress Publishers.

Marx, Karl, and Frederick Engels. 1973 [1850]. "Address of the Central Committee to the Communist League," in *Karl Marx: The Revolutions of 1848*. Harmondsworth, Middlesex: Penguin Books.

Marx, Karl, and Frederick Engels. 1998 [1848]. *The Communist Manifesto*. New York: Monthly Review Press.

Mayer, Alfred. 1970. "Theories of Convergence," in C. Johnson (ed.), *Change in Communist Systems*. Stanford: Stanford University Press.

McCarney, Joseph. 1980. *The Real World of Ideology*. Sussex: Harvester.

McIntyre, Robert S., and T. D. Coo Nguyen. 2004. *Corporate Taxes in the Bush Years*. Joint Project of Citizens for Tax Justice & the Institute on Taxation and Economic Policy.

McNally, David. 1994. *Against the Market: Political Economy, Market Socialism and the Marxist Critique*. London: Verso.

McNally, David. 2000. *Bodies of Meaning: Studies on Language, Labour, and Liberation*. Albany: State University of New York Press.

McNally, David. 2011. *Global Slump: The Economics and Politics of Crisis and Resistance*. Oakland: PM.

Meek, Ronald. 1956. *Studies in the Labor Theory of Value*. New York: Monthly Review Press.

Mepham, John, and David-Hillel Ruben (eds). 1979. *Issues in Marxist Philosophy (Volume One): Dialectics and Method.* Atlantic Highlands, NJ: Humanities.

Mészáros, István. 1970. *Marx's Theory of Alienation.* London: Merlin.

Mészáros, István. 2010. *Social Structure and Forms of Consciousness, Volume I: The Social Determination of Method.* New York: Monthly Review Press.

Miliband, Ralph. 1994. *Socialism for a Sceptical Age.* London: Verso.

Mohun, Simon. 1996. "Productive and Unproductive Labor in the Labor Theory of Value." *Review of Radical Political Economics,* 28(4).

Mohun, Simon. 2005. "On Measuring the Wealth of Nations: the U.S. Economy, 1964–2001." *Cambridge Journal of Economics,* 29.

Mohun, Simon. 2009. "Aggregate Capital Productivity in the U.S. Economy, 1964–2001." *Cambridge Journal of Economics,* 33.

Moody, Kim. 1997. *Workers in a Lean World.* London: Verso.

Moreau, Francois. 1991. "The Condition of the Working Class under Capitalism Today: The Mexican Case." *Socialist Alternatives,* 1(1).

Morrow, Felix. 1963. *Revolution and Counter-revolution in Spain.* London: New Park.

Moseley, Fred. 1991. *The Falling Rate of Profit in the Postwar United States Economy.* New York: St. Martin's.

Moseley, Fred (ed.). 1993. *Marx's Method in Capital: A Reexamination.* Atlantic Highlands, NJ: Humanities.

Murray, Patrick. 1988. *Marx's Theory of Scientific Knowledge.* Atlantic Highlands, NJ: Humanities.

Nadeau, Mary-Jo. 2006. "Migrant Farm Workers Organizing in Canada." *Arthur* (Trent University), 23(January).

Nicolaus, Martin. 1975. *Restoration of Capitalism in the USSR.* Chicago: Liberator.

Norman, Richard, and Sean Sayers. 1980. *Hegel, Marx and Dialectic: A Debate.* Brighton: Harvester.

Novack, George. 1978. "In Defense of Engels," in G. Novack, *Polemics in Marxist Philosophy.* New York: Monad.

OECD [Organisation for Economic Co-operation and Development]. 2011. *Economic Outlook.* No. 89.

Okishio, Nobuo. 1961. "Technical change and the rate of profit." *Kobe University Economic Review,* 7.

Ollman, Bertell. 1976. *Alienation: Marx's Conception of Man in Capitalist Society.* Second Edition. Cambridge: Cambridge University Press.

Ollman, Bertell. 1993. "How to Study Class Consciousness ... and Why We Should," in B. Ollman, *Dialectical Investigations.* New York: Routledge.

Ollman, Bertell (ed.). 1998. *Market Socialism: The Debate among Socialists.* New York and London: Routledge.

Ollman, Bertell. 2003. *Dance of the Dialectic: Steps in Marx's Method.* Urbana and Chicago: University of Illinois Press.

Ollman, Bertell, and Tony Smith. 1998. "Introduction," in B. Ollman and T. Smith (eds.), *Dialectics: The New Frontier*, Special Issue of *Science & Society*, 62(3).

Ontario Federation of Labour. 2001. *Report on Agricultural Workers.* Toronto.

Palmer, Bryan D. 1987. *Solidarity: The Rise and Fall of an Opposition in British Columbia.* Vancouver: New Star.

Palmer, Bryan D. 1990. *Descent into Discourse: The Reification of Language and the Writing of Social History.* Philadelphia: Temple University Press.

Palmer, Bryan D. 1992. *Working-Class Experience: Rethinking the History of Canadian Labour, 1800–1991.* Toronto: McClelland and Stewart.

Palmer, Bryan D. 2003. "What's Law Got to Do with It? Historical Considerations on Class Struggle, Boundaries of Constraint, and Capitalist Authority." *Osgoode Hall Law Journal*, 41(Summer/Fall).

Palmer, Bryan D. 2013. *Revolutionary Teamsters: The Minneapolis Truckers' Strikes of 1934.* Leiden and Boston: Brill.

Panitch, Leo. 1989. "Capitalism, Socialism and Revolution." *Socialist Register 1989.* London: Merlin.

Panitch, Leo. 2008. *Renewing Socialism.* Pontypool Wales: Merlin.

Panitch, Leo, and Donald Swartz. 2003. *From Consent to Coercion: The Assault on Trade Union Freedoms.* Third Edition. Aurora: Garamond.

Parenti, Michael. 1997. *Blackshirts and Reds.* San Francisco: City Lights Books.

Parsons, Talcott. 1953. "A Revised Analytical Approach to the Theory of Social Stratification," in R. Bendix and S. M. Lipset (eds.), *Class, Status and Power.* Glencoe, IL: Free Press.

Popper, Karl. 1974. "What is Dialectic?" in K. Popper, *Conjectures and Refutations.* London: Routledge and Kegan Paul.

Poulantzas, Nicos. 1973. *Political Power and Social Classes.* London: New Left Books.

Poulantzas, Nicos. 1975. *Classes in Contemporary Capitalism.* London: New Left Books.

Poulantzas, Nicos. 1978. *State, Power, Socialism.* London: New Left Books.

Preis, Art. 1964. *Labor's Giant Step: Twenty Years of the CIO.* New York: Pioneer.

Preobrazhensky, Evgeny. 1965. *The New Economics.* Oxford: Clarendon.

Rabinowitch, Alexander. 2007. *The Bolsheviks in Power: The First Year of Soviet Rule in Petrograd.* Bloomington: Indiana University Press.

Rakovsky, Christian. 1981. "The Five Year Plan in Crisis." *Critique,* 13.

Remnick, David. 1998. "Vladimir Ilyich Lenin." *Time,* April 13.

Resnick, Stephen, and Richard Wolff. 1994. "Between State and Private Capitalism: What was Soviet 'Socialism'?" *Rethinking Marxism,* 7(1).

Reuten, Geert. 2006. "On the quantitative homology between circulating capital and capital value: The problem of Marx's and the Marxian notion of 'variable capital.'" Paper for the *Historical Materialism* Annual Conference 2006, "New Directions in Marxist Theory," draft, November.

Reuten, Geert, and Michael Williams. 1989. *Value Form and the State.* London and New York: Routledge.

Ridley, Matt. 2004. *The Agile Gene: How Nature Turns on Nurture.* New York: Perennial.

Rizzi, Bruno. 1939. *La bureaucratisation du monde.* Paris: Impremerie Les Presses Modernes.

Roemer, John. 1982. "New Directions in the Marxist Theory of Exploitation and Class." *Politics and Society,* 11.

Roemer, John. 1988. *Free to Lose: An Introduction to Marxist Economic Philosophy.* Cambridge, MA.: Harvard University Press.

Rose, Hillary, and Steven Rose (eds.). 2000. *Alas, Poor Darwin: Arguments against Evolutionary Psychology.* London: Jonathan Cape.

Rosenberg, Gerald. 1991. *The Hollow Hope: Can Courts Bring About Social Change?* Chicago: University of Chicago Press.

Rosenthal, John. 1999. "The Escape from Hegel." *Science & Society,* 63(3).

Rubin, Isaak I. 1973. *Essays on Marx's Theory of Value.* Montreal: Black Rose Books.

Saad Filho, Alfredo. 1996. Review of: *Invisible Leviathan. Capital & Class,* 20.

Saez, Emmanuel, with Thomas Piketty. 2011. "Income Inequality in the United States, 1913–1998." Excel spreadsheet updated to 2008. Retrieved from: http://elsa.berkeley.edu/~saez/

Sanbonmatsu, John. 2004. *The Postmodern Prince.* New York: Monthly Review Press.

Sato, Takuya. 2012. "The Evolution of Service Economics as Part of the Theory of Contemporary Capitalism." *International Critical Thought,* 2(1).

Satzewich, Victor. 1991. *Racism and the Incorporation of Foreign Labour: Farm Labour Migration in Canada since 1945.* New York: Routledge.

Sayer, Derek. 1987. *The Violence of Abstraction: The Analytical Foundations of Historical Materialism.* Oxford: Basil Blackwell.

Sayer, Derek, and Philip Corrigan. 1983. "Late Marx: Continuity, Contradiction and Learning," in Teodor Shanin (ed.), *Late Marx and the Russian Road.* New York: Monthly Review Press.

Sayers, Sean. 1985. *Reality and Reason: Dialectic and the Theory of Knowledge.* Oxford: Basil Blackwell.

Schmidt, Alfred. 1971. *The Concept of Nature in Marx.* London: New Left Books.

Schweitzer, David. 1982. "Alienation, De-alienation and Change," in S. G. Shoham (ed.), *Alienation and Anomie Revisited.* Messina: Ramot Educational Systems.

Sensat, Julius. 1979. *Harbermas and Marxism: An Appraisal.* Beverly Hills and London: Sage.

Seymour, Joseph. 1997. *Lenin and the Vanguard Party.* New York: Spartacist.

Shachtman, Max. 1962. *The Bureaucratic Revolution: The Rise of the Stalinist State.* New York: Donald Press.

Shaikh, Anwar. 1978. "Political Economy and Capitalism: Notes on Dobb's Theory of Crisis." *Cambridge Journal of Economics,* 2(June).

Shaikh, Anwar. 1981. "The Poverty of Algebra," in I. Steedman (ed.), *The Value Controversy.* London: Verso.

Shaikh, Anwar. 1999. "Explaining the Global Economic Crisis: A Critique of Brenner." *Historical Materialism,* 5.

Shaikh, Anwar. 2010. "The First Great Depression of the 21st Century," in L. Panitch, G. Albo, and V. Chibber (eds.), *Socialist Register 2011: The Crisis This Time.* London: Merlin.

Shaikh, Anwar, and Ahmet E. Tonak. 1994. *Measuring the Wealth of Nations: The Political Economy of National Accounts.* Cambridge, MA: Cambridge University Press.

Shanin, Teodor (ed.). 1983. *Late Marx and the Russian Road: Marx and the "Peripheries of Capitalism."* New York: Monthly Review Press.

Sharma, Nandita. 2001. "On Being not Canadian: The Social Organization of 'Migrant Workers' in Canada." *Canadian Review of Sociology and Anthropology,* 38.

Singer, Daniel. 1991. "Privilegentsia, Property and Power." *Socialist Register 1991.* London: Merlin.

Sklar, Holly. 1995. "Economics for Everyone." *Z Magazine,* July–August.

Smith, Adam. 1976. *The Theory of Moral Sentiments.* Oxford: Clarendon Press.

Smith, Adam. 1986. *The Essential Adam Smith.* Edited and with an introduction by Robert L. Heilbroner. New York and London: W.W. Norton.

Smith, Murray E. G. 1984. *The Falling Rate of Profit*. Master's thesis, University of Manitoba, Winnipeg.

Smith, Murray E. G. 1989. *The Value Controversy and Social Theory: An Inquiry into Marx's Labour Theory of Value*. PhD Dissertation, University of British Columbia, Vancouver.

Smith, Murray E. G. 1991. Understanding Marx's Theory of Value: An Assessment of a Controversy. *The Canadian Review of Sociology and Anthropology*, 28(3).

Smith, Murray E. G. 1992. "The Value Abstraction and the Dialectic of Social Development." *Science & Society*, 56(3).

Smith, Murray E. G. 1993. "Productivity, Valorization and Crisis: Socially Necessary Unproductive Labor in Contemporary Capitalism." *Science & Society*, 57(3).

Smith, Murray E. G. 1994a. *Invisible Leviathan: The Marxist Critique of Market Despotism beyond Postmodernism*. Toronto: University of Toronto Press.

Smith, Murray E. G. 1994b. "The 'Intentional Primacy' of the Relations of Production: Further Reflections on the Dialectic of Social Development." *Science & Society*, 58(1).

Smith, Murray E. G. 1996-97. "Revisiting Trotsky: Reflections on the Stalinist Debacle and Trotskyism as Alternative." *Rethinking Marxism*, 9(3).

Smith, Murray E. G. 1999. "The Necessity of Value Theory: Brenner's Analysis of the 'Long Downturn' and Marx's Theory of Crisis." *Historical Materialism*, 4.

Smith, Murray E. G. 2000. "Political Economy and the Canadian Working Class: Marxism or Nationalist Reformism?" *Labour/Le Travail*, 46.

Smith, Murray E. G. 2010. *Global Capitalism in Crisis: Karl Marx and the Decay of the Profit System*. Halifax and Winnipeg: Fernwood.

Smith, Murray E. G. 2011. "Author's Reply to Reviews of 'Global Capitalism in Crisis: Karl Marx and the Decay of the Profit System,'" *Global Discourse*, 2(1). Retrieved from: globaldiscourse.files.wordpress.com/2011/05/smith-reply.pdf

Smith, Murray E. G., and Jonah Butovsky. 2012. "Profitability and the Roots of the Global Crisis: Marx's 'Law of the Tendency of the Rate of Profit to Fall' and the US Economy, 1950-2007." *Historical Materialism*, 20(4).

Smith, Murray E. G., and Jonah Butovsky. 2013. "The Decline of the Labour Movement: A Socialist Perspective," in T. Fowler (ed.), *From Crisis to Austerity: Neoliberalism, Organized Labour and the Canadian State*. Ottawa: Red Quill.

Smith, Murray E. G., and Joshua D. Dumont. 2011. "Socialist Strategy, Yesterday and Today: Notes on Classical Marxism and the Contemporary Radical Left," in H. Veltmeyer (ed.), *21st Century Socialism: Reinventing the Project*. Halifax: Fernwood.

Smith, Murray E. G., and K. W. Taylor. 1996. "Profitability Crisis and the Erosion of Popular Prosperity." *Studies in Political Economy*, 49.

Smith, Tony. 1990. *The Logic of Marx's Capital*. Albany: SUNY Press.

Smith, Tony. 1993a. "Hegel's Theory of the Syllogism and its Relevance for Marxism," in T. Smith, *Dialectical Social Theory and Its Critics*. Albany: SUNY Press.

Smith, Tony. 1993b. "Postmodernism: Theory and Politics." *Against the Current*, July–August.

Smith, Tony. 2000. *Technology and Capital in the Age of Lean Production*. Albany: SUNY Press.

Söhn-Rethel, Alfred. 1978a. *Intellectual and Manual Labour: A Critique of Epistemology*. London and Basingstoke: Macmillan.

Söhn-Rethel, Alfred. 1978b. *Economy and Class Structure of German Fascism*. London: CSE Books.

Spartacist. 1988. *"Market Socialism" in Eastern Europe*. New York: Spartacist Publishing.

Spartacist. 1989. "Leonard Shapiro: Lawyer for Counterrevolution," *Spartacist*, 43/44(Summer).

Spivak, G. C. 1988. "Scattered Speculations on the Question of Value," in G. Spivak, *In Other Worlds*. New York: Routledge.

Starosta, Guido. 2012. "Cognitive Commodities and the Value Form." *Science & Society*, 76(3).

Steedman, Ian. 1977. *Marx after Sraffa*. London: Verso.

Sweezy, Paul. 1968. *The Theory of Capitalist Development*. New York: Monthly Review Press.

Sweezy, Paul. 1981. *Four Lectures on Marxism*. New York and London: Monthly Review Press.

SYL [Spartacus Youth League]. 1977. *Why the USSR is Not Capitalist*. New York: Spartacus Youth Publishing.

Szymanski, Albert. 1979. *Is the Red Flag Flying?* London: Zed.

Therborn, Goran. 1980. *Science, Class and Society*. London: Verso.

Timpanaro, Sebastiano. 1980. *On Materialism*. London: Verso.

Trepper, Leopold. 1977. *The Great Game: Memoirs of a Master Spy*. New York: M.W. Books Ltd.

Trotsky, Leon. 1963 [1939]. "Introduction," in *Leon Trotsky Presents the Living Thoughts of Karl Marx*. New York: Fawcett.

Trotsky, Leon. 1967 [1934]. *History of the Russian Revolution*. Three Volumes. London: Sphere.

Trotsky, Leon. 1969 [1929]. *The Permanent Revolution*. New York: Merit.

Trotsky, Leon. 1970a [1930]. *My Life.* New York: Pathfinder.

Trotsky, Leon. 1970b [1937]. *The Revolution Betrayed.* New York: Pathfinder.

Trotsky, Leon. 1970c [1939]. *In Defense of Marxism.* New York: Pathfinder.

Trotsky, Leon. 1970d [1937]. "Not a Workers and Not a Bourgeois State?" in L. Trotsky, *Writings of Leon Trotsky, 1937–38.* New York: Pathfinder.

Trotsky, Leon. 1970e [1937]. *Stalinism and Bolshevism.* New York: Pathfinder.

Trotsky, Leon. 1970f [1928]. "The Draft Program of the Communist International—A Criticism of Fundamentals," in L. Trotsky, *The Third International after Lenin.* New York: Pathfinder.

Trotsky, Leon. 1970g [1936]. "The Dutch Section and the International," in L. Trotsky, *Writings of Leon Trotsky, 1935–36.* New York: Pathfinder.

Trotsky, Leon. 1972a [1933]. "The Class Nature of the Soviet State," in L. Trotsky, *Writings of Leon Trotsky, 1933–34.* New York: Pathfinder.

Trotsky, Leon. 1972b [1934]. "Centrism and the Fourth International," in L. Trotsky, *Writings of Leon Trotsky, 1933–34.* New York: Pathfinder.

Trotsky, Leon. 1973a [1940]. "Letter to the Workers of the USSR," in L. Trotsky, *Writings of Leon Trotsky, 1939–40.* New York: Pathfinder.

Trotsky, Leon. 1973b [1932]. "The Soviet Economy in Danger," in L. Trotsky, *Writings of Leon Trotsky, 1932.* New York: Pathfinder.

Trotsky, Leon. 1973c [1938]. "The Death Agony of Capitalism and the Tasks of the Fourth International," in L. Trotsky, *The Transitional Program for Socialist Revolution.* New York: Pathfinder.

Trotsky, Leon. 1973d [1940]. "The Class, the Party and the Leadership," in L. Trotsky, *The Spanish Revolution (1931–39).* New York: Pathfinder.

Trotsky, Leon. 1973e [1931–39]. *The Spanish Revolution, 1931–39.* New York: Pathfinder.

Trotsky, Leon. 1998. *The Transitional Program.* London: Bolshevik Publications.

UFWA-CO. 2001. *Executive Summary: Report on Migrant Farm Workers in Canada.*

United Food and Commercial Workers Canada. 2003. *Status of Migrant Farm Workers in Canada, 2003.* Toronto.

Vitkin, Mikhail. 1981. "The Asiatic Mode of Production." *Philosophy and Social Criticism,* 8(1).

Walton, Paul, and Andrew Gamble. 1972. *From Alienation to Surplus Value.* London: Sheed and Ward.

Webber, Michael, and David Rigby. 1996. *The Golden Age Illusion: Rethinking Postwar Capitalism.* New York: Guilford Press.

Weber, Max. 1949. *The Methodology of the Social Sciences.* Glencoe: The Free Press.

Weber, Max. 1958 [1905]. *The Protestant Ethic and the Spirit of Capitalism*. New York: Scribner's.

Weber, Max. 1978 [1914]. *Economy and Society: An Outline of Interpretive Sociology*. Los Angeles: University of California Press.

Weil, Robert. 1995. "Contradictory Class Definitions: Petty Bourgeoisie and the 'Classes' of Erik Olin Wright." *Critical Sociology*, 21(3).

Wood, Ellen Meiksins. 1986. *The Retreat from Class: A New 'True' Socialism*. London: Verso.

Wood, Ellen Meiksins. 1998. "History or 'Teleology'? Marx versus Weber," in M. Smith (ed.), *Early Modern Social Theory: Selected Interpretive Readings*. Toronto: Canadian Scholars Press.

Wright, Erik Olin. 1978. *Class, Crisis and the State*. London: Verso.

Yates, Michael. 2003. *Naming the System: Inequality and Work in the Global Economy*. New York: Monthly Review Press.

Zinn, Howard. 1990. *Declarations of Independence: Cross-Examining American Ideology*. HarperCollins.

INDEX

absolute surplus value, 40, 53, 345, 354n29

abstract intellect, 157–58, 160, 172, 176–77, 180

abstract labour, 22, 33, 48, 83, 85, 87, 89, 91–93, 94n5, 95–97, 99–101, 103–5, 107, 109, 125, 130, 142–43, 148, 193–94

accumulation of capital, 30, 39, 43–44, 47, 55, 66–67, 74, 89, 95, 102, 108, 119, 124, 143, 207, 328

Agricultural Labor Relations Act (California), 341

Agricultural Labour Relations Act (Ontario), 330, 342

Albo, Greg, 55, 74n1, 75n2, 276–78

alienated labour, 85, 87, 103

alienation, 50, 76, 83–87, 89, 102–3, 105–10, 147, 262

Allende, Salvador, 231

Althusser, Louis, 84

American Federation of Labor, 337, 365

Analytical Marxism, 83, 192

anarchism, 2, 273, 282n2, 311

anticipated future value (AFV), 49–50

antiquity, 159, 162

appropriative rationality, 169, 174, 180

Aron, Raymond, 212

Bakir, Ergodan, 39

Baudrillard, Jean, 87, 123, 150

Berlinguer, Enrico, 300

Bernstein, Eduard, 233, 264, 279, 299

Bolshevism, 112, 208, 214, 221, 230, 236–37, 239n1, 240n3, 244,

254–55, 268, 270–71, 282, 314–16, 318

bourgeoisie, 2, 7–8, 32, 107, 122, 217, 224, 227, 231–32, 241, 266–67, 278–79, 287–88, 290, 295, 299, 300, 305, 307, 358, 361, 363–64. *See also* capitalist class

braceros, 334–37, 353n21

Breitman, George, 246, 253–55

Brenner, Robert, 161

Brezhnev, Leonid, 220

Brown, Andrew, 135, 149n16

Brown, Jerry, 341

Bukharin, Nikolai, 146n3

bureaucracy, 2, 107–8, 185, 206–8, 210, 213, 215–20, 223–25, 230, 239n3, 241, 244–45, 247, 249–51, 254, 266, 270–72, 280–83, 293, 295, 297, 304–6, 315–17, 320, 322–25, 329, 340, 342, 347–48, 354

Burnham, James, 305

Bush, George H. W., 213

Bush, George W., 72

Brynjolfsson, Erik, 42–43

Callinicos, Alex, 240, 275–76

Campbell, Al, 39

Canada, 78–80, 274, 276, 286–87, 296, 317, 319–21, 323, 325–28, 352, 353n23, 353n24

Canadian Charter of Rights and Freedoms, 330

Cannon, James P., 236–38, 253

capital. *See* constant capital; fictitious capital; financialization;

Macy, Michael, 83–93, 95, 98, 100–2, 108
Mage, Shane, 57, 62, 64, 67, 77n6, 78n16
Mandel, Ernest, 108n1, 236–37, 240n3, 246–47, 249, 251–55, 351n8
Mao Zedong (Maoism), 75, 168, 176, 212, 251, 272, 282, 316
marginalism, 141, 143–44
market socialism, 223
Marx, Karl (Marxism), 2–7, 9, 14, 16, 83, 106, 113–15, 117, 119, 125, 129–30, 134–35, 146n6, 154, 186n2, 187–94, 197, 199–201, 209, 211–12, 221–22, 234, 246, 248–49, 252, 261, 264–67, 270–71, 273, 277–81, 282n2, 299, 306, 360
McAfee, Andrew, 42–43
McCain, John, 33–35, 43
McCarney, Joseph, 302
McNally, David, 75n2
Mészáros, István, 130
Mexico, 326–28, 335, 342, 353
middle class, 285–93, 295–312
Miliband, Ralph, 226–30, 232–36, 241n7, 241n9, 278
Minneapolis strikes (1934), 343, 365
Minsky, Hyman, 35
mode of production, 7, 15, 19, 22, 27, 52, 99, 119, 124, 129, 156, 162, 164–65, 192, 219, 250, 288, 305
ancient, 19
Asiatic, 150, 174, 175
capitalist, 15–16, 19, 21, 23, 27, 31, 48, 61, 95, 102, 131, 143, 174, 192, 260, 288, 358

communist, 19, 23
feudal, 19, 160–61
post-capitalist, 239
Mohun, Simon, 39–40, 67, 119
monism, 99, 113–14, 116–17, 119–20, 126, 128–29, 140, 145, 147n8, 150–51, 189
morality, 359–62
Moreau, Francois, 317
Moseley, Fred, 59, 78
Mussolini, Benito, 317n1

natural primacy thesis, 179
negation of the negation, 14, 15, 115
Negri, Antonio, 123–25, 294
neoliberalism, 2, 3, 28, 32, 39, 41, 48–50, 73–74, 75n2, 187, 201, 274, 298, 305, 320, 345, 347
neutral technological progress argument, 56–57
New Anti-Capitalist Party (France), 274
New Democratic Party (Canada), 321, 330, 350n4
new value (NV), 8, 22–23, 25–27, 36, 50–51, 63–65, 80, 90–93, 98, 124–25, 143, 192, 199–200, 289
non-financial rate of profit, 38, 69, 70, 80
North American Free Trade Agreement, 321

Obama, Barack, 34, 36, 285
Okishio theorem, 58
Ollman, Bertell, 113–14, 164
Ontario Federation of Labour, 331–32
opportunism, 5, 234, 238, 251–52, 266–68, 280–82

unproductive labour, 39, 41, 48,
    61–65, 67, 78–79, 293, 295
use-value, 7, 21–22, 57, 87, 92,
    99–100, 102, 104, 141–43, 194,
    196, 199
utopian socialism, 357–58

valorization, 23, 27, 33, 38–39, 42, 44,
    48–49, 100, 102, 104, 143–44,
    148, 294, 359
value abstraction, 153–54, 169–74,
    176–77, 194
value composition of capital. *See* com-
    position of capital
value composition of output, 64
value form, 22, 94, 100, 123, 189–91,
    193–94, 197–99, 240
value theory, 84, 88, 90, 93, 95–96, 98,
    101, 104, 107, 112, 130, 140–41,
    169, 188, 193, 196, 198. *See also*
    labour theory of value
variable capital, 26, 28, 41, 49, 51,
    59–60, 62–65, 67, 77–78,
    81, 241
Vietnam, 245, 249–50, 253, 271

wage-labour, 19–21, 24–26, 28, 31,
    44n2, 51, 92, 102, 108, 124,

137, 143–44, 148, 262, 287–90,
    293–96, 300, 303, 325, 327–28
Wald, Alan, 246, 253–54
Walesa, Lech, 237
Weber, Max, 121–23, 146n5, 146n7,
    151, 297–98
Weil, Robert, 287–89
Wood, Ellen Meiksins, 146n5, 223, 300
working class, 2, 4, 6, 8, 15–16, 38,
    43, 74, 107, 188, 200, 205, 217,
    219–20, 223–24, 227–31, 234,
    247–51, 255, 259–69, 271,
    274–75, 278–81, 283, 285, 288,
    290, 292–93, 295–96, 300, 308,
    320, 323, 348–50, 355, 362. *See
    also* proletariat
world capitalism, 19, 20–21, 24–26,
    28, 31, 44n2, 51, 92, 102, 108,
    124, 137, 143–44, 148, 262,
    287–90, 293–96, 300–3, 325,
    327–28
Wright, Erik Olin, 287–89

Yeltsin, Boris, 206, 220, 237, 239, 241,
    317
Yugoslavia, 212, 245, 251, 271

Zinn, Howard, 309

COPYRIGHT ACKNOWLEDGEMENTS